Migration, Diasporas and Citizenship Series

Series Editors: **Robin Cohen**, Director of the International Migration Institute and Professor of Development Studies, University of Oxford, UK; and **Zig Layton-Henry**, Professor of Politics, University of Warwick, UK.

Editorial Board: **Rainer Baubock**, European University Institute, Italy; **James F. Hollifield**, Southern Methodist University, USA; and **Jan Rath**, University of Amsterdam, The Netherlands

The *Migration, Diasporas and Citizenship* series covers three important aspects of the migration progress. Firstly, the determinants, dynamics and characteristics of international migration. Secondly, the continuing attachment of many contemporary migrants to their places of origin, signified by the word 'diaspora', and thirdly the attempt, by contrast, to belong and gain acceptance in places of settlement, signified by the word 'citizenship'. The series publishes work that shows engagement with and a lively appreciation of the wider social and political issues that are influenced by international migration.

Also published in Migration Studies by Palgrave Macmillan

Rutvica Andrijasevic
MIGRATION, AGENCY AND CITIZENSHIP IN SEX TRAFFICKING

Claudine Attias-Donfut, Joanne Cook, Jaco Hoffman and Louise Waite (*editors*)
CITIZENSHIP, BELONGING AND INTERGENERATIONAL RELATIONS IN AFRICAN MIGRATION

Grete Brochmann and Anniken Hagelund (*authors*), with Karin Borevi,
Heidi Vad Jønsson and Klaus Petersen
IMMIGRATION POLICY AND THE SCANDINAVIAN WELFARE STATE 1945–2010

Gideon Calder, Phillip Cole and Jonathan Seglow
CITIZENSHIP ACQUISITION AND NATIONAL BELONGING
Migration, Minorities and Citizenship

Enzo Colombo and Paola Rebughini (*editors*)
CHILDREN OF IMMIGRANTS IN A GLOBALIZED WORLD
A Generational Experience

Huub Dijstelbloem and Albert Meijer (*editors*)
MIGRATION AND THE NEW TECHNOLOGICAL BORDERS OF EUROPE

Thomas Faist and Andreas Ette (*editors*)
THE EUROPEANIZATION OF NATIONAL POLICIES AND POLITICS OF IMMIGRATION
Between Autonomy and the European Union

Thomas Faist and Peter Kivisto (*editors*)
DUAL CITIZENSHIP IN GLOBAL PERSPECTIVE
From Unitary to Multiple Citizenship

Katrine Fangen, Thomas Johansson and Nils Hammarén (*editors*)
YOUNG MIGRANTS
Exclusion and Belonging in Europe

Martin Geiger and Antoine Pécoud (*editors*)
THE POLITICS OF INTERNATIONAL MIGRATION MANAGEMENT

John R. Hinnells (*editor*)
RELIGIOUS RECONSTRUCTION IN THE SOUTH ASIAN DIASPORAS
From One Generation to Another

Ronit Lentin and Elena Moreo (*editors*)
MIGRANT ACTIVISM AND INTEGRATION FROM BELOW IN IRELAND

Ayhan Kaya
ISLAM, MIGRATION AND INTEGRATION
The Age of Securitization

Marie Macey and Alan H. Carling
ETHNIC, RACIAL AND RELIGIOUS INEQUALITIES
The Perils of Subjectivity

Georg Menz and Alexander Caviedes (*editors*)
LABOUR MIGRATION IN EUROPE

Laura Morales and Marco Giugni (*editors*)
SOCIAL CAPITAL, POLITICAL PARTICIPATION AND MIGRATION IN EUROPE
Making Multicultural Democracy Work

Eric Morier-Genoud and Michel Cahan (*editors*)
IMPERIAL MIGRATIONS
Colonial Communities and Diaspora in the Portuguese World

Aspasia Papadopoulou-Kourkoula
TRANSIT MIGRATION
The Missing Link between Emigration and Settlement

Ludger Pries and Zeynep Sezgin (*editors*)
CROSS BORDER MIGRANT ORGANIZATIONS IN COMPARATIVE PERSPECTIVE

Prodromos Panayiotopoulos
ETHNICITY, MIGRATION AND ENTERPRISE

Vicki Squire
THE EXCLUSIONARY POLITICS OF ASYLUM

Anna Triandafyllidou and Thanos Maroukis (*editors*)
MIGRANT SMUGGLING
Irregular Migration from Asia and Africa to Europe

Vron Ware
MILITARY MIGRANTS
Fighting for YOUR Country

Lucy Williams
GLOBAL MARRIAGE
Cross-Border Marriages and Marriage Migration in Context

Migration, Diasporas and Citizenship
Series Standing Order ISBN 978–0–230–30078–1 (hardback) and
978–0–230–30079–8 (paperback)
(*outside North America only*)

You can receive future titles in this series as they are published by placing a standing order. Please contact your bookseller or, in case of difficulty, write to us at the address below with your name and address, the title of the series and the ISBN quoted above.

Customer Services Department, Macmillan Distribution Ltd, Houndmills, Basingstoke, Hampshire RG21 6XS, England

---

Military Migrants

Fighting for YOUR Country

Vron Ware
The Open University, UK

First published 2012 by
PALGRAVE MACMILLAN

Palgrave Macmillan in the UK is an imprint of Macmillan Publishers Limited, registered in England, company number 785998, of Houndmills, Basingstoke, Hampshire RG21 6XS.

Palgrave Macmillan in the US is a division of St Martin's Press LLC, 175 Fifth Avenue, New York, NY 10010.

Palgrave Macmillan is the global academic imprint of the above companies and has companies and representatives throughout the world.

Palgrave® and Macmillan® are registered trademarks in the United States, the United Kingdom, Europe and other countries.

ISBN 978–1–137–01002–5

This book is printed on paper suitable for recycling and made from fully managed and sustained forest sources. Logging, pulping and manufacturing processes are expected to conform to the environmental regulations of the country of origin.

A catalogue record for this book is available from the British Library.

A catalog record for this book is available from the Library of Congress.

10   9   8   7   6   5   4   3   2   1
21 20 19 18 17 16 15 14 13 12

Printed and bound in Great Britain by
CPI Antony Rowe, Chippenham and Eastbourne

In loving memory of Greta Slobin

Contents

Illustrations

Images

Note: All photographs except 2 & 6 were taken by the author.

Tables

Preface

Unguarded battleground

On Saturday 11 November 2006 the Royal British Legion (RBL) initiated a new public ceremony marking the anniversary of Armistice Day. The event was held in Trafalgar Square in the heart of London, and leaflets in seven different languages were handed out to passers-by, tourists and natives alike. When the two-minute silence was broken by the bugler's Reveille and a fly-past of four Typhoon jet aircraft, the public were invited to throw their poppies into one of the fountains, creating a spectacular array of scarlet petals. The RBL, which represents veterans of all the country's wars across all services, deliberately planned the occasion as an intervention, 'to show people they can take part in a Remembrance event, perhaps on a less formal basis, but still one at which they can stop and think, and hope for the future'.[1] Entitled 'Silence in the Square', the event has become an annual fixture in the nation's commemorative calendar.

In 2010 Armistice Day fell on a rainy Thursday. Arriving at the square shortly before Big Ben struck 11, it was hard to estimate the total number present, but a few hundred umbrellas were clustered near the stage where a pop group called The Saturdays was performing. The proceedings, which had been advertised in many of London's entertainment listings, had begun at 9.30 a.m. and were orchestrated by a TV presenter called Ben Shephard. Having been in Trafalgar Square just the day before on the occasion of a mass demonstration against cuts in higher education, it was eerie to be standing there again in very different company. This time the incessant traffic came to a halt and the whole area was still. Crowds of people of all ages now lined the steps around the square, many with heads hung in reflection. A crocodile of primary schoolchildren had arrived just in time, the bemused expressions of the infants only adding to the extraordinary scene of a capital muted by an apparently consensual silence. In an attempt to create a visual component to match this audible quiet, the giant screen to the right of the stage showed the participants images of the crowd, so they could see what they looked like at that moment.

When the bugle call marked the end of the two minutes and the harmonious voices of the London Gospel Choir could be heard competing with the sound of the traffic, the screen began to show the faces of politicians and celebrities, interspersed with those of wounded soldiers.[2] It was a mixture of usual suspects, from the new prime minister to his predecessor, from sportsmen and women who had represented the UK to veterans who had suffered terrible injuries. The actors and musicians who took part in the video were a less predictable bunch: among them were Thom Yorke from Radiohead, David Tennant of Dr Who fame and Ian Wright, the ex-footballer-turned-commentator. Predominantly male but representing a range of the UK's cultural fronts, the cast enacted a reflective silence for those who had died in Britain's wars, past and current. But it was the final scene that caught my eye, and as it looped around I had to watch several times in order to decide whether my first impressions were correct.

A tall soldier dressed in a T-shirt, combats and a green beret stood on the left of the screen, his hands held behind his back and his face half hidden in shadow. The background was clearly a historic building with ornate patterns carved into golden stone. In the centre, his bulky army rucksack lay on the ground and on the right a Union Jack furled around a pole was propped against the wall. After a few seconds the man turned and walked across the set, first picking up his heavy bag and then clasping the flag as he exited on the right. The message of this brief drama was unavoidable: British soldiers will continue to risk their lives for the country despite the inherent danger. For those few who recognised him, ex-marine Ram Patten, founder of the fund raising project March for Honour, was an appropriate participant in this pageant, having spoken openly about the corrosive effects of Post-Traumatic Stress Disorder (PTSD) on his own life. But for the vast majority, he was likely to be a symbolic figure performing another role, one that was perhaps less heroic. He appeared to be an ordinary serviceman doing his job, but he was also black.[3]

Meanwhile a counteroffensive had been launched less than a mile away. As the two-minute silence began in Charing Cross, over in Kensington all hell was being let loose. Thirty odd members of the group, Muslims Against Crusades (MAC), had chosen this moment to demonstrate against the UK's wars in Afghanistan and Iraq. They set fire to a giant poppy, and began chanting slogans such as 'British soldiers burn in hell' and 'British troops are murderers'. Just yards away, representatives of the English Defence League (EDL) were holding a counter-protest, and the Metropolitan Police were attempting to keep them apart.

Oblivious to this fracas, the crowd milled about in the square, filling the pool with handfuls of poppies handed out by cadets in baggy uniforms. Here another small drama was taking place at the side of Nelson's column. A group of six infantry soldiers in green battledress stood awkwardly in a row, their backs against a giant marble lion, while members of the crowd took turns to have photos taken at their side. It was as if these men were celebrities too, like the ones who had just climbed down from the stage. I knew that it was no coincidence that of the six who were trying to maintain a polite and friendly demeanour, two were from Fiji and one from Nepal. It made me wonder how many people in the square had any idea where those soldiers were from or why those particular men had been chosen. But in this context, public ignorance provided an unguarded battleground in the struggle for hearts and minds, whether at home or in the combat zone. Regardless of any 'real' explanation as to why they happened to be there, the stealthy deployment of a group of ethnically mixed soldiers was a weapon in the war of information that stretched from Whitehall all the way to Kabul and back again.

From recruitment to representation

March towards the sound of gunfire. This has long been the standard instruction for military men trained to identify the location of their enemy and to seek them out. The convention for books written by or about soldiers seems to follow this rule as well, invariably beginning with a life-or-death struggle that catapults the reader straight into the carnage of war. Opening with this alternative scenario in the heart of London allows me to introduce the subjects of this story, Britain's migrant soldiers, within a very domestic context. The occasion also helps to mark out the territory covered in this book.

The annual ritual of commemoration provides an opportunity to focus on the changing profile of military service in British cultural life. By paying attention to the soldiers themselves, either on screen or in person, it draws the eye towards the politics of multiculturalism at work in this public arena. This point in turn is a reminder that the British Army is not just an important public institution but one that represents the nation in its historic form. Finally, by heeding the simultaneous protests from the Islamists and their opponents, the event is able to evoke the wider political context of democracy, securitisation and war.

The primary intention of this book is to document the story of Britain's twenty-first-century Commonwealth soldiers. Beginning with the mixed group in the square, we turn first to the figure from Nepal. Although not a member of the Commonwealth, Nepal supplies another group of migrants who are no less relevant to this discussion. In 2008 the public was alerted to the fact that the modern British Army still included a sizeable contingent of soldiers recruited annually from the foothills of the Himalayas. Known as Gurkhas, they could trace their connection to British military power right back to the East India Company's conquest of northern India in the early nineteenth century. Their modern profile was dramatically heightened in 2008, when Joanna Lumley took up cudgels for the Gurkha Justice Campaign, demanding settlement rights for elderly ex-servicemen who until 2009 were denied residency in the UK. The resulting media attention propelled the question of military service as a condition of citizenship into the public eye, tapping into a deep vein of support for these veterans who had spent many years fighting for Britain in distant wars. Meanwhile, from 2007 Gurkhas have enjoyed the same terms and conditions as all the other soldiers in the British Army.

In order to understand the reasons for the two Fijians' presence, knowledge of colonial history is important but it does not provide the immediate explanation. For that it is necessary to go back to 1998 when the Ministry of Defence (MoD) in the young New Labour government dropped the five-year residency requirement for applicants from Commonwealth countries. The government's aim was to widen the armed forces' recruitment pool to include citizens from more than 50 countries, allowing them to apply either from overseas by post or on the Internet, or in person while visiting the UK on temporary visas. Individual regiments, desperate to fill vacant slots, were quick to set up their own recruitment channels. The measure was immediately effective in increasing 'manning' levels to meet the demands of deployment in Northern Ireland, Kosovo, Sierra Leone and East Timor. In 2001 an official programme of Overseas Pre-Selection Teams (OPTs) began to travel to different Caribbean countries and to Fiji in order to fast-track those who had applied online. These OPTs were to continue at intervals until Lehman Brothers crashed in the late summer of 2008.

In 2010 there were 7,895 soldiers who fell in the category of Foreign and Commonwealth in the British Army.[4] Of the former, 300 were from the Republic of Ireland, 350 classed as British National (Overseas) and 450 were Nepalese ex-Gurkhas who had transferred. The largest national groups from Commonwealth countries were composed of 2,615 Fijians, 935 Ghanaians, 910 South Africans, 525 Jamaicans and 430 Zimbabweans. There were 1,185 from other African countries, just under a thousand from other Caribbean nations and the rest came from as far away as Bangladesh, New Zealand and Canada. Among the Commonwealth countries not represented at that time were Papua New Guinea, Singapore, Ascension Islands and Tonga.

The book documents this experiment in creating an integrated, culturally diverse army through conversations with men and women at different stages of their careers, from brand new recruits to seasoned soldiers and from privates to commanding officers. The chapters build on each other to investigate from different angles what it might be like to join a military organisation in someone else's country, mindful of how the organisation has responded to their presence. Part I covers the mechanics and politics of recruiting, while Part II incorporates a wide-ranging discussion of culture as a factor in integration, training and everyday life. Part III considers a variety of experiences of hostility and racism within the institution, charting the army's attempts to eradicate bullying and to reform systems of monitoring and disciplining unacceptable behaviour. Part IV includes a chapter on the experiences of army spouses living on the cusp between military and civilian worlds. This leads to a sobering investigation of the issues arising from the soldiers' status as migrants. The concluding chapter returns to a discussion of death in service, asking why and how the figure of the British soldier has become re-centred in the life of the nation.

Elephants and empire

There are three interwoven strands that run through this story, and together they pose urgent questions for anyone concerned about the place of the military in social and political life. The first of these underlines the connections between Britain's imperial past and its current status as a junior partner of the US. This dynamic can be illustrated by another encounter with soldiers. One day, when visiting a base to observe a briefing by the newly formed Fiji Support Network, I fell into conversation with a Fijian Sergeant who hosted our lunch in the Officers' Mess. As we sat at the polished oak table, surrounded by military memorabilia collected by that particular regiment over many decades, he drew my attention to an engraving of the young Queen Victoria which was hanging nearby. He wanted me to know that this very same object had once graced the walls of a British encampment near Kabul and that in 1879 it was rescued after a battle – the locally raised foot-soldiers had mutinied over pay – and eventually restored to its rightful home in the regimental base. It was an otherwise unremarkable picture and I would not have bothered to read the legend inscribed on the frame which linked it to the dismal history of British military failures in Afghanistan. Later I was able to trace the artistic details of the print as well as its dramatic 'rescue', but it was not that aspect of our exchange that was enlightening.

More telling was the Fijian Sergeant's openness to knowing about Britain's military past, his grasp of the genealogy of his own organisation and his despondency that his younger British colleagues seemed to be neither informed nor curious about their country's historic role in carving up the world. As we sat and talked, surrounded by umbrella stands made of elephant feet and countless depictions of battles in far-flung lands, I became even more convinced that we ignore the institutional politics of the armed forces at our peril. Ignorance is no defence.

Without this source of global migrant labour which addressed problems of poor retention as well as low recruitment, the British Army would not have been able to sustain continuous deployment in Iraq and Afghanistan. But the reliance on a military workforce drawn from Britain's former empire in order to fight contemporary wars has not been publicly acknowledged, nor is it often discussed in terms of the UK's aspirations to remain a global power, able to 'punch above its weight', to borrow a phrase beloved to recent governments. By placing the recruitment of migrant soldiers within a much larger historical context, seeing it as a contemporary version of the colonial armies first raised over 200 years ago, the book suggests that this is an opportunity to learn about those continuities with the past as well as to become reacquainted with the legacies of British imperialism in the present.

The second strand argues that the presence of Commonwealth soldiers in the British Army has enabled the institution to incorporate a version of diversity management in line with the rest of the public sector, informed by and under pressure from the broader shifts in HR technologies and employment law. This process of modernising a tradition-bound, hierarchical and male-dominated institution has been largely hidden from view. Combined with the effects of privatisation, financial cuts and the incessant demands of deployment, the move towards becoming a diverse, multicultural employer has been part of a rapid period of reform. But this is not merely a matter of internal management. The issue of who joins the British Army, one of the most symbolic institutions of the nation, has implications for the politics of inclusion in the wider society. This documentary account of diversifying the army proposes a re-thinking of what is meant by multiculturalism and a re-evaluation of its effects on British public life.

The third strand concerns the relationship between military service and citizenship. It is worth clarifying at the outset that foreign soldiers do not enjoy an expedited route to citizenship by virtue of military service. Needless to say, the capacity of the British Army to deal with the issues and problems entailed in employing migrants has been limited since, particularly in the early days, they were just not equipped to manage this aspect of their 'diversity'.

However, the administrative problems of employing military migrants are compounded by the wider politics of European immigration control which produces ever-tightening regulations, rising visa and naturalisation costs and, more ominously, an increasingly fearful xenophobia that sanctions further anti-immigration measures – particularly targeted at migrants from outside the EU. As a consequence, Commonwealth and Gurkha soldiers have found themselves 'caught in the crossfire', as the Fiji Support Network puts it, alternately lauded as heroes but stigmatised as immigrants.

The journey that this book has promised will flag up more questions than it has been able to address, so dense is the web of politics connecting war, empire, nationalism, security, immigration, military service, racism and citizenship. One important route not taken is the disparity between the three armed services, the British Army (BA), the Royal Navy (RN) and the Royal Air Force (RAF), which each have their own record of employing ethnic minorities as well as practices of excluding them in the past. The book does not do justice to other aspects of recruitment, such as the attitudes of 'home-grown' minorities towards military service or the phenomenon of recruits from the Republic of Ireland, who are still classified as 'foreign'. Crucially, it retains a single-minded focus on the British military experience, although, where possible, comparisons with other national armies are made in order to highlight significant discrepancies. The contrast also helps to underline that this discussion is relevant throughout the military sector worldwide.

To clarify what I have not covered is a way of emphasising some of the work that lies ahead. This study does not address the experience of combat, the job for which most soldiers are trained. I did not follow the soldiers to

Helmand since that was never my intention. This investigation of a phenomenon I have called 'militarised multiculture' begins and ends in the country that sends migrant soldiers to war. And I did not begin to touch on the after-effects of military service for those who were wounded or traumatised, including the families of those who were affected. This dimension of the story cannot be captured from the UK alone.

In 2010 a tri-service community social worker for the Eastern Caribbean was appointed; he was to be based at the British High Commission in Barbados. His role was to offer direct specialist welfare support to the families of the more than 1,200 members of the British armed forces who came from the region, holding meetings, briefing families and serving as a contact point with each of the three services. One of his duties was to support the families of casualties. He was also on hand to advise those who were medically discharged with injuries and who were eligible to claim medical costs under the Armed Forces Compensation Scheme. Learning about this new post during the finishing stages of the book, I realised that he would be speaking to the families of the men and women I first met in 2008, many of whom feature in these pages. This simple news item, buried deep inside a publication for army families, brought home one more devastating consequence of global military migration, one of the enduring features of our time.

Acknowledgements

I owe a huge debt of gratitude to Lieutenant-General Sir Freddie Viggers who, at a chance meeting in 2007, drew my attention to the predicament of Commonwealth soldiers. The fact that this book happened at all is due to his support, although he bears no responsibility for the way it is written. Colonel Mark Abraham was an inexhaustibly patient and helpful point of contact throughout, and I cannot thank him enough for his guidance as well as his trust.

It is impossible to name all the individuals who arranged and hosted my visits, explained procedures and put up with my questions. I remain deeply grateful to those who made me feel welcome and I hope I made this clear at the time. Conversations with Colonel Richard Castell, Colonel Tim Checketts, Colonel David Hayes, Major Sports Gordon, Lt Colonel Duncan Strutt and Colonel Roddy Winser were invaluable. David Cunningham facilitated my visits to the Infantry Training Camp in Catterick, and his generosity, humour and interest in the project were enormously appreciated. Thanks too to Lindsay Russell for her warmth and kindness and to Sala Smith whose hospitality during those visits to Yorkshire ensured that I had a home away from home. Her friendship, advice and support have made all the difference to this account, although again, she bears no responsibility for the result.

I am especially grateful to the committee of the Fiji Support Network for letting me attend meetings and for sharing information. Glen Lalabalavu was a gracious host and guide to Fijian culture, while the Waqavonovono family supplied a dimension to this research that was invaluable.

To these and all the others who took part in discussions and interviews, heartfelt thanks. I am aware this book only represents a fraction of the voices I heard, but I have done my best to make it representative as well as accurate.

My post as Research Fellow at the Open University, UK, enabled me to undertake this project and I remain extremely grateful to those who gave their full support, including Tony Bennett, Marie Gillespie and Sophie Watson at the ESRC Centre for Research on Socio-Economic Change (CRESC) and Engin Isin and Jef Huysmans at the Centre for Citizenship, Identities and Governance (CCIG). Thanks to my great colleagues for sympathy and solidarity throughout: especially Claudia Aradau, Mark Banks, John Clarke, Francis Dodsworth, Umut Erel, Andrew Hill, Nick Mahony, Karim Murji, Janet Newman, Sarah Neal, Evelyn Ruppert, Raia Prokhovnik, Alban Webb, Margie Wetherall and Kath Woodward. Thanks to Julia Platt for great transcriptions in the final stages. Karen Ho and Sarah Batt were an endless source of help and good cheer.

It is hard to convey enough gratitude and respect to Cynthia Enloe for her tireless work on militarisation. Her insistence on curiosity as a guiding principle and her generosity of spirit helped to set this project on its way.

Big thanks to Victoria Basham, Deb Cowen, Ozgur Heval Cinar, Paul Higate, Mark Imber, Ron R. Krebs, Annica Kronsell, Anna Leander, Phil Withington and Rachel Woodward for contributing to the 'Soldiers, Citizens and Security' workshops, and to Tarak Barkawi for advice and encouragement from an early stage. I also learned from conversations with Shane Brighton, Christopher Dandeker, Derek Gregory, Anthony Matheson, Hugh Milroy and Tony Warner.

Thanks to Daniel Conway and Melissa Steyn for inviting me to explore citizenship, racism and military service in *Ethnicities*, and to Bolette Blaagaard for her invitation to lecture in the International Programme at the Utrecht School of Critical Theory in the Netherlands. I am grateful to Jonathan Rutherford for commissioning a piece for *Soundings* and to Sandra Ponzanesi for urging me to write about soldiers and intersectionality. I was very honoured by the Danish translation of 'Lives on the Line' in *Social Kritik*, and I am grateful to Benny Lihme and Flemming Røgilds for that.

Thanks to Robin Cohen for inviting me to the BSA panel on international migration in January 2011, and for his support in publishing the book. I also want to thank Dick Hobbs and Tony Mason for other publishing conversations.

I benefited massively from Teresia Teaiwa's insightful feminist take on militarism and her own research on Fijian recruitment in the 1960s. Rosemary Bechler, Mitra Pariyar and Mark Slobin read chapters at crucial times and were invaluable, unsparing critics, and Victor Manuel Cruz dug up some priceless newspaper cuttings.

Many aspects of this book are indebted to conversations with friends over time, and I owe much to the inspiration and insights of Les Back, Anthony Barnett, Chetan Bhatt, Tricia Bohn, Debbie Bond, Rosi Braidotti, Daniel Canetti, Hazel Carby, Iain Chambers, Helen Crowley, Lidia Curti, Miranda Davies, Hedvig Ekerwald, Hoda Elsadda, Johanna Esseveld, Ruthie Gilmore, Craig Gilmore, Stuart Hall, Catherine Hall, Dan Hancox, Hermione Harris, Judith Herrin, Roger Hewitt, Dienke Hondius, Sara Ilyas, Manzu Islam, Isaac Julien, Laleh Khalili, Maki Kimura, Jill Lewis, Rebecca Lewis Smith, Achille Mbembe, Steve McQueen, Angela McRobbie, Altaf Makhiawala, Mark Nash, Sarah Nuttall, Hiroko Ogasawara, Bridget Orr, Ann Phoenix, James Rhodes, Manuela Ribeiro Sanches, Shamser Sinha, Emmanuel Raymundo, Mandy Rose, Inger Sjørslev, Lucia Trimbur, Farida Vis, Ed Vulliamy, Nick Wadham-Smith, Lilah Wayment, Georgie Wemys, Val Wilmer, Patrick Wright, Janet Wolff, Gary Younge and Thomas Zacharias.

My friend Greta Slobin, though she will not see the book in print, is part of its history. I miss her more than words can say. Cassandra Marks and Barbara Hezelgrave helped to keep body and soul together throughout.

Special thanks go to my mother, Elizabeth Ware, for providing a base with cakes and comfort and much else besides. My brother, Fran Ware, provided valuable photographic expertise and Jack Latham stepped in with design advice at a crucial moment and I am really grateful to them both.

Cora Gilroy Ware's fearless intellect and Marcus Gilroy Ware's exacting originality drove me on. The book would not have happened without the sanctuary provided by Paul Gilroy. Through the example of their own work, they open my eyes to new knowledge and creative ways of thinking. This has been one strange voyage, and without the separate anchors they each provide, I would have long been lost at sea.

All the names of those who were interviewed for this book have been changed in the interests of anonymity. Individual views do not necessarily represent current British Army policy.

Abbreviations and Acronyms

AFCAS	Armed Forces Continuous Attitudes Survey
AFF	Army Family Federation
AFMA	Armed Forces Muslim Association
ARTD	Army Recruiting and Training Division
AWS	Army Welfare Service
BARB Test	British Army Recruit Battery (test)
BDF	Belize Defence Force
BG	Brigade of Gurkhas
CGJ	Campaign for Gurkha Justice
CGS	Chief of the General Staff
CO	Commanding Officer
CRE	Commission for Racial Equality
DART	Diversity Action Recruiting Team
DASA	Defence Analytical Services Agency
DM(A)	Director(ate) Manning (Army)
E&D	Equality and Diversity
ECHR	European Court of Human Rights
EDL	English Defence League
EHRC	Equality and Human Rights Commission
F&C	Foreign and Commonwealth
FMF	Fiji Military Force
FSN	Fiji Support Network
HRM	Human Resource Management
IPA	Institute of Practitioners in Advertising
ITC	Infantry Training Centre
LGBT	lesbian, gay, bisexual and transgender
LOA	Local Overseas Allowance
LPR	Lawful Permanent Residency
LTR	Leave to Remain
MAC	Muslims Against Crusades
MATT	Military Annual Training Tests
MAVNI	Military Accessions Vital to the National Interest
MoD	Ministry of Defence
NCO	non-commissioned officer
OC	officer commanding
OPT	Overseas Pre-selection Team
ORs	other ranks

PTSD	Post-Traumatic Stress Disorder
RBL	Royal British Legion
RFMF	Republic of Fiji Military Forces
RMAS	Royal Military Academy Sandhurst
RTS	Recruit Trainees Survey
SANDF	South African National Defence Force
SAS	Special Air Service
SCC	Service Complaints Commissioner
SFA	Service Family Accommodation
SOFA	Status of Forces Agreement
TA	Territorial Army
USCIS	United States Citizenship and Immigration Services
UWO	Unit Welfare Officer
V&S	Values and Standards
VC	Victoria Cross
WO	Warrant Officer

1
Introduction: For Queen and Commonwealth

Image 1   Lance Corporal Paul Erhahiemen, Household Cavalry Mounted Regiment, 2010

When the time comes, it takes less than ten seconds to turn from a civilian into a soldier. The officers supervising the transformation make it perfectly clear that this is the most significant moment in the whole proceedings. First, however, there's the ritual of attestation. Dennis, a tall young man wearing a sweatshirt, jeans and trainers, steps forward, raises his right hand and begins:

> I...*solemnly, sincerely and truly declare and affirm that I will be faithful and bear true allegiance to Her Majesty Queen Elizabeth II, her heirs and successors*

and that I will as in duty bound honestly and faithfully defend Her Majesty, her heirs and successors in person, crown and dignity against all enemies and will observe and obey all orders of Her Majesty, her heirs and successors and of the generals and officers set over me.

As he sits down, his three companions, Ben, Carlos and Albert rise to take their turn. They too are casually dressed, and in their left hands they each hold a compact copy of the Bible. With their right hands raised they recite the Oath of Allegiance in unison, inserting their own names hesitantly as they read from the poster on the wall in front of them: '*I...swear by Almighty God that I will be faithful and bear true allegiance to Her Majesty Queen Elizabeth II, ...*'

When they finish they return to their seats, anxious to complete the whole ordeal. They know that they are not officially employees of the British Army until they have written their name on the printed contracts not once, but twice. Sign on the first dotted line as a civilian, and sign again here as a soldier.

I watch the four young men go through the motions, one by one. It is less than a week since they travelled across the Atlantic to take this step, having left their families and friends in Belize and St Lucia, not knowing when or whether they will see them again. I wonder what their parents would say and offer to photograph the ceremony so they can email the pictures home as proof that their new lives have truly begun. When they have all signed twice, I take another picture of them standing stiffly in a row in front of the Queen's portrait, each holding their attestation certificate and looking grave. Then it is all over. The officer in charge offers to hold my camera so I can be included in the group photo, then wishes them well and leaves the room. The new soldiers have little to do except pack their few belongings and wait for transport to take them to the Infantry Training Centre (ITC) in Yorkshire.

Looking at the pictures later I notice the large action posters of guns, tanks and helicopters visible in the background. The images leave no doubt as to what these recruits have signed up to and the matching blood-red carpet and crimson chairs only add to the solemnity that they clearly feel. But the pictures are a reminder of something else. When I had first met them at the beginning of the week I had encountered them as young adults barely out of their teens. Over four days I had heard about their families, their school days, their girlfriends, the pressures that had caused them to seize this opportunity and the ambitions that they nurtured beyond the life of an infantryman in the British Army. They had shared some of the shock they had felt on arriving in this new environment. Although they were already committed to this path, apprehensive but determined to excel in their new profession, we were all civilians together, strangers in a very odd world indeed.

The picture from that final day in the Johnson Beharry room captured some of the warmth generated by our conversations. But it was also a record of their first moments as paid-up members of the British armed forces. They were now heading for an intense six-month programme that was designed to transform them into small cogs in a military machine, trained to kill if not to die in the course of doing their job. Within the coming year they might well find themselves on patrol in Helmand Province. The major had made that very clear in his briefing. 'Be prepared,' he had warned them. 'These are challenging times ahead.'

Several new experiences could be guaranteed at the training establishment in Yorkshire: achingly difficult ones such as the lethal effects of freezing temperatures and physical exhaustion, homesickness and a relentlessly bland diet. There would undoubtedly be positive ones too: unexpected friendships, a sense of achievement and newfound physical and mental confidence. The major had urged them to be proud of who they were, and not to hide the fact that they represented their own countries as well as the British Army. But it was also certain that they would have to face the reality of being identified as black and treated as foreign, possibly for the first time in their lives. Inevitably they would develop a sharpened sense of being outsiders, acutely aware of not growing up in the UK and not being habituated to local ways of speaking or doing things. They would come across English, Welsh, Scottish and Irish counterparts who might never have heard of their countries and who might hold them in contempt because they were different. But they would also meet other young recruits who, like them, were not citizens of the UK.

'Broken Britain'

Although they did not know it at the time, these four young men had arrived at the tail end of a cycle of active overseas recruitment that had lasted throughout the decade, meeting the incessant demand for new sources of soldiers. Without the intake of migrant workers from the South Pacific, Africa and the Caribbean from 1998 onwards, the army would have struggled even harder with the effects of poor retention and under-recruitment.[1] In 2006, for example, it emerged that the number of soldiers had fallen by more than 15,000 in the previous 12 months, despite a rise in the number of recruits, and a survey indicated that one in five wanted to leave 'as soon as possible'.[2] The chronic shortage of soldiers was not a new state of affairs. Since the end of conscription in 1960 the armed forces had found it hard both to attract and retain workers for a range of social and demographic reasons.[3]

In more recent times negative perceptions of army life were heightened by public anger at the invasion of Iraq, fuelled by news of mounting casualties and reports of inadequate equipment. But the domestic lives of soldiers had been causing concern too. The investigations into the unexplained deaths of four recruits in Deepcut, Surrey, between 1995 and 2002 had exposed numerous instances of abuse and cover-ups. In addition, in 2005 a report by the

Adult Learning Inspectorate had found that living quarters in the training barracks were sometimes 'dilapidated, dreary and depressing'.[4] Widespread problems with sub-standard army housing across the country had impacted on the social welfare of military families who were bearing the brunt of repeated deployments. It was hardly surprising that military service did not represent an attractive career. But at the same time as filling the ranks, this apparently inexhaustible supply of eager recruits from overseas conveniently began to fix the lack of diversity that could no longer be ignored.

In 1998 there was a total of 1 per cent ethnic minorities among the armed services, with the same figure represented in the army (0.9 per cent officers and 1.1 per cent other ranks). Ethnic monitoring was not carried out on a systematic basis until 2001, by which time the level in the army had increased to 2.4 per cent (1.2 per cent Officers and 2.5 per cent Other Ranks). The 2001 census indicated that ethnic minorities made up 8 per cent of the UK population, which meant that they were significantly under-represented in the armed services. By the end of the decade, when the last recruits garnered through the Overseas Pre-selection Teams (OPTs) were filtering in, the proportion of black and ethnic minority soldiers in the army, including officers, had exceeded 9 per cent.[5] Never mind that just a third of these were citizens of the UK and had grown up there.

As minorities, Commonwealth soldiers feel the impact of entrenched patterns of racism across all sections of the institution. This is hardly surprising given predominant attitudes towards foreigners and immigrants in the wider UK society, but the fact that racist bullying and harassment has long been associated with military culture continues to present those who manage the army with a particularly difficult task in rooting it out. Commonwealth soldiers are therefore well-placed to testify to the effects of the uneven pace of reform and to contribute to the modernisation of the institution. But while they have been busy helping to transform the army, the country has been changing too.

By November 2009 when the young men that I had met were summoned from the Caribbean, British society was in the midst of a deep recession. The war in Afghanistan was entering a new phase after eight long and demoralising years. The number of fatalities that year had reached 100, over double that of the previous year, and over 150 had been seriously wounded. The general election was on the horizon, and the financial crisis had helped to propel the politics of immigration high up the crowded agenda. The term 'Broken Britain' had become a cliché, operating as an expressive metaphor of a dysfunctional national community. Massive cuts in public spending were forecast regardless of which party won, and the armed forces were no more exempt than any other sector.

As the four new recruits went through the process of signing up to a military career, they must have felt an extra layer of disbelief that they had got this far. They had passed the pre-selection tests in June 2008 when the British

Army's OPT visited Belize and St Lucia. At the time they were about to graduate from high school, worried about how they would survive financially, let alone qualify for a decent job. It would be another 14 months before they received an invitation to buy their plane tickets to London. During that interval Britain's security requirements had begun to look very different. Recruitment in the UK had soared and retention was no longer an acute problem. However although the demand for manpower had stabilised, the financial crisis was having a severe impact on plans for the army's future size and capability.

While defence was not the only sector to face radical restructuring, it had particular significance for Britain's ambitions to be a global power. Writing about the long-term effects of the recession a few months earlier, economist Will Hutton had pointed to the links between foreign policy and public spending. 'Britain is going to feel very different in the years ahead,' he warned. 'Like the empires of Venice, Spain, the Netherlands and Austria before us, Britain no longer has an economy large enough to finance our ambitions and overseas commitments.'[6] Within barely a year this prediction had become accepted as common sense, forming the basis of the new coalition government's programme to dismantle the welfare state.[7] Just a few weeks before the *Strategic Defence and Security Review* was released in October 2010, Defence Secretary Liam Fox was even blunter. 'We don't have the money as a country to protect ourselves against every potential future threat,' he told *The Daily Telegraph*. 'We just don't have it.'[8]

For new recruits entering the system this was hardly a time to consider such weighty matters, regardless of whether they had UK citizenship or not. But the link between finance and foreign policy has implications for the way that the armed forces relate to civil society as well as for the nation's role in the world at large. It may only take a few seconds to turn a civilian into a soldier but the hidden resources required to get the individual to this point, before the training has even begun, draw on far more than the question of taxpayers' money alone. Although this process requires public funds to promote the benefits of a military career within a competitive labour market, there are other less tangible costs as well.

The ideas that most of us have about soldiering today draw on a morass of complex assumptions formed as a result of historical events, traditional practices, political settlements, legal agreements, media representation and personal experience. They also depend to a large extent on what we think about the wars that soldiers are sent off to fight. As a consequence, recruitment into the armed forces is a supremely social issue as well as an intensely political one, and the line between military and civilian spheres is revealed as an unpredictable and unstable fissure. In some periods the question of who joins the army is relatively dormant as a public concern. But studied over a longer period military recruitment strategies can be seen to play an important role in shaping the politics of citizenship and the definition of the political community. This is because, at certain moments, the act of volunteering to be a soldier is thought to reach into the heart of what it means to be a citizen and to 'serve' the country. This commitment becomes especially prominent when the number of young soldiers killed in battle starts to rise and the media spotlight turns towards their grieving families before settling on the politicians who sent them there. In the UK the collective annual rituals of commemoration create a space where Britishness emerges in its sacred historical form, providing a bridge between the crumbling pillars of empire and the unstable edifice of contemporary militarism. In the presence of the coffin draped by the Union Jack, the concept of 'the ultimate sacrifice' brings the idea of the nation back to life.

Silence

By chance it happened that 11 November, Armistice Day, fell in the middle of the same week in which the four young men from the Caribbean passed through the Army Selection Centre. The first two, Dennis and Ben, had arrived early on Monday morning, but Albert and Carlos had barely been in the country for 24 hours, since their flight from Belize had been delayed and they had missed their connection in Miami. That day I found them all in recovery after finishing their timed run, laughing about the excruciating head and chest pains they had experienced as a result of breathing in cold air for the first time in their lives. The conversation was cut short when we were summoned to go to the main reception area just after 10.30 a.m. We sat in the back row, continuing our exchange in rather more hushed tones as we watched the BBC coverage of the service in Westminster Abbey on a large screen. The breaking-news ribbon along the bottom was distracting, but strangely relevant too. 'Youth unemployment has reached a record 20%,' it repeated, as if drawing our attention to the reasons why army recruitment had soared in recent months.

While we waited for the clock to strike 11, 30 or so half-dressed young men in numbered bibs, who had been interrupted at different stages of their pre-selection tests, fidgeted in the front rows. Civilian medical and administrative staff filed in at the back of the room, uniforms appeared from all directions and gradually the entire workforce was assembled. At the appointed time a voice behind us barked, 'People: stand up!' Facing the screen we stood and watched in silence as the camera panned over the faces of the congregation in Westminster, pausing on those of politicians, veterans, royalty and clergy. As it lingered over the Tomb of the Unknown Soldier, the words 'British Warrior' were visible under the scarlet poppies scattered on the flat grey surface.

Elsewhere on the base all activity had stopped. There was a palpable sense of stillness across the parade grounds nearby and throughout the accommodation and teaching blocks on the far side. The preparations for this year's

Remembrance ceremonies had seen the usual controversy about the significance of wearing (or not wearing) poppies. As the fatality rate in Afghanistan continued to rise, Gordon Brown had been in trouble for writing a clumsy, misspelt letter to a grieving mother, an error he had compounded when he failed to bow his head after placing a wreath at the Cenotaph on Remembrance Sunday. But there were two other reasons why 2009 was significantly different from previous years. The first was that the service we were watching in Westminster Abbey marked the passing of the generation that had fought in the First World War. That summer, Harry Patch, the last surviving soldier to have fought in the trenches, had died at the age of 111. The second was that there was a greater emphasis on the casualties being sustained in the course of Britain's latest wars. In the grounds outside the Abbey the Royal British Legion had created a Field of Remembrance containing 60,000 small wooden crosses, stars and crescents bearing a poppy and a personal message, each dedicated to friends and relatives who had died in service during the twentieth century. For the first time a special area had been set aside for soldiers killed in Iraq and Afghanistan. When it was opened by the Duke of Edinburgh a few days earlier two widows had been invited to plant crosses in honour of their husbands. The plot also included memorials to the five British soldiers killed in Afghanistan that same week.

The end of the period of silence was registered by the commentator's voice and the movement of the congregation in the Abbey. The sergeant was the first to speak in our gathering, this time to apologise for his gruffness towards the civilians present. The breaking-news tape announced: 'Sainsburys see a 32% jump in profits.' The crowd dissolved and the normal pace of the centre resumed as if nothing had happened, but there was no doubt in my mind that the silence had resonated very differently in this environment. It was far too simplistic to think that everyone in the building shared the same attitudes, the same misgivings and the same convictions just because it was a military base, but since the whole rationale of the centre was to turn young civilians into new soldiers I imagined that many of the staff were aware of the poignancy of this moment.

When we reassembled I asked the newcomers what they had thought of the Armistice Day ceremony. It is a date that is commemorated throughout the Commonwealth, but I wondered what they made of this ritual in honour of fallen soldiers when they were just about to put on uniforms themselves. They agreed that it was important to know that soldiers were not forgotten in Britain. 'It's good because people remember you after you die,' said Albert. 'It's a very good thing. It makes the family of the individual feel proud.' Then he added, 'It helps us to have the drive to join the army.' They had also heard about Harry Patch whose death had been reported globally, and were aware not just that he had died, but that he had decided to speak out about his traumatic experiences in the war after keeping silent for 80 years.

I asked them if they had noticed the two soldiers who had stepped forward to hand the Queen a wreath to place on the tomb of the Unknown British Warrior that we had glimpsed earlier. One of these soldiers was Lance Corporal Johnson Beharry VC. Originally a citizen of Grenada, he had passed through this same selection centre in 2001 shortly before being sent to Catterick in Yorkshire, where many of the young recruits now watching the ceremony were bound as well. While on deployment in Al-Amarah, Iraq, in 2004 he had distinguished himself by driving members of his unit to safety on two occasions when they came under heavy fire. He had been awarded the Victoria Cross the following year, becoming the first living person to receive it since 1965 and certainly one of the youngest. He was 24 at the time. The citation for this award commended him: 'For his repeated extreme gallantry and unquestioned valour, despite intense direct attacks, personal injury and damage to his vehicle in the face of relentless enemy action.'9

It was no surprise to see Beharry playing such an important role on this occasion, but it was unlikely that these latest Commonwealth recruits would be aware of his significance as a military figure. As we stood observing the two minutes' silence, this seemed an especially rich moment to think about the forces that had brought them into this room. They had barely been in the country for 48 hours before being confronted with one of the nation's most sacred ceremonies. Although the figure of the fallen soldier was the focus of remembrance, made more sombre than ever by the escalating fatality rate in Afghanistan, there were other aspects of this nationalist event that bound the history of Commonwealth countries to Britain's imperial past.

Echoes of empire

After the carnage of the 1914–1918 war, the idea of creating tombs for the Unknown Soldier had been discussed across Europe, particularly in Britain and France where there was growing pressure to provide a national focus for dealing with the aftermath of so many deaths. In each country, the rituals that accompanied the construction of the memorials took place within a 'riot of symbolism', according to historian George Mosse. The details, however, represented political agendas that were nationally specific, though often long forgotten in the turmoil of subsequent wars.

In his book *Fallen Soldiers: Reshaping the Memory of the World Wars*, Mosse describes the attention given to every aspect of collection and burial. The bodies intended for Britain were collected from the most important First World War battlefields such as Ypres and Somme. A high-ranking officer chose the individual to be buried in London – unlike in France where a sergeant wounded in the war selected the body to be interred at the Arc de Triomphe. The coffin for the British soldier was made from an oak tree at the Royal Palace at Hampton Court, and the body was placed inside with a trench helmet and khaki belt together with a medieval sword used in the

Crusades. The Unknown Soldier was taken by a horse-drawn gun carriage from Whitehall to Westminster Abbey immediately after the unveiling of the Cenotaph (a Greek term meaning 'empty tomb'). Mosse emphasised the significance of the fact that the king followed the coffin on foot, a dramatic performance that was intended to evoke the spirit of the times. 'There was a new consciousness at the war's end that a democratic age had dawned,' he wrote, 'an age of mass politics, where national symbols – if they were to work – had to engage popular attention and enthusiasm.'[10]

Benedict Anderson begins his famous book *Imagined Communities* with a discussion of the Tomb of the Unknown Soldier and its role in establishing collective identities at pivotal historical moments. 'There were no more arresting emblems,' he said, 'because...void as these tombs are of identifiable mortal remains or immortal souls, they are nonetheless saturated with ghostly national imaginings.'[11] In both countries, the anonymity of the dead body was able to invoke the nation as a natural, organic entity whose origins lay in the distant past. Where the French memorial symbolised the secular values of the country, the location of the British tomb in the Abbey infused the notion of death in service with Christian ideals of sacrifice and duty. The inscription on the tomb that we had glimpsed on the giant TV screen revealed how the nation projected its identity on to the rest of the world too. The British Warrior interred within offered a memorial to all those who had died in 'the Great War' of 1914–1918, who had given their lives for God, for King and for Country as well as 'For Loved Ones', 'Home and Empire' and 'For the Sacred Cause of Justice and Freedom of the World'. The ghostly *national* imaginings that Anderson describes were also *imperial*, formed in an age in which the major European powers took for granted their right to rule over large areas of the globe.

In his book *The Great War: An Imperial History*, John H. Morrow explains that the 'Great War' had originated in imperialism and cannot be fully analysed without understanding contributory factors such as the European fear of the 'lesser races'. His study provides an altogether different account of the conditions that gave rise to the war, which he describes as 'an orgy of violence', stoked by the xenophobic nationalism of European populations.[12] 'The victors gained in empire but the losers not only lost their empires but also their own imperial states,' he writes. And the aftermath was almost impossible to comprehend. 'Disillusion and despair gripped all, because any reason, any aim, any goal, any gain, and any commemoration paled before the havoc they had wrought.'[13]

In 1920, in the days of King and Empire, the forbears of the Commonwealth citizens now in the Army Selection Centre were regarded as British subjects within this particular imperial nation. Millions had been drawn into the war either directly or indirectly, as soldiers, labourers, munition workers, nurses and other kinds of workers in support roles. In 1914 the British Army had been ill-equipped for a major campaign in the trenches in northern

France and Belgium, and had turned to contingents of Gurkhas, Pathans, Sikhs, Punjabi Muslims and other groups from the Indian Army who were brought over as the Indian Corps to fight the Germans in the first two years of the war. Although not widely remembered today, the deployment of colonial manpower in Europe had been represented to home audiences as an organic feature of the empire's ability to command loyalty from its numerous subjects around the world.

A film made in the late winter of 1915 shows a unit of Sikhs performing tasks away from the battles zones, shortly after the Corps was disbanded and replaced by soldiers from Britain.[14] Meanwhile the Brighton Pavilion had been turned into a hospital on the grounds that its orientalist architecture would make the Indian casualties feel more at home. Those who died of their wounds were commemorated locally. In 1921, the Chattri Memorial to the Indian Army was built on the Sussex Downs to mark the place where 53 Sikh and Hindu soldiers were cremated. The graves of the Muslim soldiers can be seen today in the Muslim Burial Ground in Brookwood, Surrey, less than a mile away from the Centre in Pirbright. The continuing relevance of this history was indicated by the opening, in September 2010, of a new addition to the Chattri memorial, built by the Commonwealth War Graves Commission. The monument names the 53 soldiers who died on the Western Front, and serves as an educational resource promoted by the Commission.

In the case of the Caribbean nations, there is a long history of raising battalions of black soldiers, a tradition that goes back to 1793 when British military recruiters saw the advantages in recruiting 'slaves in red coats' to fight against the French.[15] After 1795, black battalions were formed in several islands and thousands of slave soldiers were purchased by the British Army to help suppress local rebellions. Although they were former slaves, they were paid the same wages as whites and highly prized for superior fitness and resilience in the tropical climate. They were also promised their freedom when they left the army. In practice this was rarely the case, largely due to the objections of plantation owners whose interests were represented in Westminster. As a result the slave rebellions were often followed by slave soldier mutinies, both leading to a litany of floggings and executions.[16]

Over the next 100 years or so, the West India Regiments were widely used in other parts of the empire, particularly in the notorious 'scramble for Africa', where they supported the French and British against the Germans. At the start of the First World War hundreds of young men from the British West Indies were enticed or persuaded to travel to 'the Mother Country' to undertake further selection and training. West Indian troops were deployed in Europe, the Middle East and Africa, although they were frequently used as 'pioneers' or labourers performing demeaning jobs such as cleaning the latrines of the British soldiers, who referred to them as 'West Indian "niggers" '.[17] By the end of hostilities they were treated in such a menial capacity that one battalion, the 9WIR, mutinied. In order to deter others the British imprisoned the ringleaders and repatriated the other battalions. None of the West Indian regiments marched among the British forces in the 1919 victory parade in Paris.[18]

These historical details are bare fragments of a complex and multi-layered account of Europe's imperialist wars. As historians like Morrow have shown, the fact that so many colonised people fought for and alongside Europeans led inexorably to the break-up of empires. In a study of the impact of Jamaican volunteers in the First World War, for example, Richard Smith illustrates how the language of military service and sacrifice had a significant impact on demands for national sovereignty in Jamaica.[19] Today's Commonwealth soldiers, now integrated within the ranks of the modern British Army, are the direct descendants of this history. Their presence should make us ask why it is that the contribution of colonial troops to Britain's former status as an imperial power remains relevant to its current predicament in the twenty-first century. To be more precise, as the military analyst Christopher Dandeker put it, how was it that the government's current recruitment strategies for its armed forces depended so much on these multivocal 'echoes of empire'?[20]

Running in the blood

It is worth taking a brief detour here to connect the recruitment of Commonwealth soldiers to those earlier patterns of immigration that were designed to support the reconstruction of Britain in the post-war period. In 1948 the Labour government led by Clement Attlee passed the British Nationality Act which granted rights of citizenship to all members of the Commonwealth countries, whether still under colonial rule or newly independent.[21] The law was undoubtedly an extraordinary compromise, designed to satisfy the competing claims to nationalism within the Commonwealth while preserving the status of British subjecthood throughout its territories. Although the extension of British citizenship to all members of what are now Commonwealth countries is often forgotten in revisionist accounts of post-1971 immigration control, it provided the legal and constitutional context for the subsequent negotiation of restrictive policies by successive governments.

Dandeker, together with David Mason, a theorist of race and ethnicity, is one of the few commentators to have tracked the UK armed forces' development as a multicultural employer since the 1990s. On the one hand, they point out, the minority ethnic citizens whom the armed forces have sought to recruit locally are predominantly the descendants of Britain's former imperial subjects who were summoned in the post-war period. On the other, the vast majority of non-British citizens admitted to make up numbers have been drawn from former colonial dependencies.[22] The history of British colonial rule, common to both these categories of potential recruits, continues to be a salient factor in explaining their attitudes to military service, qualified of course by where they were born and raised. Although they might not have known the details, the new recruits with whom I was watching the rituals of Armistice Day definitely had a sense of their countries having been involved in and deeply affected by past conflicts between European powers. This was certainly true of the Second World War, as the young men from Belize testified. Some of their parents and grandparents had served in the Allied forces, and this was a significant factor in their sense of connection to the UK.

Albert, for example, told me that he wanted to be a soldier because 'it runs in the blood'.

'My grandfather was in REME and fought in WW2,' he explained, 'somewhere in the desert. He was a UK citizen. My father was in the Belize Defence Force (BDF) as a captain and went to do the officer training course in London. He is a UK citizen too.'

When he was asked to write his full name on his contract, he revealed that his middle name was Rommel, much to the amusement of the major who was signing him up.[23] Dennis too had personal connections with the British armed forces, not least because his maternal grandfather had been a British soldier who had been deployed in Belize in the 1970s. His step-grandfather had also served in the Second World War with the British Army and his mother, now in her early forties, had often told her children she wanted to raise them as British. 'My mother drinks tea and has toast and jam in the morning,' he told me. 'We ate sardines and crackers. She feels connected to England. Almost everything in our household is in the British way.'

These connections were not just inherited, however, since British soldiers had been a familiar sight to Dennis during his childhood. 'When I was a boy, the British Army used to train near my house. We live in a valley and our nearest neighbours are a mile-and-a-half away. The British used to come there and train.' He pointed to a nondescript building we could see out of the window. 'There's a mountain over there and a river. They gave us rations and my sister loved them.'

Belize had once been a British colony, known as British Honduras, famed for its mahogany and the opportunities for rich pickings by outside investors. Although the country had gained independence in 1981 Britain had maintained a military presence there until 1994, when Guatemala finally agreed to recognise the territory as a sovereign state. After the British Army officially left, a specialist training centre was established in exchange for supporting the Belize Defence Force (BDF).

Carlos, whose father was born in Guatemala, and who was from a Creole-speaking community, had recently volunteered to join the BDF and would have attended the officer-training course for overseas cadets at Sandhurst, had he not been selected for the British Army at the last minute. Unlike his fellow Belizeans, however, he had no familial links with the UK. Guatemala had originally been a Spanish colony, but in Carlos's lifetime the country

had suffered a civil war, involving state-sponsored genocide against indigenous ethnic groups, a situation that had required prolonged international
intervention. Carlos's father was one of thousands of Guatemalans who had
fled to Belize to escape the violence.

'There is no army in my family,' he told me. 'I am the only one.' He was
quite candid about his perceptions of the UK when he had first decided to
apply. 'I have no connection with Britain as a country,' he said cheerfully.
'I barely know anything about it.'

The situation was entirely different for Ben, whose mother lived in
London. Although he had not visited the UK before, and his mother had
left St Lucia when he was young, Ben was eager to join her in an attempt
to make a new life away from home. While the strength of their individual
ties to Britain varied with family history, this group of young Caribbean citizens personified the deep colonial and military connections between their
countries and the UK. But this was the twenty-first century. These particular
credentials made them eligible to join the British Army at a time when stringent immigration controls were aimed at blocking the flow of non-skilled
workers from outside the European Union. So how was it that these young
men, armed only with their high-school diplomas, had been invited to make
this journey? What exactly was the framework of the Commonwealth that
had enabled this source of migrant workers to qualify for military work on
Britain's behalf?

Commonwealth of Nations

The term 'British Commonwealth of Nations' was first uttered by the South
African statesman and polymath, Jan Christiaan Smuts, in 1917. The concept, however, had been in use ever since the white settler countries – South
Africa, Australia, New Zealand, Newfoundland, Canada and the Irish Free
State – began agitating for greater independence from Britain before the end
of the nineteenth century. The arrangement of the Dominions, as they were
then called, to have a separate but equal status within the Commonwealth
was formalised by the Balfour Declaration delivered at the Imperial Conference in 1926 and then ratified by the Statute of Westminster in 1931.
Although each country struggled to negotiate its own distance and degree of
independence from Britain, the Declaration established that the Dominions
were 'in no way subordinate one to another in any aspect of their domestic
or external affairs, though united by common allegiance to the Crown, and
freely associated as members of the British Commonwealth of Nations'.

As the process of decolonisation accelerated after the end of British rule
in India in 1947, the word 'British' was dropped from the official title, and
the anachronistic structure of the Empire gave way to the Commonwealth
which promised new relationships between Britain and its former colonies.
Inevitably the process of joining, opting out or being accepted within the
new framework varied according to the political formations within each

territory, but the hierarchy between 'old' and 'new' Commonwealth had already been established by the precedent of recognising the Dominions earlier in the century.

Regardless of whether individual nations opted for republican status or not, the role of the British Crown was a pivotal element within the development of the Commonwealth as a political entity, and since the coronation of Queen Elizabeth II in 1953, an occasion marked and celebrated throughout the former empire, the monarch has maintained a symbolic position as the centrepiece of this postcolonial, global re-alignment. One index of the continuing role of military history within this formation was the construction of the Memorial Gates on Constitution Hill in London in 2002 in recognition of the five million men and women from the Indian subcontinent, Africa and the Caribbean who had served with the Armed Forces during the First and Second World Wars. The official website for the structure makes this connection between the colonial past and the multicultural present explicit. It explains that the memorial also celebrates 'the contribution that these men and women and their descendants continue to make to the rich diversity of British society'.[24]

It became clear through talking to soldiers recruited from a wide range of Commonwealth countries that the Queen was not just a familiar figure because she was the nominal head of the Commonwealth and a historical figure in her own right. Her picture was recognisable from their national banknotes and postage stamps, from history textbooks, portraits gracing the walls of ordinary front rooms, administrative buildings and educational buildings as well as local media accounts of Royal Family gossip, just as it was in the UK. In 16 of the independent sovereign states, including Belize, St Lucia and Grenada, Elizabeth was also the reigning queen, although Jamaica had started the process of becoming a republic. In the Remembrance Service we watched on that day, LCpl Beharry effectively handed the wreath to the Queen of Grenada as well as to the head of the British state. But the historical significance of the Queen's role in the Commonwealth goes far beyond her position as monarch of several nations. More importantly for those recruits in the room it would be to *Her Majesty Queen Elizabeth II, her heirs and successors* that they would swear allegiance when they signed their contracts with the British Army, and not, as many would assume, to the country of Great Britain or the United Kingdom. In the eyes of some British citizens, however, no amount of constitutional history could make up for the fact that these young men were still immigrants, plain and simple, and therefore targets for all kinds of racist and nationalist resentment.

True Brits

In 2008 a senior leader of the far-right British National Party referred to Johnson Beharry as 'an immigrant from Grenada who entered the UK in

1999 and controversially won a VC in Iraq'. Andrew Brons, a former member of the equally repugnant National Front who was elected to the European Parliament as a representative of the BNP in 2009, claimed that the reason Beharry was 'singled out' for a Victoria Cross was because of 'positive discrimination' by a 'PC mad government'.

These attacks on Beharry's reputation were part of a campaign within the BNP to brand the party as 'pro-soldier' but opposed to Britain's involvement in Afghanistan.[25] In his notorious appearance on the BBC programme *Question Time* in October 2009, for example, BNP leader Nick Griffin claimed that the party was successfully targeting charities that supported army veterans. The organisation had recently changed tactics to deploy Churchill as one of their inspirational figures, turning to mawkish representations of the Brits at war to assert that the only people who truly belonged in the country were those whose forefathers' names were on British war memorials. Their attempts to reclaim the history of this global war as white Britain's 'finest hour' were intended to disqualify all but 'true Brits' from having a right to belong. And by smearing Beharry's record on grounds of political correctness they were attacking the government *and* the army for employing migrants in the pursuit of a futile war.

That same month (October 2009) there was a brief flurry of media attention when several former military chiefs drafted an open letter directed at the BNP in response. The letter was signed by General Sir Mike Jackson and General Sir Richard Dannatt, the former heads of the Army; General The Lord Guthrie of Craigiebank, former Chief of the Defence Staff; and Major-General Patrick Cordingley, commander of the Desert Rats in the Gulf War.[26] They called on 'those who seek to hijack the good name of Britain's military for their own advantage' to 'cease and desist'. They declared: 'The values of these extremists – many of whom are essentially racist – are fundamentally at odds with the values of the modern British military, such as tolerance and fairness.'

As proof of their commitment to their opposition to racism, the generals cited the fact that 10 per cent of the army was from Commonwealth countries. 'The reputation of our Armed Forces was won over centuries of service in some of the most difficult areas of the world,' they claimed. 'Political extremists should claim no right to share in this proud heritage.'

While the BNP continued to boast of support from serving soldiers who expressed sympathetic views on internet forums or who encountered BNP leafletters in garrison towns like Catterick, the increasingly vociferous English Defence League (EDL) was beginning to mobilise in larger numbers, motivated by what they claimed to be opposition to Islamic Jihad. The catalyst was an anti-war demonstration in Luton held in response to a local regiment's homecoming parade through the town in March 2009. Placards denouncing the troops as 'child killers' and 'butchers of Basra' were brandished by members and supporters of a group calling itself Ahle

Sunnah al Jamah, whose spokesman Anjem Choudary was already known to police through his involvement in other Islamist groups, including Al-Muhajiroun.[27] The EDL was formed that same month, and began holding their own demonstrations in the name of an outraged, patriotic stand against the tyranny of political Islam.

Quick to prove their populist credentials by seizing on topical issues of the day, the organisation posed as defenders of the ordinary men and women in the armed forces. When the BNP failed to achieve success in the general election in May 2010 and began a period of recrimination and leadership struggles, the EDL, whose membership included many disgruntled BNP sympathisers, emerged as an alternative focus for the far right, one which was potentially more dangerous since it was not interested in the electoral process. Despite the difference between the public images of the two groups, their joint ability to articulate a visceral hatred of anything Islamic and to combine this with an appeal to disaffected soldiers deployed in a Muslim country helps to explain why the military chiefs took a stand. But the chiefs' support of Beharry could not be written off as a scandalised reaction at the disrespect shown to a recipient of the highest military award for bravery, nor was it prompted solely by Griffin's attempt to ventriloquise Churchill as a retrospective spokesman for the BNP. It was an outcome of a prolonged struggle within the armed forces, especially the army, to prove themselves a modern, multi-faith and culturally diverse institution. As we will see, the far-reaching consequences of this 'culture war' could be glimpsed on the battlefield as well as in the barracks and bases at home.

Beharry, who was indeed an 'immigrant' when he joined up, was part of this corporate transformation, although by 2009 he had been naturalised as a UK citizen. The four young recruits watching the ceremony in Westminster were about to enter a workforce that included a significant number of fellow migrants, some of whom would, in time, spend a large proportion of their salary on the citizenship process with the aim of gaining 'the red passport'. There would also be many others who had no intention of relinquishing their own nationalities and becoming British. The question of citizenship and all the technical and legal issues raised by Britain's immigration restrictions threw several spanners into the conventional mechanisms that articulated what it meant to be a soldier in the service of the country. In the meantime, despite the phenomenon of Commonwealth soldiers remaining largely out of sight, an important principle was established as the result of an emotive campaign on behalf of a particular group of soldiers who were neither British by nationality nor Commonwealth in origin.

Deserving citizens

Every year at the end of September the parade ground at the Infantry Training Camp in Catterick (ITC) is the setting for the final 'passing off' ceremony for a new batch of Gurkha soldiers. The event follows the same formula as the equivalent occasion for infantry recruits who have successfully arrived at the same stage of their training: a sequence of drill manoeuvres to the accompaniment of a military band, an address by a senior officer who then carries out an inspection, a prize-giving and more marching past the proud relatives sitting in the pavilion. The difference is that all of the young soldiers and most of the audience are citizens of Nepal.

There are important procedures too that mark this rite of passage as unique in the British Army. The formal part of the day over, the new soldiers and their guests are treated to a sumptuous 'curry lunch' in a marquee erected especially for the purpose. At one end, a gallery of photographs showing pictures of the recruits during training is perused by some of the older male relatives. The young men are beaming, unrecognizable from the stiff marching units seen earlier on the parade ground and now decked in garlands of flowers. The lucky ones are reunited with families whom they have not seen since they left Kathmandu in December the previous year. But at the end of the afternoon, they prepare to bid farewell once more as they get their bags, ready to move on.

They have known for about a month where their next destination lies, since their new positions were revealed in another formal ceremony a month earlier. Most of them now belong to one of the two battalions of the Royal Gurkha Rifles. A small number will also work within the Gurkha Signals or other smaller contingents. The 'traditional' elements of their drawn-out graduation process might have been different from the routine followed by their peers in the same garrison, but one important discrepancy was abolished just a few years earlier. Although they had trained separately from their British Army counterparts and were bound for special Gurkha units, they are now entitled to the same terms and conditions relating to pay, pensions and other benefits after a government ruling that came into effect in 2007.

The year that I attended the 'pass off' parade saw the full quota of young Gurkhas graduate from the training centre. In 2009 exactly 230 had arrived and 230 were leaving, although two were prevented from finishing on time because of injury. The guest of honour on that occasion, Kevan Jones, MP for Durham and then Parliamentary Under-Secretary for Defence, made a short formulaic speech congratulating the recruits on their efforts and thanking their families for coming to support them. 'You are now going to join the best army in the world,' he told them, with little expression in his voice. 'You will have great opportunities. It will be dangerous as well, but the training you have received will stand you in good stead.' The minister also made a brief reference to the Gurkhas' historical connection to Britain, adding that he was humbled by the great contribution that they were continuing to make to 'the defence of my country'. Listening to his perfunctory remarks about pride and tradition I thought back to my encounter with five of these young men just a few weeks earlier.

Although they had little experience of speaking conversational English we had covered a fair amount of ground. I had asked them whether they had any idea about British culture and society before they had travelled to London on the plane together, 230 apprehensive and excited lads bound for a military career in a foreign country. They had seen England on TV, they assured me, at football matches – Liverpool being the team of choice – and in cricket coverage. They had also watched the Channel Four soap 'Hollyoaks' with great interest, and seen most of the *Harry Potter* films. One of their recurring concerns now that they had lived in north Yorkshire for eight months was that they had not been able to communicate with young people whom they had met on their rare trips to Darlington. They were puzzled that people of their own age did not recognise them for who they were and often mistook them for foreign students.

> They don't have knowledge – they do not care.
> The younger generation need to know more about us.
> They don't know about the battle with the East India Company.
>   We have history in our syllabus.
> We have our history; our parents, grandparents were British
>   soldiers. It's a good opportunity to have the opportunity to
>   prove we are as good.

I assured them that the Gurkhas' reputation might have bypassed the young people in Darlington but they had recently become famous throughout the country, thanks to the extraordinary publicity achieved by the Gurkha Justice Campaign (GJC). In 2003 Folkestone Councillor Peter Carroll was asked to support a retired former Gurkha soldier who was facing deportation from the UK after 22 years of service in the British Army. In 2004 the government agreed to change the law to allow any Gurkha who had retired since 1997 the right to stay in the UK. But the GJC continued to draw attention to the plight of those elderly Gurkha ex-servicemen who had retired before this date and who were being denied residency in the UK, regardless of the length of time they had served with the British Army or the honours they had received in return.

Media attention reached a pitch during 2008 when actor and TV star Joanna Lumley stepped in. Numerous online forums, phone-ins and other sources of public reaction testified to the popularity of the Gurkhas in contrast to the wrong kind of claimants: those economic migrants and spongers who had nothing to contribute in return. A dramatic reversal of government policy followed in 2009 which meant that all Gurkha ex-servicemen and their families would be permitted to return to Britain to be cared for in their old age. The decision was hailed as a triumph, a salve for the nation's conscience, and the public appeared to be satisfied.

The tears of shame and then joy that flowed down Lumley's famous cheeks not only stemmed from an emotive struggle to recognise the 'moral debt of honour' owed to a group of people still tied to Britain through residual and anachronistic colonial settlements.[28] They also signalled the triumph of a powerful principle derived from the perceived value of military service. During a time when the noxious politics of immigration control had become re-centred as an electoral issue, the groundswell of public opinion indicated that those who had fought for Britain deserved the right to live there, regardless of nationality or cost to the public purse. However, far from proving that racism had disappeared, the episode simply demonstrated that it was necessary to distinguish between good immigrants and bad ones. The BNP, for example, caught between the logic of loyalty to soldiers and an agenda that favours only citizens of 'ancestral stock', dodged the contradiction by announcing: 'We would actually be happy to have the Gurkhas if we can swap them, for instance, for the very significant number from the Muslim population in this country who identify with al Qaida and who are not loyal to this country.'[29]

The striking image of Lumley waving a *kukheri*, the iconic Gurkha knife, and shouting a Nepalese war cry at the top of her voice, dramatised the existence of Britain's Gurkha soldiers to a global audience. Up to that point, however, few British citizens under the age of 40 had any idea who the Gurkhas were or understood how or why a fighting force from Nepal was still part of their country's defence arrangements in the twenty-first century. Young people in Darlington or anywhere else could be forgiven for not recognising the Gurkha recruits because, for a start, the history of the British Empire would probably not have featured in their school curriculum. But the aim of the campaign was not to educate the rising generation of British citizens. While Lumley herself received extraordinary publicity, the people whom she was representing were reduced to props in a pageant of national self-recrimination. The guilt and shame expressed by papers such as the *Daily Mail* were not really addressed to the Gurkhas' situation at all, but rather expressive of a convulsion of anxiety about what sort of country Britain had turned into.

Doing right by these warriors because they were living evidence of the former glory of empire seemed suddenly very important in the context of economic collapse and a steady stream of casualties sustained in an unwinnable war. The annals of imperial history could be collapsed into a single uncomplicated narrative in which the details did not really matter, to the protagonists at least. But Britain's modern armed forces are products of that long history and the tangible memory of empire is evident throughout the institution, and enshrined as well as commemorated within the chronicles of individual services and regiments. While the current employment of these two groups – citizens of Commonwealth countries and Nepal – emerges from a common history of blood-soaked imperial warfare, the terms of their inclusion in the British Army today can be traced through the braided fibres of the 'Golden Thread' of continuity.

The golden thread

The stained-glass windows in the Indian Army Memorial Room at the Royal Military Academy at Sandhurst (RMAS) offer a panorama of imperial history that is infused with sacred memory. The rich colours invoke an almost religious atmosphere of reverence and awe, presenting a mosaic of geographical and regimental records that depict images of soldiers from all over the empire. Each section is inscribed with the name and date of a campaign or battle, such as Burma, Eritrea, Palestine, Mesopotamia, Persia, Gallipoli or Flanders. In the middle of one of these windows, a fierce, turbaned warrior, rifle in powerful hands, glowers at those who look up at him. Underneath is written in large capitals: AFGHANISTAN 1919.

'My grandfather has medals from fighting in Waziristan,' said Ollie, the young English captain who was showing me round the premises. There was a panel marking that campaign too, just above the one on Afghanistan, and between the ones on the Arab Rebellion and the North West Frontier. Ollie had brought me to the memorial to begin our tour of the academy where officer cadets are trained. At first I thought it was a diversion from my mission to compare how the officer class was educated in relation to the ordinary soldiers I had been meeting. By the end of the day I had learned a great deal more than I had bargained for, not least that studying the military history of the British Empire was a core part of the syllabus for young officers today. It was also in the fabric of their physical environment, woven into their training experience through direct contact with the memorials, paintings, artefacts, traditions and ceremonies that reference the myths and legends of Britain's heyday as a global power.

Our visit to the Indian Army memorial was neither sentimental nor procedural. The room was situated in the oldest building on the campus, which was built in 1812, and was originally designed as the chapel. Ollie took me over to a glass case, saying there was something that he wanted me to see. He pointed to two pictures that recorded the dining habits of one of the Punjab regiments, back in the day. The first scene depicted a platoon of Indian soldiers with shaved heads, sitting on low blocks and served by two chefs with what looked like a basin of curry and a bucket of chapattis. The second was a photo taken in their officers' mess, the men resplendent in uniform as they posed at a polished dining table that was groaning with silverware. Sikh waiters, dressed in white from turban to toe, stood stiffly in the background. Ollie drew my attention to the racial segregation illustrated by the faded images. 'That's absolutely not how we do things now,' he told me. 'I show this to all my visitors.'

As we walked over to a more modern building, constructed in 1911, he talked enthusiastically about some beautiful cannons, captured by the East India Company in the course of their conquest of India. I was not holding my breath at the prospect, but indeed, when we arrived at the cannons situated next to a scarlet post box, I had to concede he had a point. The bronze had long ago turned green, and close inspection showed that they were inscribed with Koranic verses and decorated with ornate tigers' heads. I was more intrigued that they looked identical, in fact, to the ones that feature in the opening pages of Rudyard Kipling's novel *Kim*, a book that Ollie had not read. But the continuities with the colonial era were not just to be found in archival form or literary references, nor was it just my host who was obsessed with knowing his history.

Unlike the training establishments for the regular infantry and corps, RMAS offers courses for Overseas Cadets who are recruits from other national armies selected to complete part of their training in the UK.[30] Now integral to the UK's Defence Diplomacy strategy, the practice of training young officers from foreign militaries began during the bloody process of decolonisation after 1947. As the British Army became embroiled in counter-insurgency operations in south-east Asia, east Africa and parts of Arabia, the military academy at Sandhurst was used as a training centre for a new cadre of military allies. Malaya, Pakistan and Afghanistan were among the countries that began sending officer cadets in the 1950s and 1960s, and the practice continues to this day. Earlier on, a high-ranking officer had told me that it was very much part of the British exit strategy to leave a well-trained democratic army. 'Like Afghanistan now,' he remarked, 'although there's not really enough of them [coming through] to make a difference.'

In April 2011 the historical connection was perfectly illustrated when Chief of the General Staff of the Afghan National Army, General Sher Mohammad Karimi, visited Sandhurst 43 years after he had graduated in 1968. The Ministry of Defence (MoD) news bulletin reported that he met two young officer cadets of the Academy's intake of 103 who were both members of the Afghan security forces.[31]

As the tour led through the institution, my guide pointing with irrepressible pride at historic objects, furniture, paintings and ornaments, we arrived at the Royal Memorial Chapel. Originally erected in 1879 and later modified after 1919, it is not a particularly beautiful building, but it is here above all else that the pulse of institutional memory can be found.[32] Its walls are covered with stone tablets and commemorative plaques, and there is a smaller room on the side, known as the South African chapel, that commemorates all officer deaths after 1945. As we approached the front door of the building, Ollie had suggested that we stop and turn to look back at a monument dedicated to all the soldiers who had died in the First and the Second World Wars. 'When we have commemorations for officers we see this when we come out, and it shows us what it's really about.'

He was at pains to show me how important this institution was for the young officers-in-training. 'This place is known as the chapel of death,' he said, 'but it is also a place of thanksgiving and worship.' All former cadets are eligible to use the building to get married, have christenings or hold funerals. 'It seats about one thousand at a time,' he said. 'Cadets have to come twice a year, and when you hear the national anthem being sung it sends a shiver down your spine.'

Ollie was talking about his own sense of awe at these moments, but his image neatly conjured up the staunch militarism characterising Britain's national identity. For him, as for countless others, the Royal Memorial Chapel was not just a space of death and historical memory but a shrine to the British military ethos, that particular blend of patriotism, military training and Christian heritage that has shaped the internal culture of the armed forces. It was a way of illustrating the fact that 'The British military...represents and serves the state in its sovereign and nationalistic form.'[33] Military historian Stephen Deakin spelled out what this might mean in a paper published by the RMAS:

> Of all institutions within the British state the military is likely to be the most nationalistic because its job is to protect and if necessary to die for the nation state. The military have an unlimited liability to protect their nation state even at the cost of their own minds, bodies or lives. To express this commitment and to help them to do this service, the military experience symbols of national identity and statehood to a much greater extent than do the civilians that they protect. The national flag, the Union Flag is flown in military bases and on military vehicles and it is worn as a badge on personal uniforms. Pictures of the Monarch and her family hang on the walls of military buildings. The Monarch is toasted at formal dinners; the national anthem is played whilst the military stand at attention. Worship services are held in the state church, the Church of England. The military is heavily engaged at symbolic state rituals such as trooping the colour and state funerals.[34]

This description of the conventions of British militarism are important for this book, not least because it might help the civilian reader to visualise just how different it might be to work in the army, rather than, say, a school, hospital, police station or private corporation. In due course we return to a discussion of military culture and ethos from another angle. For now, the warriors in the stained glass windows direct us back to the deep imperialist foundations of British nationalism. It is here, in the ideological cement of white, Christian supremacy that we find the continuities and disjunctures that explain why the modern British Army is able to recruit soldiers from all over the world.

Fighting races

The memorial to the Gurkhas stands outside the soulless Ministry of Defence building in Horse Guards Avenue. Barring the memorial to women's war work round the corner in Whitehall and the statue of Edith Cavell on Charing Cross Road, it must be one of the only statues in the immediate neighbourhood not featuring a white man on a horse. The monument features a Gurkha soldier wearing the trademark broad-rimmed hat, and bears an inscription composed by Sir Ralph Turner, a former Gurkha officer: 'THE GURKHA SOLDIER: Bravest of the brave, most generous of the generous, never had country more faithful friends than you'. It was only unveiled in 1997, but the historical relationship between Gurkhas and the British Army had begun almost two centuries earlier in the foothills of the Himalayas. Since then it has spanned a wider topography of British military activity that has remained global in its scope: the early expeditions of the East India Company, subsequent colonisation and the growth of Empire, two World Wars, decolonisation, the Cold War, and the War on Terror and its manifestation as the multinational counter-insurgency operation in Afghanistan. It is a relationship characterised to this day by a strange combination of sentiment, mutual dependency and pragmatism, both economic and military. But dig deeper into the past, and the Victorian theory of martial races is able to provide the crucial explanation as to why Gurkhas have been so valued within British military calculations.

The word 'Gurkha' is derived from Gorkha, the state in west-central Nepal that dominated the region throughout the eighteenth century.[35] The unification of Nepal, carried out by a Gorkhali army of legendary force, brought the kingdom into conflict with the East India Company, leading to the Anglo-Gorkha war in 1814–1816. The pact drawn up at the end of hostilities granted independence to Nepal. In return, Nepal's rulers agreed to allow Gorkhali soldiers (as they were then known), who were greatly feared and admired by British troops, to enlist as mercenary volunteers in the service of the East India Company.[36]

This period of expansion into the northern Indian territories in the first half of the nineteenth century was a testing ground for the belief that 'some communities possessed inherited traits which made them better soldiers'.[37] Now under British command, the Gurkha mercenaries, who were recruited from a small number of local castes, proved invaluable in policing the unruly tribal groups, particularly in the mountainous regions of the area known as the North West Frontier. In 1857 the two Gurkha regiments played a key role in suppressing the 'Sepoy Revolt' which came to be known as India's First War of Independence. Their loyalty to the colonial administration in the face of the nation-wide insurgency guaranteed them a role in the British Indian Army which was reorganised after the British Crown took over. Gurkhas retained their separate regimental structures within this larger organisation, and were employed alongside many other ethnic and religious groups as part of a 'highly effective, well-trained, all-volunteer force of professional regulars' that supported the wider colonial military order.[38]

Martial race theory was codified from the late 1890s in a series of official *Recruiting Handbooks* for the different 'classes' of the Indian Army. One of the authors, a Captain H. Bingley, argued that 'fighting ability depended not just on race but also on the hereditary instinct and social status of the men enlisted'.[39] The theory did not refer solely to the selection of effective sources of manpower, however. It was also about the manipulation of ethnic differences in the army, as Tarak Barkawi explains, by 'keeping it divided by grouping men in companies of their "own kind" and catering to their religious, dietary and other customs'.[40] At the same time, he continues, it was thought that no situation would arise that would render all the different groups of troops simultaneously unreliable, 'so should there be problems with one class of troops, the others would be available to check them'.

By the end of the nineteenth century, these principles of military organisation had been applied far beyond the tribal areas of northern India and were intrinsic to the whole science of colonial warfare. In 1888 an article on 'The Negro as a soldier' was published by *The Fortnightly Review,* a literary publication of liberal persuasion that attracted 'almost every distinguished English writer and critic of the day'.[41] The author, General Garnet Wolseley, was a household name according to the National Army Museum, having taken part in battles in all over the Empire including Natal where he had been instrumental in capturing the Zulu king Cetshwayo in 1879. His distinguished military career ensured that he was regarded as an expert on the martial characteristics of Britain's allies as well as their enemies. An extraordinary testament to the ideology of white supremacy that animated nineteenth-century Englishness, his article is worth pausing over as it illuminates the historical practice of designating particular groups as inherently equipped for war.

It begins with an assessment of the ranks of the West India regiments which 'until recent years' had been filled with 'fairly good fighting material'. Although 'generally wanting in intelligence', continued the general, 'the private who could bear fatigue, who was brave, absolutely obedient, and who was to be depended upon to stand by his officer under all circumstances, possessed the best qualities which go to make up a really good soldier'.

When it came to the 'savage from the interior of Africa', the author declared that his natural instinct made up for his want of intelligence as a solider. He illustrated this with an analogy that seems reprehensible today, but which was perfectly acceptable within the terms of late Victorian 'muscular' masculinity.

The instinct of some breed of dogs – the setter, pointer and retriever – renders it easy to teach them their special work, which other species, though equally intelligent, cannot be effectively taught. So it is with races of men. There are some to whom drill and the ordinary duties of the soldier in the field can be more easily imparted to than others. That sort of work seems natural to them, and in accordance with their instincts.

For Wolseley it was an inconvenience that slavery had been abolished, because 'we can no longer obtain the wild negro from the interior of Africa, as we formerly did, to fill the ranks of our West India regiments'. Suffice it to say that his argument then began a long and colourful disquisition on the effects of civilisation on the 'negro nations' in Africa and the warrior traditions within certain tribes, such as the Zulus and the Ashanti – with whom he was well acquainted. In one passage he speculated that 'the nature of the country or district the negro inhabits has certainly some influence upon his fighting qualities and national character'.[42] It would be easier to consign these theories to the past if there was not ample evidence that they were instrumental in more recent times.[43] The driving force of racial categorisation that shaped the 'polyglot' colonial armies throughout the twentieth century has since mutated into what sometimes passes for 'common sense' in today's military culture.

Tides of history

Commenting on Britain's contemporary difficulties in attracting and retaining a military workforce at the end of the twentieth century, military historian Hew Strachan looked back over the country's tradition of employing mercenaries to supplement its manpower, as well as the use of colonial troops.[44] 'The Gurkhas are the surviving embodiment of both traditions,' he pointed out. As remnants of the colonial armed services, 'they are held in deep affection and high esteem in Britain'.[45] But, he continued, although mercenaries have had a bad press because they fight for reward rather than a cause, 'the sort of conflict which we are currently confronting is entirely appropriate to warriors who sell their skills'.

Strachan was writing before the events of 11 September 2001, but as the press coverage of Lumley's campaign showed, Gurkhas are still valued for their reputation for fearlessness, physical endurance and courage. On many occasions I was to hear that Fijians were appreciated in the British Army because they had an instinctive sense of hierarchy and that South Africans and Zimbabweans, both white and black, were great warrior material. But there are other genealogies of military history that have produced categories of enemies as well as allies. While instinct and environment were thought to shape the variable skills of the African warrior, Wolseley was also convinced of the importance of faith as a key component, or, as he put it, 'intensely bigoted religious enthusiasm'. '[O]ur men would much pre-fer to fight the best European troops,' he thundered, 'rather than the same number of African warriors who were under the influence of Mahommedan fanaticism.'

The general's fear of Islamic militarism, expressed in typically voluble terms at the end of the nineteenth century, allows a glimpse of antago-nisms that both preceded and long outlived his Victorian version of white supremacy. He was precise about what was at stake: 'Pride of race, patri-otism, fervid loyalty, intense love of liberty, in fact, all the noblest and strongest feelings of the civilised European are weak and poor when com-pared with the religious frenzy which can convert the peaceful camel-driver near Suakim into the most terrible and most dreaded of foes.'[46] This clearly defined polarisation between the benefits of Christian civilisation and the evils of Islamic fanaticism harked back to enmities that virtually shaped Europe in the Middle Ages, symbolised by the Crusades in the eleventh and twelfth centuries. The reference to this gargantuan struggle so memo-rably evoked by George Bush Jr in 2001 in his declaration of the war on terror brings us back to the Tomb of the Unknown Soldier in the recesses of Westminster Abbey.

As I sat with the jet-lagged recruits from the Caribbean, watching the Remembrance Service on TV, it was hard not to think about the trusty medieval sword under the marble slab and the tides of history that had deposited it there. These young men, and countless others, had decided to join the British Army in the hope of a better life for themselves and their families. Descendants of Britain's colonial past, and of the barbarism of racial slavery before that, they were employees in an organisation that had its own historic battles with racism and segregation.[47] As minorities they were par-ticipants in an experiment about which the British public knows very little, summoned as part of a governmental project to create a more diverse mili-tary that would 'represent' the troubled nation in its 'ethnic composition'. But as migrants they would be caught up in another dimension of war where battles over belonging, citizenship and national identity were being fought on more familiar terrain. Although they would be trained to fight far from Britain's shores, the reasons for their enlistment in the first place – both political and pragmatic – must be sought much closer to home, mired in a very domestic quarrel about what it means to be British.

Part I

Recruitment

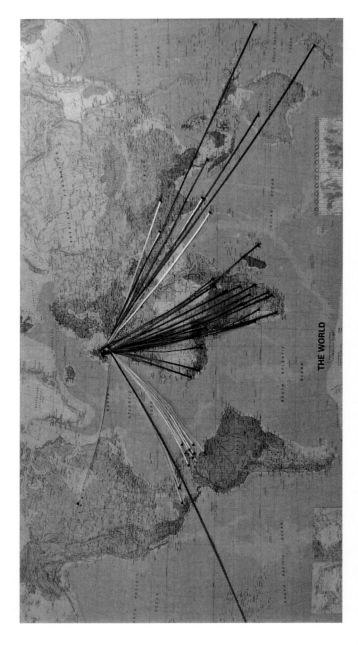

Image 2 Map showing home countries of Commonwealth recruits at ITC, 2008–2010
Crown copyright 2011.

2
The Race to Recruit

By August 2009 Carlos had almost given up hope of hearing from the British Army. He was enjoying an evening out in Belize City after he had been paid and needed to buy a new phone, so he went into a shop and picked one out for $99. It occurred to him that he should retain his old sim card and keep the same phone number he had given the British Army recruiters the previous summer. As it happened, he was carrying it in his pocket.

> As I inserted the sim card into the phone and put the battery in and turned it on, I could hear the phone ringing. Shucks, I hear this English voice in the shop! The happiness I felt at this moment! There and then she asked me: are you checking emails? She was trying to get in touch with me!

The voice that Carlos heard belonged to one of the administrators who worked from Army Careers Office in central London. Before the recruiters left Belize they had assured him that he would hear as soon as they had fixed a date for him to come to the UK to begin training. Weeks turned into months, and Carlos thought that they had either forgotten him or there was a problem with his contact details. He hadn't completely given up, but in the meantime he joined the Belize Defence Force (BDF) as a volunteer in the reserves. He showed an aptitude for the work and soon became attached to the regular force. He was four weeks into regular training when he finally received the offer of a position in a British Army Infantry regiment he had never heard of. His response was immediate. Although he had applied to join the Royal Artillery, he was not about to argue. 'Sign me up, I don't care what you give me,' he had told them. 'Once I have a job and pay, that's it.'

Carlos told this story as we sat in the Spartan accommodation block in Pirbright, Surrey, confident that he had passed the final selection test and would therefore be eligible to start Phase 1 training the following week. His travel companions from the Caribbean, whom he had met for the first time a couple of days earlier, were sharing similar accounts of waiting, hoping and never quite giving up.

Albert, like Carlos, was finishing high school in Belize City when he heard that the British Army was looking for recruits. 'The recruiters came at the right time,' he said. 'I graduated and made sure I passed so I didn't have to do an extra year.' After he was accepted he found an electrical job to tide him over until he got his letter inviting him to buy his open return ticket to London. But then in January he left his job, convinced that the call would come any day. He waited a whole month but there was no news. He took another electrical job and worked until July. 'Then I got a letter on email,' he said. 'I nearly gave up!'

He too had originally signed up for the Royal Artillery, and was told the regiment did not have any vacancies. Like Carlos he felt he wasn't in a position to argue. 'I didn't really sign up for the Infantry. Nonetheless I wanted to be in the army, but if possible I will change.'

Dennis, who was from the south of Belize, spent the intervening year between initial selection and the summons to come to the UK working for his mother's business. He too had left school thinking that he would soon be on his way to a new life in the Royal Artillery. Although he was just 21, he had previously contemplated joining the US Army, hoping to use family contacts in California to get himself over there to qualify for a green card. He had heard rumours that the US Marines occasionally sneaked small groups out of Belize, although he was prepared to try the longer route by gaining residency first. Unusual for someone of his age, he had done extensive research on the relative policies of healthcare and compensation due to injured soldiers. In the end, a combination of factors had persuaded him to apply to the British Army. Fascinated by ancient history, he was keen to come to Europe, encouraged to apply by English expatriate neighbours who had known him since he was a child.

The fourth member of the group, Ben, assured us that St Lucia was a very different country from Belize. He had been the first to arrive that week and I had found him hunched in a corner, his face hidden under a hooded jacket. It was early November and the sky was heavy with cloud all that week. Coming to England from the Caribbean must have been like stepping into a dark room with a low ceiling and not being able to find the light switch.

He was interested in architecture and hoping to study at college, but felt he could not expect his father to support him when there were other family members to take care of. His parents had separated when he was an infant, and Ben was the youngest of three children left behind when his mother moved to the UK. He alluded frequently to his difficult relationship with his step-mother and seemed anxious to distance himself from an unhappy childhood. Apart from joining his mother in London, he had hoped to study engineering in the army and had applied to join the Royal Engineers. But then, when he had almost given up hope, he got the call. 'I accepted it,' he said, 'Anything that's worth doing is worth doing well. Maybe I'll try and get a transfer.'

He mentioned this again on several occasions: 'They gave us infantry, but I would still try to get education…go to college and do a part time course, do a degree. I still have my goals.'

It was hard to understand why they were expected to wait for so long at such a crucial juncture in their lives, especially when the army had made the journey to their countries to fast-track their applications. It was hardly an attempt to 'keep them warm', as army jargon put it, referring to the process of juggling potential recruits while they waited for their jobs to start. But these four from the Caribbean were soon to discover that they were the penultimate 'batch' selected by the OPT to receive this summons, and that all further pre-selection drives in the region had been suspended later that year. In effect, their new careers were starting just as this historic operation to recruit from Commonwealth countries was coming to an end. In order to appreciate why they were there at all, we must go back more than a decade to unravel the complex history behind the making of Britain's multi-national army.

The topping on the ice cream

In August 1998 the Royal Edinburgh Military Tattoo hosted the spectacular marching band from the Republic of Fiji Military Forces (RFMF) which had been invited to take part in the customary programme of international performers from Commonwealth countries. Sitting in the audience were some senior officers from what was then the Royal Scots who were particularly eager to make the Fijians' acquaintance. The oldest regiment in the British Army, the Royal Scots was first raised in 1633 when Charles 1 issued a warrant for Sir John Hepburn to recruit 1200 men from Scotland, but by the end of the twentieth century it was woefully undermanned and, like many other units across the UK, unable to attract new recruits. After a brief consultation, the commanding officers formally invited the visitors to join them. As a result, 15 bandsmen returned to Fiji, resigned their posts in the RFMF and returned to the UK to work as British soldiers in the Royal Scots.

There was little publicity at the time, although the local media gave the transaction a predictably colourful slant. According to the *Herald*, 'a troop of South Pacific soldiers [were] abandoning their grass skirts in favour of kilts after visiting the Edinburgh Military Tattoo'.[1] The report, which was regurgitated in the *Independent* seven years later, suggested that the 'military band from the South Pacific island [sic] was so struck by the event that they applied to transfer to British regiments'.[2] Although this version was not supported by those who took the decision to come to Scotland, there was no doubt that this single episode acquired apocryphal proportions as the moment of entry for Commonwealth soldiers.

Another brief report in the Scottish press, dated a few weeks later in December 1998, perpetuated the story that the soldiers were 'smitten by the rich military heritage' of the Scottish regiments which were raised in the decade before European explorers 'discovered' Fiji in 1643.[3] That was not quite how it was, according to Jo, one of the first cohort of Fijians to join the British Army and therefore well qualified to tell his own version of the Edinburgh Tattoo legend. At that time, Jo was employed in the RFMF as a military clerk attached to the marching bands. When the bandsmen returned from their trip, full of enticing details of pay and pensions available in the British Army, Jo too was immediately attracted to the idea of transferring. He had been in his job since he was 16 and was ready for a change.

> They came back home and mentioned about everything they had gone through. They said the regiment can sponsor everybody. I thought I'm going to have a go.

But by then he was 28 and married with two young children. With these family responsibilities he was not convinced that it could be as promising as it sounded, so he took precautions.

> I applied for leave in the Fijian army, for one month leave, with the thinking: I will come up here and have a look; go through my interview; see how it feels. If I'm not happy I will go back home. My job will be secure. On the other side, I wrote a resignation letter to my commanding officer who knows me well. He said, 'As soon as you're happy give me a phone call and I will do whatever next to process your resignation. If not happy, come back and soldier on.' So I thought, I haven't got anything to lose.

Like the other recruits from overseas, Jo paid for his own flight to come over and was persuaded by the recruiting staff to transfer into the Royal Scots. 'They told us it would be like the topping on the ice-cream, compared to the FMF,' he said, with a trace of scorn in his voice. It was only after he had taken the Oath of Allegiance that he realised he had been lured with 'false promises'.

He soon discovered that his contract was valid only for 12 years. He was particularly annoyed because he was committed to spending the rest of his working life with the British Army on the promise of a full pension at the end of it. That had all been part of the brief from the recruiting officer: 'you will have a good pension – imagine when you are living in Fiji you will get this!' he had assured them.

Jo spent the next five years attempting to transfer out of the infantry into another cap badge, or trade, where he would be eligible for a full-length army career. His experience was in no way unusual, and it demonstrates that rather than being the result of any strategic policy decision, the early recruitment of Commonwealth soldiers took place through a mixture of contingency and opportunism. The bandsmen from Fiji were the right men in the right place. The army was struggling to recruit; combined with the new rules allowing citizens from Commonwealth countries to join, this crisis effectively gave the Scottish regiment, which faced particular difficulties, the signal to proceed. But the fact that these new soldiers could be classified as ethnic minorities was another bonus – the real topping on the ice-cream. The politics of tackling institutional racism in the 1990s had resulted in a programme of reform that was about to be put into practice. The invitation issued to the bandsmen from Fiji, a pragmatic response to an acute shortage of soldiers, effectively signalled the beginning of a new drive to increase minorities as well.

1998 and all that

It would be difficult to dispute that 1998 was a turning point in the history of the British Army as a public institution. By tracking the relevant developments that took place during that year, including the legendary Edinburgh Tattoo episode, we can glimpse the convergence of intense pressures emanating from outside the institution as well as the forces of reaction operating within. With hindsight this process is too easily subsumed under a coherent-sounding ideology of multiculturalism, at least in its corporate or public sector versions.[4] It is worth pausing, however, to consider how we might picture the army as an organisation that is amenable to social and political pressure. After all, by their very nature, military institutions are rigidly hierarchical, inaccessible to outsiders and notorious for communicating through specialist language and terminology. Taking one year at a time reveals just how much can happen in a relatively short period but it requires a historical perspective to assess the grinding effects of gear change.

There are several vectors running across this timeline of 12 months that need to be considered independently, but the first was the reformist energy of the New Labour government, elected into office in May 1997 with a huge majority after 18 years of Tory rule, and with a mandate that promised a substantial review of Britain's defence sector. Dealing with the legacy of racial discrimination and harassment in the armed forces was one aspect of this programme, and challenging its reputation as a harsh employer another. In October that year, John Reid, Minister for the Armed Forces, told the House of Commons that the Chief of the General Staff had recently issued a press release confirming 'the Army's view that there was a perception of racism inside the Army. The Chief of the General Staff – not politicians – made it plain that he would not tolerate it.'[5]

In his speech outlining the new administration's policies on all aspects of defence and foreign policy, Reid admitted: 'We face a greater challenge in recruitment from the ethnic minorities. The armed forces have until relatively recently remained distanced from the progress in racial awareness made in other areas of society.'

The government and the armed forces were aware of their responsibility, he went on, and regretted the fact that only 1 per cent of service men and women were from an ethnic minority background.

> We are examining the image of the services among ethnic minorities to see what more can be done to unlock barriers and remove misconceptions. We must also satisfy ourselves that there is no scope for discrimination or exclusion, and that we create a culture in which all personnel value, respect and learn from one another.[6]

During the same debate MPs also learned of the deficit of at least five thousand men in the armed forces, a situation inherited from the previous government. 'The matter is not open to simple solutions,' Reid told MPs. 'It involves a range of problems not only of numbers but of culture, retention, the nature of the modern armed forces and the nature of the community from which they draw their raw material.'[7]

A few weeks later, on January 22, the minister outlined the government's plan to increase the proportion of ethnic minorities in each service by setting new targets: 'For the year starting in April,' he announced,

> the goal for each Service will be that 2 per cent of new recruits should be from the ethnic minorities, with that figure rising annually by 1 per cent so that it reaches 5 per cent by the end of the financial year 2000–02 and in time reflects the proportion of people from ethnic minority communities in the wider population.[8]

The next development passed virtually unnoticed in the national media although it paved the way for something much more significant, in practical terms at least. On 18 February the government reported that the review of nationality issues for employment in the armed forces was complete, and, as a result, Reid told the House of Commons, the rules concerning the nationality of an applicant's parents would be relaxed to bring them into line with employees in the civil service. As long as the applicants themselves were British or Commonwealth citizens, or Republic of Ireland nationals, their parents' nationality was not relevant except where security issues were involved. More importantly, the five-year residency rule which was previously in operation was to be relaxed 'to allow those who have spent less than five years in the UK entry into the armed forces'.[9] Reid continued,

> I believe that these rule changes will ensure that the Armed Forces become more open for potential recruits, particularly amongst the ethnic minorities.

Diana, tanks and foreign travel

To begin with, the Royal Scots set up their own channel to recruit the young men directly from their home country, acting as sponsors who hosted them while they waited for their employment to begin, and as the numbers increased, the British Army formalised the arrangement by appointing a British Army contact within the British High Commission in Suva. News of the initiative spread quickly throughout the Fijian army, especially after other British regiments sent word that they were also recruiting. Will, who applied in early 1999, explained how he first became interested.

> When the British Army started enrolling back at home, I was still working in a government firm as a draftsman. I then heard someone ... the opportunity came for sons and daughters who are in the RFMF, so they were the ones who distributed the invitation and they extended it according to the British Army's wishes. They started giving out application forms, and I took the opportunity from a son of a Fijian army man who was issuing the leaflets.

Will's family was supportive of the plan and he applied from Fiji by corresponding with the army recruiting centre in Upavon, Wiltshire. By then the system of dealing with overseas recruits was in place, although sending forms back and forth by post took time and determination on the part of the applicant. Initially the information required was a basic medical test and a declaration that there was no criminal record or any other reason to prevent their employment. But in order to travel to the UK for further tests, individuals needed a sponsor to support them while they were waiting to go through their various selection procedures. Luckily Will's family history offered a precedent for joining up as well as a reliable port of call on the other side of the world.

> My father told me that there was a relative in the UK who resides in London. He was ex-British Army, and he managed to get into contact with him. We needed sponsors so he accepted, and the ball started rolling then. In the winter of '99 I got the nod from the recruiting centre that they've given me ok, and the interview date set up. I paid for my fare and flew across.

'What did you apply to be?' I asked. 'Were you given a choice?' Just minutes earlier Will had been telling me how his life and outlook had changed during the 12 years he had lived in the UK. At first it was extremely disorienting, even though he was a member of the ruling elite in Fiji and had been educated in an English-speaking boarding school. 'When I joined, I was like a marginal man, being as this was the first time coming out of my country.' Since Fiji is so small, he explained, it was hard to adapt to the different scale of things in the UK.

That's another thing, I just applied to be in the army, you see. Like I said, my mind was small, I was looking at the Fijian military forces, which is a small contingent. I was in shock. It was like someone trying to sell me something – 'here you go – you sit your BARB test' they told me.

This was the British Army Recruit Battery test, carried out on the computer, which was designed to screen for what was known as 'trainability', and to determine what kind of job might be most suitable for the candidate.

'Look, do you know Princess Diana? ' they said. Yeah, yeah. 'Well Princess Diana is colonel-in-chief of this regiment. Do you like tanks?' Er, yes. 'Well, believe it or not this regiment has tanks, do you like to travel abroad?' Well, those were my wishes for joining up – I like to travel abroad. 'Well, they are in Kosovo at the moment. So would you like to join them?'
   Me knowing less about the army then, so I said yes, and they said, 'right, sign on the dotted line.' So I signed up for the infantry as first battalion of the Princess of Wales Royal Regiment (PWRR).[10]

Will later found he had been steered into the infantry without being given a chance to explore other options, one of about eight young Fijians who had been actively recruited by the regiment. He recalled how the group had been looked after, accommodated and provided with transport between interviews in Blackheath, south-east London, where the army careers centre was located, and the regimental base in Canterbury. One measure of the urgency of the recruitment drive was the short turnaround between training and deployment. After six months in Bassingbourn and Catterick the new recruits were sent to their unit in Tidworth and then deployed to Kosovo five weeks later during the winter of 2000. Will returned to Kosovo the following year and in 2004 his regiment was deployed in Iraq. He later transferred into the Royal Engineers where he was demoted from sergeant to private, but at least he was able to resume the professional training he began as a draftsman in Fiji.
   These testimonies of individuals, often highly motivated to pursue a full career in the British armed forces, provide one example of the recruitment pattern. But there were others. As individual regiments began to advertise further afield, the applications started to flood in by mail. The practice of sending teams to fast-track recruits who had contacted the recruiting offices, and to attract those who might not yet have thought of it, began almost immediately. OPTs were sent to several countries in the Caribbean, such as Jamaica, St Vincent and Antigua. It is difficult to obtain figures for people recruited in this way, but in an illustrative aside, one officer mentioned to me that in 2004–2005 his regiment was 'backfilled with Jamaicans'. Information is available on costs for flights, transport and accommodation charges

for staff from 2005 onwards, but the comprehensive history of these OPT expeditions has not yet been compiled.[11] Before looking in more detail at the consequences of mass recruitment in Fiji and the Caribbean, we must return to the narrative of institutional reform taking place in 1998.

Your country needs YOU

In July 1998 the government published the Strategic Defence Review (SDR) which was hailed as the most radical plan to rationalise the country's defence policy since the end of the Cold War.[12] Compiled over the first 14 months of New Labour's administration, the proposals ranged from matters of global security to the minutiae of equipment to be used by each of the three services, and from the future shape of the armed forces to the conditions of service for both civilian and military personnel working within the defence sector. Contained inside this last section was the familiar statement that the government was 'determined that the Armed Forces should better reflect the ethnic composition of the British population'. This was followed by a reiteration of the target-oriented approach.

> Currently some 6% of the general population are from ethnic minority backgrounds, but they make up just 1% of the Services. This must not continue. We have set a goal of attracting 2% of new recruits this year from ethnic minority communities for each Service. We want that goal to increase by 1% each year so that, eventually, the composition of our Armed Forces reflects that of the population as a whole.[13]

The rationale for increasing the percentage of ethnic minority recruits was presented in the context of employing 'our fair share of the best people this country has to offer'. This was connected to the theory that public bodies should reflect the socio-demographic mix of the country, an idea that had gained credibility as an instrument for promoting 'equal opportunities' and addressing discrimination inside the workforce. A paper outlining the policy shifts referred, somewhat obliquely, to the reasons why the current figure was so low:

> We are also committed to making real progress on improving our record on equal opportunities through tackling the complex web of underlying factors which have inhibited people from various backgrounds choosing to join us in the past.[14]

Although it is important to unravel this 'complex web' to understand why British citizens from ethnic minority backgrounds might not be drawn to military service, we learn more about the army as an institution if we consider why the pressure to improve its past record had become such a critical issue. In other words, one of the major explanations was that the history of under-recruitment simply reflected patterns of outright discrimination and exclusion which identified the armed forces as a particularly negligent employer. In 1997, for instance, the Office of Public Management released a damning report that found evidence of widespread racism in the armed forces.[15] However, it is difficult to grasp why the new government pressed the issue of raising ethnic minority recruitment so hard without first examining the disciplinary role of the Commission for Racial Equality (CRE) earlier in the decade. Documenting this story of institutional racism and the external pressure to reform provides another important vector of analysis needed to make sense of 1998 as a critical year.

The CRE was established in 1976 under the Race Relations Act to work for the improvement of 'race relations' in Britain, and to ensure that employment practice was not only subject to principles of equality but also free of discrimination and harassment. In a submission to the Defence Committee in the House of Commons in 2000, it was noted that the CRE had been concerned about reports of racism and discrimination in the armed forces over a considerable period.[16] The organisation had intervened in the army's grievance procedures in 1991 in order to give complainants an opportunity to sidestep internal procedures which were not considered impartial. In 1994 the CRE initiated a more formal inquiry into the Household Cavalry after two serious incidents of discrimination and bullying. Corporal Jake Malcolm was awarded £6,500 as compensation after it emerged that his transfer from the Royal Electrical and Mechanical Engineers had been refused on the grounds that he was black.[17]

A year later, Mark Campbell, the first black trooper to join the Household Cavalry, was discharged from the Queen's Life Guards on medical grounds. In his evidence he claimed that he had faced taunts of 'nigger', had been handed a note saying 'there is no black in the Union Jack' and had his bed soaked with urine.[18] The regiment had come under scrutiny before for its suspected policy of hiring an all-white workforce, and it was no surprise that the resulting investigation found it to have contravened the law on several counts: direct and indirect discrimination in recruitment and selection; abuse and harassment of ethnic minority soldiers; inducement and instructions to discriminate.[19]

One of the results of this inquiry was to threaten the Ministry of Defence (MoD) with a non-discrimination notice, but in 1997 this was deferred after the MoD agreed to work with the CRE to implement a campaign for equality across the armed forces. At the centre of this was the formation of a special team to examine 'cases of alleged racism' outside the routine channels, referred to within the armed forces as the 'chain of command' and a support hotline offering counselling and advice to those who were experiencing discrimination.[20] The agreement also instigated 'greater awareness training' for recruits and officers and a special recruitment cell drawn from ethnic minority personnel. By the end of 1997, pilot initiatives to target members of ethnic minority groups had been set up in Newham, East London, and Sandwell in the West Midlands, supported by the expertise of Focus Consultancy which specialised in advising organisations, both public and private, on how to implement equality and diversity policies. As a consequence, when Reid spoke in January of the new goals for recruiting ethnic minorities into the armed forces, he was confident that all the right measures were in place. The decision to admit Commonwealth citizens that he announced the following month served as the back-up plan in case the local minorities proved reluctant to enlist.

On 25 March 1998, the MoD and the CRE joined forces to sign a five-year Partnership Agreement which included a further 'action plan' with a series of fresh initiatives intended to eliminate discrimination and harassment from the three services. Among these was the collection of data on minority recruitment to be presented and analysed in quarterly reports. Other forms of monitoring were to be introduced, along with new models of equality training and outreach schemes targeted at ethnic minority communities in the UK. An exhibition, entitled 'We Were There', was prepared by the MoD 'to honour the invaluable contribution made by the ethnic minorities to the Armed Forces for more than 200 years'.[21] The same year, the army issued a set of recruitment posters based on Alfred Leese's well known 'Your Country Needs YOU' image of Lord Kitchener from the First World War. In one of these, Kitchener's face had been replaced by that of Ghanaian-born Captain Fedelix Datson of the Royal Artillery,[22] producing a composite image with rather a startling effect – not least because the figure of the contemporary black British soldier was just so unfamiliar. A second version featured the face of Warrant Officer Ashok Kumar Chauhan, also of the Royal Artillery, who would later become a recruiting officer in his own right.

Whether intentionally or not, the slogan 'Your Country Needs YOU' harked back to the recruitment propaganda for volunteer workers in the Caribbean in the 1940s.[23] By the end of the twentieth century it was clearly intended to invoke a patriotic response from those who might otherwise have felt excluded from the national collective. 'Britain is a multi-racial country', the poster declared in small print at the bottom of the picture. 'It needs a multi-racial Army.' Interested parties were told to ring one telephone number to 'find out how we are making the Army a better place for ethnic minorities to work' and another to 'talk directly to a Black or Asian soldier'.

Rights of the individual

The posters were part of a wider recruitment campaign launched by the advertising agency Saatchi and Saatchi, aimed at increasing not just the number of new soldiers but also improving the calibre of those who applied.

Entitled 'Putting the Army back in business', the campaign earned the Effectiveness Award from the Institute of Practitioners in Advertising (IPA) because it was seen to be instrumental in raising numbers to meet the 15,000 target that had been set at that time. This was the third factor needed to comprehend the drive to recruit ethnic minorities to the armed forces: the army, in particular, had long been plagued by a chronic labour shortage, particularly in the post-Cold-War period. It is important to bear in mind that the armed forces as a whole, but the army in particular, desperately needed to change the public image of military service in order to present it as an attractive career choice. Allegations of bullying, harassment, discrimination, entrenched prejudices about gender and sexuality, and a general culture of violence throughout the ranks presented huge obstacles to performing this PR operation, and the army, as the largest and most visible of the three services, needed all the help and expertise it could get.

The IPA award was just one index of a sea-change of corporate policy taking place within the armed forces as military chiefs struggled to keep up with the demands placed by Blair's government. Not surprisingly this was a busy time for the new consultancies that had sprung up during the 1990s, promising to bring 'diversity expertise' to the wide public sector. As a result of their successful co-operation in 1997, Focus was contracted on a longer-term basis in 1999 to act as broker between the British Army and the ethnic minority communities in the UK, and to continue assisting with the recruitment campaign, 'one of the largest multiculturalisation initiatives in Europe'.[24] Other awards were to follow: in November 1999 the MoD won the Gold Award for Best Diversity Practice by a Government Department at the British Diversity Awards after success in both the 1998 British Diversity Awards and 1999 Windrush Awards. The online version of the MoD's 'We Were There' exhibition won a Race in the Media award in 2002. The British Army was on a roll. Looking back at this period, Sir Herman Ouseley, former chair of the CRE, described the Partnership Agreement as 'a good, ground-breaking model for other employers'.[25] He was full of praise for the exemplary reforms being carried out by the armed forces which had recognised that 'equality and diversity are positive strengths for an organisation and their work in this area is setting standards that other sections of society should follow'.

The commitment of senior officers to reform the institution seems to have offered genuine proof that the army, at least, was ready to become part of multicultural Britain, or at least to co-operate with the newly dominant culture of equality and diversity management. Admittedly, with the threat of legal action from the CRE it was not as though it had a choice, but in any case, the term 'institutional racism', was becoming officially identified as a problem at the heart of British public life. In 1997 the New Labour government had commissioned Sir William Macpherson to conduct an inquiry into the Metropolitan Police handling of the murder of Stephen Lawrence, and this was due to report in early 1999.[26] One of the direct consequences of this investigation was a formal recognition that public bodies had a duty not just to prevent racism within their own employment practices and professional duties but also to be actively involved in endorsing diversity as a public good. This partly explains the slogan on the recruitment posters: 'Britain...needs a multi-racial Army'. The meaning of the word 'need' was clearly intended to be self-evident though it was soon to be enshrined in law.

The Macpherson Report was followed by the Race Relations (Amendment) Act in 2000. This new bill extended the definition of 'public authorities' which had been encoded in the 1976 Race Relations Act to cover the police, prison service and also for the first time, the armed forces.[27] It also gave the CRE further powers to promote race equality, whether by issuing tighter codes of practice or by imposing specific duties on public authorities. From this point, the British Army had a statutory obligation to 'eliminate unlawful racial discrimination' and 'to promote equality of opportunity and good relations between persons of different racial groups'.[28]

Allowing Commonwealth citizens to join the army meant that the figures for ethnic minorities started to rise exponentially, exceeding planned recruitment targets set by the SDR. However, as defence analysts pointed out in the months that followed, these minorities brought diversity into the ranks, but in what way did they 'represent' the ethnic make-up of the UK? Writing in a cross-national comparison of cultural diversity in the armed forces, Dandeker and Mason argued that the category of 'ethnic minority', enshrined in this legal obligation to diversify, took no account of the different socio-demographic profiles, levels of social mobility, educational attainment and cultural traditions of Britain's actually existing ethnic minority population. For this reason, they suggested,

> It is entirely conceivable that the gross target of increasing ethnic minority representation to a level commensurate with the proportion of the population classified as belonging to an 'ethnic minority' could be reached without representativeness being achieved for some of the communities involved.[29]

We will return to this issue later but the fact of the matter was that Commonwealth citizens conveniently provided both a new source of soldiers and minorities to boot. However, we should not forget that there were other battles over inclusion and 'representativeness' happening at the same time. Racism and cultural diversity were only two dimensions of the reforms dragging the employment policies of the armed forces into the twenty-first century.

'Cultural subversion'

The parallel history of women in the armed forces was also under review as the MoD grappled with the obligation to re-think the conditions necessary for 'combat effectiveness'.[30] April 1 saw the effects of another significant layer of reform intended to expand the recruitment pool as well as to conform to equality and diversity legislation within the armed forces. From that date, the British Army widened access to female recruits from 47 to 70 per cent to include all jobs with the exception of units whose primary role was to 'close with and kill the enemy'. These included the Infantry, the Royal Marines General Services, the RAF Regiment and the Household Cavalry, which were part of the Royal Armoured Corps.[31] The change was accompanied by the adoption of a new physical selection system for all recruits that was designed to be both gender-free and job-related. This used 'a battery of nine physiological tests' to predict and test performance.[32] Recognising that the continuing bar on women in combat roles was not only controversial but also potentially unlawful, the MoD undertook to monitor and review the situation over the next three years.[33]

Collating the interventions and initiatives that took place in the late 1990s brings into view the convergence of legal, administrative, political and constitutional motors of reform that challenged the MoD's claim to be an exceptional form of employer. A House of Commons research report, published as a background paper for the 2000–2001 Armed Forces Bill, reiterated that 'it has become increasingly apparent that the armed forces are no longer immune to the wider changes that have taken place in society'.[34] The report was not confined to questions of ethnicity. It continued: 'As the rights of the individual have been accorded greater importance, equal opportunities issues, dealing with gender, race, sexuality and disability have increased in prominence over the past few years.'

The emphasis on individual rights referred partly to the new legal environment prohibiting forms of discrimination in the workplace. The European Court of Human Rights (ECHR), for example, had declared in 1999 that the ban on homosexuals serving in the armed forces was illegal. Unlike the protracted process in the USA where the tentative Don't Ask Don't Tell policy, introduced by the Clinton administration in 1993, was not lifted by President Obama until 2011, this ruling had an almost immediate effect. The British public were not party to the deliberations behind closed doors, but when Secretary of State for Defence Geoff Hoon announced in 2000 that the armed forces would henceforth recognise sexuality as a private matter, he did so in the full knowledge that the heads of all three services had been involved in consultation and were prepared to support the new code of conduct, in public at least.

There were deep reservations in private, of course, as the Chief of Defence Staff, Sir Charles Guthrie, noted on the eve of his retirement in 2001. In a comment about potential damage caused by placing the rights of the individual over those of the team, he said, 'the chiefs of staff must make it quite clear that, if they introduce women into the SAS or blind people into the Coldstream Guards, if they put social engineering and equal opportunities in front of combat effectiveness, there is a real danger of damaging something that works really well'.[35]

The prompt lifting of the ban on serving homosexuals meant that the MoD's employment policies were changed overnight to be brought in line with the rest of the public sector. Combined with the widening of posts available to women in the armed forces, these measures were predictably characterised as the insidious effects of political correctness enforced by those with no experience and knowledge of military culture. Thatcherite defence pundit Gerald Frost complained bitterly about the destructive consequences of applying civil law in the military sphere, referring to it as 'cultural subversion'.[36] How would he have reacted, a decade later, at the news that the accolades had kept on coming? In September 2011, for example, the MoD announced that Proud2Serve.net, the networking website used by serving lesbian, gay, bisexual and transgender (LGBT) military personnel, had won the 'European Diversity Award for Outstanding Employee Network Group of the Year'.[37]

Frost's dyspeptic reaction is useful though because it illustrates how the line between civil and military spheres was still imagined as impervious, even at the end of the twentieth century. Until then, military culture had rested on a fixed set of ideas about how soldiers were supposed to behave within a disciplined and class-bound order. Issues of sexuality and women's rights were anathema in this world, and any reforms enforced by civilian politicians with no experience of service life were denounced as inappropriate and intrusive. At the heart of this refusal to modernise was the perennial question of who was fit to be a soldier. As immigration from Commonwealth countries in the post-1950 period began to produce a new generation of black and Asian Britons, racism remained a decisive factor in determining whether these postcolonial citizens were either eligible or suitable to serve in the armed forces. The decision to extend recruitment to Commonwealth citizens emerged out of this murky history, sometimes in the most unexpected places.

Fitness for soldiering

The Lt Colonel responsible for recruiting Will was commanding an infantry unit in Canterbury at the time. He too had heard vague reports about the Royal Scots recruiting Fijians after the Military Tattoo and was wondering how to solve his own manpower crisis since he was a hundred men short and was expecting to be deployed to Kosovo. One day in early 1999, visiting the local recruiting office in Blackheath, he came across Will's uncle who had gone there to make enquiries after hearing about his nephew's desire to join up. The two men fell into conversation, and Will's uncle told the officer that his nephew had already applied, and that he knew of several others keen to join. As a result of this fortuitous encounter, the regiment not only created its own channel for recruiting young Fijian men but provided continuity among families as well.

It was not as though Fiji was a new solution to the British Army's recruiting problems. In 1961 Will's uncle had been one of 200 men and 12 women recruited directly from Fiji and the Seychelles to fill critical shortages throughout the organisation. The timing was significant. National service had just ended after prolonged and anguished debates about the effects of its abolition for the moral and physical health of the nation. The British Army was faced with the task of recruiting an all-volunteer force, competing with an expanding higher education sector as well as a booming economy, and stretched by insurgencies in Malaya, Borneo, Brunei and Kenya. A brief diversion into this historical period reveals that official policies on 'fitness for soldiering' were shaped as much by prevailing attitudes to immigration as they were by the historic contribution of colonial troops in the 1940s.

In a discussion about recruitment in the House of Commons in 1961, George Wigg, Labour MP for Dudley and ex-army man who styled himself as a defence expert, gave his opinion of how the organisation might react to institutional reform. He observed that it was a humbling thought that 'nothing that was said today, and nothing that the Secretary of State could do tomorrow', would have any effect on the Army for a considerable time. 'The Army is a vast organisation,' he continued, 'spread all over the world, with thousands of men in the pipeline and thousands more joining and leaving. It is a vast, amorphous organisation, administered as much by hope and faith as anything else.'[38] As an insider he knew how entrenched military procedures and attitudes were. As a politician he realised that the government had no choice but to approach the question of widening recruitment as a social and political issue.

In many ways, summoning a contingent from Fiji in 1961 was an anomaly, not least because in 1946 the Army Council, the governing body of the British Army at the time, had produced regulations recommending that 'Men not of pure European descent should not be allowed to enlist in UK regiments or corps of the Regular Army' on the grounds that they were considered 'a threat to the discipline and well-being'.[39] Despite the shortages of manpower that followed the end of national service, there remained strong reservations in some quarters about recruiting from the pool of Commonwealth immigrants who had been arriving in the UK throughout the 1950s. In his exhaustive historical account of British national identity from 1945 to 2000, Richard Weight discusses the transition from national service to an all-volunteer army at length since this was a pivotal event in the country's transition.[40] Conscription had begun on 1 January 1949 as a way of ensuring that troop levels were maintained in Britain's large garrisons overseas. All British males between the ages of 17 and 21 who passed the basic fitness tests were expected to serve in the armed forces for 24 months and remain on the reserve list for an additional four years. By the late 1950s, however, there were economic reasons why it was no longer practical to continue, as well as political and social tensions.

Weight suggests that there was a growing acceptance that the empire was no longer a viable concern and the arguments for nuclear power were undermining the rationale for a large-standing army. After the Sandys White Paper in 1957 the decision was made to abolish conscription as part of the cuts in public spending. There were many voices expressing fear that without a system of national service, feelings of patriotism and national cohesion would diminish. But there were countless others who celebrated the decision, not least the young men whose lives were about to be disrupted by enlistment. National service was identified as a rather 'European' practice and something to be satirised in public culture. Among some quarters, however, racism and hostility to immigrants were implicated in arguments to end conscription as well.

A document from the Army Council, cited by Weight, voiced the concern that 'the loyalty of black and Asian soldiers could not be relied upon in wartime'. This was a particular worry since a new generation of British-born children of migrants would soon be liable for the call-up. 'The enlistment of black Britons into the professional army could be controlled by prejudicial selection,' it continued, 'but statutory national service was another matter.'[41] In 1961 the Council released a document on the 'Recruitment of Coloured Personnel' which again emphasised the link between ethnicity, loyalty and reliability:

> The strength of the British Army has always depended on the reliability of the individual soldier. The reliability of coloured soldiers is not certain and therefore too great a dilution of British units would be dangerous.[42]

For this reason the War Office planned to restrict numbers, according to a report in *The Times*, to 'about 3,500', recruiting 'men and women from Commonwealth territories...in England' along with targeted drives in the Caribbean, Fiji and the Seychelles.[43] The same report in *The Times* revealed that 'the men from Fiji will bring the number of coloured soldiers in the British Army to about 1,200'.[44]

The army's reluctance to increase its minority troops is corroborated by the National Army Museum which records that, despite the growth in immigration from the New Commonwealth during this period, there was an unofficial quota limiting the number of ethnic minority personnel to a maximum of 3 per cent which lasted until the late 1960s.[45] However, documentary evidence has since proved that the MoD, established in 1971, continued to condone racist recruitment practices at the highest level.

Documents released under the Freedom of information Act in 2005 revealed that 30 years earlier the army was still adhering to its unsavoury method of identifying non-European recruits, while claiming at the same time that a more formal system of racial monitoring was counter-productive to the ethos of the army.[46] One internal paper claimed: 'In keeping with the spirit of non-discrimination no statistics are held identifying coloured personnel.' Another memo said that although they did not officially keep statistics of 'coloured soldiers', the medical officer would routinely comment on the features of recruits at the attestation ceremony. This system was known as the 'D-factor', and had been in use since 1957 as a strategy to maintain quotas. The term included attributes such as 'Mediterranean, Asiatic, African, Negroid or other' which often boiled down to a crude distinction between 'white' and everyone else.

Gender was a discriminatory factor in its own right as female recruits were segregated from male soldiers and ascribed different characteristics. The Women's Royal Army Corps, formed in 1949, produced a collective prayer that read:

> Oh merciful God and Father of us all, whose will it is that we should help one another; give us, the members of the Women's Royal Army Corps, grace that we may fulfill the same. Make us gentle, courteous and forbearing. Direct our lives so that we may have courage and resolution in the performance of our duty and hallow all our comradeship by the blessing of Thy spirit for His sake who loved us and gave Himself for us, Jesus Christ our Lord.[47]

In 1961 there were 'already about 50 coloured girls' in the WRAC and 23 in Queen Alexandra's Royal Army Nursing Corps who were integrated into their units and 'employed according to their aptitude'.[48] In her interviews with some of the 12 Fijian 'girls' recruited into the WRAC, almost 50 years later, Teresia Teaiwa discovered that they had received less pay than their male compatriots and were given contracts lasting only three years. One member of the group was found to be pregnant on her arrival, and after a hasty marriage to the child's father – a fellow Fijian recruit – organised by the British Army, she was forbidden to start her basic training.[49]

The expediency of tradition

The integration of a small number of Fijians in the British Army in 1961–1962 therefore amounted to something of an experiment, in terms of breaking the homogeneity of white British nationals at least. The Fijians' reputation for soldiering, however, was not in question. As a Crown colony since 1874, Fiji had supplied cohorts to support the Britain's military operations throughout the twentieth century. In May 1917, for example, a group of 101 Fijian men and 6 European officers served as a Labour Corps unloading ships in Calais and Marseilles in France and Taranto in Italy.[50] Approximately 8,000 Fijians from the Fiji Military Force (FMF) fought against the Japanese in the Solomon Islands in 1942–1943, and a contingent from the FMF fought for the British in Malaya during the so-called Emergency which lasted from 1948 to 1960. There they were particularly valued for their ability to perform in a tropical environment.[51]

This historical background is important not least because it provided the rationale for extending Britain's recruiting pool even if that entailed incorporating soldiers of 'non-European' descent. It becomes instrumental where it supplies a pretext for targeting selected national or ethnic groups on the basis of their perceived affinity for military work and it directly contradicts the view espoused by the Army Council that black and Asian soldiers could not be relied upon in war. In 1963, MPs held a lengthy parliamentary debate on the proposed Army Act, providing a fascinating record of the ethics, logistics and problems entailed in establishing an all-volunteer army at that time.[52] The issue of employing 'foreigners' was discussed at length and it was clear that the track records of contingents from Commonwealth countries were viewed as a positive reason to invite them into the British Army. Brian Harrison, Conservative MP for Maldon, for example, warned about the political problems that might occur if non-British troops were used but, he continued:

> There are, however, lots of other areas within the Commonwealth where we have had experience of the magnificent fighting qualities of the local troops, and from which we could surely recruit people for the Army. The Seychelles have produced a number of recruits who have been successfully absorbed into the British Army, and so has Fiji. During the Emergency in Malaya the Fijian battalions proved themselves to be exceptional.[53]

Referring to the recruitment drive that had recently taken place in Fiji, Harrison went on to argue that the successful 'absorption' of Fijians into the Army gave the green light to pursue this further. He hoped that the government would sanction increasing the numbers of Fijian recruits, even establishing a battalion 'out there to carry out the preliminary training for the Army so that the recruits are partly trained before joining their regiments here...'.

As it happened, Harrison's suggestion was not taken up and the numbers recruited from Fiji in the early 1960s – originally supposed to be 100 but increased to 200 'in view of the enthusiastic response and the quality of the applicants' – were capped, despite the positive reactions evident in both countries.[54] It is also worth noting that the House of Commons saw regular debates about the retention of Gurkha soldiers as an inexhaustible supply of proven military assets, ready to step into the empty boots left by Britain's reluctant youth.[55] During this same debate on the shortfall in recruitment in 1963, MPs were informed that the proposed reduction from

14,600 to 10,000 Gurkhas would be postponed, but some urged that the number should actually be increased to 20,000. The infamous Conservative MP, Sir Gerald Nabarro, who was leading the charge, stated that the increase would 'make a contribution to overcoming the marginal manpower deficit from which we are suffering, and, secondly, it would be additional insurance against continuing or even expanding trouble in the far east as a result of the creation of Malaysia and the activities of President Sukarno'.[56]

Recruiting and retention crises were to continue throughout the period of decolonisation and after the end of the Cold War as well. Strachan records that the recruiting problems in 1995 were so serious that there was talk of using Gurkhas to make up for the shortfalls in infantry battalions. He commented that 'the notion of drafting Nepalese into regiments with British regional titles showed once again how the system cut across the need for flexibility'.[57]

Even after the 1998 decision to admit Commonwealth recruits from their countries of origin, a similar argument continued about the historic value of colonial troops. Asked to comment on the then-current phase of importing Fijians into the British Army in 2004, Major Charles Heyman, senior defence analyst for Jane's Consultancy Group, said:

> There is a long military tradition in Fiji and many serve today because their fathers and grandfathers did.
>
> The Fijians have been an essential part of the British empire and what they are doing, basically, is filling the vacant slots in the British Army because we cannot recruit enough from the UK itself.
>
> This happened very successfully in the 1960s and 70s and is working very well again today. The truth is they are just normal guys, just like our guys. They make very, very good infantry soldiers.[58]

Heyman's *verdict* on the trend of importing fighting men from the South Pacific – which by then had been continuing for five solid years – amounted to a virtual shrug of the shoulders, reflecting the extent to which the changes in the British Army's recruiting strategies were overshadowed by war itself. By 2004 the armed forces were embroiled in Iraq and the recruitment shortage was compounded by the poor rate of retention. The pressure to monitor ethnic minorities was still on the agenda but had become less of an issue since so many of the new recruits arriving directly from Fiji, the Caribbean and Africa qualified statistically despite not being UK nationals. There had been a few newspaper articles about the phenomenon, but little sense that anyone was systematically monitoring the relationship between recruitment strategies and the colour of the recruits' passports.[59]

For any large organisation, sustaining a workforce is a complex scientific process and the army is no different in principle. Although the modern British Army is considerably more streamlined today than it was in the early

1960s, it can still arguably be described as amorphous and constantly in flux. One thing that has definitely not changed, however, is George Wigg's analogy of the pipeline which remains the standard way of representing the flow of labour in and out of the organisation.

In the pipeline

'On the left you've got a civilian,' said Bob, the officer charged with the job of explaining the structure of army recruitment.

> On the right you've got a trained soldier, who's joining his unit in the field army. Unfortunately in between there are lots of leaks in the pipe and people leave. Either because we ask them to leave – we deem them unsuitable – or they ask to leave themselves, or a medical condition which we were previously unaware of comes up and they have no choice but to leave.

The image of flowing water is not normally associated with the cut and thrust of military culture, but water – or at any rate, liquid – provides a potent metaphor for describing the production method through which new soldiers are made. The art of recruitment is a matter of adjusting the intake and the outflow in order to regulate the volume of liquid that passes through. The pipeline has taps, leaks and 'pinch points' which have to be monitored closely as well as fixed at short notice. The potential recruits are seen as the raw material funnelled into the opening where they face a barrage of selection tests before being primed and sorted for their minimum four-year commitment to army life.

'Running a pipeline is a complex business,' Bob continued. This was my first official day of interviews, and as it turned out, his last day in service. In the room next door the admin staff were preparing a farewell lunch for him. He pointed to the diagram projected on to the screen.

> For every 100 that go into the careers office on the high street, 57 will pass through the army development and selection centre. 34 will turn up for Phase 1 training, 22 will actually arrive to do Phase 2, and 20 will turn up to join the field army.

I was already beginning to feel like Bart Simpson doing his maths test, but my guide went on to interpret the sums for me.

> When you convert that into real figures – this complicated diagram shows you from April 07 to the end of March 08: you've got 21,804 turning up to the army development and selection centres, and this is how many joined the field army: 7,000. So in that part of pipeline, that many people

were lost, and it's not because our standards are too high – there's a whole range of reasons why.

Although it was hard to take in all this information in one sitting, it was true that imagining the recruitment process in this way certainly helped to convey the risks and calculations required to maintain the desired flow. Resorting to a more conventional language of output targets, efficiency and throughput, Bob went on to describe how the whole operation required a staggering amount of effort and money each year. My notebook on that day was almost indecipherable. I scribbled phrases like '8.7 million man-training-days', and 'operational costs of more than £1,000 million'; 'the army employs 10, 432 staff, with a throughput of 13,000 in phases one and two'. As an introduction it was overwhelming, but the basic principles of the pipeline were made crystal clear. The annual budget is finite but the numbers of actual human beings passing through the system fluctuate enormously. Trying to maintain the organisation's workforce at full capacity is a thankless task because so many factors are beyond the army's control. But the extent to which the army is under-manned has potentially grave repercussions in terms of 'operational effectiveness'. In other words, if the government commits the army to war at a time when they are having difficulties with recruiting and retention, this puts additional strain on their capacity to do their job, let alone provide adequate conditions for the soldiers to operate under. This in turn affects the representation of military service as an attractive career choice.

At this point, the simple analogy of the pipeline drawing from an infinite pool of eligible but unenthusiastic citizens does not really do justice to the mechanics of military recruitment. Maintaining the army at an operational level is partly a matter of mathematics, of working out complex formulae and creating algorithms involving elements of risk and probability. The overall size of the army often comes as a surprise, however, and many civilians are often amazed to find out how it compares to other organisations and institutions. Tesco, the UK's biggest private sector employer, has over 360,000 employees, for example.[60] At that time, the army had less than a third of this number, but it is more difficult to imagine its total workforce partly because most people do not have any reason to encounter soldiers in the course of their daily lives, unless they live in a garrison town. It once helped to hear a numeracy tutor teach a group of unschooled infantry trainees how to visualise what big numbers look like. If the army has 100,000 soldiers, 90,000 would fit inside Wembley stadium with 10,000 sitting on the pitch. You don't really need to visit Wembley to be able to picture that in your mind. (If you go to the stadium website it tells you that 'The rows of seating, if placed end to end, would stretch 54 kilometers'.) The point is that while the numbers are supremely important, it is the statistics that really count.

All in the numbers

Like all state-funded institutions in the public sector, the armed forces are obliged to conform to legal and administrative norms which include the collection and presentation of data that break down the different components of the workforce. As a result, military statistics can provide a rich source of material for analysts who want to investigate the relationship between the armed forces and the society from which they recruit. The copious information to the public via the Defence Analytical Services Agency (DASA) website presents a numerical representation of the armed forces broken down by service, age, location, ethnic origin, rank, gender and so on. This information is freely available online and in theory members of the public are able to monitor the size and composition of the armed forces at regular intervals.

Here the lyrical imagery of water must give way to a more measurable analogy that is no less fluid but considerably more complex than hydrogen and oxygen combined. The ingredients of the 'intake', as it is called in official parlance, come from a range of sources which are tapped according to a complex science of social, economic and political factors. It is this mixture that makes up the 'outflow' which is calculated on a regular basis. Graphs and tables can be employed at any point in time to support or undermine a claim that the army is successfully maintaining the required size of its workforce. Viewed over a longer period the figures are able to demonstrate other features that reflect its image as an employer, such as the fits and starts of recruiting from ethnic minorities or the slow progress of women up the ranks. But even when accompanied by simple charts showing some of this distilled information, the statistics alone are unable to explain the complex methodologies involved in the political science of recruitment.

Since 2001 DASA has published regular reports revealing the intake and outflow of different categories across the three services separately and as a whole. Calibrated as a series of graphs, this information is able to demonstrate the fluctuating levels of ethnic minority personnel entering each of the three services.[61] For example, Table 2.1 shows the rate at which they have been successfully recruited into the army since 2004 when the information was first available in this form. It is clear that the pre-selection drives in the Caribbean and other places resulted in a sharp increase from 2007 until spring 2009 when numbers began to fall again.[62] The graph does not explain why there is this pattern, but it provides a simple illustration of the unevenness of ethnic minority recruitment.[63]

The second diagram (Table 2.2) tells a slightly different story because it indicates that there has been a steady increase in the number of ethnic minority personnel entering the Army. The peaks and troughs are absent, suggesting that there are other factors, not visible in this graph, relating to differential rates of retention as well as recruitment. It reveals a successful

Table 2.1   Ethnic minorities as a percentage of intake of UK Regular Forces by service 2004–2010

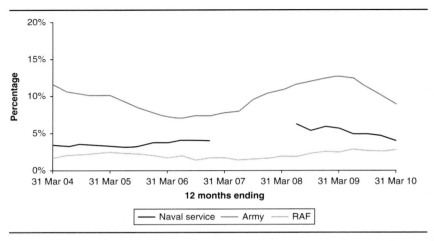

Source: Naval Services intake by ethnic origin is currently unavailable from the 12-month period ending 31 March 2007 to period ending 31 March 2008 due to poor data coverage.

Table 2.2   Ethnic minorities as a percentage of strength by service 2003–2010

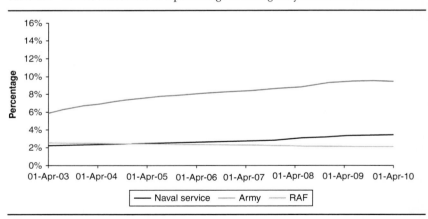

Source: Ethnic minority percentage figures are based on those with a known ethnic origin. Tables showing date on strength split by sex and ethnic origin from 1 April 2003 to 1 April 2006 are shown in TSP4 Table 3 and 3a which can be found at www.dasa.mod.uk.

rise in the percentage of ethnic minority soldiers to a level commensurate with the national population, for the army at least.[64]

But although these two diagrams reveal that there are striking differences between the three services, they offer no explanation for the changes which are visible at a quick glance. While the army constitutes a world of its own in so many ways, the analogy of the pipeline is especially useful because it can be made to reveal the complicated dynamics that deter, propel and attract prospective candidates who are drawn from the wider society. At times it is also appropriate to think of it as an underground channel since army recruitment receives wider attention in the media only when there is some controversy, whether as a result of general protests against war or when the army is accused of targeting or misleading vulnerable groups.

During the same month that I sat through the Power Point briefing with Bob, the Defence Committee was debating the fact that 'Recent research by the MoD found that 56% or parents or guardians would discourage their children or dependents from a career in the Army and 41% would discourage a career in the RAF, in part because of the United Kingdom's involvement in Iraq and Afghanistan.'[65] A few weeks earlier, a comprehensive report claimed that young people under the age of 17 were especially vulnerable to misleading recruitment strategies routinely employed by the armed forces. David Gee, author of *Informed choice? Armed forces recruitment practice in the United Kingdom*, argued that the desperate measures being used by the military recruiters were far from healthy; in fact they were unethical and in severe need of reform.[66] His suggestion that the recruiting materials and methods of the armed forces were deliberately obscuring the realities of military work was particularly powerful. 'The literature rarely refers to the dangers of combat and never mentions the risk of being killed, seriously injured or chronically traumatized,' Gee concluded. 'The absence of the word "kill" suggests a policy decision to avoid it.'[67]

Gee's research caused a furore by questioning the way in which young people were being drawn to a career that might involve the taking of human lives. At the same time, reports of regular targeting of recruiting offices by anti-war protestors were confined to the occasional item in the local media. Although there is a wealth of statistical information about army recruitment which is freely and regularly available online, the larger stories about who is joining (or leaving) the army tend to be submerged, which is one reason why the phenomenon of recruiting large numbers of soldiers directly from Commonwealth countries has gone almost unnoticed. Yet as the first diagram indicated, the rate of their recruitment between 2004 and 2010 was also uneven, ranging from about 6 per cent at its lowest in March 2006 to around 12 per cent three years later.

Unexpected surge

The Army Selection Centre in Pirbright witnessed these peaks and troughs at first hand since it handled all the candidates arriving through the OPT system. After the four young men from Belize and St Lucia who arrived in November 2009, there would be one more group, also from Belize, which was due to arrive the following January. The situation had been very different just 12 months before. 'This time last year,' said the Major, who had been in charge since 2006, 'we were collecting 30 a week, from each airport, Gatwick and Heathrow, from five different carriers.'

He explained that as a result of renewed operations in Iraq and Afghanistan, OPTs were sent out to Fiji and the Caribbean in 2007 and 2008. As a result, all through the summer and autumn of 2008, coachloads of young men and women passed through the selection centre, arrived in the country on Monday, signed their contracts on Friday and began their training the following Monday morning. But the selection centre was not physically equipped to deal with more than a certain number, and the large groups of newcomers arriving straight off long-haul flights presented ethical problems in addition to administrative ones.

Since they had not yet signed their contracts they were still civilians, which meant that the centre was liable under civilian law for their safety. They could not simply be crammed into accommodation blocks and left to sort themselves out unsupervised, but the tempo of testing and selecting meant that staff were not readily available to act as chaperons. Solutions had to be found fast, and often with local improvisation such as moving them to temporary dorms nearby. Each recruit had been obliged to raise significant sums to purchase their open return ticket, a condition of their admission into the country, so their motivation to succeed was strong.

The Major was selected to accompany the team on a further OPT trip to Jamaica in December 2008, but in the meantime the situation had altered drastically as a result of the financial crisis at home.

I had my passport ready but we knew we had turned a corner. Recruits were coming through. The numbers of indigenous went up ballistically in February. They started coming through in April, then till summer – we were stretched. By December last year, we were getting 50 a day indigenous.

The imagery of the pipeline helps to illustrate the fact that the intake was only one part of the equation. The numbers entering the army had to be calculated in relation to those who were leaving, and at what points in their careers they dropped out. The outflow had been running at 5.6 per cent but by November 2009 it had dropped to 1 per cent. This rapidly changing situation posed a problem for the administration because they still had significant numbers of successful Commonwealth applicants waiting for instructions to fly to the UK. The unexpected surge in numbers of domestic applicants threatened to overwhelm the whole process.

'Things were almost changing on a weekly basis,' the Major recalled. 'We would call people a week early for the Monday, but by the time they landed, those jobs have disappeared. We had to give them whatever jobs that were available. We couldn't live on a day-to-day basis ... It was a massive fraught, frenetic period.'

There was disagreement about how to respond to this unexpected crisis. The Directorate of Manning (Army) (DM(A)) called a temporary halt to bringing the Commonwealth applicants over in order to look at the issues, but there were many, like the Major, who argued that they should honour the job offers that had been made. Since they had been approved for selection by the OPTs before the new system was introduced, they were given 'grandfather rights'. Solutions such as re-screening were proposed by the DM(A) but appear to have been dropped when the whole system was overhauled. Nonetheless those who were on the books were carefully scrutinised to examine whether they were the right calibre as it was regarded as important to screen out potential drop-outs. The Major confided how relieved he was when it was agreed to 'ringfence' the vacancies that were open to the remaining candidates who qualified.

'The MoD has taken its responsibilities seriously,' he said. 'Although it was a provisional offer, this has been honoured.' Reflecting on those hectic times over our asparagus soup in the Officers Mess, he seemed almost wistful about the past. 'Now that the OPTs have stopped we are sad to see them go,' he said. 'They added another dynamic. The pace of life was faster here than other selection centres, but the manpower bill was heavy.'

The Major had also overseen changes in the final selection process which were devised to reduce the drop-out rates in the early stages of training. From January 2009, 'we put in a bit of science', he explained. A new set of selection tools was introduced, focusing on the individual's abilities and aptitude and concluding with a formal one-to-one interview. This explained why the young hopefuls I had seen in the centre had changed out of their sportswear and into rather incongruous-looking suits, their faces scrubbed and damp hair plastered as they lined the corridor, nervously waiting for their turn. Those who were given Grade A were given first priority depending on the vacancies available and their chosen career. The rest were to be held in the queue.

Breaking the ice

One of the hoops that the prospective recruits had to jump through at the Army Selection Centre was called the Icebreaker. I first assumed this to be a team-building exercise intended to cut through formalities and to make the young men feel more at ease. Many of them would understandably be feeling insecure, possibly away from home for the first time or just apprehensive about taking this drastic step into a career they could only dream about. During their two-day ordeal candidates were required to wait in the reception room where the screen showed a rolling programme of documentary footage illustrating the realities of being 'on tour' in Afghanistan as well as some of the glories involved in military work at home. Watching this for five minutes it was not hard to imagine that a proportion of applicants might go home having decided that this was not the life for them after all.

Dennis and Ben had completed this part of the pre-selection at home, but the opportunity to listen to others served as a way to observe their peers and get used to the sound of English voices – since this was the regional centre for the south of England, the only northern accents belonged to the centre staff. We sat with a group of about 15 young men and listened as the training instructor ran over the rules. It quickly became apparent that this had nothing to do with shyness and group dynamics. It was an assessed individual presentation, and an important part of the final selection.

'The best way not to fidget with your hands is to put them behind your back. Speak clearly and loudly so that everyone can hear. You have five minutes . . . ' said the instructor who made it clear that he would be grading their efforts.

He read out the headings that each person was supposed to cover, pointing to the list on the flip chart in case they needed prompting. Earlier they had been given a questionnaire which would be the basis of their presentation. Where did they grow up? Why did they want to join the army? What did their friends and family think? What was their goal in life, their ambition? The candidates were required to memorise their answers as they took turns to stand in front of the room and introduce themselves to the other candidates. This was not just about confidence as there was homework involved too. They were supposed to have researched the regiment that they were applying to join and to know something about the work they might be doing.

The first boy was from Essex.

My parents are separated and I'm a football player. My friends say I am mad. But I think that service to your country is the most rewarding thing you can do. My ambition is to get to the highest rank possible. The British Army is the best in the world.

The second was from Kent.

I have three older sisters, two much older and they all have kids. My friends and family feel it is right, they can see it suits my character. I like being outdoors, keeping fit. I want to be in a job that'll keep me fit, being with the lads. I hope to achieve a career, be the best I can be. With a group of lads, good mates.

The third was from Plymouth. He was 22, so a little older than the two previous boys, and his family was familiar with life in the forces.

My step-dad was in the RAF, and I live with mum. My half brother is in 2 Para. My family is happy. My 16-year-old brother is joining the Paras next year too. I want to make something of myself. I dropped out of uni where I was studying law. I want to serve in 1 Para, the Pathfinders.

He professed great love and admiration for the Paras but he spoke more gravely about the risks involved in war. 'I know 30 per cent come back mentally affected, but I am prepared to take this risk.'

Jamie was 18 and lived with his mum and two sisters, one of whom was at university, the other at home. 'My family is happy,' he said. 'My dad was in the navy in the Falklands.' But then he added, 'Mum is not happy.' Like several of the others, he too wanted to join the Paras, the 'best of the best'.

The sergeant corrected him. The 'best of the best' is the SAS, not the Paras. The next was from Eastbourne.

It's a nice place to live. I am not satisfied by any job. I did cadets when I was younger as I had an itch for the army, and you can get qualifications.

Then he admitted something more surprising.

I have a 15-month-old daughter and I want her to be proud of me.

The final question they had to address was about their Most Memorable Moment. A few of them told anecdotes about being selected to play football for a club or alcohol-related incidents with mates, but for many of them this was a chance to say something really personal. For this young father, for example, his Moment was watching his daughter being born.

It was gruesome, but would bring tears to any man's eyes, Paras or SAS.

Another boy admitted that his occurred when he went to play rugby for his school in New Zealand at the age of 16.

I got a phone call from my mum, saying she was leaving my dad after 32 years of marriage. It was shit, but definitely my Most Memorable Moment.

One other young man's story stayed with me from that occasion. He was from Cameroon and told us that he had done voluntary work in South Africa before travelling to the UK as a student. He talked about his interest in human rights, something that had motivated him to join the army. His Most Memorable Moment, he said, was in South Africa, saying goodbye to a 12-year-old girl he had met, whose mother had HIV/Aids. He was slightly older than most of the English boys, and his life experience had evidently given him a wider perspective and a greater sense of idealism.

Afterwards I asked Dennis what his Moment had been. He replied, 'when my sister heard she got a place to study law at the University of the West Indies'. I turned to Ben. 'Seeing my mother for the first time when I was fifteen.' The presentations had indeed given them a chance to hear why their UK-born counterparts in the UK had decided to join the army, and to compare their own ambitions with local recruits. But there was one question they were discussing among themselves. How was it that the local candidates could choose what job they wanted, whether it was clerical, specialist ammunition technician or a member of the infamous Paras, whereas they were only offered posts in an infantry regiment they had never heard of?

As migrants were they being discriminated against, held in a queue only to be given the jobs that no one else wanted? Their suspicions resonated with the experience of the first entrants from Fiji, men such as Jo and Will who, as we heard earlier, were not properly informed about alternatives to infantry. In the next chapter we will look more closely at the logistics of the recruiting process as we explore the hopes, dreams and motivations of some of the individuals who followed those first pioneers.

3
The Promised Land

'There she is on the end, two along from the coloured girl,' whispers an excited voice behind me. A child corrects her, 'no, that's not her, she's over there on the other side'. I was glad to hear them disagree as I was having trouble identifying people too, although there was no one in my family on the parade ground waiting for inspection. The platoon, whose 'pass-out' ceremony we had all come to watch, had just completed their Phase 1 training. For many, this event would be one of the highlights of their army career, and a memorable one for their families as well. The reason why relatives were having trouble picking their daughters out of the troop marching back and forth was not so much that they all looked the same in their khaki uniforms. It was more that they looked *different*. After only three months they had been turned into soldiers, and at that moment they were no longer individuals but figures within a synchronised unit, their heavy skirts swinging in step as they marched past, steel rifles held in white-gloved hands and eyes raised solemnly to the right.

I had come along to see some of the recruits I had met whose families were not able to travel to the UK. But it was almost impossible to tell who was who, especially the ones with the large peaks pulled down over their foreheads. Before the familiar strains of the marching band could be heard in the distance, the master of ceremonies had tried to work on the crowd, urging them to refrain from applause throughout the earlier part but to cheer as loudly as they liked during the final march past. Watching the long process of speeches, inspections and prize-giving gave the audience plenty of opportunity to ponder the new world into which they too were being inducted as new members of the 'service community'. The parade was, after all, partly for their benefit. Unlike other graduations at which students are congratulated and sent on their way, this event was a rite of passage into an institution that would undoubtedly change the successful candidates for life. Those families with no prior experience of military culture were unlikely ever to see an army uniform in the same light, or react to a media story about soldiers with indifference.

After the parade was over, the proud parents, friends and relatives drifted over to the canteen area where they could drink tea out of polystyrene cups before taking their offspring away for a long weekend. For most of these newly qualified recruits, Phase 2 of their training would begin the following week and they would be moving on to other establishments. The array of headgear that they wore during the parade indicated their 'cap badge', revealing whether they were destined for medical corps, signals, engineering, clerical or logistical support – in fact any form of employment within the army except for ground close combat roles in the Infantry and Amoured Corps.[1]

The young women passing out on this occasion had found their way into the British Army through a variety of routes. Four of them were young women from St Vincent who had gone through the pre-selection process in their home country. The OPT had run a four-day basic skills course for over a hundred people, taking over a hotel in the capital, Kingstown, and using a local playing field to put the applicants through their paces. Seven women had flown to London two months later in one 'batch', together with a number of men and some 17-year-olds who were sent to Bassingbourn near Cambridge for the 24-week course designed for those who were under 18.[2]

In addition to these four from the Caribbean, there were two from Zimbabwe in this particular troop, one from Malawi and another from Kenya. At that time, when applicants from the Caribbean and Fiji were arriving on a regular basis, it was not unusual for Commonwealth recruits to make up a quarter of a platoon of over 40 trainees. There was no mechanism for distributing numbers evenly, and there was no ethnic monitoring in the training centre on the grounds that it was not relevant, at least as far as the instructors were concerned. Some platoons were comprised of almost one third of Commonwealth citizens, many of whom were in the UK for the first time. They were often older than their UK peers and many had already begun to acquire civilian qualifications. The ages of this group ranged from 21 to 32. We first met one afternoon, halfway through their training, when they had been there long enough to reflect on this particular life choice. I asked what made them want to join the British Army.

'Money!' laughed Louise, who was from St Vincent. She explained that the exchange rate meant that she could send home a reasonable amount each month. But then she added that she had other motives. 'I always wanted to follow my studies. I am going to Royal Military Police (RMP) – it was given to me after the BARB test.'

Cherry had a degree in Business Management and Accounting from university in St Vincent, and Eva too had impressive qualifications. She was from Kenya and was clear about the career path she wanted to take:

I am going to the Royal Mechanical and Electrical Engineers (REME) as a mechanic, but I want to do air tech. I have a diploma in aeronautical engineering and worked for 2 years with Royal Dutch Airline. In Kenya I was doing civil aviation exams.

Security clearance issues meant that, as a Commonwealth applicant, she was unable to go straight into military aviation, but she was determined to transfer as soon as she could.[3] Her plan was eventually to return to Kenya with her qualifications and put them to good use there. She had no intention of leaving her family and settling in the UK for good.

Like Dennis, who had researched the possibility of joining the US Army, these young women had also checked whether it would be feasible. They had looked online and discovered that there were different restrictions. Yvonne, from Zimbabwe, had certainly found rules that disqualified her, apart from not having US citizenship or a green card. 'You have to be a specific age and family size,' she said. 'They won't take anyone with more than two kids.' That ruled her out as she had three.

Kat, also from St Vincent, explained her reason for applying to work in the British Army.

I had a job as a data entry clerk which would have been permanent after a year. But I loved adventures since I was a child. I am joining the Royal Artillery (RA) but I didn't want to at first. I wanted military clerk, but there were no vacancies so I have to stick with it for a couple of years.

I had first met Kat when I was sitting outside the Spa shop one afternoon waiting to see the Padre. Her troop had arrived back from exercise and were given a moment to relax. I had been watching new male recruits emerging one by one from the barbers, all rubbing their heads as if they had been through some kind of initiation procedure. As the women sat there smoking, eating energy bars and chatting in groups, Kat asked if she could join me at my table. At that moment another troop of men slunk past, strangely attired in black undershorts and long khaki jackets. Needless to say, the 'females' all had a good laugh. Seeing my puzzled look, Kat explained that the men had been to the quartermaster's stores to try on their ceremonial uniforms. We began to talk. She told me she had been not been selected through the OPT in Kingstown but had applied while on a visit to the UK.

There was a consensus that the British Army offered the promise of qualifications as well as a steady salary. But there had been plenty of people warning them off too. When we met again with the others in her troop, Kat said that before she came from St Vincent she was warned to expect racist treatment in the British Army. 'It was different once I was here,' she said. 'People say the instructors will call you names but it hasn't happened.'

Yvonne confessed that 'they always told us it would be hard so I thought it would be harder'. She had twins of 10 and a 13-year-old. For her the whole experience was 'a new world, completely different, a totally 360 degree new world'.

Before she applied she was working towards a degree and hoping to do a masters. 'And here we are starting in the army at a basic level...'

'So what made you want to join?' I asked.

A lot of my family is in the army – my brothers and cousins are in the army. Initially I was getting over a divorce, looking for a new start and I had a thought. I came here from Zimbabwe in 2006 but couldn't join because of my age. Then they were taking people up to 29–30 and my 31st birthday was coming up. Two weeks later they advertised that they were taking people up to 33.

I had so many ups and downs. There was a correspondence breakdown too. It took a long time. But I had a fantastic team from the recruiting office who helped with my application.

My cap badge is the Royal Logistics Corps (RLC) where I will be a chef, but I really wanted to do nursing and want to change to Royal Army Medical Corps (RAMC) – I am working on it.

It became clear that there was considerable frustration at not being able to follow the paths of their choice. Sometimes the discrepancy between an individual's existing qualifications and their job offer could be nonsensical, although the promise of transferring halfway through Phase 1 made many people take whatever came their way. Mary who was also Zimbabwean was told to be a driver. 'Definitely not!' she said with evident disdain as she had her heart set on a medical training. She was in her mid-twenties. She had come to the UK in 1999 on a two-year family illness visa, and had subsequently found employment as a healthcare worker.

My sister was very ill and I came as a carer. I was working in Ipswich for Suffolk County Council. I was trying to make ends meet and I thought my life would be much easier if I joined.

I first met her in September 2008, in the third week of her training at Pirbright. At that time she was in a different platoon with several young women from Gambia and South Africa, all of whom had joined while they were living in or visiting the UK. Mary was already finding the PT very hard and would shortly be back-trooped in order to work on her fitness levels. Three months later, she would definitely be one of those I had trouble recognising on the parade ground. At our first meeting, however, she had already become firm friends with Anni and Ntabi from South Africa. Anni was 21. 'I was a healthcare assistant, and here in UK for 2 years on a working holiday visa,' she explained when I asked about her route into the army.

> I had a friend in the UK who was in the army already and he recommended it to me.
> My first feeling was that I had a lot of information through my friend, and then I went to the careers office. I was nervous. I would have liked to have studied more. I did an accounting course at home, in East London (South Africa). I am the youngest in my family.

Ntabi was a little older. Aged 24 she had two children, aged 5 and 1, who were living with her parents in Bloemfontein. She had originally applied to join the South African army and was disappointed not to hear back from them. 'There are not many jobs in South Africa,' she said, 'and a lot of corruption.' She came to the UK on a holiday visa in 2006 and was impressed by the opportunities offered by the army. I subsequently learned that her brother had joined ahead of her.

> Everywhere you go, the army is promoted. Especially recently.

As she spoke, her friend Anni stroked her ear affectionately. Mary noticed, and smiled. 'We were happy to find each other – we are like sisters – it makes life easier.'

I asked if they were worried that the Mercenary Act might affect their future if it became law. Since 2007 the South African government had threatened to enact the Prohibition of Mercenary Activities and Regulation of Certain Activities in Country of Armed Conflict Act, aimed at preventing citizens from joining other national armed forces as well as private security services.[4] Although the law was not specifically aimed at discouraging South Africans from joining the British Army on the basis of their Commonwealth status, the implications were that soldiers might lose their South African citizenship or risk arrest if they went home.

The young women were vaguely aware of the bill which was awaiting further public consultation, but they were not unduly concerned. 'Things are uncertain,' they said. 'We can't put our lives on hold. We will deal with it when it arises.'

Living by the gun

I began meeting army recruits in Pirbright early August 2008, at the peak of the influx that was causing headaches for the Major next door. The five young men sitting round the obligatory polished table had arrived in large groups of 30 plus from St Vincent and Grenada the previous Monday and had spent the week shivering in the English summer as they went through the final process of selection. Predictably we began by chatting about the weather and they were happy to complain about feeling cold. Once we started to talk about their reasons for coming to the UK, they became slightly less reserved. As we went round the table each one explained what had motivated them.

> I wanted something different in life. Most of the time we have to stay in the same job. I wish to go far. I completed a community college course and did three A levels – physics, geography and maths. I want to go as far as I can in five years. Many people in St Vincent go to the US or Canada.

> I am an adventurous guy and I like working with machines. The army has good pay and you get fit.

> I have been a chef for a while. I don't have money for more studies. I got information about the (British) army and it blew my mind. I made a decision to be a chef, but now I am here there are many different things.

> I work in a brewery at home. It was nice learning how it all worked but it becomes monotonous, too boring, doing the same thing every day. In the army you move around and meet new cultures. You stay fit, wear uniform.

> They give you training and educational opportunities. I will be in the Royal Engineers now, but want to do IT in five years.

Most had heard about the British Army's recruitment drive from friends, but the OPT that came to St Vincent and Grenada in 2008 was not the first to visit, and some remembered that there had been an earlier mission in 2001. I was curious about the local response.

> At first there was uproar [in St Vincent]. People said: 'Why would you go to fight for another man's country?' But then people reported back home, and word of mouth spread. The Government was annoyed because they lost a lot of police officers. They had to drop their standards to recruit and raise pay.

I asked what the status of policing was, and whether it provided an alternative form of employment.

'You can't join the police there for political reasons,' they explained.

In Grenada reaction had also been mixed. 'People thought that Brits didn't want to join because of Iraq and Afghanistan.'

One of the moot points was the fact that recruits had to purchase their own plane tickets. This often meant borrowing money from friends and family, putting more pressure on individuals to succeed so that they could start earning a salary to repay their debt. Opinion was divided as to whether this was fair.

Shortly before this I had met some of the recruiting officers who had been involved in selecting these cohorts. They had talked enthusiastically about the benefits of travelling to locations where there were significant numbers of potential applicants. 'We generally bring back 150 plus from an OPT trip,' said Jim, a warrant officer who routinely travelled with the team. 'It costs around £1,000 per recruit which compared to here is a lot cheaper.' Not only was it economical for the army, but it also provided a way to filter them, saving everyone a lot of time, money and effort.

He ran through some medical problems which disqualified hopefuls, and which might not have been picked up had they travelled to the UK for their initial selection. 'Their protein levels might be too high, they might have heart problems, asthma ... '.

He also appreciated the chance to weed out those who were ambivalent.

Parents put kids under pressure in the Caribbean, often for financial reasons. When kids are put forward to apply and they are not genuine, *you can see it in their eyes.*

Another major problem was language levels.

We tell them it's better to spend another month speaking English. There were two British kids who had lived in Belize for eight years who failed the test. We couldn't understand a word they said!

Mine come in and can start training after a week. It can be tougher because they can't acclimatise unlike the others who are already here. The climatic change and jet lag is difficult for Fijians especially.

I asked him whether they ever encountered criticism or hostility from host countries. 'We meet criticism from inside and out,' he admitted. In Grenada they had been approached by people from 'Middle England' on their winter break.

They said we shouldn't be recruiting. But people from all round the world have built this country. It is their right to join. I get upset by this – I am emotionally attached to the Foreign and Commonwealth (F&C). We will be mobbed in Jamaica, that's for sure.

Jim was referring to the OPT that had been planned for December 2008, which was later cancelled. He was convinced that the F&Cs were 'far more robust, willing to undertake challenge and get an education'. The fact that they paid remittances was proof that they had strong values, particularly in relation to family, law and order and religion. 'The average Brit will have spent his salary in the first week!' he told me.

But F&Cs are proud to serve. You should really try to witness them taking the oath and see how some of them burst into tears. Guys from St Vincent, Grenada, Fiji, they mean it.

One reason for his confidence in the process was that he had heard a great deal about conditions for young people in some of the countries they had visited. 'St Vincent: it's very poor, there's no real income, it's under-developed. In Grenada, there's nothing much except tourism. In Belize there are no opportunities, it's not a nice place. St Lucia is not so bad. In Jamaica they live by the gun,' he said ominously.

Over a year later I was to hear Dennis, Carlos and Albert talking about the pernicious influence of gangs in Belize, and how networks of MS13, and Bloods and Crips dominated throughout the region. Every town and village in Belize was divided, they told me, and there were only certain areas where you were safe.

'It's all about the money,' explained Carlos. 'If I see you making more money than me I want to kill you.'

They talked about how dangerous it has been for them personally, Carlos and Albert talking at once.

If I stayed I would have been killed, it was one reason I joined . . .
If you look at someone, or say one thing . . .
Girls can't wear jewelry even, someone will just pull it off them.

The stories started to come out, about stepping on someone's shoes, looking at them the wrong way, having to confront possible assailants who are armed with knives. Albert laughed as he recounted how he had seen gang members use bicycles as get-away vehicles after robbing people.

Carlos was more serious. 'Most people respect you if you are into religion,' he conceded. 'The gangs don't really pick on you that much – it's about peer pressure. The younger heads in the gang want to do things, they are more senseless.'

Later he told me how he had intervened to protect his brother who had run into trouble, and how his family had to raise money for the boy to attend a school in the mountains to keep him out of harm's way. Part of his motive in joining the British Army was to send money home to contribute.

It was difficult to ascertain to what extent these cultures of violence, particularly among young men, had been a contributing factor in their decisions to leave home, and whether this was any different from many of their UK counterparts. When the Belizeans were regaling me with stories about gang warfare in their country, I couldn't help thinking about parallels with some parts of London, Liverpool or Manchester. The previous year had seen a substantial rise in deaths of young men from stabbings which had led the government to launch the Tackling Knives and Serious Youth Violence Action Programme (TKAP).[5] To many it would seem counter-intuitive to join the army in order to escape the threat of violence, but this is by no means uncommon. I once met a civilian welfare worker who said she was glad her own daughter had joined the army as she was less likely to get killed there than if she had stayed in her home-town in northern England. An English soldier told me that he had joined the army so that he would not have to raise his children on the same council estate in Sheffield where he grew up. Coincidentally he had just been on a course where the instructor had asked participants why they had joined the army. Out of 20 people in the room, he told me, more than half had expressed the same reason: to get away from home.

This anecdotal evidence was commonly accepted in the army, and there was a general perception that the majority of UK recruits came from 'broken homes' or from economically deprived backgrounds.[6] In 2005, just three months after the publication of Nicholas Blake's Deepcut Review, the Select Committee on Defence reported that there was little evidence to substantiate the view that the Army recruited most of its soldiers from the least privileged socio-economic groups, partly because the MoD did not collect the relevant statistical information.[7] However, it was noted that a survey carried out on Infantry recruits from the Cardiff area between 1998 and 2000 had found that the majority of recruits had left school with minimal qualifications. One third came from poor housing conditions and 45 per cent came from 'broken homes'. This survey was to have significant impact not so much on the recruitment process but on the army's strategy of training and education.

Since there was no corresponding collection of data on the socio-economic background of Commonwealth soldiers, it was impossible to draw a comparison with UK recruits. However, although the costs in financial and emotional terms might be higher the further the recruit has to travel, there was no doubt that joining the army provided an escape route, not just to get away but also to get on. But just as there were many comparable motivating factors, there were also discernible differences. As Jim had suggested, perhaps the biggest discrepancy between recruits from the UK and from Commonwealth countries was that for the latter the job also represented a chance to provide families at home with a regular income. One young man from Grenada was able to illustrate all these factors when I met him on his own.

He was 23 when the OPT came to his country, and a friend persuaded him to go along. He explained why he went:

I was learning buffing and cleaning cars. Doing labouring, working with concrete... Where I come from there ain't nothing good for young people... For example, if you have a job, you leave home at 7 and work till 4.30, everything is the same every day and the boss man is hassling you, you want to cuss and walk away. You go and drink, smoke weed, want to make yourself feel better.

On civvy street a lot of boys can end up in a lot of trouble, in jail or getting killed. The army is a good thing for young men. You have to have goals, ambition.

My mother has high blood pressure and diabetes. Another sister does dental care and looks after her at night. A friend comes in the day time. The main thing is to help my mother as best as I can. Without her I can never become who I am ... but without education it ain't good.

The mechanics of sending money home to parents and other dependants is not always easy. One of the problems incurred in processing so many recruits coming from the OPT trips was the inexperience of the staff in dealing with the international banking system, particularly in the eastern Caribbean. According to staff in the Selection Centre in Pirbright, individuals were not able to get loans for their flights in St Lucia and St Vincent because there was no way to pay them back through UK banks. The only solution was to set up accounts with the Bank of Nova Scotia which has branches in those countries. Watching the young men from Belize go through the paperwork after their final selection at the centre, it was clear that, while opening a bank account was likely to be a novelty for most recruits, setting up a system for remittances was by then accepted as an integral part of the administrative process.

Short-term visas

One of the reasons why local attitudes to British Army recruitment in Grenada might be different than in other islands was the prominence of former Grenadan citizen Johnson Beharry after he was awarded the VC in 2006. In his autobiography *Barefoot Soldier*, Beharry, who was not selected through the OPT, gave an account of how he made his decision to join. His boyhood in Grenada was marked by extreme poverty and hardship, but his life changed in 1999 when he came to London for a holiday to stay with relatives. At his aunt's suggestion he successfully applied for a student visa intending to take a course on motor mechanics. Finding the course too basic to hold his attention – he had been obsessed with cars since a boy – he soon dropped out, and with help from his cousins found jobs on building sites to keep him going. It was then that his life began to fall apart. Terrified of becoming like his alcoholic father who had terrorised his family back in Grenada, he noticed an advert for the army in a newspaper left on the seat next to him as he travelled to work by tube. There was one sentence that grabbed his attention:

Recruits don't have to be British to apply; Foreign and Commonwealth applicants will be considered on their merits.

Realising he was eligible he made up his mind there and then. 'If I joined the army,' he thought, 'it would solve my problems at a stroke. I can remain in the UK. I might even get a British passport. I'll also get a reasonable wage, but best of all, I'll break completely with the past.'[8]

Beharry's resolve was tested by scepticism from his workmates and his family but he found his way to the nearest recruiting centre in north-west London. Here it was not his immigration status that caused a problem but the fact that he was wearing an earring in the shape of a marijuana leaf. The recruiting sergeant sent him away for six months to get fit, and when he reapplied, he was able to complete the forms and pass the initial tests with no further problems. Introduced to another Grenadan soldier working in the careers centre, Beharry opted for the same regiment, particularly as it promised the chance of driving armoured tanks. The Princess of Wales Royal Regiment (PWRR) was recruiting at that time which meant only a short delay between final selection and the start of training.

This route into the army, applying directly through recruiting offices in the UK, remains an option for Commonwealth citizens who are in the country on temporary visas and who have a minimum of four years to run on their passports. Like the young women from Southern Africa whom I met in Pirbright, many find temporary work in private care homes which employ significant numbers of Commonwealth workers – by no means all female. I spoke to one young man from Mauritius who had come to the UK three years earlier to study Business Administration. He explained:

> For foreign students it's a lot of money. I stopped college for six months and got a job in a nursing home. My family is having financial difficulties back home, and I was sending money back every month…Then I got the idea of joining the army – you don't pay rent or buy food, and you get loads of qualifications and it's the easiest way to send money back home. You need to work hard obviously…so I went for selection and everything.

It was only his third week in training but he was already looking forward to finishing the course and starting his job in the medical corps. I asked what he thought he would be doing.

'I will be acting like a combat medical technician, working alongside doctors and nurses like a paramedic…evacuating casualties, soldiers and civilians,' he replied enthusiastically. His only qualifications consisted of a first aid course with St Johns Ambulance and an NVQ in health and social care.

The chance to follow a medical career also attracted Paul who had joined from the UK where his sister was living. Before that he completed his university degree in bio-science in Ghana and then applied to the British Army while in the UK on a visiting visa. Since he knew exactly what job he wanted to do he was prepared to wait for a vacancy in the medical corps.

> I was waiting to join – I want to be a bio-medical scientist. I did temporary warehouse jobs, and clerical work in a shipping company. I wanted to join the army, wanted to be a soldier. I liked the uniform, the discipline. I will work in labs with doctors, on operations, on diseases, research, help monitor treatments – I won't be fighting. I have always been interested in helping to save lives as well so it's a double win. It's not to kill but to save casualties.

Word of mouth

As we saw in the previous chapter, the decision to admit applicants from Commonwealth countries in 1998 was partly driven by the need to increase the number of ethnic minorities in the armed forces. Dispatching the OPTs to countries where there was significant interest was an effective way to accelerate the rate at which they joined. Targeted advertising within the UK was another, along with touring Sikh and Muslim community centres. A lasting legacy of the CRE's involvement in the early period of reform was the creation of the Diversity Action Recruiting Team (DART) which argued for the importance of role models to encourage minorities. As the decade wore on, its remit expanded to include gender as well as ethnicity. When I visited the DART offices in 2008 there was a simple way of gauging the organisation's track record of increasing the number of UK-born minority recruits. Among a group of eight soldiers seconded for a year to work as role models, only one was what they called 'indigenous', while the rest had joined as Commonwealth citizens. Despite the fact they had not grown up in the UK, they were still considered an effective tool for communicating with young people.

'It is very difficult for white males, engaging with minorities,' said the officer in charge, speaking with the weight of experience.

> It is not something they grew up with. There is a degree of fear and ignorance. DART is supposed to help mainstream recruitment and our business is in the inner city. The ignorance of uniformed personnel is our biggest drawback – it is very difficult to educate military personnel.

Carla, a 23-year-old Jamaican, was a technical supplies specialist who had applied to join in 2003 when she was in the country on a student visa. One of those seconded to work with DART, she agreed to meet in a shopping mall in Slough, just outside London, where she was part of a team running an army recruitment stand. As we sat talking in the open-plan café within sight of her colleagues, she explained how her family in Jamaica felt about her being a soldier in the British Army:

> They were pleased. It's a job at the end of the day, but you feel proud of it, going back there.
>
> Lots of people think it's new for Commonwealth to be in the army. Young soldiers don't know their history; they ask, 'Why do you want to join the British Army?' – I say why not? The Queen is head of our government, we have British values and standards. Technically we are British, Commonwealth British.

Carla's sense of historical continuity was partly based on her perspective as a Jamaican citizen. However, as a recruiter she was well aware that young British people born in the UK were not attracted to the army, particularly those of Caribbean or South Asian descent: 'There's not a lot of ethnic Brits joining the army,' she said. It was evident to her that her fellow Commonwealth soldiers had a different approach. One reason was that 'we don't have a long history (here) so it is easier for us to join. Parents have a big role to play in terms of recruiting ethnic minorities in Britain. My family didn't have experience of living in the UK. I didn't have a barrier in my head.'

Free advertising

Karim, the Community Liaison Officer for the Home Counties, was more than happy for me to observe their work at the recruiting stand. He was born in Kenya and his family moved to the UK when he was a boy. After joining the army in 1978 he was posted to Germany with a Royal Artillery regiment. There was a lot of name-calling, he said, it was a huge culture shock. But he never thought anything of it, assuming it was part of army life. 'I liked the old days, you knew where you stood,' he admitted.

As we began to talk, it was clear he was fervent about his mission to recruit more minorities. 'Recruitment is best done one to one,' he said, 'much more effective than ads.' A passing shopper caught his eye and he turned his full attention towards him. 'Do you want to join the army? Where are you from?' He rattled off questions. The guy looked startled by the attention, but he replied, saying in hesitant English that he was from Nigeria. At 38 years he was too old for the regular army, but when he learned he was eligible for the Territorial Army (TA) he began to show more interest. The questions continued:

> When does your passport expire? How long is your visa for?

The man muttered something about his brother. His own passport was due to run out in two years which was not good enough – applicants were required to have at least four years left. His visa was good for six months, which was more than adequate, but he seemed keen to join now.

The brother appeared and was drawn into the conversation. He was in his early thirties but more portly. He was doing an MA in banking and finance and had to renew his visa every year. He had just renewed his passport so there was no problem there. Karim told him he could move fast and join either the regular army or the TA. With those skills he might apply to work in the Adjutant General's Corps.

Can you run 1.5 km in 13 minutes?
Yes.
Any tattoos? Criminal record?
No, no.

He took their contact details and the brothers moved off with some brochures. He then showed me a supply of army pencils which he offered to a little girl passing with her mother. The child's eyes lit up, but she was too shy to accept one.

'This is free advertising,' he grinned. 'We put our literature out because I know the woman who runs the centre. We are supposed to get permission otherwise.' He pointed to a large stand with stacks of glossy literature, placed just far enough away so people could browse without engaging. Nearby there was another temporary stand advertising a Polish bank, in Polish, and the familiar voice of Sade could be heard crooning in the background.

A healthcare worker from Zimbabwe had stopped to talk to Carla. She was 32 but seemed genuinely interested. Karim stepped in and made a phone call. He passed his phone to her so she could ask about doing a health-related job in the TA.

Meanwhile I talked to one of the other soldiers on the stand. 'The main problem is the medicals,' he told me.

Even if they've come to the UK for some time they won't have registered with a GP. When we give them the form, they have to send it home and it can take months. Some give up. It's absolutely ridiculous in my opinion.

During the course of my interview with Carla, I watched the recruiting group out of the corner of my eye. The three white men in green uniform did their best to solicit interest from passers by, intermittently chatting to each other and looking bored, and not doing very much business. When Carla rejoined them I was immediately struck by the way that the addition of a young black woman wearing the same uniform transformed their display. It was undeniably more dynamic, underlining Carla's priceless value as a recruiting tool. She had talked at some length about her conversations with young people, black and white, out of earshot of her colleagues, and it became clearer why her role was not just about meeting minority recruitment targets. 'My job is to talk to the kids,' she said, 'and I tell them like it is.' Looking over at the stand, she added, 'I wouldn't stop if I was them. But it's good to have me and ethnic minorities in the army.'

Not all minority recruiters enjoyed their mission, however. Mel was from Yorkshire. Her mother was white and her father, who died before she joined the army, was Jamaican. She had volunteered to work with DART a few years earlier but found that she hated it. 'I think being on the ethnic recruiting team was probably the worst thing I ever did. I got pulled around like a dancing bear!'

Although she enjoyed talking to young people at special events and conferences, and telling them about her experiences in the army, she felt more ambivalent when she was part of a recruiting group in a public place. It felt all wrong to target passing black kids on the basis that she was also black. Wincing at the memory, she said:

> I didn't like it at all. I just felt as though we may as well have had a big belisha beacon on our head saying, 'We *don't* want to talk to you,' because the guy I used to work for used to say, 'There's one of yours, go talk to him.' I didn't know what to talk to him about, it was difficult but especially because I don't have any friends who are black so it was hard for me to just go and chat – to go and talk to people, just to... why would they want to talk to me? It was only a year, thank god.

Learning a trade

On my following visit to Pirbright I arranged to meet some British trainees to get some sense of why they had chosen a military career. Although this was early days I had heard enough to know that those who selected the Corps, as opposed to the Infantry, were often keen to get further qualifications and training which would equip them for civilian life at some later point. Billy, who was 18, spoke with a strong Lancashire accent and was a newcomer to this platoon as he had recently been held back for a few weeks, or 'back-trooped'. Since he had already admitted this, I asked if he minded telling me why.

'My administrative skills were not up to standard,' he said somewhat sheepishly. Personal administration is army code for sorting out your belongings, keeping uniform pressed and boots polished, and cleaning your block.

'Did you iron at home?' I asked him. I had been told that most British kids had no idea how to look after themselves when they turned up for training.

'No!' he replied. There were three other young men in the room and they agreed that it was a common occurrence, being back-trooped. Several members of their platoon had failed a shooting test the previous day.

> You have to learn all over again. You have three chances, but after two attempts there are so many people they don't have time to wait for you to do it right.

After you have been back-trooped three times you are declared unfit for army purposes. I asked Billy what made him want to join?

'I was always interested,' he said, evidently shy at talking about himself in front of the others.

I had an uncle in the army who has been to Afghanistan. I want to travel, do things.

When I inquired what his friends at home thought about his decision, he became more animated.

Back home everyone treats you with more respect. So many people can't believe I have joined.

Andy, from Basingstoke in the south of England, was also 18. 'I wanted a career,' he explained. 'My cap badge will be military clerk.' He was clear about two things. 'I don't want to go to Afghanistan,' he said firmly, 'it's not for me. I want a qualification.' Before he applied he was doing labouring jobs. His parents were supportive but he seemed tentative. 'I'll wait and see how it is.'

Mike, who was 24 and much more laid back, described himself as an RAF brat.

I was born in Belgium and my father was in the air force. I've never stayed anywhere long so I am used to the life. I had friends in the army and I am going to the Army Air Corps.

He seemed resigned to joining the army, almost as though it was beneath him.

I put it off for ages. I went to college to do sports coaching but got bored. I did odd jobs. I planned to go back to college but couldn't be bothered to be poor.

The fourth young man was also in his mid-twenties and unlike the others he had completed his university education studying social sciences. He said modestly,

I considered a career in prison or probation office but I fancied something more hard-core. This is one of the most intense careers – it gives you a real sense of achievement.

The mix of different backgrounds and motivations among this randomly selected group inhibited our conversation, but I was struck by the pride with which the young man from Bolton spoke about the way his friends looked up to him when he went home for his first long weekend. 'They said I couldn't do it,' he told us.

While it was difficult to find out from him why they thought he would fail – what choices the friends were making for themselves, what their prospects were or their general attitudes to the army for that matter – his sense of self-esteem had obviously rocketed in spite of his battle with the ironing board. And talking to this small group revealed a wider point: that joining the trade corps was an attractive option for those who were anxious to get qualifications, as well as for those who were not necessarily committed to combat roles. I was told many times by recruits who had taken this path that the Infantry did not offer any training or qualifications that would be of use in civilian society. This was just as true for British trainees as it was for the young men and women born outside the UK.

Questions of choice

The four young men from Belize and St Lucia, recruited through the OPT in 2008, were all destined for different battalions in the Yorkshire Regiment, founded on over 300 years of 'Yorkshire Warrior' tradition. When we first met they had no idea about the history of the regiment, having been told they had jobs in the Kings Division which includes the Yorkshire regiments. 'We recruit soldiers with a strong sense of unity, duty and high sporting prowess from Yorkshire, the North East and all Commonwealth Countries,' claims the website. In 2009 17.7 per cent of the Wiltshire-based battalion of the Yorkshire regiment were soldiers from Commonwealth countries.[9] The majority had been assigned to the regiment in response to staff shortages, not because they identified with the North-east. At least the young men had a choice between units in Wiltshire and Germany, where in both cases they would meet other young men from the Caribbean.

Although many individuals expressed frustrations and disappointments at not being able to join their desired trade, the question of choice could be a luxury when visas were running out and the alternative was to return home or risk overstaying. Many recruits I spoke to expressed their intention to transfer to a different trade at the earliest opportunity, having been reassured by recruiting officers that this would be a straightforward process. But given the resources that it takes to train each individual to perform the basic roles of their allocated trade, allowing for all the 'wastage' involved in losing those who drop out or fail at earlier stages, the reality is that transferring is a great deal more difficult than simply making an application and waiting for the administration to deal with it.

The model of the pipeline which represents the constant flow of employees in and out of the organisation – or any component part – suggests that this is a logistical matter. But there are other barriers that not only make the transfer process frustrating and drawn out but also likely to cause resentment and possibly worse. Again, this is a complex issue which derives from the particular demands of the organisation. There are two main reasons why it might be problematic to request a transfer. The first is that the trade (or whatever the post that the individual wants to leave) might have difficulties attracting recruits, and therefore be reluctant to lose trained employees. But a second reason stems from the structural elements of the army itself. Each regiment, company and area of expertise cultivates forms of attachment and identification that make it more difficult to move freely between different jobs.

Jo, for example, whom we met in the previous chapter, had spent 12 years as a military clerk in Fiji, applied for a transfer from his regimental position as an infantryman after only three months. He felt aggrieved not to have been informed about jobs in administration or the medical corps when he applied in 1998, but the regiment that was recruiting him was woefully undermanned and therefore reluctant to let any of the promising new Fijian recruits go elsewhere. His first application to transfer was chucked in the bin, he told me, and he became alarmed when he was told he only had two more chances. Eventually he was able to move to the RLC becoming the first Fijian to transfer out of his regiment. 'Everyone tried to follow,' he said. 'Four succeeded, but after that there was a temporary stop.'

There are numerous factors deterring individuals from opting out of the section or regiment that first recruited them, and as we have seen, these are not all to do with resources and numbers. After meeting recruits at the ITC, the formidable internal hierarchies within the organisation came more clearly into view. Young men with only a few weeks' experience of army life were quick to internalise the strong lines of demarcation that exist not just between trade corps and infantry but between different regiments as well. Important distinctions were made on the basis of history, geography, expertise and reputation.

Tribal training

'We train tribally,' I was told by the officer in charge of the Infantry Training Centre (ITC). Despite historical precedents of raising regiments from diverse groups, the regimental system continues to place a value on local identities, retaining strong connections to place in spite of constant amalgamations. I was subsequently given a recruiting map which divides the country into areas where different regimental units carry out their own outreach. The Wars of the Roses had ended in 1485, but 'a Yorkshire accent in the Lancashire regiments stands out', I was informed on another occasion. 'It's a rarity.' The idea of 'tribalism', of emphasising regional commonalities and identities, is thought to 'add colour' to army life in much the same way as sport, although rivalries between supporters of different football clubs within the same city could be a problem. The spread of regional accents, affinities and identifications also encompasses a north–south divide in England as well. One recruiting officer admitted that they would not send southern soldiers up north because their accents made them identifiable and they were seen as 'soft'.

A quick glance through the British Army website reveals the vestigial emphasis on place, identity and tradition where it is still expedient or feasible. The Mercians, for instance, are described as 'A proud, close-knit local regiment with three centuries of operational success behind us'. Formed only in September 2007, the regiment draws 'our fighting strength from the history and traditions of our antecedent regiments, and the strong family ties we maintain with our counties and communities'.[10] Looking at the names of the antecedents, such as the Sherwood Foresters Regiment, it becomes more evident how modernisation proceeds to flatten out those differences, operating on a different socio-economic scale. The Mercian regiment now claims to be 'the modern heart of England – confident, diverse and forward-looking'. The stress on England is significant because it draws attention to the internal dynamics of the UK. In this sense the army is a truly British institution, and some would also argue that it is already multinational since it places emphasis on the component nations of the UK.

The Welsh Guards were set up in 1915 and have retained a strong identification with Wales and the Welsh language. On their recruiting page they offer 'the chance to join Welsh Guards and serve alongside fellow Welshman (99 per cent of Welsh Guardsman are Welsh, coming from both North and South Wales)'.[11] The Scots Guards make no mention of Scottish ancestry or historical roots, emphasising instead the combat infantry role played by their battalions. The Royal Regiment of Scotland, however, which was an amalgamation of 14 original regiments raised in the seventeenth and eighteenth centuries, makes a different claim. 'We are fiercely proud of our heritage ... Scotland has a tradition of producing courageous, resilient, tenacious and tough Infantry soldiers.'[12] The Irish Guards, known 'affectionately' as 'the Micks' according to the Army website, have regional recruiters in Northern Ireland, Manchester, Liverpool, the Midlands and London.[13] Similarly, the Royal Irish Regiment recruits 'soldiers of Irish origin or background' and 'suitable recruits from across the whole of Ireland, Great Britain and Commonwealth countries'. A report from Belfast in 2008 noted that '16% of all those enlisting since April were from south of the border – up from the 10.5% recorded in the previous year'.[14]

As we saw in the Icebreaker sessions at the Army Selection Centre in Pirbright, candidates were required to explain why they had chosen a particular job or regiment. By that time they would have taken various tests to determine whether they were qualified, and many would have been steered in particular directions by parents and recruiting staff, if not by army ads,

Andy McNab books or TV documentaries. On several occasions the instructor grading the presentations cross-questioned the recruits on their grasp of the history or expertise of their regiment of choice, but in most cases the young men appeared to know what it was they wanted from an army career, whether it was excitement and glory in the Paras or a more specific role as an 'ammo-tech' in the RLC. Hearing the prospective recruits gush enthusiastically about their desired jobs, it was not hard to see why the boys summoned from the Caribbean to fill vacancies in Infantry regiments they had never heard of felt that they were being discriminated against from the very start. But for many British boys, too, it was the Infantry or nothing.

That's what it's all about

The young men from south Wales were all clear about their career choice. 'Infantry is soldiering for me,' said one, and the others murmured in agreement, including one who had re-enlisted after leaving the RLC because he was bored. The four were approaching the end of their course, and having been together for nearly six months they were easy in each other's company, chipping in and laughing at each other's responses. They were also very pleased with themselves for having survived this far.

Dan was from Carmarthenshire. He wanted to join the army from a young age, he told us, but he finished his education and went to Cardiff University where he did a degree in BA in leisure and sports management. After that he was unable to find work.

> I had family problems too, and used that as a reason to go off the rails, and then I had a problem with the police. I thought the army would be a good career move, to try and get some normality back in my life. That's basically how I ended up here.
> *Did your friends think it odd?*
> No. The crowd I was hanging around with – they were going nowhere. For my university friends – it was a bit of a shock. They thought I'd be doing something more like administration... Reconnaissance. That's what attracted me. I'm not frightened about going on operations; it's all part of it.

'That's what it all about,' added someone.

Dave began to talk about his motivation.

> It gives me a lot of excitement. Every day is something different. I always wanted to join the army as a child, my uncle being in the army. My family? They agreed with me though my girlfriend wasn't happy. It was kind of mixed between my family and my girlfriend and daughter.

It turned out he had a one-year-old child, and I was intrigued to know whether his girlfriend was ready to become an army wife with all that this entailed.

'We are not married yet,' he replied quickly. The others laughed – 'don't do it!'

'I don't recommend it for a squaddie,' said Nicky, who seemed to know. 'You don't have time to be together. I got married when I was in my unit. We still couldn't see each other as much as we wanted to.'

He was what is called a 're-enlister', and had first joined at 17. 'I was in the Logistics, based in Abingdon,' he explained, 'in the driving unit. I didn't like it at all, to be honest. It was boring, sitting around in a car all day.'

I turned to Ian, the fourth one. He described how he had wanted to join since he left school but when he did try to join they told him to come back when he had put on some weight.

> I wanted to join as a vehicle mechanic – that's something I done at college. They said I needed qualifications and to put on weight. I worked on construction. One day I just popped into the office, and ended up joining. I needed to get away from the crowd I was with. The only thing I could do was move away or … I just decided to join the army. It was either the army or prison.

I heard someone murmuring, 'better yourself … '.

> Yes, I wanted to try to better myself, to show my parents I can be a better person.

As they all seemed to share this motivation I asked whether their friends had the same experience. 'A lot,' they said in unison.

> It's something to fall back on. After the training they put you through, it does make you grow up quick.'
> You're forced to grow up!
> There are going to be more because of the recession now – there's lots of re-enlisters.
> I've heard there's a three month waiting list.
> Six month waiting list for the infantry!

They all talked at once, about people they knew who were wanting to join – how they joined at the right time. There was a definite element of smugness about getting in before the recession really began to bite.

Later I discovered that while Wales contributes 5 per cent of the total population in the UK, it makes up 7–8 per cent of the army's recruitment target. Figures obtained under the Freedom of Information Act showed that during the financial year 2008–2009, the armed forces recruited 1377 people from Wales – an increase of over 15 per cent on the previous year.[15]

Elite forces

Four young men from two different continents were sitting round the table. They were two thirds of the way through their training as infantrymen, and all were destined for Guards regiments when they left in a few weeks time. The Guards are considered to be among the elite sections of the infantry along with the famous Parachute regiments which require an extra level of mental and physical strength of their recruits. I had begun the conversation by asking whether they had all chosen to be Guardsmen when they applied. Their response was a unanimous 'No!', led by Simon, from New Zealand.

Chike, from Nigeria, attempted to clarify this collective response. He had applied to join the army while studying for a Masters in Disaster Management at Aberdeen University. He was halfway through the course when he learned that he was eligible for officer training in the British Army.

> When I got to the recruiting office they told me that you had to stay for four years in the country and that the short cut was for me to enlist as a soldier first, do my four years as a soldier then I'd be recommended as an officer, which I was comfortable with. But at that point, I didn't want to go into the Guards, I wanted to go into the medics. When I came to the UK I was studying as well and I was working in a hospital, so I had that interest as well, you know, the medics sector and helping out.

Chike explained that he had been told that there were no openings in the medics at that time, but he had not been convinced and had done some of his own research to find out if it was true. Even though he was doubtful, he still felt he had been lured into joining the Guards.

> But when I got in, I fell in love with it – (although)...I'll just wait and see what the battalion holds for us, because they tell us that the battalion is the promised land. When we get there things are better. I am just waiting to see if this is really the life I want to lead.

Mbizi, who was born in Malawi, had a cousin in the Coldstream Guards who encouraged him to apply. He was actually more interested in the Paras but they told him he would have to wait for a vacancy unless he joined the Guards first and applied to move later.

'If I am in the army, maybe I have a future because I might go to school through the army as well,' he added.

While the two West Africans were motivated by a desire for further education, the other two seemed drawn to a soldier's life for its own rewards. Simon told us about his goal:

> I always wanted to join the military, I always wanted to come over here and try. I held off for a few years but when I was 25 I thought I'd better get over here. I came here because you have the best training in the world, so many different regiments... all sort of different options, things like that.

'What's wrong with the New Zealand Army?' I asked. 'Did you consider joining that?'
'No,' he replied, with some feeling.

> It's under-funded and under-manned. And it's boring, they never get to do anything. I know people who've been in for five years, never seen any combat or anything.

Simon was from Ashburton, just below Christchurch in the South Island. I asked whether it was widely known that New Zealanders were eligible to join the British Army, and what people thought about that.

> Yes it is. We're still part of Britain really, and still haven't severed ties. New Zealand is still a colony of Britain, especially the town where I'm from. A lot of people leave and come over here. There are a lot of retired people there who are paratroopers, things like that.

'What about the Australian army,' I asked. 'Was that an option?' I was struck by the discrepancy between his gentle manner and his evident enthusiasm for excitement and danger.

> No! Too many Aussies! Too many snakes and spiders and crocodiles. There's more chance of being killed by a snake in the Australian army than in armed combat!

Jan was from South Africa and the most experienced of the group. He became aware that the British Army had recruiting stations in his country, and that it was also possible to pick up forms from the British Embassy and apply online. His story was surprisingly complex considering his previous military training.

> I applied two times. I was in the South African army and thought that my chances would be better, but nothing came of it. I went two times for

selection and waited six months, seven months, and heard nothing from them, But I knew they were recruiting foreign people.

Then I came here, got myself a stupid little job just to make some money – went to a recruiting office, did my selection, everything, and applied for Royal Regiment of Scotland. I came here and today I am in the Scots Guards.

Outside there was an incessant sound of marching boots and the high-pitched 'Eff! Ight!' of the platoon sergeant. The room we were sitting in looked out over the parade ground where a batch of recruits was preparing for their passing off ceremony the following day.

Jan was evidently determined to leave the country of his birth to join the British Army, and admitted to being quite at home.

Now I have no problem, I have adapted. I like it a lot. I like the friends, the traditions, obviously I think the Guards are the best.

I asked what he did in the South African National Defence Force (SANDF).

I was in the infantry, ma'am. I went on tour to Congo for six months, for peace keeping with UN, but I only did two years. After that I finished my contract and came over.

'Would you join them again?' I asked.

Never again ma'am. There's no way. If you consider the training, the pay, the equipment, the food ... people moan about the food here, but this is five-star food, seriously.

Jan explained that after he left, he had been contacted many times by his former employers. 'They have to have 20 per cent white people ... and young white people don't want to join army any more, that's the problem with them.' He said that out of 2000 soldiers he was one of five who were classified as white.

Later that day I met four South Africans who had been placed with the Parachute Regiment. They were also well over half way through their training, though two of them had suffered significant injuries and were waiting to find out where else they might work. Having heard about Jan's experiences in the SANDF, I asked whether any of this group had considered joining.

'No chance!' They chorused, laughing at the thought of it. I asked why.

'If you ask any South African,' said Franz, from Bloemfontein, 'It's in a state, it's not clever for you to do that. You wouldn't get promoted.'

'Is that because you're white?' I asked.

'Yes!' They laughed again. Sam, from Cape Town, explained:

It's not a professional army. The pay would be pathetic, you don't go on ops. The British Army invests a lot more money in you, obviously, as they have better funding.

There seemed to be a consensus that their prospects in the country were limited. I asked Thabo, from Johannesburg, what he thought. 'The blacks ... I am dark skinned but just stating the facts.' He spoke in resigned tones about the way in which politicians were known to put their families first. His family lived in Hillboro, an area of the city which had remained relatively integrated throughout the apartheid period.

I lived there when it was still like the centre of Jo'burg, a nice place to go to, but slowly more people came. And it turned into what it is today. Loads of migrants – Nigerians, Zimbabweans, Botswanans.

Thabo explained that he had originally intended to join the SANDF, but while visiting his extended family in Reading during a visit to the UK, he learned about the opportunity to apply to join the British Army.

My family knew about people joining. My aunt was going out with someone from Jamaica and one of his relatives had joined.

'What was your first thought?' I asked him.

To be honest, with the opportunities the British Army offers, I thought fair enough, it might be a better choice than to go back to a corrupt country and hope for the best. Like I said, everyone there looks out for their own relatives.

I didn't see myself doing an office job. The Engineers were full. The best option in the Infantry is the Parachute regiments.

Thabo had sustained an injury in his lower back as a result of weight-bearing exercises. He was about to have a medical to see if he was fit enough to join the RLC. The ambition to join an elite regiment clearly did not come without risk. Recruits are obliged to pass an extra course, known as Pegasus, consisting of a series of eight tests carried out over a period of seven days.[16] This demands intensive preparation beforehand, resulting in a high dropout rate. 'You have to accept that in Paras, 'cos it's hard. It's the hardest course you can do,' Franz said proudly.

More than half get injured, and only 30 per cent pass out. If you fail you can either transfer or wait out until the next one. It's an elite regiment. It's meant to be the hardest physical test the army has to offer.

Franz took a certain pride from the fact that, in his observation, the majority of white South Africans were directed to the Paras when they applied, possibly because they showed a real enthusiasm for tough combat training.

'Most of us look for hands on,' said Franz. 'And Paras are motivated to go to Afghan, to be on ops. If you are training to be a soldier you want to use your skills. Everyone's up for Afghan.'

Months later I recalled what the South Africans had said when I listened to the young English boys performing their Icebreaker tests at the selection centre. The majority had expressed their excitement at joining the Paras because they viewed it as the most prestigious job, largely thanks to the numerous memoirs and war documentaries that have proliferated since the war in Iraq. For some it promised a glittering route out of an uncertain and often unhappy childhood, one that led towards a more exciting career where they would be the envy of their friends in civvy street.

Loaded questions

I had heard that recruits from Southern Africa were particularly valued, even that they made great warriors. At a briefing on Commonwealth soldiers from senior infantry personnel, I once asked if some nationalities were considered more valuable than others. The Colonel leading the meeting answered cautiously, aware that this was a loaded question. 'Less so,' he replied, and then paused. 'But I still get people who say give me 50 white South Africans and you can have all my West Africans.'

He offered an explanation of how different nationalities were regarded within the army:

> Some cultures adapt to the British mentality better. Fijians have a respect of hierarchy, and they are easier to adapt. There is anecdotal evidence that New Zealanders, Australians, and South Africans are more ambitious. The Special Forces have lots of white South Africans and New Zealanders. And the odd Fijian.

By then I was aware of the connection between Fijian soldiers and the armed forces' rugby teams. More than once I had been told that you could place bets depending on how many Fijian players there were, and I had met many individuals who played for their regimental units. One young recruit, interviewed on his first day of training, mentioned that he was a member of Fiji's national team, a fact which he seemed to think had secured him a place in the army.[17] *The Sunday Times* reported on 'the Fijians' prowess at rugby' in April 2009, pointing out that 'Last year the army's 12-man sevens squad included 10 Fijians and a South African. Its captain, Mark Lee, was the only British player.'[18]

The Colonel's remark about Fijians having a respect of hierarchy was also a familiar theme, and one to which we will return. In the context of recruitment, however, I had been trying to ascertain if Commonwealth applicants were being routed into particular jobs on the basis of assumed qualities or characteristics relating to their countries of origin, or whether it was just a matter of contingency at the level of regimental requirements. I was also testing the idea that they were being routed into more menial or unpopular jobs that were particularly hard to fill because they offered neither qualifications nor prestige – and were therefore unpopular with British nationals.

There is no doubt that there is a solid internal hierarchy of occupations and expertise within the army, which offers an incentive for individuals to transfer in or out of designated posts but also militates against this being a simple administrative process. There are numerous other factors, such as the desire to follow family or friends' recommendations (and footsteps), that indicate how difficult it might be to draw any conclusions without a more systematic survey. However, the extent to which non-UK nationals were over-represented in certain jobs – proved uncontrovertibly by the statistics – came to light as a result of an extraordinary agreement reached between the MoD and the Equality and Human Rights Commission (EHRC). After a decade of recruiting Commonwealth citizens, during which their numbers had risen from 360 to more than 6,600, a decision was announced that reflected mounting unease that there might be *too many* of them accumulating in particular sections of the army.

Armed to the teeth

On 3 February 2009 Defence Secretary John Hutton told the House of Commons that a limit of 15 per cent would be imposed on Commonwealth soldiers in selected trades. This was being done in the 'interests of operational effectiveness'.[19] The cap would henceforth apply to the RLC, the Royal Army Dental Corps (RADC) and the Queen Alexandra's Royal Army Nursing Corps (QARANC), where the number of Commonwealth citizens was already approaching or had exceeded the 15 per cent mark. The point, Hutton explained, was to restrict the number of personnel whose foreign citizenship could leave them 'potentially subject to legislation contrary to our own decisions – on, for example, operational deployments'. The South African Mercenary Act, as we noted earlier, was clearly an example of this potential danger since if it was enacted it would require soldiers to choose between resigning from the armed forces to avoid criminalisation at home or relinquishing their South African nationality. There were other anxieties about the behaviour of foreign governments which had more to do with the status of British foreign policy. The Army recognised the 'controversial nature' of recent operations in Iraq and Afghanistan, Hutton continued. 'Britain's military presence in the latter country is likely to continue for many years.'

On the day that the cap was officially announced in the national media, Captain N, who was then the recruiting officer for the RADC, first spotted the news on the BBC home page. Later that morning he received an email with a briefing note. 'It was all rather unfortunate,' he told me several weeks later. 'It was very rare that the RADC was in the news. There we were, large as life. It was a complete shock.'

In the initial panic he was contacted by all those who were in the process of training to find out if their jobs were safe. The answer depended on how close they were to completing Phase 1 and whether they had been offered firm places in the second phase of the course. Unlike many of the other cap badges, the RADC processed a finite number of new applicants each year, the maximum being 39. Out of these, about half were usually from Commonwealth backgrounds. But the captain was unsure of the exact figures, as he explained. The RADC did not monitor ethnicity or nationality because it had never been an issue until that point.

He was about to process another batch of applications from Commonwealth citizens which he had to turn down immediately, giving precedence to UK nationals, many of whom were applying to transfer from other trades. The RADC had been identified as one of the sectors that was over-recruiting foreign nationals and there was little he could do about it. He was clear, however, about the reasons why it was an attractive career for those seeking a vocational training, and particularly for women. He admitted,

> Dentistry is not seen as a manly trade, and it's not a run-around-the-woods sort of job. It requires a different sort of recruit from other sections, such as the Infantry. There is no specific qualification to join the RADC but applicants have to convince recruiting staff that dentistry is their vocation.

He had examined the qualifications of those who were applying, and saw that people with higher qualifications tended to come from Commonwealth countries. They were also older and more mature, often quite well-grounded.

> Most Brits are 17–18, but you might get someone from Ghana who is 26 who will have a lot of life skills. The army generally is not interested in character and experience and they want to mould people into what they need. We are not trying to mould, though. The attraction of dentistry is that it offers great civilian qualifications.
>
> In the army you would earn £22,000 as a hygienist, while as a civilian you might be on £40–45,000. So a lot do leave when they have finished the training to do this. It's a big incentive – to do three years service to increase your earning power.

The decision to cap numbers of foreign nationals in the RADC provoked a certain amount of anxiety that overall numbers would fall dramatically, but so far that had not been the case. Meanwhile, of the 17 who were turned down because of the cap, three or four had applied to transfer to dental work as soon as they began training as chefs. 'So somewhere out there,' said the Captain, 'there are three or four disaffected individuals.'

Diluting Britishness

The RLC employed 16,000 men and women of all ranks who worked in 14 different trades, from chefs and specialist drivers to mariners, port operators, suppliers and postal workers. In theory it offered a wide range of training and qualifications that transferred more easily into civilian employment than combat-related skills. After the Infantry, the RLC was the second largest section, constituting 15 per cent of the organisation. In early 2009 I spent some time with one of the Training Squadrons at Deepcut, where recruits in their second phase of training were learning skills required for suppliers, petroleum operators and engineers. There I learned that over 50 per cent of the intake at that time was from Commonwealth backgrounds, and that across supply units in the army as a whole, the figure was then 38 per cent.

For the RLC Chief of Staff the notion of a cap was a complete contradiction of the army's basic doctrine. 'The army view is that we don't give a stuff,' he said.

> If someone is recruited we treat them as a British soldier. It's no different if you come from Liverpool or anywhere else. It's got to be the only way.
>
> We would be massively under-recruited if we didn't take Foreign and Commonwealth soldiers. They are doing jobs British people are not prepared to do.

His frankness was matched by his assessment of diversity as an issue for the army. 'The army is a great leveller,' he said. 'It doesn't matter who a soldier is, someone either responds to training or they don't.' He admitted that when he took that particular office a year earlier he had been alarmed by the high proportion, but having just been to a Commanding Officers' conference, where it was listed as one of the top ten issues, he was glad to see that 'the feedback was universally "So What? Why is it a problem?"' But this pragmatic response was not shared by his employers.

Although the cap was only announced in 2009, anxieties began leaking out as early as 2005. An article drawing attention to the presence of Commonwealth troops, written by the *Times* Defence Editor Michael Evans, was entitled 'How the British Army is fast becoming foreign legion'.[20] 'The Army has stopped actively recruiting Commonwealth and foreign soldiers,' he wrote, 'because the numbers joining up have risen by nearly 3,000 per cent in seven years.'

The term 'foreign legion' referred to the infamous French unit of foreign nationals who were not otherwise eligible to join the French armed forces. First formed in 1830, it quickly acquired a fierce reputation as an elite fighting group with a strong ethos of its own. It was often seen as a bastion of ex-criminals, escaped convicts and other dubious characters eager to start their lives afresh, an image sustained by the fact that all applicants, including French citizens, were permitted to join under a false identity. Although it has undergone extensive modernisation in recent years, the term 'foreign legion' still evokes a practice which is itself 'foreign': in other words, a military unit made up of desperate men whose backgrounds cannot be checked, and who might have ambivalent loyalties to the country in whose name they fight. Needless to say, it is a phrase that cropped up in the British media soon after the recruitment of UK non-nationals began in 1998.[21]

Evans' article in November 2005 shows how quickly the prospect of a cap had arisen, and how, at this stage, it was the infantry regiments that were under scrutiny. He quoted a 'defence source' as saying: 'It is after all supposed to be the British Army, not the Commonwealth Army.' Evidence for the rapid intake of 'foreigners' was provided by the example of the 1st Battalion The Princess of Wales's Royal Regiment, one in five of whose members were not UK citizens. Evans also mentioned the fact that 'The Black Watch had 31 Commonwealth soldiers, most of them Fijian.'

The subject of capping emerged once more in 2007 when a report headed by General Sir Richard Dannatt had suggested that numbers be limited to 10 per cent throughout the army. The following year the issue was raised again when the then Liberal Democrat defence spokesman, Nick Harvey, asked a question in the House of Commons about the statistical profile of non-UK soldiers. Statistics revealed that the figure had risen from 0.4 per cent in 1998 to 6.7 per cent in 2007, which meant that if present trends continued, the proportion of soldiers recruited from the Commonwealth would be 10 per cent by 2012 at the latest.[22] Commenting on the projected increase over the next three years, Harvey said: 'There must be some sort of natural limit to quite how far it's desirable for this to go. One hesitates to use emotive terms like mercenaries but clearly you're beginning to travel somewhere onto that spectrum.'[23] By that time the numbers had risen to just over 8 per cent, with many more applications in the pipeline and a new round of OPTs planned for 2008.

Initial reactions were varied. The army was still 7,000 short of its recruitment target and the proposal to curb the number of Commonwealth citizens was seen by many as defiance of common sense. Tory Defence spokesman Mark Harper was reported as saying:

> It seems to be limiting our options at a time when we have such a shortfall in the Army and are struggling to recruit and retain British citizens. The problem is the inability of the MoD to recruit British citizens, not the number of Commonwealth soldiers we are recruiting in itself.[24]

A statement from the MoD attempted to defend the cap while at the same time praising the calibre of the soldiers and emphasising the country's historical links with the Commonwealth. What it did not reveal was that the Ministry was negotiating with the EHRC over the legal implications of restricting numbers of recruits from overseas. The decision to apply the cap to certain trades was an outcome of extensive calculations aimed at steering a path between breaking the law of the land and damaging the army's attempts to be seen as an enthusiastic Equal Rights employer. Introducing the decision to restrict foreign nationals in certain parts of the army, Hutton told the Commons that they had also borne in mind 'the importance of ensuring that the armed forces continue to be identified with and representative of the UK'. This euphemistically worded phrase referred back to discussions that were far more inflammatory than any talk of hostile foreign governments.

In April 2007 the *Daily Mail* reported that 'Defence chiefs want to limit the number of Commonwealth troops in the Army to retain its "Britishness".'[25] Under the headline: 'Race uproar over Army troop quota', it reported that 'confidential papers prepared by the Army General Staff, headed by General Sir Richard Dannatt, suggest Commonwealth troops – mostly non-white – should be limited to 10 per cent of the 99,000 total'. One of the main reasons for restricting the number of Commonwealth troops was 'cultural'. The article only hinted at what this actually meant:

> One source said: The main reason is this view of Britishness, ensuring that the norms and values of society are reflected in its armed forces.
>
> For example, gender equality in Britain means that the dominant view is that women should have a role in the armed forces. It's different in other countries.

The implications of this statement were that some nationalities had issues serving alongside women, and that this was causing problems within the organisation. It was exactly the kind of statement that might feed the idea that foreigners were less enlightened about gender equality than British nationals. But there was more. The article continued with another quote from 'Army chiefs':

> There are also practical issues, like, for example, a Fijian soldier getting killed in Iraq, keeping the family informed in Fiji and flying the body back to Fiji is logistically more difficult than dealing with people who live locally.

This reference implied that, despite reassurances from the MoD that 'these soldiers bring a range of skills and talents which enrich the Service as a whole,' the result of employing foreign nationals had effectively produced more administrative work. Combined with the earlier point about 'norms and values' there was clearly a more substantial charge being made: that dealing with the different cultures of some of the Commonwealth soldiers was proving an additional burden that had not been anticipated. It was fortuitous that the rhetoric of Britishness promoted by Brown's government allowed the legitimacy of a cap on migrant soldiers to pass as an imperative of social cohesion in the nation as a whole as well as a requirement for 'operational effectiveness' in the armed forces. In the next chapter we consider the way in which 'culture' is both defined and utilised in military terms.

Part II

Culture

Image 3   Recruits on parade at pass-off ceremony, ATC Pirbright, November 2008

4
Culture Shock

'Socially immature, lacking mutual respect and having led self-indulgent, materialistic lives, they are all too easily shocked by the close confines of military life.'[1] This verdict on the calibre of British Army recruits was the result of a research project entitled 'Culture Shock and the British Infantry Recruit', published in 2006. The study found that recruits were 'increasingly self-absorbed and undisciplined' and that 'they come from backgrounds that have suffered from the decline of the traditional family'. Leaving school 'without any set of moral values', many young men were simply unable to cope with military life and were failing as a result. The report concluded that recruit training centres were 'sites of cultural collisions, between the infantry, with a clear focus on the task and the team, and a civil society that is increasingly focused on image and the individual'.

It was not hard to see that the army was encountering problems derived from the society it was supposed to be defending. Research published the same year provided further evidence that the physical state of Britain's youth might be a source of concern, particularly after a report by the National Audit Office (NAO) warned that 'increasing levels of obesity and resultant health problems reduces the number of young people able to join the services'.[2] The NAO cited research carried out by the army in 2005 which showed that only a third of all 16-year-olds would pass the body mass index set for all recruits to the forces. The idea that the army was struggling to find suitable material to sustain its workforce was more than an embarrassment for the Ministry of Defence which was already up to its neck in deeply unpopular wars on two fronts.

The documented shortcomings of the 'play-station generation' and their lack of ethical or moral orientation matched corresponding research on young people's sense of identity, particularly in relation to Britishness.[3] Meanwhile, many of the Commonwealth recruits, often older than their UK counterparts, were also grappling with the physical and mental rigors of the training regime in addition to adapting to a new country. In this chapter we examine the unique demands of military culture as we consider how the army struggled to develop a coherent, functional approach to the concept of 'difference'.

The Army Selection Centre at Pirbright provided a fitting introduction to military culture regardless of whether prospective soldiers had travelled from the southern hemisphere or the south of England. I first met Dennis when he arrived at the airport after the long transatlantic flight, and was with him when the officer showed him the room where he would spend the next few days. I don't know what I was expecting, but the sight of several unmade bunk beds shoved together in a corner of what looked like a gym changing-room represented a minimal attempt at British hospitality. The message of the stark accommodation was clear: welcome to the army, the life you have chosen. You will start as you are expected to go on. Hard, narrow beds, no privacy and few creature comforts.

Twenty-four hours later, Dennis and the other young men who had journeyed the long haul from the Caribbean appeared to be taking their new surroundings in their stride. When they were called to go to the cafeteria for meals, they had no problem following instructions to form ranks and march in step. Apart from the relentlessly grey skies, there were more shocking aspects of life in Britain that they had not anticipated. They were reeling from the fact that one of the younger members of the local contingent in the selection centre had already fathered one child and had another on the way. They couldn't get over the fact that he was boasting about it too. To them it was unthinkable since the age of consent in Belize was 16 which meant that the young man would have been prosecuted at home. They were also taken aback by the swearing, references to alcohol and the coarse sense of humour they detected among the boys they had encountered during the evening's activities. This came as no surprise to me as I had heard it all many times before.

Swearing, being disrespectful to elders, boasting about sex, drink and drugs – these were among the first points of contrast that Commonwealth recruits seemed to encounter among their UK peers. This was the same for women as it was for men, although there was often a more cliquey atmosphere when it came to the social life of female platoons. When I first met the three Southern African women training to be dental nurses, they made it plain that they preferred their own company to that of their fellow recruits, male or female. Differences in age and experience were likely explanations, but there were cultural and behavioural issues too.

'They are definitely different in all aspects!' exclaimed Anni when I asked how they were getting on with their UK-born colleagues. Although they were a little reticent at that stage, they were clearly shocked to see young women swearing, smoking and talking back to their superiors. Ntabi added:

If something happens they want to know how and why... culturally they are not brought up like us. Africans are easy going, we adapt quickly.

The way people speak is different. For example, if we swear in front of an older person, our mum would give it to us. We are brought up to speak to an elderly person as if it was our parent – we would never call them by name.

Attitudes towards religion provided another factor that distanced the young women from their peers. They expected to attend a church service every Sunday, and one was investigating the possibility of joining the Fijian choir. More than anything, they confessed to finding the PT lessons the hardest thing to deal with. Mary especially was struggling. 'We were not fit when we joined,' she explained, 'and they push you to extremes.'

They laughed as they recalled their attempts to do the required number of press ups the previous day. 'I thought I was going to die,' said Mary, 'but you feel good afterwards.'

Two weeks later I had the chance to see for myself how the combination of age, experience, familiarity and comfort influenced the relations between the young women training together in one platoon. Sometimes referred to as a troop, a platoon is made up of approximately 40–50 individuals separated into 12 or so sections. A section consists of eight people and, as the smallest unit of administration in the organisation, is led by a corporal who will have a lance-corporal as his or her deputy. It is important to form bonds within the section first and then the platoon, as all tests and examinations take place together. Relationships within these groups are often dependent on personalities of the recruits as well as the personal skills (or lack of them) possessed by the section commanders.

I had arranged to visit the platoon while they were carrying out their first overnight exercise in the Surrey woods. When I arrived, I found I was the only person not wearing make-up or a helmet festooned with bracken. Even the driver who had picked me up from the station had taken out his grease-stick and was busy daubing his cheeks with dark green face-paint. It had taken some time for him to track the platoon down, not because they were camouflaged effectively, but because there were several other troops in the woods involved in similar activities.

The mobile phone coverage was patchy and at one point he had to stop a young male soldier who was hiding behind a tree to ask if he had seen the group of females. I was struck by the dazed expression of bewilderment and shock on this particular recruit's face, and I realised subsequently that he must have been one of the new arrivals recruited by the OPT in the Caribbean a few months earlier. If so, he would have only been in the country a few weeks and would have had no experience of British life outside the military base. Stumbling through the Surrey undergrowth armed with a rifle, dodging the joggers and dog walkers sharing the facilities and having had little or no sleep the previous night, he probably felt that he was on a different planet.

When we found the women, they had just come together for a short break. Many of the girls took the opportunity to have a smoke, and several were rearranging each other's hair, scraping it off the face and tying it in a knot to fit under the helmet. This was the first time I had met female English soldiers, let alone raw recruits and I was struck by the cross-section of regional accents from London to Lanarkshire. This was a chance to observe the day-to-day experience of basic training, but as they relaxed it was also possible to see how they managed potential divisions and conflicts. The young African women I had already met sat together in a group slightly apart from the rest, and were joined by two sisters from Gambia and another South African who was white. Although there was no discernible tension, it was evident that they felt more comfortable in each other's company.

After a lesson in hand signals delivered by an affable sergeant, I found myself sitting with Ntabi in a hollow she had made in the ground. She had spent the previous night taking turns to snatch short spells of sleep and to guard the camp, and she was tired as well as cold. She had already told me how much she missed her two children who were in the care of her parents in South Africa while she completed her training. Mixing her rations in the tin pan she carried on her belt, she confided, 'Sometimes I really don't know what I am doing here.' She tried the various items of food that were allocated for her meal: packet mushroom soup which she heated in the pan over what looked like a firelighter, also produced from a pocket, a tin of pate, a chocolate bar for later. I watched as she cleaned the pan using dry soil and water from her canister, aware that this was a relatively gentle exercise designed to prepare them for greater ordeals ahead when they would be a lot further from hot showers and proper food.

A week later I found the same group in a tetchy mood, arguing among themselves about why they always found themselves sitting separately. Diana, a white South African also training to be a dental technician, was critical of the others for insisting the white girls were shunning them. 'You segregate yourselves!' She retorted. 'I go wherever I like.'

Ntabi remonstrated with her. 'If I go and sit with them, one will move away. It happened in Belgium and I reported it to the corporal.'

Diana was adamant that she was just as guilty as anyone else. 'It's your fault just as much,' she said. This was the first time I had met Diana although the others had mentioned her before. She was going through very much the same adjustments, although on this occasion it was clear that she was in a different position. 'I am in the middle,' she said, exasperated.

I love you guys and I love them. Africans are narrow-minded. We have a chip on our shoulders.

I speak to everyone, but some things irritate me. Like their cliques.

The group began to discuss an incident that had happened on the platoon's trip to the war cemeteries in Belgium, one of the highlights of the three-month course. It turned out that the younger of the two Gambian sisters, who was only 17, was rather unceremoniously pushed out of a group photo pose by some of the English girls.

Anni, who had been arguing with Diana about the reasons for the animosity, said, 'I don't want to be childish but there are a lot of factors. It's not my talk: sex, smoking and clubbing. I would rather talk about serious things.' Diana agreed with her on that. 'Anything under 20 gets me,' she said. I asked them again about how they got on with men at the centre. This time they didn't laugh, although they acknowledged that they had met a few. Diana complained that they were patronising: 'they ask, "oh, do you want a hug then?"'

Their reactions and those of many others who had not grown up in the UK often expressed a marked sense of difference between themselves and the British-born recruits. On another occasion Abi, who was from Malawi, expressed the problem succinctly.

> Sometimes they complain so much about little things. Whereas if something comes, we take it. If we have punishment we take it, we know we've come a long way and can't complain. Some things that they say are hard for *them* are not hard for *us*. In my country, when we are growing up they are very strict on discipline. When an older person is talking you are not supposed to [interrupt]...you have to be able to listen to what they have to say. Here the problem is that when the corporals and sergeants are talking, they answer back and then we all get punished.

Individuals often expressed a sense of urgency too, of knowing what was important. Yvonne had three children and at the upper age limit of joining was understandably finding the training regime and the social relations all too reminiscent of her high school in Zimbabwe. Despite this she was trying hard to be positive and understanding. 'It's all right,' she said with a tone of determination:

> Everyone's really sweet. Some can be annoying. It's all right but...they are too much like little children, there's too much childish behaviour. Most girls come straight from their parents' house [whereas] I had experience before I came. But they don't adapt – it's like they are wrapped in cotton wool. We've made up our minds, got objectives, we are not going to mess around. They have options.

The differences in age and life experience had been a particular issue in her platoon, but there was no doubt that men and women from a wide variety of countries and social backgrounds felt that they had more in common with each other than they had with their British-born equals, whose behaviour they often found alienating or baffling. In the last chapter we saw that defence chiefs justified their decision to cap numbers of migrant soldiers by stating their concern that British norms and values should be reflected in its armed forces. In the next section we glimpse the deep imprint of British imperialism that partly explains the shared cultural traits among Commonwealth recruits.

People you can call your own

If you grow up in a Commonwealth country you often feel you have been exposed to elements of British culture despite never having been there. Paul, from Ghana, explained that you felt a bit British because everything you are taught was also British. 'We know poems, nursery rhymes, British history,' he said. 'Some Ghanaians are more British than the Brits.' The era of colonial rule had left a legacy of educational, legal and political infrastructure that continued to bind the two countries together, but Paul had been surprised to learn that a lot of British people he had met had no idea about the history of empire, and certainly had little sense of a connection to Britain's former colonies.

Speaking to the group of Guardsmen assembled from Malawi, Nigeria, South Africa and New Zealand, I asked them outright how important the notion of the Commonwealth was to them. To what extent did they consider themselves connected to Britain through common cultural and historical ties?

Simon was clear about the fact that he was 'totally British descent'.

> I am only three generations New Zealand. I've lived in other countries but I actually feel at home over here with the old British people. You get a bit of stick, from other countries and that, but I give stick back. You've got Welsh and Scots and that, but if they call you 'foreign bugger' you say what about you? You are not even in your own country.

Chike, from Nigeria, was more reflexive, appreciating the fact that intolerance and segregation were problems in his country too.

> From my experience – I've lived in this country for four years – I think that British people are really tolerant of foreigners compared to other countries. I mean even in my country, in the north, people don't tolerate you the way they do here.

Chike had married a woman from Scotland just before starting training. He had not told his parents about his plans and was terrified his mother would be angry. Fortunately when he took his bride back to Nigeria the two women had become fast friends, helped by the fact that his wife was a committed Christian. His mother still had to be appraised of her son's decision to become a British soldier though.

'At some point you can say that some things come up that are out of hand,' he said diplomatically, 'but still a foreigner is a foreigner, and when those issues – who you are, where you are from...that's where you stick to people you can call your own.'

As he said this he gestured towards Simon. 'Still he is white, but at some point you just cling to him, get some hope from him, when things happen that go out of hand.' He elaborated,

> Just like now, just the two of us in the platoon are blacks, so even when things happen, we look at Simon and think that he is a foreigner here and has adapted, so why can't I? So [there is] that sense of us getting hope from each other, for the fact that we have come from a very far place and found ourselves here.

In the evenings recruits are not permitted to leave the centre but have the option to socialise, watch TV or use computers. Military bases have received substantial investment following revelations of dilapidated housing stock and training facilities, and it was noticeable that most of the bases I visited, like many university campuses, had a newly inaugurated building known as the Hub, offering dining rooms, coffee areas and small supermarkets, all run commercially by corporations such as Sodexo. The 'Hub' at ITC had been named after LCpl Johnson Beharry VC and a commemorative plaque marking his presence at the opening of the building enscribed his name in the brickwork of military history. The dining room, or in army jargon the 'scoff house', is on the ground floor, but the first floor offers a large recreational area where recruits can gather in the evenings. The night I dropped in, a group of young men were taking turns playing table tennis. One was from the Philippines, another West African. The third, who was English, was reading an article in the *Sun* about a drive-by shooting of two soldiers in Northern Ireland. 'It makes me sick,' he said to his friends. 'It's murder.'

They lingered over the naked woman on page three, murmuring in approval. The place was unusually quiet as it was a big football night and there were other venues with screens available. The computers were all occupied by users deep in Facebook and several people were queuing to see the F&C advisor who was appointed as part of the welfare services. One of those waiting his turn was a young Gambian. As we talked about his attempts to make friends he revealed how sex could prove divisive as well as supplying common ground.

> English guys can swear at their mums and for the first six weeks I found that hard. They say [things like] – do you want to date my mum?
> I hate that. It's an insult to me. In my country it would [mean] the whole day fighting! Bastard is a big insult. Here they can say anything.

He was not the only one to find that hard. People had asked him why the other Gambian in the platoon was always on his own. He told them that he objected to the swearing. 'His best mate is now someone he never coped with before. When he explained [what was bothering him] they could understand.'

A separate conversation with young men from St Vincent revealed that ideas about acceptable masculine behaviour could also vary widely. I asked them what were the most surprising things that they had encountered.

'The culture is different from what we are used to and what we expect,' said one hesitantly. I had a feeling that they were alluding to something specific this time but they clearly felt awkward describing what troubled them.

> The games the lads play . . . touching each other.
> It's meant as a joke. They come up behind you and spank you.
> They kiss you on the neck, pretend to be gay. In our country it is against the law.
> Sometimes it winds you up. Sometimes you get used to it – you realise . . .

Language could prove alienating too, as these young men testified.

> We blend in, but have our own groups as well. But they don't understand how we talk. Some of them are offended. But sometimes they speak too fast.

Although 'foreigners' were expected to speak English, there was little understanding that they not only studied English at school to a high standard that was incomparable to language teaching in the UK, but that they were obliged to pass an English exam in order to complete their secondary education. Evidently the monolingual UK-born recruits were resentful if their colleagues fell into a pattern of speaking they did not recognise, whether it was Fijian, Twi or even a dialect of English from another country. Often the provocation would be caused by the sight of two or more men who looked the same talking to each other in private. Those from Caribbean countries complained that they were frequently reprimanded by their peers as well as instructors who told them to 'speak English!' Naturally this same rule did not apply to those who communicated in strong regional accents that were recognisably British.

While talking in any language other than English was forbidden during the course of work or training, there were situations when it was simply unrealistic to expect people to obey. During meal times, recruits would grab their trays laden with protein and carbohydrates and head for a table to sit with their friends. This was a time to catch up with people one might know from home or who might be in a different platoon, but the element of choice laid bare the underlying social dynamics. On my first visit to ITC, I was told categorically that everyone mixed in the dining halls, but when we went in to check, the situation was the same as it had been at Pirbright: visible segregation along colour lines. The only exception was a couple of tables in one corner where a platoon had evidently been ordered to sit together.

Individuals coped in different ways. Many accepted that it was normal to go wherever they felt comfortable, although others insisted that they sat with their friends, black and white, and that they never thought about the difference. Some reported that if they were the first to sit at a table, none of the whites would join them. The Fijians had their own solution, having established a firm tradition that they ate together. For them it made sense to converse in Fijian unless there was an English-speaking friend on the table, in which case they would translate, or speak English too.

Early on I asked Ravu about this, having sat with a group of his friends at lunch on a couple of occasions. By this time he had been at Pirbright for nearly three months and was looking forward to passing off.

'Fijians find it hard to talk to each other in English,' he explained.

> The Corporal asked us not to talk in Fijian but I told him: we don't want to sell our language – not like the Hawaians who lost theirs because of America.

As we cleared our trays, I noticed that the women who worked there were mainly Nepalese. Because of the common Hindi elements of their two languages the Fijians were able to communicate with them, and they greeted each other warmly on their way out.

Ignorance about basic geography and crude assumptions about other cultures often caused offence. Recruits of African origin, male and female, were often asked if the countries where they came from had electric lights, whether they carried water on their heads, whether they wore clothes at home and other questions which revealed more about the level of education in the UK than anything else. These extracts and observations from many hours of conversation indicate a widespread degree of antipathy, or certainly disparity, between Commonwealth recruits and their UK-born counterparts. Of course this was not always the case.

There were also stories about the cumulative effects of familiarity that stemmed from sharing rooms, facing the same difficulties, discovering common interests in music, sport or religion. In fact, recruits would often volunteer remarks about how barriers were breaking down within sections, claiming that 'we are becoming a family'. There were anecdotes too about unlikely friendships emerging, as with the young Gambian at ITC or Ravu who mentioned that one of their English mates was trying to learn Fijian. But if the Commonwealth recruits were prepared to discuss what they found shocking or strange in the majority culture, how were they perceived, as minorities and outsiders, by their peers? Did the distinction between 'them' and 'us' that they often voiced hold true for the rest of the recruits too?

A bit of a rough country

The four young men from south Wales agreed that they felt a strong connection with each other because they were all from the same part of the country, but they were forthcoming about their relationships with other members of their platoon. At first they found it difficult mixing with strangers. 'We all wanted to beat each other up at the start,' said one.

> Everyone pulls together.
> We bicker, we bicker a lot.
> Especially on exercise we perform well.

They admitted to finding it especially hard to relate to some of their fellow recruits, 'especially the Commonwealth, when they first got here'. They talked over each other as they gained confidence in speaking their minds.

> They didn't want to speak to us!
> I couldn't bear them.
> Terrible at first.
> When we all stood around they'd stand separate from us.
> Some of the stuff we do to each other... You do that to them, they really don't like it.
> I didn't want to socialise with them at the start but...
> As the course has moved on they've lightened up, started joking... even B... has lightened up the last couple of weeks.

It emerged that one reason for resenting the Commonwealth recruits was that they were perceived to be keeping themselves separate. After a few minutes of complaining, however, the four young men began to distinguish between different individuals, naming some who had been more willing to 'mix in' than others.

> Different countries, different cultures.
> Some of them still separate from us. We get on though.
> Mike – he's one of us lot. One of [us] British lads, he's ok, loves it.

This last remark implied that Mike was black but born in the UK and not therefore a stranger. I had heard a corresponding refrain listening to women from several different African countries arguing about segregation. Diana had pointed out that the black British girl in their platoon was quite happily integrated. To her fellow South Africans, the girl did not 'count' as she was not from the same background as them. Her colour was irrelevant.

The ambivalence expressed by the young Welshmen included a tacit acknowledgement that the family circumstances of Commonwealth recruits were different.

> It's hard for them as well – they can't go home as well.
> Caribbeans, some of them can't go home every week to see their families.
>   Darren can't go home no more.
> Haven't seen their children for six months. Can't understand that.
> One Fijian can't go back – he got kicked out, can't go back.
> It's 'cos of the coup – it's not just him, it's all the Fijians.

Their attempts to empathise with those who were far from home were an insight into the group's somewhat reluctant or hesitant acceptance of behaviour that was different from anything they had encountered before. When I asked directly whether they had found it a positive experience to meet Commonwealth recruits, they made an effort to think about their answers.

> We get to experience different cultures for a start. Seeing how people act. We get to socialise with people we wouldn't normally socialise with in south Wales. In my school, in my area, there were maybe one or two black people. It's the first time I've really mixed with Commonwealth.

One of them muttered, 'We are all god's children!' This produced the response, 'What crayons have you been eating?' which was greeted with nervous giggles. I turned to one of the four who had been relatively quiet, asking if he had been surprised to find so many people from other countries in Catterick.

> No, I don't mind them I don't. I get on with them.

He was dismissive of my next question about whether they'd heard the view that the British Army should only be employing British people.
  'No! That's gone a long time ago,' he said. 'It's a multicultural society now isn't it? You know what I mean? One third of the army...'
  'Not just for certain people, it's for everyone,' chimed in the others.

> If we didn't have Commonwealth we'd be so small.

As they relaxed they started to reflect among themselves about the pros and cons of working with foreigners.

> They're all quite fit – especially Al in my troop, he is so fit – he's designed for the army – they're all well built, shoot well.

> Can't really fault them, performance wise.
> They don't like the cold though. They're used to 40 degrees and then
>   they come over here.

They laughed among themselves remembering how some of the recruits
reacted to snow during a recent exercise. This raised a serious point since
many soldiers who were not used to sub-zero temperatures were particularly vulnerable to 'cold injuries'. If the symptoms were not recognised early
enough, there could be lasting damage from frostbite which would in turn
lead to disability and medical discharge. This being the army, complaining
about being cold was regarded as a sign of being soft, and codes of masculinity made it harder to speak up.[4] But the Welshmen's good humour
remembering their colleagues' shock did not mean that they were uniformly
positive about what they perceived as difference. One voice was quick to
point out that 'You have one or two that are really terrible as well.'

I wondered how much of their training was spent discussing the issues
involved in interpersonal conflict.

> Yes, we had a lot of that in the first six weeks.
> Basically lectures by our platoon commander, basically telling us how to
>   approach them, equality, diversity and all that.

I asked outright whether they thought that it did any good.

> No, not really, 'cos half of us, some of us, struggle with learning.
> I can't sit still for longer than ten minutes.
> Not everybody's a prototype, not everybody's the same, can be
>   approached the same way.
> It's taken me a good six months, we are at the end of training only now, to
>   have a proper conversation with someone in the Commonwealth.
>   That's basically six months of *trying* to talk to them. I don't know if
>   they are ignorant. Or it's just . . .
> They don't open up like.
> Britain is a bit of a rough country, for them to come in here, with all the
>   things that go on, it must be difficult for them.
> They've got to adjust more than us.
> They've got their own culture. They feel secluded.
> It is tough, mentally, upstairs in your mind. Gets pretty rough.

Listening to the young men's reflections on their encounter with difference was helpful in providing a sense of the complicated social relations
within a multinational cohort, especially when placed alongside conversations with groups of Commonwealth recruits. Army training is not like
other educational experiences since recruits are virtually locked in the camp

for weeks at a time. It is designed to create tight-knit bonds within units, which means that there are many issues posed by 'mixing' individuals from different backgrounds, particularly when all recruits are struggling to adapt to a life-changing regime. This is not a new problem caused by importing non-British recruits, nor is it confined to the British armed forces. Within the scholarship on military organisations there are long-running debates about the most effective strategies to create forms of comradeship and mutual trust. Countless empirical studies can be found discussing the merits of creating bonding through enforced tasks as opposed to an emphasis on the intensely social ties that are fostered by shared experience. It is worth looking at these diverging theories because they offer insights into military ways of working that are not always visible from outside.

Bonds and cohesion

While it is easy to refer to military culture as a coherent whole, it is also important to consider how it is internally divided as well. The separate components of the institution – from ranks and regiments to tasks and training establishments – each produce and sustain features that might be termed 'subcultural' within the general military organism. In common with other occupational environments, notably the police, the institution also fosters forms of clannish behaviour within and across the hierarchies, often referred to as canteen culture, or barrack-room culture.[5] This complex organisational structure presents particular problems for analysts studying the optimum ways of teaching disparate individuals and groups to work together.

The journal *Armed Forces and Society* hosted a recent exchange that demonstrates the extent of disagreement among specialist researchers, particularly in the US and the UK. In the first article, UK-based sociologist Anthony King argued that there had been too much emphasis on the interpersonal aspects of soldiers' relationships. He explained, 'Although sustainable, there is an unfortunate bias in the work of military sociologists. They focus almost exclusively on informal rituals in which personal bonds are forged.'[6] By this he was referring to the friendships that are made outside, or alongside, the actual physical requirements of military training. Factors such as humour, cultural backgrounds, attitudes and beliefs stemming from gender and social class, degrees of mutual trust, all contribute to the formation of intimate bonds which provide the basis of group cohesion. But, King suggested, there was also evidence to show that 'comradeship' did not always produce effective performance. Likewise, the success of military operations did not necessarily depend on a social cohesion within a unit but on the unit's ability to function collectively.

'In fact,' he declared, 'the decisive rituals that bind military groups together are the formal processes of training.' Citing early sociological theory on the importance of physical activity in producing social cohesion, he pointed to specific military practices such as drill which have also been shown to induce a collective ethos:

> Through coordinated bodily movements, a social group appears out of the diverse interests and activities of individuals. Disparate individuals are physically united toward a common goal. In the orders process, British forces have deliberately sought to engage in ritualized forms of movement to encourage collective action.[7]

Having watched the not-quite-yet soldiers at the army selection centre being herded into ranks and marched around in their hooded sweatshirts, I could well believe that this aspect of recruit education is fundamental in all sorts of ways. Drill demands a high degree of physical co-ordination, of synchronising arms and legs with the head, an exercise that has to be practised until it becomes perfect. Visiting training centres provides ample evidence of how this element of physical instruction is literally drummed into individuals.

Any recruit in uniform caught walking normally, as opposed to marching with stiff arms swinging in exaggerated rhythm, or found slouching, as opposed to standing bolt upright, particularly in the presence of a superior, was likely to be reprimanded or at least stopped and corrected. It was no surprise that many commented that their families were struck by the difference in their appearance when they went home for their first long weekend. As we saw in the pass-off parade, they were even unrecognisable to their own parents when performing with their platoon. However, the extent to which ritualised activities such as drill prepared individuals to act as components of a larger machine continues to be a matter of debate.

Countering King's analysis a few months later, Guy L. Siebold, who worked for the US Army Research Institute for the Behavioral and Social Sciences, referred to research carried out in the US military which indicated that social relations were of supreme importance and that the picture was far more complex than had been represented.[8] He criticised King's empirical material as weak, arguing that the structure of military institutions also played a part in creating bonds of trust and loyalty between members on many different levels. For him, cohesion was not an entity or thing, nor was it easily recognised or its level readily agreed on by knowledgeable military observers.

> Cohesion, in its horizontal, vertical, organizational, and institutional components, is a social-relationship product or form generated by the interactions and experiences of the group members in the context of their daily military activities, combat and noncombat.[9]

In other words, bonds emerged between soldiers in the course of their common tasks, regardless of whether they were on operations or anywhere else.

In a third contribution to the debate, Charles Kirke attempted to move beyond the dichotomy of either rituals or social relations by breaking down the elements of what he called 'military organizational culture'.[10] Presenting himself as a former commissioned officer in the British Army who had also trained as a social anthropologist, he offered a framework of four interlocking structures that range from formal to informal, professional to interpersonal. This model, he explained, allowed the ethnographer to approach the cultural life of the whole army as 'a unique assembly' of different contexts where behaviour, attitudes and expectations could be assessed, across all ranks as well as among peers. Making a distinction between the various social structures that a soldier had to negotiate in the course of her or his working day is useful in other ways. It helps to demonstrate to the civilian observer how the institution is supposed to function as well as throwing light onto some of its internal procedures.

The first of these strands is what Kirke calls the structure of formal command, otherwise known as the chain of command. The chain of command is a deceptively simple term for an organisational principle that underpins all relationships between individuals and ranks within the army. The command structure of the institution as a whole is more readily explained by a diagram than a sentence since it is essentially a vast pyramid, with the Chief of the General Staff at the peak and the Lance Corporals, who represent the lowest levels of Command, distributed along the bottom. The significance of the chain, however, is that all personnel, whatever their rank and in whatever unit of operation, know where they stand relative to power, authority and responsibility for decision-making. Individuals are expected to report any problems or seek advice from the authority figure immediately above them, or in some cases, parallel to them. If this proves unsatisfactory, they are then permitted to go 'above the head' of their superior to the next link in the chain, although this is a step that inevitably provokes resentment. Understanding how the chain operates as a fundamental element of military discipline explains why educating, or re-educating, those in positions of authority, from the lowest rank to the highest, remains a priority.

The second structure that Kirke identified was the informal version of the command chain, which he defined as situations guided by 'conventions of behavior permitted in the absence of formal constraints'.[11] This might include periods where soldiers are either off duty or in relaxed duty contexts, and so encompasses some of the situations that have been described so far. The timetables of Phase 1 recruits do not permit as many opportunities to relax away from the gaze of authority since they are still in the duty of care, but the reports of sitting separately at mealtimes and socialising in cliques during leisure hours tell their own story.

The two remaining structural elements of army life identified by Kirke point forward to discussions with more experienced soldiers which will emerge later in this book. The next component of the 'assembly' demonstrated the structure of 'belonging', where bonds of shared identity and loyalty were forged. At each level of organisation, from section to regiment, the extent of membership that any individual might feel was likely to depend on what the particular group was being compared to. 'These attitudes and feelings,' wrote Kirke, 'can commonly be captured in the concept that "we are the best," at whatever organizational level the "we" is placed.'[12]

The final element was the functional structure, which encompassed the jobs that soldiers were trained to do. It directs attention to areas of working life where individuals carry out military tasks, whether in the course of training exercises or on combat operations. These might range from drill and other ritualised activities to the expertise of more specialised cap badges such as medical, logistical or engineering corps. It also entailed the more extreme ordeals encountered in dangerous, life-threatening circumstances.

As a former soldier, Kirke was able to test his framework by using empirical information gleaned from inside the organisation, based on his own observations and expectations in addition to more formal anthropological methods. As a result, he was confident that the model of four distinct social structures was useful in visualising cohesion as 'the product of positive interaction among the *social structures* within a British military group'. In other words, the greater the cohesion in any one structure, he suggested, the greater the level of cohesion in the whole. But it was also clear that the conditions under which people bonded were neither guaranteed nor constant.

Kirke's theory leaves observers with a better sense of how the structures fitted together as well as the certainty that levels of cohesion would inevitably vary between groups and within a single group at different times. More important, it suggests that what was initially perceived as cultural difference during military training might prove less of a problem once individuals were forming work-based relationships in their units. But was it all a matter of human chemistry and martial discipline? What is missing from all three theories is a sense of how military organisations themselves have adapted to requirements from civil society, especially in the realm of cultural pluralism and human rights.

The official directive on Equality and Diversity for the British Army, issued in 2008, attempted to clarify how the institution regarded these broader directives. For a start, it presented its own case for being 'different'. Equality and diversity were viewed as 'critical components in the generation and maintenance of Operational Effectiveness', it declared, and were important 'not for reasons of political correctness'. The policy was based on recognising 'the inherent qualities in every individual', respecting their differences and enabling them 'to make the selfless commitment that the Army demands, in the knowledge that they will be treated fairly'.[13] However, placing a value on individual rights was thought to present specific challenges to a military way of working which demanded teamwork and mutual dependence.[14] In other words, being 'different' was only permissible if it didn't interfere with your work as a soldier. This prompts the question, how has the British Army been able to square its own claim to be 'different' with its obligation to get in step with the rest of society?[15]

Gone soft

By the time 'Culture Shock' had made headlines in the national media, the army's approach to training infantry recruits had already begun to shift. The author of the report was a Commanding Officer at ITC and well placed to intervene in the way that beginners were handled throughout the six-month course. With the help of civilian consultants such as sports psychologist Professor Lew Hardy of Bangor University, the Centre introduced what was known as 'value-based learning', a system first applied to the Royal Marines after revelations of systematic bullying. Borrowed from the US military model but widely used in other spheres such as sport and business, it is an educational method developed primarily by psychologists, and one that focuses on the principle of motivation rather than coercion. One of its principles involves persuading instructors to lead through example and encouragement rather than administering humiliation and punishment to those who fail.

In theory, this was a radically different method of handling Britain's school leavers who had proved increasingly unable to cope with the mental and physical rigours of army training. For a start, it demanded that senior staff 'unlearn' the rudiments of military culture that shaped them as soldiers since it placed emphasis on leadership skills. Belief that the army had gone 'soft' was commonplace for this reason alone, compounded by a general irritation at all reform measures associated with 'political correctness', such as equality and diversity, health and safety, and human rights.

It was around this time that Gordon Brown initiated a controversial debate on the need to define Britishness as a renewed focus of national identity. In January 2006 he made an important speech pitching his ideas for a new civic patriotism that would re-orient Britain in the wider world. Referring to the London bombings that took place in July 2005, but without mentioning the two wars in Iraq and Afghanistan, he declared, 'we have to face uncomfortable facts that there were British citizens, British born, apparently integrated into our communities, who were prepared to maim and kill fellow British citizens, irrespective of their religion – and this must lead us to ask how successful we have been in balancing the need for diversity with the obvious requirements of integration in our society'.[16] His solution was to identify 'shared values' that would help determine the responsibilities of citizenship and discover the 'essential common purpose' underlying modern Britishness.

Brown's project of foregrounding national values as a way to address different aspects of social and political malaise clearly resonated with the new strategy to adopt value-based learning in military training. In both cases, the focus on core values was little different from the conventional language of corporate social responsibility. It is routine for commercial corporations, for example, to declare their brand values as a guide for workers, customers and investors alike. Tesco values consist of two simple commands: 'No one tries harder for customers' and 'Treat people as we like to be treated'.[17] Values and ethical statements were also prominent on the website of the UK wing of Sodexo, a multinational company that provides food and management services to a wide range of clients across the public sector including the MoD. The 'corporate citizenship' statement lists the company's values as 'Service spirit; team spirit and spirit of progress'.[18] The introduction of value-based learning into army training demonstrated the extent to which neo-liberal management theory (based on corporate structures as opposed to democratic institutions) had converged with military techniques aimed at inducing a mindset prepared to take human life.

Martial values

The emphasis on value-based learning in response to the shortcomings of British youth stems from a tried and tested system of military education imported from the US, where the Armed Forces had been training an ethnically and culturally diverse workforce for considerably longer. In 2000 the Defence Committee examined the implementation of the 1998 Strategic Defence Review (SDR), which addressed the problem of how to recruit, motivate and retain people with the right skills at a time when the armed forces were finding it increasingly hard to compete in the labour market. The policy of targeting ethnic minorities and women was not just a strategy to locate new sources of personnel, it was also a sign that the science of human resource management (HRM), first developed in the US corporate world, was about to transform the British military workplace as well.

Now taught in business schools globally, HRM emerged in the last quarter of the twentieth century as a diverse set of theoretical and practical methods aimed at getting the best out of employees in the interests of improving productivity. In an essay on the impact of HRM in the defence environment, Alex Alexandrou and Roger Darby, who have followed the rationalisation of the UK armed forces for more than a decade, emphasise that this development has had far-reaching effects in many parts of the world:

> It is fair to state that many nations' armed services are experiencing rationalisation and restructuring that has occurred as a result of the ending of the Cold War, changes in defence budgets, and new defence priorities since 2001.[19]

Identifying organisational values was an important component of HRM because it acknowledged the need for employees to be incorporated into and to co-operate with a shared sense of mission and ethos, whatever the sector or type of work. This was especially pertinent for the armed forces, write Alexandrou and Danby, 'for values form the core of the moral component of fighting power'.[20]

> Values are basically guiding principles (which must not be confused with specific cultural or operating practices) and they must not be compromised for financial gain or short-term expediency. Values are not goals, specific targets or mission statements. They are beliefs that a particular end-state (such as honesty, liberty or justice) is a good thing in its own right... Values are timeless principles that drive the manner in which an organization operates.

During 2000, the same year that the Defence Committee reviewed the HRM developments in the UK Armed Forces, the army formally adopted the concept of Values and Standards (V&S) as a vehicle for modernisation. Two pamphlets were published, one for all army personnel and one for commanders, explaining the importance of the six core values that formed the basis of the organisation's ethos: selfless commitment, courage, discipline, integrity, loyalty and respect for others.[21]

A review paper issued in 2008 revealed that the underlying tenets were not new, but in the past 'their comprehension and application was assumed rather than explicitly stated'.[22] After 2001 the situation had changed dramatically as troops were dispatched to new war zones. The internal document continued: 'The changed strategic and operational context and the incidences of the deliberate abuse of Iraqi civilians during operations in 2003–2004 demonstrated that the understanding and perhaps more the application of V&S was not as comprehensive as required.'

That same year, the army issued a new pamphlet outlining the importance of V&S as the 'lifeblood' that sustained the institution. In the introduction, General Sir Richard Dannatt wrote:

> Our Values and Standards are vital to operational effectiveness...They have to be more than just words, we must believe in them and live by them. Therefore, it is the effective and coherent translation of these Values and Standards into actions that must penetrate every command and organisation until they are instinctive.[23]

This edition was rewritten in order to 'improve readability and understanding at more junior levels' and published along with promotional materials such as posters, a DVD and a mouse mat. The aim was to ensure that the contents were inculcated in a more systematic way through improved training methods, regular inspection and a new focus on leadership throughout the organisation.

Learning loyalty

I was not expecting that a lesson on loyalty and integrity with the Padre would be illustrated by pictures of Iraqi detainees being tortured by British soldiers. He showed several slides of sadistic abuse: one of a boy tied up and used as surfboard, another of two naked men forced to simulate sex with thumbs up, with a tank decorated with an England flag in the background identifying the perpetrators.

'Terrible things happen to other people when the British Army loses its integrity,' he said. 'If that was my brother I would go and buy an AK47. I'd kill someone for that. Don't do it! This is what happens . . . if you ever see it, report it.'

His students, approximately 30 members of Taku Forts platoon, were facing the prospect of a drill test that afternoon and feeling nervous since failure would lead to the ignominy of being back-trooped. It was a Monday morning in week 7, at the end of which they were due to have their first long weekend leave. Earlier the Padre had been trying desperately to inject some energy into the room, with little success.

'Are you happy to be in the army?' he began, and without waiting for a reply he told them it was great to see them in church the previous day and hoped they'd had a good Sunday after that. Recruits were occasionally required to attend a Sunday church service in their platoon, although faith was considered an individual issue. There is a multi-faith room in the centre, but the Padre had told me that people of all religious backgrounds generally preferred the church.

One or two young men muttered that Sunday had been boring as they had to do admin, or in other words, cleaning, ironing and polishing, but there was little sign that Monday was proving any more exciting. The lesson continued with a Power Point presentation, a format which the Padre had inherited, he told me, rather than designing it himself. A Methodist minister, he was one of the three Christian Padres responsible for providing spiritual welfare throughout the week as well as Sunday worship. His teaching methods relied on constant interaction, repetition and prodding the audience to react. There was no sign of anyone taking notes or asking for clarification.

After listing all the core values, he called out, 'What is integrity?' This was the first topic of the lecture.

'Not lying!' said one. 'Not grassing yourself up,' said another.

'You are soldiers with integrity,' he replied. 'This means strength of character. What's on the inside is displayed on the outside. Most of all, people you can trust. Walking the walk.'

He talked about the need for trust, starting with the importance of looking after your own possessions. 'But you need to be able to trust the people you are with. If you can't trust them with your things, how can you trust them with your life?'

The recruits were then shown a film clip of a US army general giving a motivational speech to his troops as they prepared to go into battle. It was impossible to tell where in the world they were going to fight, but the gist of the message was clear. 'Look around you,' exhorted the commander, 'you will see people from Ukraine, Spain (he reeled off several other countries), Jews, gentiles, blacks and whites. We are all Americans!'

As the camera panned round the assembled troops he went on,

> Some men may experience discrimination, but for you and me all that is gone. We are moving into the shadow of the valley of death. You have to watch the back of the man in front of you, and you won't care what colour he is.

The camera showed a row of white women and their daughters looking on. The officer raised his voice to a crescendo, swearing to the men and their relatives that he would not desert them, even in death. 'Dead or alive we will all come home together! So help me God.'

'Is he a man of integrity?' asked the Padre when he had turned it off. 'He could be talking about this troop. You are black, white, ('Scouse!' shouted someone) – all from different backgrounds.' He went on to explain the need for self-respect and the importance of building team spirit at Pirbright. The lesson's second topic was then projected on the screen. Loyalty: unshakeable commitment to person or cause that will stand the test of time.

What are we loyal to?

This produced a more animated response:

> 'The British Army?'
> 'Football teams?' *Which one?*

The answer – Millwall – was inevitably met with derisive laughter.

> 'Stella!' *How old are you?* '19'.
> 'Family and friends!' *Where are you from?* 'Belfast'.
> 'Girlfriend!' *Where are you from?* 'From Salisbury'. (It turned out the individual didn't have a girlfriend and didn't like Salisbury either.)
> '*Beliefs?*'

It was noticeable that none of the Commonwealth recruits spoke at all. This platoon had a relatively high proportion, and I had met some of them before in their first week at Pirbright. Among them were several Fijians and a group of young men from St Vincent. I had subsequently interviewed other members: a Sikh from Punjab who had been working as a traffic warden in the UK before applying, and a Nigerian who had joined while on an international student visa. The instructors had warned me that these two had to be housed apart, at different ends of the block. 'They hate each other because of their religions.' I was told, darkly. The young man from Lagos was from a Muslim background, but he did not seem to hold any grievances when we sat down together to talk. 'My parents are strict Muslims,' he told us, 'but I make my own decisions.' The Sikh had been complaining that his turban attracted hostility in his previous job because people assumed he was Muslim but his main problem was trying to lose weight.

I wondered if the two men were aware of the administrative headaches their presence was causing. This over-sensitivity – or so it seemed – to religious affiliation as an index of difference derived from an idea that individuals from other countries arrived at the centre with their cultures packaged neatly in a suitcase. While it was permissible to keep hold of the suitcase, like a possession, it was also expected that it would be kept out of sight during the business of military work. Its contents, however, might still explode out into the open if the owner was not handled properly. The concept of culture as something that had to be 'managed' will be addressed later, but it was not immediately relevant to this lecture. Cultural and religious difference would come under another core value: respect for others.

Teaching core values was part of the Padre's job description, but there was nothing overtly religious about the syllabus.[24] He had invited me to sit in his class as this was the only place where recruits encountered any formal instruction on identity, whether individual, collective or national. I had learned early on that Britishness was not a familiar concept in army education, partly because the assumption was, as the adverts claimed, that the British Army was simply the best. It was intriguing then, though not particularly surprising, that most of the illustrative material consisted of either US military or Hollywood film clips. The second extract shown in this session was a scene from *Saving Private Ryan*. Selected to demonstrate the value of loyalty, it showed a young man making a stirring speech about having found a new family where he felt he belonged, rejecting his mother's pleas to come home since she had already lost two sons in war.

The film elicited a short discussion on the character's behaviour and priorities. Was he displaying loyalty?

'His mum is being selfish,' was one response. 'She should have known.'

'But don't most mums worry?' asked the Padre. 'Are we loyal to our Queen and Country?'

'No!' was the answer. 'To our mates and to ourselves'.

The man who had earlier called out 'Scouse' was moved to speak again, 'My grandfather fought in WW2, and he said that they were fighting to get home. That's the only I time I heard him swear when some one said we were fighting for Queen and Country. Bollocks!'[25]

Earlier the Padre had mentioned that those from Commonwealth backgrounds were more likely to admit to having joined for Queen and Country since they often expressed 'a high view of the monarchy'.

'A lot have a nostalgic view of England,' he had said, 'and they think of it as the mother country.' He had once met a Gambian recruit who had 'a very romantic picture. He had been led to believe that the Englishman's word was his bond!'

On this occasion there was little feedback from the class. It ended with the Padre reinforcing elements of the lesson, summed up as 'Doing the right thing on a difficult day when no one is looking'. Loyalty as soldiers means being different, he told them, being prepared to make the ultimate sacrifice. And among the benefits is an army that people are pleased to see. As the young men filed out of the room with more enthusiasm than they had shown during the entire lecture, he called out, 'Don't forget to use your ID cards to get discounts at Burger King or Subway!'

'Subway? I'm not going there!' I heard someone say.

Mosques, markets and suicide bombers

The Padre's Power Point slide of abused and tortured detainees in Iraq, combined with his remark that 'terrible things happen when the British Army loses its integrity', was not just a warning to recruits to refrain from excessive violence beyond the rules of combat. The reputations of national armies are mediated by a heavily controlled information system directed at the electorate back home.[26] Under the conditions of counter-insurgency, unchecked and overt racism towards civilians has serious implications in a remote combat zone in which the management of news and spin is paramount and the focus of global media selectively vigilant.

In 2008 the Aitken Report published the results of an inquiry into the documented abuse and unlawful killing carried out by British soldiers during military operations in Iraq in 2003 and 2004, including the activities at Camp Breadbasket near Basra on 15 May 2003, graphically portrayed in the Padre's slides.[27] The author, Brigadier Aitken, downplayed the extent of the abuse, noting, for example, that no one had been convicted for killing Iraqi civilians, including Baha Mousa, who died as a result of a beating while in British custody. However, he stressed, although 'criminal activity of one sort or another often happens on operations', just as it occurs in the UK, there is no doubt 'that such behaviour is particularly damaging when committed by the British Army, in the 21st Century, on operations where we were meant to be improving the lot of the Iraqi people, under the immediate gaze of the world's media'.[28]

In his introduction to the report, CGS Dannatt made a similar point about the potential damage caused to the organisation as well as the mission: 'If we are genuinely to live up to our world class name, we must never allow a few of our people to besmirch the reputation of the majority in this manner again.'

The Aitken Report resulted in the adoption of three main strategies intended to strengthen the organisation's internal procedures to deal with 'breaches of discipline'. First was a renewed focus on the army's V&S as a means to 'sustain the moral component of fighting power'; second, the instigation of more effective training on issues of military law and the handling of detainees; and third, a greater attention to the issue of cultural awareness.[29]

Each of these recommendations could be traced back to significant shifts in the wider project of global counter-insurgency in which the UK armed forces were deeply embroiled. The definition and promotion of values such as 'respect for others' addressed the growing ethnic, sexual and cultural diversity among the workforce in accordance with the civilian principle of individual rights. But what weight did this same value have in a combat situation? Making cultural awareness a component of military education was not just aimed at improving relations between soldiers themselves. Instead, the report made clear, this was about teaching them that culture was also a weapon.

Writing about what he calls 'the cultural turn in the War on Terror', anthropologist Hugh Gusterson describes how US troops came to find themselves

> fighting an intermittently violent guerrilla war and trying to discern friend from foe in a country that speaks a different language and worships a different god, where real men hold hands, where free and open American body language can lead to serious trouble, where familiar hand signals can have unfamiliar meanings, where loyalties defy American intuitions, and where the political map is one in which Republicans and Democrats have no place.[30]

For British troops, the degree of estrangement was scarcely any different, despite their country's long-running history of military engagement both in Mesopotamia and Afghanistan. But the discomfort of soldiers occupying an unfamiliar, unpredictable country was not the point.

During the middle of the decade, the tactical direction of the war itself had begun to change. As the NATO-led ISAF (International Security Assistance Force) operations acknowledged that their mission in Afghanistan could stretch far into the future, counter-insurgency theorist David Kilcullen called for a new strategy which he termed 'armed social work'.[31] Military leaders like General Petraeus spoke of the need for a 'better knowledge of the cultural terrain', echoing the Defence Department's insistence on better intelligence gathering.[32] In 2006, the US government authorised a new pilot programme called 'Military Accessions Vital to the National Interest' (MAVNI), passing a statute that allowed the separate services to recruit up to hundreds of legal non-citizens who were deemed to have critical skills.[33] Anthropologists were brought in to work for special military units known as the Human Terrain System, a development with profound implications for the US academic profession.[34] Another development was the distribution of hi-tech apps and smart cards designed for use in the field. Cultural knowledge was seen as something that could be learned and preferably kept in the pocket in the event of face-to-face encounters with local people. These measures were replicated in some of the NATO forces which began systematically to acquire linguistic and cultural expertise.

The reforms outlined by Brigadier Aitken can therefore be seen as a response to this shift in military tactics as well as an attempt to prevent the abuse of detainees. His report outlined the need for theoretical and practical training, aided by Iraqi and Afghan nationals, which would imbue all ranks 'with an understanding of the culture, customs and philosophy of the indigenous peoples'. Further support would be provided by special pre-operation training centres through the delivery of language training and 'the use of interactive e-based cultural awareness training packages'.

In May the following year, the MoD announced the opening of a replica Afghan village in the Norfolk countryside, complete with 'mosques, markets and suicide bombers' at a cost of £14 million.[35] The precedent for building foreign settlements in order to train soldiers had been set many years previously when the site was used to create a replica German village in 1942. This was later amended to resemble Northern Ireland and Bosnia before becoming Sindh Kalay, which the *Telegraph* referred to as a 'Middle East settlement'. Media reports described how the houses were arranged around 'a traditional courtyard and vegetable patch' and the village was populated by 'volunteers dressed as insurgents in traditional Taliban robes'. Retired Gurkhas and amputees from the charity Amputees for Action were hired to act as villagers, insurgents and injured soldiers.

The first infantry group to use the village for training was the 1st Battalion Coldstream Guards, whose commanding officer, Lieutenant Colonel Toby Gray, reported that the facilities were superb.

Not only is the physical infrastructure strikingly realistic, but the attention to detail is second-to-none. The bazaar, which is peopled by Dari-speaking, retired Gurkhas is as close as we can get to the real thing outside Afghanistan.[36]

In addition to hiring retired Nepalese servicemen to add authenticity, the MoD regularly employed Afghan nationals as advisers and to perform the roles of interpreters and civilians. This practice had been flagged up as early as 2007 in a *Daily Mail* article which warned that refugees were being 'paid up to £200 a day by taxpayers to help to train our soldiers to fight the Taliban'.[37] However, the custom of using 'foreigners' to augment the experience of training was not a particularly new one since Gurkhas routinely performed roles as 'the enemy' in situations where infantry troops trained for battle. Fijian soldiers were sometimes called upon to play the parts of Iraqi or Afghans too, wearing appropriate clothes and acting as civilians in exercises where their colleagues were practising interacting with locals with whom they were unable to communicate.[38] This example made me curious about the extent to which the British Army followed the US army's lead in making use of different language skills and cultural expertise among its workforce.

'The British Army is *so* bad at this,' sighed the Commanding Officer when I asked him about this in early 2009. He looked despairing. 'I had a friend,' he went on, 'a Muslim who could speak Urdu fluently. He put his name forward when Afghanistan started and no one took any notice!' Although this situation had begun to change towards the end of the decade, the officer's comment suggested that there were conflicting policies regarding the cultural attributes of minorities serving in the army. Leaving aside the disruptive effects of ignorance, prejudice or stereotyping, the concept of 'culture' remained central to the way that the British Army had responded to the demands of an increasingly diverse workforce. In the next chapter we look more closely at cultural difference as a factor in 'operational effectiveness' as we continue to chart the role that Commonwealth soldiers have played in the making of a multicultural military.

5
Keeping the Faith

The chemistry in the photograph has an explosive quality, but the dynamism might only be visible to those who are aware of the anomaly. The picture shows a group of eight young male soldiers wearing the green battledress of the British Army, some with matching helmets and some without. They are posing for the camera, but unlike the conventional pictures of men in uniform these guys look unusually relaxed and cheerful, as though they had just completed a difficult task together. Their faces are smeared with greasepaint and some have their arms draped around each other like old friends. You can tell at a glance that most of these soldiers are from Fiji, Africa or the Caribbean. But there are two who do not fall into this category which is why this image of camaraderie is so compelling.

Two young Nepalese men grin happily from the middle of the group, both looking comfortable and very much at ease. The caption explains that they missed out on a training module due to injury and fell behind in the schedule. By joining a platoon of Infantry recruits on a temporary basis they could catch up with their peers, who by that time had been dispersed into the Brigade of Gurkhas following their pass-off parade. What makes this photograph so electric is that normally these two categories of recruits would not get a chance to meet in the course of their training. Later, on operations and in exercises things might be different, but in Catterick there is almost total separation between the young Gurkhas and the British Army recruits in their respective training centres. Keeping young Nepali recruits away from peers helps to inculcate a sense of how they are different, but the solidarity that the young men evidently feel towards each other suggests it might be the reason why they are kept apart. The photo is significant because it tells two important stories.

The first reflects the simple fact that all recruits who have travelled a long way from home to join the British Army are likely to find much in common with each other as outsiders, despite differences in language and cultural backgrounds. The second story is more complex as it indicates two apparently contradictory methods of organising minority ethnic groups within the army. Where those from Nepal are trained to think of themselves as culturally distinct in the interests of enhancing their 'operational effectiveness', young men and women from Commonwealth countries, from the South Pacific to the Caribbean, from southern Africa to Pakistan, are integrated with their UK-born peers from the moment they put on their uniforms. Institutional reform might now demand that the objectives of equality and diversity are recognised and valued in the army, but the demand for efficient soldiers also requires an ethos of discipline, loyalty and self-sacrifice that overrides any notion of ethnic or locally based distinctiveness between groups or individuals.

These two approaches to minority culture might seem incompatible in one organisation, or at least, one might appear outdated and the other recognisably modern, but in fact they both derive from long-standing models of military practice. The young Commonwealth soldiers photographed with the smiling Gurkha recruits were the beneficiaries of a more co-ordinated approach to 'diversity management', but they too owed their presence to Britain's historic recruiting traditions. For a start, the practice of melding disparate individuals, ethnic groups, mercenaries and even different nationalities into one army has been illustrated countless times in British history, as it has been in many other countries. It is a little known fact, for example, that Europeans volunteered to fight in the cosmopolitan army of the Sikh leader Ranjit Singh in the early part of the nineteenth century. More famous were the multinational forces amassed by Wellington to fight the Napoleonic Wars in Europe during the same period. In 1813, two years before the Battle of Waterloo, Britain's 75,000 troops were made up of 26,000 Portuguese, 5,000 German and 1,000 French.[1] Their defeat of France's republican army of citizen-soldiers meant that there was no automatic consensus that fighting nationalist causes would be more likely to be motivated by patriotism and common culture. Punitive training and professionalism continued to be seen throughout Europe as the basis of a united army even though mercenaries themselves came to be viewed with suspicion.[2]

The distinction between Gurkhas and the rest of the army is also complicated by the fact that, just as the Nepalese soldiers are organised along culturally distinct lines, British infantry regiments are also, in theory, assembled on the basis of regional, 'tribal' identities, as we have seen in Chapter 4. We have already noted that the local cultural ties that are fostered in the interests of group cohesion do not apply to those who grew up in another country altogether and who are not necessarily aware of Britain's internal geography. Today, neither mercenaries nor colonial subjects, and definitely not citizens – at least not until they have satisfied the requisite criteria – Commonwealth soldiers have not always been equipped or allowed to make informed choices about which regiments they join, particularly when they apply from outside the country.

The practice of maintaining infantry regiments on a geographical basis proves that the link between culture, identity and ethnic characteristics, which is the historic rationale justifying the Brigade of Gurkhas (BG), has strong traces in other parts of the institution, even though it is very unevenly applied and increasingly hard to maintain as regiments are amalgamated, cut and relocated. Dennis and his cohort found themselves joining the King's Division which draws recruits from 'the North of England, from the fells of Cumbria and the mill towns of Lancashire, across the Pennines to the Yorkshire Dales and the large cities of Yorkshire. Its soldiers compliment [*sic*] the geography being tough, gritty and plain speaking … no-nonsense northern soldiers with a proud history of uncompromising service to both Queen and country.'[3] Increasingly, however, in a modern 'progressive' army, infantry recruits are to be enticed by the prospect of an exciting career leading to a sense of personal achievement. Geography is still a significant factor, but residual rather than definitive, as it is for Gurkhas.

Thus the distinction between the young Nepalese and Commonwealth soldiers in the photograph can be made to demonstrate the uneven effects of modernisation on the British Army. The stress on separate development and cultural authenticity, also echoed in modern forms of ethnic stereotyping, derives from the dubious theory of martial races, as we noted in Chapter 1. Originally used as a divide-and-rule tactic in the colonial setting, martial race theory casts a long historical shadow over the modern BG even as it is forced to adapt to meet the standard terms and conditions of the army as a whole.

Education and brawn

There is no mistaking the young Nepalese recruits in Catterick, especially in the evenings when they are dressed like inmates of a strict boarding school with crisp white shirts and grey v-neck jumpers. They are physically segregated, and not only are there few opportunities for meeting their counterparts in the grounds of the garrison, they are also actively discouraged from mingling with them. Housed in a separate part of the ITC campus, in a modern set of buildings with its own enclosed parade ground, dining facilities, teaching rooms and religious buildings, young Gurkha recruits are more likely to watch Hindi films together as a way of relaxing than trying to improve their English by seeking out new friends of their own age. This might seem to contradict the evidence of the photograph that non-UK recruits are drawn to each other's company, but by examining the conditions of Gurkha recruitment and training it becomes clearer how notions of distinctiveness are fostered from the start.

Instead of a rolling programme whereby new recruits turn up on a weekly basis for their six-month training, as they do in the ITC, the Gurkha schedule begins each year with up to 230 new trainees who start in early January and then graduate together in late September. Although the selection procedures have been centralised in one place, it is still the case that thousands apply and only a couple of hundred are selected.[4] Today the physical aspects of selection are still intense – the historic 'doko carry' test consists of a two-mile run up a hill carrying 35kg – but recruits are also required to pass English language and maths exams at the Brigade's centre in Pokhara. As one senior officer put it, 'we need to mix education and brawn'.

The Gurkha Learning Centre in Catterick sends representatives to Nepal to take part in the educational selection process. Roughly seven hundred candidates who successfully pass the physical tests sit the exams in British Army basic skills, which include listening, speaking and reading in English. In addition they are required to write an essay in half an hour on a choice of topics. But if a candidate exhibits exceptional physical skills, recruiters will argue for his inclusion regardless of lower academic scores.

'The regiment want good shooters,' explained one of the examiners, explaining how the final selection is often a question of haggling round a table with all the grades in front of them. 'So even if they've not got very good English but are the best shot they've had in 20 years, they'll take him.'

The level of educational qualifications is determined in accordance with NATO guidelines which have been set to ensure standards internationally. The BG requires level 2 and 3 in English which is the level required to do tasks such as writing internal memos. Since 2002, the army has also been using ESOL (English as a Second Language) courses since it was decided that soldiers should have qualifications that are valid in civilian life. For that reason the Gurkha Learning Centre also offers City and Guild ESOL certificates as the education system is standardised across the armed forces.

Their language tutors are acutely aware of the reason why there is such competition. One explained:

> Generally speaking they join for money – Nepal's a very poor country, and there are no jobs, no opportunities for self-advancement. Young men are reduced to hanging around the streets. I often ask them, 'What did you do at home?' They tell me, 'I roamed around.' There are no jobs, no money, strikes in colleges. They don't have much of a life. And the richer ones are problems to parents, with motorbikes and drugs. It's not much fun being a Nepalese teenager, there's nothing to do. A bit like Stockton on Saturday night.

While there have traditionally been strong caste and family networks supplying many of the young men,[5] the economic opportunities represented by joining the British Army have made the recruitment process more competitive than ever. Recruiters report that candidates are now more likely to be from urban areas where they have access to better education, rather than the remote hill areas favoured in the past. 'However, because our standards are extremely stringent,' I was told, 'in particular physical standards and educational standards – they tend to come from these regions in which the Gurkhas have traditionally been found . . . The boys themselves are generally up in the more remote hill areas, providing the more robust, durable Gurkha. That has been traditional but now there are a number of academies who will train up the more urban-oriented man.'

Since the BG is part of the wider British Army, equality legislation means that recruitment must be offered to females as well. In 2008, 20 women applied, two of whom passed the educational tests, but none passed the physical. This is partly because they are excluded from the academies set up in recruiting towns and run by ex-Gurkhas who train young men to pass the tests.

'If you go to Pokhara,' said another tutor who takes part in the annual selection process, 'you see boys running up and down the hill practising. Girls have not been to these crammers and therefore are not prepared for the tests in the same way . . . . Boys know they will have to do this and this, and will practice with their friends or father.'

Of the five young men I met, four identified themselves as 'city boys'. Sandesh had been to boarding school in India because, 'in our country education is not so strong'. He was accepted the third time he applied to join the Brigade and was now at the upper-age limit of 21. If he had failed again, he said, he would have tried to go abroad.

'I am a city boy,' said Pratap. He had been successful his second time and had family connections. 'My brother is in Signals and my uncle is retired in Kent.'

Chitraraj was only 18, and younger than the rest of the group. He had been successful on his first attempt, and was one of three pairs of brothers undertaking the course at the same time. 'I am from the hills,' he told us shyly, 'although I came to the city for my education.'

Their military curriculum is more or less identical to the six-month Infantry training, but as well as extra English language classes they also have a cultural orientation programme, known as the 'Three Steps', which introduces them to life in the UK, or at least some of the practicalities in moving around. Our conversation took place in a storeroom as I had asked if we could go somewhere quiet, and we were surrounded by shelves stocked with picks and shovels, toilet rolls and unidentifiable cardboard boxes. Straight ahead of me on the opposite wall was a deer's head mounted on a shield. I had been in incongruous settings before but this felt quite appropriate as a backdrop for contemplating Britishness, especially since their views had been shaped by a mishmash of Hollyoaks, David Beckham and Harry Potter before they arrived. Being in the windowless storeroom was a bit like a metaphor for them too.

Like the British recruits, the boys had been confined to barracks for the first five weeks. 'We feel like a bird going out of a cage,' they told me, remembering their first step which began with an introduction to the pelican crossing and traffic lights – 'there are not so many in our country' – and a trip to the giant local branch of Tesco – 'we have supermarkets but we don't have chains' – where they were taught how to buy things with a bankcard. A whole day was spent touring the area, including the adjacent towns of Richmond and Darlington.

The second step took place in the seventh and eighth week when the recruits were taken further afield to visit museums in York, Manchester or Newcastle. The third and final step, which these young men had recently completed, involved a weekend trip to London where they were shown how to use public transport and taken to sites such as the Imperial War Museum. The exercise also included a test in which they had to visit certain points on the underground system within a certain time. They seemed genuinely surprised that London was so much more crowded than they had imagined after seeing it on the TV.

The procedures for training the young Nepalese soldiers were designed to foster a sense of their unique capabilities as Gurkha warriors. In military terms, the role of the Centre was 'To mould a Nepalese youth into a Gurkha soldier trained to the standards of the British Army, who retains his Nepalese identity and will live up to the traditions of the Brigade of Gurkhas.'[6] Earlier I had been briefed by a senior instructor, also from Nepal, who explained how the cultural element of the training was devised, by which he meant Gurkha culture rather than British. Some boys know how to shop and how to behave, he told me, but our concept is to start from the beginning. 'We have our own ethos,' he went on, 'our own way of doing things. Half of them have spent their lives in boarding school, and some are like British kids. Here is what it's all about.'

The cultural training included cooking and eating traditional food and carrying out ceremonies according to the Nepali religious calendar.[7] Both Hindu and Buddhist spiritual advisers were on hand and there was a small Hindu temple within the grounds of the Centre. Recruits were encouraged to call their instructors 'guruji' and to think of them as paternal figures. All instruction was carried out in Nepalese, and this applied to the British Gurkha officers who were required to learn the language as part of their own training.

Instilling a sense of military history was important too, as it was for recruits in the regular army. This usually took the form of a battlefield tour in northern Europe, carried out during the first phase of training. The Gurkha class of 2009 had been to the Indian memorial at Neuve-Chapelle in France, dedicated to the Indian and Nepalese troops who had died fighting for the British in 1914–1916. 'Every evening we do a parade,' said the instructor. 'It shows them that being a soldier is still respected even though they died a long time ago.'

The overall impression is that the young men are nurtured throughout the training as they are inducted into this elite profession. However, visiting the Gurkha Learning Centre I could not help noticing one essay that revealed how hard this experience was for many individuals, especially at the beginning of the training regime:

> Sometimes I even felt that I made a great mistake by joining the army. We didn't get any respect. The Gurujis were very furious and I felt that we were animal and not human. I found myself very lonely.

This extract suggests that the 'culture shock' encountered in the early stages of training is not confined to those who have grown up in the UK, indicating that new army recruits might have much in common, regardless of which regiment, cap badge or nationality they belong to. The principles of maintaining the BG as a separate entity today should not be allowed to obscure the continuities with the wider army as well. One of these overlapping areas can be found by looking at the level of basic education expected of all recruits. In 2007 a report entitled 'Army Basic Skills Provision: Whole Organisation Approach, Lessons Learnt' found that while half of army recruits had the basic skills of primary school leavers, up to 9 per cent were at the lower standard expected of seven and eight-year-olds:

> Up to 50% of the 10,000 to 12,000 Army recruits join the service with literacy or numeracy skills at national Entry Level 3 or below. About 8 to 9% are at Entry Level 2 and, before the recent introduction of an Entry Level 2 recruit entry standard, around 1% were at Entry Level 1. This situation has been fairly consistent over the last four years.[8]

Those with poor basic skills were concentrated in particular sections of the army. 'Those technical trades with higher entry qualifications have a much smaller percentage of recruits with skills below Level 1 than those Army specializations (e.g. Infantry and Artillery) that set few or no academic/vocational entry qualifications.' The same report noted that most foreign nationals, who at that time numbered 9,500 (including 'significant numbers from Nepal and Fiji') had English language needs: 'very many join with English speaking and listening skills at Entry Level 3 and below'.

Dumb and dumber

While the young Gurkhas' learning needs were taken care of during their training, those infantrymen who completed their six-month course at ITC but who were identified as having inadequate literacy and numeracy skills were required to complete an extra two-week package at Darlington College. The aim was to reach Level 1 (grades D-G at GCSE) which is the standard needed to stay in the army after their first term of three years, and to be considered for promotion.[9] The course was apparently referred to as 'dumb and dumber' but the specially designed programme was sometimes the first opportunity that some of the young men had had to enjoy small classes and individual attention.

On the morning I visited, the literacy group was already at work. It consisted of Chris (Gambia), Sam (Ghana), Bryan (St Vincent) and Jimmy (Dewsbury) who were shortly joined by Saul from Ghana who had been at the dentist's, and Andy from Sunderland who seemed to have more of an attitude. He said he had missed the bus, complaining he had been told the wrong time, and he didn't have a pen either. The tutor began by asking if they knew what vowels were – Jimmy rattled them off, but the others recited them as well. They were given a sheet of paper and told they were going to do a spelling exercise rather than a test. The tutor then asked if they knew what a syllable was. 'Use syllables when you are marching,' she advised. 'Get used to the beat of the word.' She called them out, accentuating the syllables for them: Army – unit – guard – duty – soldier – training (train with ing at the end) – rifle (any riflemen?) – barracks (bar racks) – military – Catterick. Although they were words that any soldier would see or hear every day, they were not the easiest to spell.

After they had finished they were asked to read out their attempts. Chris used the standard military alphabet. Duty: delta, uniform, tango, yankee. Sam spelled them all perfectly, explaining that he had done lots of spelling and writing back home. Some had written entirely in capital letters, and the tutor clarified where and when they should be used. 'Victoria Road and down the road'. She gave them clues for spelling some of the harder words: green uniforms are rarely dirty. The latecomer from Sunderland said he could spell all those words but I noticed that Jimmy was struggling. Shortly after this he was taken off to work with another tutor.

Looking round the classroom as they continued their studies, it was clear that the staff made an effort to acknowledge the students' different backgrounds. One of the posters on display had the word 'diversity' written as an acrostic: Different Individuals Valuing Each Other Regardless of Skin, Intellect, Talents or Years. Another had a list of 'army learners 2009' registered by country of origin: Gambia, Kenya, Fiji, Iceland, India, St Vincent, Grenada, Jamaica, Namibia, Ghana, Cameroon, Zambia. The UK was well represented with a spread from all over the country.

When I returned, the class was playing a computer spelling game designed for adults and Andy was being given help by one of the Ghanaians. I asked him where he was headed and he told me he was in the Coldstream Guards, volunteering the information that he would be going to 'Afghan' in October. His words tumbled out as though he was both excited and terrified. Meanwhile the numeracy tutor was teaching a group how to work out the time difference between Darlington and Camp Bastion. Being unable to read figures, such as serial numbers on equipment, or to do basic arithmetic would endanger their own lives, let alone the safety of others.

Later I learned that Andy McNab had been a regular visitor to the ITC where he would try to inspire recruits to use the educational opportunities provided for them. Apparently he was able to reach young people who were alienated from the world of books, using his own experience in the army to encourage soldiers to improve their basic literacy skills and to take pleasure from reading.[10] Judging from the fact that his books were all marked as 'out' on the college lending list his words evidently had an impact.

Training not to be British

The teachers in the Gurkha Learning Centre were frustrated that their students were reluctant to venture into the rest of the camp to practise their English. They were perplexed too that they resisted their advice to read English magazines about sport, or to watch TV programmes like 'Top Gear' which normally appealed to young men. These habits were partly attributed to youthful reticence and laziness, but it was also evident that their training was designed to produce a particular mindset. Their 'gurujis' did not encourage them to be independent at that stage of their career. Visiting some of the same young men in the regimental base in Folkestone, Kent, a few months later, I asked them about life in their new surroundings. One or two admitted to going into town to see girlfriends whom they confessed to have met on the internet, but they were not allowed to stay out much after 9.30 p.m. Afterwards their instructor told me that they didn't want the young men going to pubs and behaving like British soldiers. They were regarded as their children, he said, and the instructors felt a duty of care.

Earlier that day I had asked Adam, the young English Captain who was hosting my visit, how long he had been in the army and why he had chosen to be a Gurkha officer. Now in his thirties, he told me he had made the decision when he was 17 after winning an army scholarship to Sandhurst and learning about Gurkhas at an open day: 'I had found the soldiers I wanted to command!' he said imperiously.

That week, he explained, the regiment was desperately busy as it was due to deploy in a few months time. Many were away on training exercises, 'basically learning the culture and how to shoot straight, so they would be ready to hit the ground running when they arrived'. This remark was another reminder that 'culture' was an equally important element of military expertise, a fact illustrated by the army's Equality and Diversity Directive. 'Operationally, we face increasingly complex challenges worldwide, particularly when dealing with people of different cultures, traditions and language.'[11] Having a culturally diverse workforce was therefore regarded as an asset: 'The ability to draw on a diverse population from society and from within our own ranks will help us to meet those challenges.'

While the British Army had taken its time to appreciate the value of diversity on a day-to-day level, the presence of the Gurkhas had long provided a useful tool in exploiting the British lack of cultural expertise. Their specific aptitudes and affinities were seen as integral to their fighting skills, a combination that has undoubtedly played a part in their retention in the present.

'What makes Gurkhas Gurkhas,' continued Adam, 'is that they maintain their cultural identity. We find it important to making them as good as they are, their strengths inherent from Nepal.'

'We appreciate and respect their cultural sensibilities. For example,' he reached for a publication and showed me a section on cultural guidelines, 'their family background helps them grieve appropriately. The eldest son has to go back to Nepal.'

He pointed to a list of do's and don't's. I noticed that whistling indoors is forbidden in Nepalese culture as it is a way of calling ghosts.

He went on: 'What makes Gurkhas strong and the cohesion work is the fact that we want them to maintain their cultural links back to Nepal. We don't want to turn them into British individuals!'

I had heard this sentiment before from English officers in the BG. 'We don't want brown Brits!' was another version.

'The [British] army really isn't a reflection of society,' he said. 'The 3,000 Gurkhas are not a reflection of society in Nepal [either]. They are handpicked, 230 out of 17,000, each year.'

Captain P, who was Nepalese, was hovering as he was going to escort me for a while until he had to drive up to Yorkshire. His phone kept ringing and he would answer in Nepalese but switch back to English at certain points in the conversation. He explained that English is used to discuss rules and regulations as they don't have the same terms in Nepalese. 'You have to use English for official things or people will say they haven't understood.'

Cultures within cultures

In 2008 the army produced a significant document that finally acknowledged the importance of cultural differences among its many national groups. This represented quite a turnaround from the *laissez faire* attitude which favoured osmosis as the easiest route, placing the burden of adapting to UK culture on the shoulders of those who had travelled from furthest away.[12] The new guidelines were intended to promote sources of information and advice in order to support Gurkhas as well as Commonwealth citizens and their families. 'Respect lies at the very heart of our fighting power', the document explained, '...it is built on understanding of other people, taking time to find out who they are, what their background may be and how that background affects how they think and act.'[13] The historical ties that explained the contemporary employment of Nepalese and Commonwealth citizens were made explicit: 'This shared past history is the basis for a common bond and shared respect. We go back a long way together, we have done a lot together and we can be proud to continue to do so.'

The most salient feature, however, was not the obligatory remark about the joint commitment of Commonwealth countries (with their 'people of different races and origins' [sic]) to world peace and democracy, but the attempt to break down the cultural properties of the different nationalities now working in the British Army. The document provided information that had been compiled 'from the viewpoint of the British person looking at each individual national culture' but also included a section on the United Kingdom written 'from the viewpoint of a foreign or Commonwealth soldier looking at the British'.

> The sheets cannot tell you everything about a country's culture and there will of course be things that you do not agree with or recognise. This is good. This is diversity. It is often easy to see our differences, but our similarities are often only found out in conversation. We must get to know each other and work together towards our common ground – the Army's culture and its Values and Standards.[14]

As well as providing basic demographic information about each Commonwealth nation, the notes gave more detailed facts about those supplying significant numbers of recruits, organised under headings: what is similar (what is the common ground), what is different (what seems strange or may be uncomfortable), what is hidden (what lies beneath) and what is critical (what may cause tension and misunderstanding). Welfare staff often mentioned that the guides were useful in dealing with family issues, and in some instances they were helpful in explaining behaviour that could be misunderstood, such as a refusal to look superiors in the eye or touching parts of the body inappropriately. Space does not allow a thorough analysis of the contents of this document which contain fascinating insights into the way that 'culture' becomes an umbrella-word for any recognisable patterns of group behaviour. Listed as common ground, for example, are the observations 'Kenyans generally love to party' and 'The British, like most people, seek to identify themselves with people similar to themselves'. Under the 'hidden' section on St Vincentians, the notes suggest that 'leaving home and travelling across the world to join the Army is a big step and shows huge commitment and determination to achieve'.[15] It goes on:

> This keenness to get into the Army and get on has sometimes lead people to enter the more widely available trades sooner, rather then waiting for vacancies in other trades that may better match their qualifications and trade-test results. This needs to be carefully managed; it is better to encourage transfer to the right cap badge and trade than risk loosing [sic] the soldier altogether.

Comparing the references to religion, family or attitudes to women in authority would make another interesting study, but perhaps the most significant finding was that the existence of the guide was not widely known and the information was certainly not designed for ordinary soldiers. As a tool for welfare and training staff, the notes provided a reference point, but the testimony of Fijian and Nepalese support workers suggested that a written summary was not sufficient for those who worked with dependants in the UK and families in countries of origin as well. However, the concept of cultural difference was not always one that entailed potential difficulties and misunderstanding, as far as personnel policies were concerned at least. There were some instances where it became an important medium for negotiating the right to act as a group, a process likely to be initiated and led by members of well-established communities with long memories of British colonial rule in their own countries.

Culture as exchange

The first part of the ceremony marking Fiji Day was formal, and we slipped into the back of the room just in time to hear the welcoming speech being delivered by a British officer. Coloured cloths and balloons hung from the windows, giving the community hall a festive atmosphere. There were two rows of dignitaries from the three UK services on a raised platform at the front, while the audience sat on straw mats in respectful silence. The men were grouped together, dressed in the bright cotton shirts they would wear at home, while the women and children, some with flowers in their hair, were clustered at the back. A two-year-old in a bright blue and orange shirt bearing the words Fiji and Paradise wandered around looking bemused. The glistening shoulders of the male dancers sitting at the front were just visible through the sea of heads, and I wondered if I had missed the performance or whether it would take place after I had left.

The officer was speaking appreciatively of the contribution that Fijians had made to the British Army over the years, a garland of flowers round his neck and his wife placed next to him demurely on the stage. My host, Will, who was a respected figure in the community, leaned over to whisper what was going on. We had arrived after a significant moment when a dish of meat was passed forward to the army representative, offered as symbolic thanks to the organisation for allowing the ceremony marking the anniversary of Fiji Independence Day to take place on their premises. Kava had been drunk too, in symbolic quantities, but it was broad daylight outside and the festivities would continue long into the night.

As we sat listening to the speeches, small children moved around ceaselessly. One tripped over and fell, banging his head and shrieking with pain. A man whom I presumed to be his father picked him up and the child stopped crying almost straight away. No one seemed put out by the din although it threatened to drown out the speaker, for those at the back of the room at least. The dad held him perfectly still until he cheered up and started to play with his father's ear.

We all rose to our feet for the Fiji national anthem, sung in English. Then the formalities were over and it was time to eat. Outside in the bar area there were tables set for a feast: huge silver bowls of fish, seafood, meat, yam and cassava. This was the women's work, and they also served and supervised the meal. Families and friends sat together, although I noticed that there were many single men sitting together too. The children ran around or played on the bouncy castle outside.

Celebrations to mark this day were held regionally throughout the UK wherever there was a large enough Fijian community to organise them. Will was a veteran of British military culture having joined in 1998, and he had witnessed the way in which the institution had struggled to adapt to the presence of different national and cultural groups. He had also observed how the waves of recruits from Fiji had fared over the years, playing his own part in easing their transition to the UK. As an older man and more experienced soldier he had earned the respect clearly emanating from colleagues and their spouses. But as he explained to me, he was also a member not just of a high-caste family, but one of the three ruling families which had retained power in spite of several coups. His father was not only one of the high chiefs in Fiji, but he also had a ministerial position. Will was from the equivalent, he told me, of the royal family.

When we first entered the hall, I had noticed that we had caused a bit of a stir by sitting on the floor at the back. Will's rightful place, where he had sat in previous years, was on the dais, but on this occasion he was perfectly content to remain on the margins and confessed that I had provided the perfect excuse. The social structure in Fiji is based on a caste system which once distributed power among the chiefly clans who were protected by the caste of warriors. The chiefs provided protection and welfare to those within their jurisdictions, right down to the smallest village units where inhabitants were divided among three more castes. Although the upheavals of the last two decades had curbed the political authority of the chiefs, the underlying hierarchies had remained, modified by the inevitable social transitions caused by modernisation and migration. Fijians encountering each other outside the country were likely to defer to protocols of social rank, not unlike citizens of any small country who meet compatriots away from home. However, the patterns of deference acknowledged by Fijians within the confines of the British Army community suggested the possibility of an alternative chain of command, especially among recruits from rural areas. In the early days this was identified as a problem that qualified the prized assets of Fijians as ideal warriors and sportsmen. There was a possibility that a member of the chiefly clan would refuse to obey orders from someone beneath him in rank, thereby putting other people's lives at risk.

Will knew all about this anxiety from above. 'In the army, work is work,' he told me. 'But people revert in social situations.' The lack of knowledge about cultural differences throughout the institution, coupled with inexperience on the part of NCOs, officers and welfare services, has meant that soldiers from Fiji have had to develop their own channels for advising newcomers about how to behave in the new environment. Acting as unofficial mentors was encouraged by the chain of command too, especially once Fijians began to gain promotion to the rank of corporal and higher. But there was also the question of educating the bosses as well. As the ritual of passing meat to the army chiefs had indicated, the concept of exchange was extremely important, not just in symbolic form, but also in terms of diplomatic relations between the two countries.

Will was the best person to illustrate this, as it turned out. His wife, who had joined the army in 2001, was a sergeant in the AGC but had passed away in 2008 shortly after being posted to another base near Southampton. Will decided that rather than take the traditional route and repatriate her body, he would hold her funeral in England where he planned to bring up their infant daughter. This meant going to the CO of her unit to ask permission to hold what would have been a state funeral in Fiji, transferred to a British military setting. Will was aware that the request involved a two-way transaction.

> They have to work with tradition and I have to respect where the army comes into play. They asked me for my agreeing to this, to use [the experience] as a template, so in future, if this case arise at least they have a template to work with, [to show] how tradition works with the army.

Since the two families had to travel from Fiji the funeral was delayed by almost a week. In the meantime, the CO allowed Will to take over the welfare hall and decorate it according to customary practice.

> When the monarch passes away, they have the guards guarding over where the casket is going to be laid a week or so before the actual casket is laid there for the funeral day. That is exactly what we went through: the drapes were there, we had all the big traditional mats, just waiting for the casket to be brought in.
>
> In the end there were nearly 500 that turned up for day of the funeral. It was like a state funeral, a good sending off for her. The locals down there saw it as a big eye opener. I've studied their version, as I've been ten years here. If a member of a family or a close friend passes away, it's more of a case of going into church, burying him and going to pub and celebrate there, or have family and friends come together, shed a few tears and off they go. In our case, we treat with high esteem our loved ones who've passed away.

I had brigadiers, commandants came down there, beautiful I would say. Not a pleasant thing for me, but beautiful overall because the army's seen how we work as a culture, and us Fijians see how the army respects our culture. That was the living example, it was such a beautiful thing for us.

I had heard about the occasion from different sources several months before I met Will. A senior officer had used it as an example of the strength of the Fiji community in the area. Because the unit specialised in port operations it was permanently stationed on the coast, not far from naval bases where Fijians were also employed. As a result, he said, the area had become a magnet for Fijians, and the funeral was an extraordinary event in the life of this community. But it also brought people together on a national basis. Owing to the status of Will's family, Fijians arrived from all over the UK in order to mourn and pay their respects. But there were other procedural issues involved in bringing the parents from Fiji to attend the funeral.

'The army normally pays for two family members to fly to the UK to attend a funeral in the case of a death in service,' explained the officer. After protestations, the army agreed to pay for four members to travel and the regiment agreed to fund three more. It was not unusual for regiments to raise funds to contribute to their own community's needs, but in this case there were diplomatic factors as well. As Will revealed later, the fact that his father was in a ministerial post meant that his travel to the UK was elevated to a state visit rather than a private trip.

'My father looked at it as an opportunity to see things in a way that we worked together, with Fijian culture,' he said as he described the symbolic exchange that took place the evening before the funeral service. In Fiji it was customary for the family of the deceased to hand over the body to the party that would be conducting the ceremony.

Our way of offering the body to the army was done in Fijian manner. The Colonel was present from my regiment, the Colonel from her regiment and the Regimental Sgt Majors were sat there. It was explained to them: this is how it is done when the body from her parents' side is handed over to my dad and my dad handed it over the army and then the army ... whatever is done with her, is done.

The different rituals practiced at times of bereavement had caused particular difficulties within the tight confines of military culture. Fijian men customarily grew beards in the period after a parent's death, for example, which was not normally permitted. It was no coincidence that Adam, the British officer in a Gurkha regiment, had mentioned the significance of Nepali practices of grieving, suggesting that the army had learned the importance of respecting their beliefs despite the inconvenience of allowing individuals the occasional unplanned leave. Nurturing the particular set of mental and physical characteristics attributed to Gurkha soldiers was thought to bring 'added value' to the armed forces, justifying their existence as a renowned military asset. But as we saw in the previous chapter, culture had also become weaponised in the course of the counter-insurgency in Afghanistan. As the decade wore on, the combination of a British Army uniform, a language other than English and a religious identity other than Christian began to acquire its own value in the combat zone.

A good monk

> *At the meeting, all in attendance agreed that there was much to admire and learn from each other's religions. Mullah Ahdin was particularly interested to learn about the UK's multi-faith society, and that soldiers from all faiths are eligible, and do, join the Armed Forces.*
>
> (People in Defence News article, 2011)[16]

The Hindu and Buddhist spiritual advisers, or 'pundits' as they are known, are important members of the Gurkha community in the UK, but they are also required to perform a valuable role in presenting the MoD as a multi-faith employer, presenting an aspect of defence diplomacy that is addressed to civilian populations in the UK as well as in Afghanistan itself.[17] In October 2010, for example, the Joint Media Operations Centre in Camp Bastion featured an illustrated account of Gurkha soldiers celebrating the Hindu festival Dashain in Southern Helmand, where temples used for weekly worship and blessings had been erected in each of their patrol bases. 'During the Dashain festival,' it explained, 'offerings of fruit are placed in the temples and services held each morning for the soldiers. Many Gurkhas are seen with red tikkas during Dashain – blessings for safety and prosperity as they approach the end of their operational tour and return home to their families.'[18]

Earlier in 2010 the relationship between Buddhism and the wider British Army surfaced after the Dalai Lama sent a personal message of support for Armed Forces Day, the second one to be held since it was announced by Gordon Brown in 2008. The statement began by declaring how much the Dalai Lama admired the courage and determination shown by those who were prepared to fight for others, drawing comparison between the life of a monk and a military servant.

Although the public may think that physical strength is what is most important, I believe that what makes a good soldier, sailor or airman, just as what makes a good monk, is inner strength. And inner strength depends on having a firm positive motivation. The difference lies in whether ultimately you want to ensure others' well being or whether you want only wish to do them harm.[19]

Along with more conventional messages from other celebrities such as Joanna Lumley, the statement was important publicity for this new event in the national calendar, but I had already heard it being read out to members of the Armed Forces Buddhist Society, held just a few days earlier in the Chaplaincy Centre at Amport House, one of the MoD's 'finest assets'.[20] In the shimmering sun of a midsummer afternoon, the idyllic Hampshire countryside stretching as far as the eye could see, the combination of Tibetan robes, lighted candles and military uniforms seemed quite surreal. But the support for Buddhists reflected across all three services was just another day in the life of the institution. 'There are 55 different faiths and beliefs in the services,' said the army's diversity officer in his welcoming address, 'and all of them need support.' As an employer, he said, the army was concerned to create a tolerant atmosphere in which individuals could be open about their cultural preferences without fear of harassment.[21] He explained that the Royal Mail had provided an example of how a multicultural organisation can operate, citing the provision of staff notice boards where minorities like Buddhists could communicate with each other as a way of being open about their faith.

'From our perspective,' he said, 'we are interested in going beyond the uniform to see differences – gender, sexual orientation, faith – and to support differences to ensure a supportive, cohesive environment. We believe this gets a better officer, a better soldier.'

A similar message was reiterated by the equivalent staff in the RAF and the RN although Buddhists were mainly associated with the army as a result of the Gurkha contingent. The Buddhist chaplain had been appointed in 2005 along with Muslim, Sikh and Hindu chaplains. The four new posts, filled by non-uniformed civilians working for the Ministry of Defence, joined 300 commissioned Christian chaplains who, until then, bore responsibility for providing spiritual care for all members of the armed forces. The appointment of the civilian chaplains replaced a system whereby religious leaders were engaged as advisers on issues specific to each faith group. This was a direct consequence of the Employment Equality Regulations which came into force in December 2003, incorporating the religion and belief elements of the European Employment Framework Directive into UK legislation. As the MoD 'Guide on Religion and Belief' made clear, this new legal obligation made it unlawful to discriminate against personnel on the grounds of religion or belief.[22]

> The Armed Forces and MOD Civil Service have been practising policies that respect individuals' religion or belief for some time. However, it is important to understand that, where in the past MOD as a matter of policy aimed not to discriminate, the new Regulations make discrimination on the grounds of religion or belief unlawful and give individuals a right to bring Employment Tribunal claims for breaches of the Regulations.[23]

This step towards becoming an official multi-faith employer was thus mandated by law, reflecting the extent to which, as a national institution, the armed forces were simply conforming to the demands of a corporate multiculturalist script. But the question of religion and personal beliefs was known to have particular significance for those engaged in military work.

Addressing the assembled Buddhists, the chaplain presented himself as a man with no prior military experience but as one who was concerned about the neglect of spirituality in the materialistic world. The vast majority of people, he suggested, were looking for some form of the beyond. 'They do not see this world as the end.'[24] His speech was memorable because he acknowledged the particular role that religion plays in military culture despite high levels of agnosticism among the majority of soldiers. Figures from the year 2010 showed that 88 per cent of army personnel were Christian, and nearly 10 per cent admitted to 'no religion'.[25] However, given the evidence that church attendance in the UK was dropping year by year, only a minority of those who ticked the box 'Christian' would be likely to identify as 'religious'.[26]

Outside the formalities of church services and official religious ceremonies, many individuals turned to religion when they were in what he called 'extreme situations'. In Afghanistan, he said, it was common practice for the padre to hand out prayers to sections before going out on patrol.[27]

The men would often form a circle and the corporal would read out the 23rd psalm: 'Even though I walk through the darkest valley, I will fear no evil, for you are with me . . . '.

These are men who would normally be going to the pub and they wouldn't be thinking about God or spirituality.

The point of lighting candles, he told us, was to dispel the darkness in the mind. Full of jokes and anecdotes, his message was simple: refrain from killing, and stay trembling for the welfare of all beings. He had recently been to the Falklands on a Forces visit, itself an indication of the diplomatic value of promoting the military as a multi-faith employer. At one high school, all the main world religions were represented on a panel.

The kids are asking about beards, turbans and so on. Then one girl says: 'the Buddhist is very quiet, what do you believe?'

'I don't believe in anything!' I said. Buddha is one teacher who said, 'don't believe a word I say'. It's all about experience. It's experiential science. With all due respect to other religions.

The list of other faiths recorded in the annual survey of religious backgrounds for 2010 included Buddhist (0.3%), Sikh and Christian tradition, meaning Seventh Day Adventists, Jehovah's Witnesses, Mormons and others

(0.1%), Hindu (0.6%), Muslim and other religions (0.5%). Minority religions included Druid, Pagan, Rastafarian, Spiritualist, Zoroastrian (Parsee), Wicca and Baha'i.[28] Humanists were not included in this list, despite their claim that one in seven members had no religious faith, making it the second largest belief group.[29] In 2011, their campaign to be represented at the Cenotaph was turned down on grounds of insufficient space.[30]

The interests of army personnel identifying as Jewish were looked after by the Jewish Committee for HM Armed Forces, which appointed the first full-time civilian chaplain in 2010. That year there were 50, up from 40 two years earlier, making a total of 80 across the armed forces and the lowest figure on the list of named world religions. Jewish forces meet for a weekend every year as well as at the Jewish Remembrance Day Parade at the Cenotaph, but their presence is rarely noted or discussed in mainstream media. Speaking to a journalist for the publication *Renaissance*, an army captain articulated the official view of the army's diversity management policy: '...the army will always bend over backwards to facilitate individual requirements and needs, whether that's religious or personal...It is absolutely hammered into us now...that what matter is that everyone is able to bring their skills to the party regardless of sexual orientation and background and all that jazz.' Asked directly about his relationship with Muslim colleagues he replied that it had been 'a real non-issue.' Although there were no British Muslims with him at Sandhurst, his group included 'a Muslim recruit and four black recruits from Commonwealth countries'.

We pull together very much as a team because ultimately, what matters when you're under fire is whether the bloke next to you can shoot straight and knows his tactics.[31]

Pomp and pageantry

The Padre's white surplice seemed scant protection against the cold wind as he stepped forward to bless the assembled troops. Unlike the Gurkha pass-off parade, the equivalent ceremonies at ITC and Pirbright both involve the presence of the military chaplain who accompanies the senior commanders on to the parade ground. His words of prayer, addressed to those in front of him rather than to the audience in the pavilion behind him, floated in and out of earshot: I could make out the words, 'Peace', 'Father', and 'Christ'. There was no doubt that this important ritual in the life of the British soldier was taking place within a strongly marked Christian framework. Although the army's own cultural guidance notes observe that 'Religion is important to many individuals but it does not play an obvious part in British society in general', the foundational alliance between church and state continues to manifest itself in national institutions such as the armed forces.

The annual ceremonies of commemorating the war dead constitute important iterations of national identity in all its historic glory. It is at these moments that Britishness is aligned with its Christian heritage, when the armed forces, the church, the state and public institutions such as the BBC assemble to pay tribute to the idea of Britain as a particular kind of country whose survival has depended on the success of its military to defend its shores. The convergence of these elements is also found on more celebratory occasions, notably the wedding of Prince William and Kate Middleton in 2011 which was dubbed Britain's 'finest moment' by the trusty *Daily Mail*.[32]

The 'pomp and pageantry' involved hundreds of (mainly) men from all three services and the centre of London was festooned with union jack bunting and banners. Highlights of the spectacle were provided by the elaborate uniforms worn by the male members of the royal family, the Guard of Honour and more than 1000 military personnel and musicians pathlining the procession from Westminster Abbey to the Palace. The Household Cavalry escorted the Queen and Prince Philip, the Band of the Coldstream Guards played the national anthem and there was a fly-pass by Tornado jets and vintage fighter planes used in the Second World War. At the end of the day the bridal bouquet was deposited on a white pillow on the Tomb of the Unknown Soldier in accordance with a 'tradition' that began in 1923.[33]

Viewed from a military perspective, the performance of the wedding procession and related festivities can be used to illustrate what Stephen Deakin has defined as the British military ethos. For hundreds of years, he writes, this has consisted of three principal interwoven strands which cannot easily be separated. These three are martial virtues, military allegiance to the state and Christianity.[34] It was only relatively recently, however, that the word 'ethos' was used by the military as an attempt to define the essential spirit of the institution outside the terms of Christianity. It was used, for example, in the Discipline and Standards Paper of 1993 which acknowledged the declining influence of religion in an increasingly secular age: 'Within society the formative influences in promoting positive attitudes towards authority have been in steady decline: religion, education and the family no longer always provide the framework of behaviour, social structure and responsibility they have in the past.'[35] Two years later, Field Marshall Sir Peter Inge, Chief of the Defence Staff, argued that 'ethos is ... a very difficult subject to talk about ... but is something that is fundamentally important for Armed Forces to believe in ... '.[36]

The 1993 Paper marked a significant point in institutional history because it paved the way for a transition towards the secular Values and Standards that would be introduced in 2000. The tone of the document revealed a sense of uncertainty caused by the effects of social and cultural change: 'More liberal attitudes prevail, leading many parts of society to reflect or reduce in importance those values which the Armed Forces seek to maintain or regard so highly: sense of duty, loyalty, self-discipline, self-sacrifice, respect and concern for others.'

Backward Christian soldier

The policy implications of these different approaches to faith presented the British military ethos with something even more dangerous than a double-edged sword. The medieval Crusader's blade secured in the tomb of the Unknown Warrior was a spectral reminder of certain other historic legacies, like the atavistic antagonism between Christianity and Islam that we noted in Chapter 1. In our current era, the army must maintain its adherence to a nominally Christian and British identity in its role as a public institution while at the same time offering support to practitioners of many different varieties of faith-based beliefs, customs and observances. This might seem a familiar dilemma within the shortish history of diversity management in Britain's public sector, but there were specific demands facing military organ-isations which placed them in a different category. And, to put it plainly, the army had spent over a decade engaged in a long-running war in which religion – specifically Islam – was widely seen as the Enemy, whether in the guise of the Taliban or the impenetrability and intransigence of Afghan cul-ture. For this reason, General Sir Richard Dannatt's remark that 'The broader Judaeo-Christian tradition ... underpins the British Army', made shortly after his appointment as head of the army in 2006, provoked embarrassment as well as outrage.[37]

The general's typically forthright remarks, made in an interview in the *Daily Mail*, were controversial not because he declared his own devout Christian faith – for which he had earned the nickname 'backward Christian soldier' – but because he also went on to say, 'When I see the Islamist threat in this country I hope it doesn't make undue progress because there is a moral and spiritual vacuum in this country.' Echoing the anxieties expressed in the 1993 Paper on Discipline and Standards he said, 'Our society has always been embedded in Christian values; once you have pulled the anchor up there is a danger that our society moves with the prevailing wind.'

The newly appointed Muslim chaplain to the armed forces was not impressed. 'British Muslims were affected by this,' said the Imam Asim Hafiz when we met three years later in 2009. 'It made them ask, "are we serving in a Christian army?"' The *Mail* interviewer had asked Dannatt what his state-ment meant for Muslim soldiers and their allegiance. He had replied, 'These are British Muslims who are also British soldiers. If they are prepared to take the Queen's shilling they will go wherever the mission requires them to go.'

The Imam knew from the military discussion forum ARmy Rumour SErvice (or ARRSE, as it is known) that the general's words had been inflammatory. 'People felt excluded when he described it as a Christian army. They felt that they hadn't been recognised.' He personally had no problem with the idea

that the army had a Christian heritage or that Britain was a Christian country, and was prepared to accept that the media had misrepresented Dannatt's
comments. He was more concerned that they had made individuals feel
excluded and isolated. On the forum they were asking why their skills, qualities, languages, cultural awareness weren't being appreciated. 'We are here
to serve Britain and the Queen, we do the job as good as anyone else.'

In 2005, when the Imam took up the post of Muslim chaplain, there was
an estimated 300 Muslims serving in the armed forces.[38] A more accurate
picture emerged in 2007 after more comprehensive statistics were systematically collected.[39] By 2009, when there were 500 Muslims in the regular
armed forces, 410 of whom were in the army, the Imam had founded the
Armed Forces Muslim Association (AFMA). Apart from providing a support
network for individual Muslims scattered across the institution, he also felt
that the military would benefit from their collective presence. This was a
view that was apparently shared among the army leadership as well. Speaking at the launch in RAF Northolt, the new chief, General Sir David Richards,
endorsed the new organisation, saying that Muslim soldiers, sailors and air-
men were 'serving the United Kingdom with such distinction today and
I have no doubt, in the future'.[40] At the same event, Imam Asim explained
that AFMA would help to further boost the morale and confidence of Muslim
servicemen and women, as well as playing an important role in helping the
armed forces 'better understand and meet the needs of Muslims within the
demands of service life'.

The Imam had been well aware that his appointment to work for the
armed forces was controversial. His Muslim colleagues in his previous post
left him in no doubt that he was in danger of compromising his faith. He
explained how it happened.

> A copy of *Muslim News* landed on my desk and I saw this job: chaplain to
> HM armed forces. I thought, wow, that would be interesting, and it sat on
> my desk for a couple of days. I ordered the application forms, and they
> sat on my desk for a few more days. I pushed it to one side. I went to my
> colleagues, and asked if any of them were applying. I said I thought we
> needed to get involved and think we should contribute. They all said 'No!
> We can't work for the armed forces. We just can't.' 'Why not?' I asked.
> 'Because they are killing Muslims' – the army was in Iraq and Afghanistan
> then.

Asim was convinced that he had the right experience and his colleagues'
aversion to the post only made him more determined to apply. This was
partly due a stubborn streak, he admitted, but he also felt a sense of duty
and responsibility. In his mind there was no contradiction. Muslims serving
in the armed forces needed access to spiritual care just like anyone else, and
being there to provide that role did not mean that he condoned the conflicts.

'After all,' he reasoned, 'soldiers are not given a choice. The armed forces are for the defence of Britain, for everybody who lives in this island. It's my army as well as anybody else's.'

The opposition Asim faced from his peers demonstrated why the position of Muslims within the British Army was such a contentious and politically significant matter. The personal endorsement of AFMA by Richards was proof that he was fully committed to this position, and unlike his predecessor was ready to throw his weight behind new support structures for Muslims in service. He was also more diplomatic in acknowledging the political implications of engaging young British Muslims in a war against a foe that was widely perceived to be driven by Islamist ideology. An interview in *The Muslim News* in 2009 cited Richards' attempts to repair the damage created by the prospect of a Christian army fighting the infidel within as well the 'fanatic' without.

> Britain, Richards said, had a commitment to Afghanistan and the region and all those Muslims with whom we have a natural identity, given our own core values reflect very strongly to those of Muslim faith. The army should not be perceived as the enemy force, he said. Although there is a very small number of Muslims who are doing as much damage to Muslims as anybody else, we have got together to fight that and we can succeed.[41]

Richards' remark about core values suggests a more co-ordinated and well-rehearsed approach to cultural pluralism inside the army, which is not to deny that the new leader was not genuine in his support. Needless to say, a quick check on ARRSE forum to see how news of AFMA was being received revealed business as usual. One comment read, 'Pampering the fuckers? Why? I thought we were all the same in the forces.'[42] There were several along the same lines, articulating the usual resentment against minority networks within larger organisations, such as the police force. One or two were more positive, however, like this comment that underscored the link between Muslims in the army and the perception of war work:

> The young muslim lad I had in my unit on Ops was a cracking bloke and bloody useful when trying to understand the locals and the jundies. He taught us all quite a lot about Islam and everyone was the better for it.

By the end of 2010, five years after the Imam was appointed and six since General Dannatt's controversial claims, the strategic importance of acknowledging Muslims within the British armed forces was demonstrated in Helmand Province itself. On November 16 that year Imam Hafiz gave a sermon to a multi-national congregation in the Muslim festival of Eid ul Adha in conjunction with the Imam of the local 205 Corps of the Afghan National Army (ANA). A lengthy report in the MoD's Defence News site revealed that there were 600 Muslims present, including representatives from across ISAF military forces, defence contractors and civilian workers as well as 'local Afghans'. The occasion was hailed as a reflection of 'the united relationship' between ISAF and the Afghan National Army.[43]

The report stated that 'The sight of ISAF troops and the local community joining together to celebrate their faith offered some respite for the whole camp from the difficulties being faced in Afghanistan.' Linking the timing of the occasion to the services of remembrance held to mark Armistice Day, the Imam also played his part in emphasising that Muslims were integral to the mission 'to stabilise Afghanistan'.[44]

'This mission,' he continued, 'need not be a combat one but could be a partnership of development and progress for ordinary Afghans. ISAF has again demonstrated that Islam and the West are compatible, and that Muslims are proud citizens of their countries – they fly their flags with pride and willingly serve their nations.'

Meanwhile back in London, Muslims Against Crusades had achieved notoriety by burning a model of a red poppy during the two minutes silence on Armistice Day. Holding placards that read 'Hands off Muslim Lands' and 'Islam will dominate', they had faced a counter-demonstration by members of the English Defence League (EDL).[45] The mobilisation of the EDL under the banner of fighting Islamic extremism in turn widened the political space where racism and Islamophobia were infused with militaristic expressions of patriotism, masculinity and whiteness.

Muslims on the front line

The issue of diversity reinforces the centrality of culture in the 'war on terror' as well as the importance of propaganda, providing a link between the management of information about the aims and objectives of the global counter-insurgency and the negotiation of social and cultural conflicts within civil society. These issues came to public attention briefly in 2009, when a British Muslim soldier claimed he was racially abused and physically attacked by a sergeant.[46] The incident was potentially damaging not just because it involved a senior NCO but also because the individual's ethnicity – he was a UK citizen born to parents of Pakistani origin – was directly connected to his work for the special forces in Afghanistan. His family alleged that he had been made ill by the racist attacks.[47] Unlike other employment tribunals hearing cases by minority soldiers, the hearing was held in private. The media was permitted to report the basic details of the young man's charge, but there was no discussion of his ethno-religious identity as a factor either in his ability to be a soldier or his suitability for intelligence work in Afghanistan.

Nevertheless this case is useful, despite the lack of details, because it is a reminder that the negative publicity surrounding one Muslim soldier's treatment threatens to damage the carefully constructed narrative of the valuable work performed by other British soldiers who are also Muslims. Racist treatment of Muslims inside the army would, for many observers, simply confirm the fact that the occupation of Afghanistan is part of a global war against Muslims in general, a war that includes the repression and demonisation of Muslims at home. Conversely, a positive representation of Muslim soldiers in the British armed forces can arguably reinforce Muslims' claim to belong within UK civil society as well as spinning the military project of bringing security to a country that happens to be Islamic.

The BBC, which plays a strategic role in airing UK defence and security issues, demonstrated the salience of these calculations in a report in 2011 entitled 'UK's Muslim soldiers "fighting extremists not Muslims" ' published the same day as a radio documentary, broadcast through its Asian network, called 'Muslims on the frontline'.[48] In both items, journalist Poonam Taneja interviewed a number of British Muslim servicemen and women in Afghanistan as well as British Muslim opponents of the war. Cpl Raziya Aslam, for example, a citizen of the UK whose parents migrated from Pakistan before she was born, talked enthusiastically about her work as a linguist, acting as interpreter in negotiations with villagers. 'I don't see it as a war against Islam,' she said. Pte Shehab El-Din Ahmed El-Miniawi was reportedly even more emphatic: 'My home is the UK,' he said. 'As a Muslim, that's the place I'd happily die for and kill for. That's the same way it's going to remain until my dying day.'

Another interviewee was Zeeshan Hashmi, one of the first British Muslim servicemen to be deployed to Afghanistan in 2002 and a member of the Intelligence Corps for five years. In 2006 his brother Jabron Hashmi became the first British Muslim soldier to die in Afghanistan. Zeeshan spoke of the pride his family felt when they were asked to lay the foundation stone for the National Memorial Arboretum which was opened in 2007. Since his brother's death they had received over 100 letters from well-wishers of all faith and backgrounds, which, he said, were a great source of comfort. However, he also described how 'There were certain remarks put on the internet, on a given website, certain people see my brother as a traitor because of his role as a soldier, because of his role in the armed forces, in Afghanistan.'

The premise of this media intervention repeated the contention that Muslims who joined the armed forces were expressing an unequivocal commitment to their identity as UK citizens as well as performing a strategic role in the 'battle for hearts and minds' in Helmand Province. This was in contrast to those who contested the basis of the ISAF operations in Afghanistan on the grounds that it constituted the killing of (fellow) Muslims. But what about attitudes to and treatment of Muslim soldiers inside the army? The employment tribunal mentioned earlier might have been low key and anonymous, but in this final section we consider an event that brought the issue of racism in the army right back into the limelight.

A royal scandal

In January 2009 the *News of the World* published a story based on a leaked video diary made by Prince Harry while training at Sandhurst. The paper revealed that Harry had referred to his fellow officer cadet, Ahmed Raza Khan, as 'our little Paki friend, Ahmed' and told a friend wearing a camouflaged hood that he looked like a 'raghead'.[49] When celebrities or public figures are caught being racist or anti-semitic on camera their employers are normally obliged to act swiftly to distance themselves or risk damage to their brand by association. Whether the culprit works for the BBC, a fashion house or even the government, he or she faces public shaming in the national media in a show of practised outrage that has its own momentum. Since he was a member of the royal family, the choice of words used by the prince might be thought to reflect negatively on the institution of the monarchy itself. In addition, Harry was not merely a soldier when he made the video; he was also in the process of training to become an officer. When the story broke he was working as a junior manager charged with responsibility to set an example. As well as his family, he had managed to drag his employer into the spotlight of negative publicity.

The fact that it was a uniformed prince caught uttering such casually racist terms meant that the monarchy, the government and the armed forces were obliged to take a stand on the limits of acceptable speech. In other words, the British military ethos stood in danger of being compromised if there was no official criticism of the prince's remarks. In the event, Harry's behaviour was more readily dismissed by his family as a youthful indiscretion as the incident had occurred three years earlier. The quick apology issued by St James' Palace also sought to condone the use of the term 'Paki', stressing that it was a 'nickname about a very popular member of the platoon', and 'used without malice'.[50]

By the time the video diary was leaked, Prince Harry, who had once caused a scandal by attending a fancy dress party in Nazi uniform, was already on the road to rehabilitation after his stint in Helmand Province had been revealed to the world's attendant media.[51] At least, this was the basis on which Prime Minister Gordon Brown was ready to downplay the incident. 'I think the British people are good enough to give someone who has actually been a role model for young people...the benefit of the doubt,' he said.[52] Cabinet minister John Denham gave him a qualified knuckle rap: 'This sort of language can be seen as offensive, is offensive, is gradually going out of use in our society, and he's apologised for it.' The opposition also took the opportunity to criticise Harry's use of language. From the sidelines, Tory leader David Cameron declared that it was 'completely unacceptable' and Liberal Democrat leader Nick Clegg said the comment had caused 'considerable offence'.

The *Daily Mail* was less ready to be forgiving, stating that Harry's apology was insufficient for his 'incredible crassness' especially since Khan, an award-winning cadet at Sandhurst, was by then serving in the Pakistan Army where he had a 'captain's role in the war on terror'.[53] Seen in this context, Harry's use of the racist terms 'Paki' and 'raghead' had more severe implications than a casual example of army banter. It represented an example of behaviour that could, in theory, lead to far more serious breach of the law if it was not publicly condemned. Pakistan was one of the UK's strategic allies in the global counter-insurgency and this was a potential blow for the cause of defence diplomacy, an aspect of foreign policy in which the RMAS plays a pivotal role.

The episode, trivial in some lights yet potentially explosive, can be made useful precisely because it brought all these issues together: the British military ethos, defence diplomacy, racism directed at Muslims. In the next chapter we look at the harm that racism does inside the organisation. How far have the reforms ushered in by a commitment to cultural diversity managed to create an environment where abuse and discrimination are confronted, not for reasons of political correctness but as obstacles to functional working relationships?

Part III
Racism

Image 4 Drama workshop organised by Garnett Foundation, February 2011

6
Crossing the Line

The day after the Prince Harry scandal broke was just another Monday morning at the Phase 2 training centre. It was less than six months since some of my earlier acquaintances from basic training had left their homes in Fiji or the Caribbean and they had still not joined their regimental unit, but the Royal Artillery training establishment in Salisbury Plain was a step nearer to regular army life than the regime at Pirbright had been. Tracking them down had not been easy and finding a time to talk was even harder. The course was modular which meant that everyone had different timetables and in addition the syllabus was constantly being adapted to prepare soldiers for Afghanistan.

'We used to train them in basic skills,' the officer in charge of the programme told me. 'But with the current operations, the commanding officers out there in the field request all soldiers to be able to drive and communicate by radio.' Over a year later the centre would be using the Apple iPad in an effort to tailor their teaching methods not just to the contingencies of war but also to the expectations and abilities of their recruits.[1] Incorporating the latest digital technology meant that instructors were often learning at the same rate as their trainees who meanwhile had been upgraded to the 'iPod generation'.[2] On this particular day in 2009, a fair number of staff seemed to be off sick or on leave and it took a while to locate suitable interviewees. I was invited to wait in the senior NCOs' office and this gave me the opportunity to ask how they had handled the media attention.

'We got emails from the top stating our equality and diversity policies, telling us what to say,' said one of the instructors. He explained that when they did the induction talks they always 'made a thing' of equality and diversity – racism, sexism and bullying. He was not aware that Harry's incriminating video was on YouTube, but after I mentioned it he surreptitiously viewed the clip on his phone and showed it to the others.

There was a radio on in the background and as I sat drinking my tea it dawned on me that between the music tracks we were listening to Jeremy Vine's BBC Radio Two phone-in. The topic was the psychological condition

149

known as combat stress. Men were ringing in one after the other, speaking of the after-effects of their 'confirmed kills', most of which took place during the Falklands war.[3] They spoke of their difficulties in returning to 'normal life', describing how certain smells could trigger the memories. One revealed he had 27 'kills'. Another was traumatised by his experiences in Iraq. All this was interspersed with vapid pop music and there was no comment from the three men sitting at their computers, one of whom was working his way through a large jam sandwich. Earlier he had asked me if I was planning to go to Afghanistan to interview soldiers, and I had told him that I hoped to talk to them after they got back. 'Probably safer!' he had replied. I wondered if he was listening to the phone-in.

'Lady Madonna' played in the background, and then someone rang in to say he had 70 confirmed 'kills'. 'I took one guy out with a knife. I was expected to get on with my life after that.'

A welcome distraction was provided by one of the sergeants attempting to contact a soldier who had failed to report to his unit after finishing his Phase 2 training. This was a window to another dimension of military employment: the difficulty of leaving when you want to get out. This particular man had been AWOL (Absent without Leave) for five weeks, which meant there was a warrant out for his arrest. His parents had confirmed that there was no compassionate reason for his absence and he was rejecting calls from anyone identifiably military. By using someone else's mobile, the Sergeant managed to reach him in an effort to persuade him to report to his unit. He reasoned that if the police found him he would be arrested, so it would be better to go and own up, whatever his difficulties. Evidently the young man was sticking to a story of a car accident and problems with insurance.

The Sergeant was not particularly sympathetic, but, as he explained when he finished the call, he was trying to help him see that he was putting himself in greater danger by staying away. Although this incident did not involve a Commonwealth soldier, it flagged up the conditions of employment in the armed forces that made it very different from other kinds of jobs. One of these was the difficulty of quitting, especially in the first four years. The Prince Harry scandal had drawn attention to the army's reputation for racial harassment and bullying at the same time as allowing the MoD to assert a policy of 'zero tolerance'. A decade earlier, in 1998, the new recruitment poster aimed at ethnic minorities had promised that the army was becoming 'a better place for ethnic minorities'. The intake of thousands of Commonwealth soldiers had provided the organisation with ample opportunity to put reforms into practice. Was it really a better place, and how would anyone know? This chapter recounts some of the multiple ways that racism is both perceived and experienced inside a military institution.

The way they live

I spotted Mission on my way through the building as he was on a break from his course in signalling. We first met on his very first day of training, barely a week out of Fiji and not yet in uniform, and I had talked to him several times since then. It was his suggestion that I call him Mission instead of his real name, and I assumed that it reflected his identity as a Seventh Day Adventist which was clearly very important to him. In this new environment we both responded to seeing a recognisable face and I was able to grab him for a quick chat. As we sat down at the long polished table under the gaze of regimental portraits, I couldn't resist bringing up the subject of the Prince Harry scandal.

'Most people here think he's done nothing wrong,' he replied gloomily. I asked him whether life had been any different at Pirbright.

'Many British lads, where there were arguments and disagreements they would normally use "black bastard"....' He shrugged his shoulders and added,

> When we complained they ignored us. Most of us had education and qualifications, compared to British lads. There are lots of school drop outs. They got bored of education, they joined the army because there were no other options. That's one of the main reasons they create problems at Pirbright.

The revelations in Prince Harry's video the previous day had offered the army the chance to announce that it took all allegations of inappropriate behaviour 'very seriously'.[4] However, some voices were equally quick to excuse Harry's choice of words on the grounds that soldiers relied on particular forms of ritual insults, often referred to as banter, in the face of uniquely stressful working conditions. One senior NCO interviewed by the *Guardian* explained that 'Within the armed forces, because we are dealing with a lot emotionally – seeing your friends killed, people losing body parts – we take things more lightly and you can handle a bit of flak about where you come from or what colour you are.'[5]

This point brings us back to the particular nature of military culture, implying that it is difficult to assess the significance of banter without taking into account the conditions in which soldiers are required to work. As we saw in Chapter 4, one of the reasons why military culture differs from civilian culture is that the armed services exist to deal with the control and use of physical force.[6] Anthropologist Donna Winslow, who has studied military culture in different settings, underlines the fact that the organisation requires its employees to be warriors who can kill and be killed while operating in a very irrational environment. Since combat is its *raison d'etre*, she writes, it is essential that 'the mechanisms designed to produce order, such as hierarchy and discipline, are effective in the fragmentary, fluctuating and fluid environment that characterizes (the fog of) war'.[7] Those attempting to analyse the internal culture of the organisation must be alert to the interplay between order and chaos at every level. According to Winslow, bullying, initiation rituals and skiving, while being routine activities in other authoritarian organisations such as the police, perform a particular role in the army as a reaction to internal disciplinary codes, strict hierarchies and the demands of battle-skill training.[8]

Accepting that military culture has its own standards and codes of behaviour appropriate for the work that soldiers are required to do presents obstacles in adjudicating how far 'a bit of flak' can go. There are also cultural dimensions that have implications for soldiers who are not habituated to the nuances of local speech and who have to learn to confront racist and sexist banter almost as a new language.[9] The cultural guidance document issued in 2008 warned that the British sense of humour is 'complicated'. The British have a habit 'of laughing at just about anything and anyone, especially themselves and each other, however strange or insensitive this may seem'.[10] Under the heading, 'What is critical? (What may cause tension and misunderstanding)' the guide pointed out: 'The British are generally just as happy to laugh *at* someone as laugh *with* someone. Sometimes this does appear disrespectful but is usually not meant to be (emphasis in original)'. And the practice of 'friendly "banter" or "teasing" is a great military tradition'.[11]

According to the same briefing paper on cultural awareness, banter is 'part of our culture, it helps to bond us as soldiers and is a way of hardening ourselves to the tough job that we do'. In a section entitled 'What we have in common', the advice continues, however, 'we have all experienced a moment when it has gone too far...Most of us will not accept people insulting our families or things that we hold dear, and for some this is an especially serious issue.' While soldiers are expected to engage in banter as part of their job, deciding where the line falls between playful speech and gratuitous insult is a matter of interpretation. The notes suggest that 'When someone has gone too far with banter the first thing they lose is respect.'

In 1999 the Macpherson Report had defined institutional racism as 'the collective failure of an organisation to provide an appropriate and professional service to people because of their colour, culture, or ethnic origin [which] can be seen or detected in processes, attitudes and behaviour which amount to discrimination through unwitting prejudice, ignorance, thoughtlessness and racist stereotyping which disadvantage minority ethnic people'.[12] If abusive practices considered unacceptable in civilian life were likely to be condoned within the army on the grounds that they had different meanings, then this raised the question, what exactly was zero tolerance? The British sense of humour may well be culturally distinct from that of many ethnic groups joining the army, but this made it all the harder to distinguish between genuine forms of harassment and the racist 'processes, attitudes and behaviour' that soldiers might encounter on a daily basis.

Mission had originally been hoping for a job in education or administration, having been a teacher back in Fiji. Now he was planning to transfer to the Royal Military Police (RMP) because he considered himself 'very disciplined'.

'Take the core values,' he continued. 'From what I've seen, most of British citizens – the way they live – they don't have those values. We do have values, customs, we brought them along with us.'

I asked him for an example.

> Some lads don't have respect. They are very fast at pointing out our weaknesses. When we tell them something good for their own benefit they never listen, they ignore us. As a result we are more separate, most of us will say no, but the reality is that the separation is always there.
>
> In the barracks they never listen. They say 'that's rubbish, bullshit', they never listen. For us, coming to the big world, there must be something we want to take back home. We bring morals with us.

Mission revealed that the Pirbright training staff had warned them that UK culture was 'broken'. 'It's because of human rights,' he said. 'We were warned: don't expect things to be like they are in your home countries.'

He was finding solace in the company of fellow Fijians in the evenings but he knew that they were resented for keeping to themselves. However, he had observed that 'One good thing about Brits is that they come straight to us and tell us. They want to sort things out. But with Fijians – big differences don't get sorted out. They hide their feelings.'

Pulling their socks up

The age differential and the increased freedom at weekends were proving a problem for Tom as well. Like Mission he was from Fiji, but he had preferred life in Pirbright since in the new establishment he had the ill fortune to have been placed in a troop of teenagers. When we met a few weeks earlier he had expressed his annoyance at the regular 'beasting' his troop was receiving as a result of the misdemeanours of a few individuals. He had described how 'two young English kids' had gone to Salisbury at the weekend and got drunk. When they returned to camp, one boy had attacked another with an iron bar, he said, giving graphic details of their state of inebriation.

It was common knowledge that British Army policy did not permit or tolerate physical violence as a means of discipline or punishment, under any circumstances, yet beasting was a familiar term, widely used to cover a range of disciplinary measures and punishment rituals metered out by anyone of superior rank to an individual or group.[13] As in Tom's example of collective punishment, beasting also referred to methods used by instructors to reinforce discipline within a group by holding all members responsible for one person's failure, a practice that was also not officially sanctioned. His entire section of eight men was ordered to submit to extra room inspections, but worse still, to be on parade every hour, throughout the afternoon. This was not the first time, and it was really making it harder for the rest who were understandably resentful. 'The kids can't pull their socks up,' he said, exasperated.

A few weeks later, he seemed a lot more cheerful but it was still hard to sustain a conversation. By then I had discovered that talking to army recruits over a period of time was an exercise of diminishing value. The initial shyness combined with a sense of optimism was replaced by a more resigned attitude, suggesting that it was getting harder and harder to convey to a civilian what army life was like. Tom had already been away from home for six months although he had spent Christmas on an army base in Germany with his brother, also a soldier. All he would say was that 'It was cold, and they didn't go out much.'

The group punishments had also stopped but 'the same kids are being a problem', he reported. Now the worst thing was the food and having to eat the same bland things every day.

I asked him about reaction to the Prince Harry incident and he replied that he had talked to a friend outside the army who had been far more shocked than anyone inside. This led to a discussion of British attitudes and incidents of name-calling by fellow recruits that he had personally experienced.

'I was out in a pub in Salisbury and a lad from the troop came over and said, "Are you black or white – what are you?" I said, "Are you trying to be racist?"'

He shook his head. 'Individuals give you problems.'

Unlike Mission, Tom had become more sociable and was able to make friends, partly through trips to Salisbury at weekends. 'It has become like a home town,' he said. By now we had been joined by Ash, also from Fiji, who was very quiet. I asked them about the Fijians' reputation for drinking beer. They both grinned, 'Fijians love to drink! It's a matter of controlling ourselves when we are drunk though.'

Ash remarked that a civilian had said to him in a pub, 'Are you Fijian? You people like your beers!'

The suggestion that Fijians had acquired a reputation that matched their UK peers reminded me of a story that I had heard in the garrison town of Catterick. Some well-known troublemakers in nearby Darlington, a town notorious for brawls between soldiers and locals, had attacked a group of off-duty Fijians on a Saturday night. This was unfortunate for two reasons. First, because they didn't stand a chance against the soldiers, and second, because the incident was recorded on CCTV. The local police, according to my reliable source, were grateful not to have to intervene and no arrests were made.

Fellow human beings

Michael had just passed his driving test that morning, and was looking suitably cheerful. He was from St Vincent, and we had met several times before. I asked him about the Harry thing. 'It's not really a big deal,' he said noncommittally.

> Lots of people get called that. If the guy don't like it, he should have reported it. If he didn't then he can't complain. It's made political because he's a royal.

We were discussing the issue of politics and the media when Ernest entered the room. He was from Ghana, and although subdued at first he opened up quickly, particularly when we began to talk about racism.

> The army's all right for me. You don't expect them to know your culture – it's you who are in a new world. Some have not travelled out of the country before. People say: you are here now.
> I just overlook some things. I am not here to argue about culture. Sometimes it hurts though. Like when someone younger than you swears at you.

As the conversation moved on to the question of cultural differences, both men began to laugh about the issues posed by showering together.
'To us Ghanaians it's normal,' said Ernest, 'especially when you are in a hurry.'
Michael replied, 'For us, if two guys are in the shower together we think they must be gay.'
'We have to educate each other,' they agreed, admitting that there were often fights. 'Because some people are racist.'
Ernest said he was used to racist abuse. 'Pirbright, at first, was a problem. Back on the streets of London it was like that [too]. You can't change the person. I try to see the distance. It's not anything you can report – otherwise people would not like you.'
He was reflexive about his colleagues' general ignorance and lack of imagination.

> It's not bullying exactly. More like, do you have lights in your country? Do you have ambulances? For example, I was showing pictures of Ghana and someone said 'is it true that you sleep on trees?'
> I was not that offended. But if you said, 'Fuck off, go back to your tree', I would be offended.
> They say 'Africa' – But I don't say 'Europe'. They don't know any countries. They say things like, 'are you African or Ghanaian?'

You have to learn how to talk to them as fellow human beings. If they are speaking the way you don't like, you have to calm them down. It's wrong to show how tough you are.

He described how he had learned this recently when a fellow recruit came up to him in a pub and tried to start a fight. He had told him to calm down and refused to go along with it, and the next day the guy had apologised.

Ernest's readiness to make a distinction between bullying and the effects of what Macpherson might have included as 'unwitting prejudice, ignorance, thoughtlessness and racist stereotyping' stemmed partly from the fact that he had not encountered any disadvantages or discrimination as a result of his fellow recruits' behaviour, obnoxious as it was. Since he was only in Phase 2 of his training and was not yet placed within his unit, his relationship with most of his peers was temporary, but at the same time he was clearly learning tactics that would stand him in good stead when he moved to a more permanent home in his regiment. But what if he had found it unacceptable to live with those who insulted and threatened him? The earliest he would be able to leave by legal right would be four years and three months after he enlisted, and even then he would have been required to give a year's notice in writing.

Signing off

'Everyone has an ulterior motive for joining the army,' said Frank, a captain from South Africa. 'The motivation is to have a better life – not a sense of duty towards Britain. It's a job!'

I had been in the RLC base for two hours and had already learned a great deal about life in the unit. The captain's forthright opinion was not exactly a revelation since it was hardly controversial and I had heard variations many times before. His reason for stating it so baldly was a sense of irritation that Commonwealth soldiers were often viewed as having 'only' joined to get citizenship. Twelve months' notice is required before leaving, a process known as 'signing off'. I had just been finding out that once it is known that an individual has made this decision, it was likely that they would be treated differently.

Rob had served for seven years and had recently signed off after completing a two-year Masters course, paid for by the army, a fact which had caused some resentment. He did not appear to be bothered as he had already secured a job as a manager working for a large supermarket chain, claiming that he had always planned to do four years and then go back to being 'a civvy'. Although he had no intention of relinquishing his South African citizenship, he admitted to having joined in order to get a British passport. 'We all know of soldiers who've joined to do nothing for four years,' he observed.

'There's a split between them and the Commonwealth who have joined and are keen.'

A fellow South African, Chris, who was a lance corporal, agreed that it was very hard to get kicked out of the army in four years, 'One thing I can say: a lot of people in the army don't like it if you get citizenship! People see it as taking advantage. I see it all the time.'

He had signed off after returning from Afghanistan, giving the impression that his job had not been good for his marriage. 'I think Commonwealth who have signed off, those guys can be picked on. The chain of command will give them extra [jobs].'

On that particular day I also learnt more about people absconding on the grounds that they were being bullied. The individuals in question were not Commonwealth soldiers but two 22-year-old men from South Wales, whose reasons for fleeing had been widely reported in the media.[14] The unit welfare officer, who was from the same part of the country, had just returned from visiting them, having spent three hours trying to persuade them to return. He tried to reassure them that the only penalty would be having their leave docked and that the people responsible for bullying would be moved away. But it was almost lunchtime and there was no sign that the young men had turned up. In the event, they went into hiding and were finally arrested a month later. At that point they were handed over to the RMP while their case was investigated. Their allegations of bullying were extremely serious and warranted full investigation. As with most instances, however, the results were never reported so it was impossible to find out what happened, either to the victims or the alleged culprits. But, unlike the incident with the young man who dropped out after his 'car accident', the case attracted enormous media coverage as well as underlining the exceptional conditions of military employment.

In 2007 a BBC Panorama programme investigated claims that more than a thousand soldiers were permanently missing, some of them since 2001, and that the number of those temporarily AWOL was more than double this figure. Research indicated that the trauma of serving in Iraq was contributing to current rates of desertion, coupled with inadequate mental healthcare on return. The MoD had rejected these claims, issuing a statement that denied that operations in Iraq were having discernible impact on the overall rate. In fact, they claimed that the number of new AWOL cases had declined over the past two years. 'In 2006, the military had its lowest number of AWOL cases for seven years.'[15]

The reasons why soldiers absconded were primarily family and relationship difficulties, according to the official response. The figures were also higher because many AWOL cases involved repeated incidents by the same people. The army had insisted that it had effective measures for supporting and dealing with such individuals, including adequate mental health provision and a confidential advice line. In 2010, however, figures obtained from the MoD showed that there were more than 2,000 cases of soldiers going absent without leave in 2009, with 17,470 incidents recorded since the Iraq invasion in 2003.[16] But it was the situation of 16- to 17-year-olds that was the most shocking. Not only was Britain the only European country to recruit into the regular army at 16, but those under 18 had no right to discharge (after the first six months) until turning 22, relying on the discretion of commanding officers to get a discharge.[17] In December 2010, five under-18-year-olds were serving sentences in the Military Corrective Training Centre, Colchester, for having gone absent without leave.[18] As a result of the campaign, the ability to be discharged was made a right, up to the age of 18, 'subject to an appropriate period of consideration or cooling off'.[19]

It was curious, as I began my interviews with soldiers embedded in their units, to find that the main topic of conversation was either about absconding or the penalties associated with leaving the army with what some considered to be indecent haste – especially if their motives for joining in the first place were judged to be questionable. As the day wore on, I became acquainted with the tedium associated with working full-time in any institution, compounded by the rigid disciplinary structure and authoritarianism associated with military life. The following discussion is worth recalling in some detail, not because it is particularly shocking in its revelations, but because it provides an insight into an individual's perception of unfair treatment on the basis of ethnic and national identity. Hearing one person's grounds for unhappiness does not mean that it provides an index of all Commonwealth soldiers' experience. The example is useful for two main reasons. First, it illustrates the way in which problems that appear not to be particularly significant in themselves can lead to an accumulated sense of grievance which then results in feelings of victimisation, either by peers or by someone of superior rank. Second, it suggests that the language of cultural awareness and cultural diversity, adapted as a vehicle for promoting forms of military multiculture, neither negated nor diminished levels of racism inside the organisation.

Better you leave the army

Kwaku, who was originally from Ghana, came to see me on his own in a break between group interviews. He was 23 years old and had joined the army in 2005 at the suggestion of a cousin who had since left. He was a driver in the RLC and lived in married quarters locally with his wife, a fellow Ghanaian who worked in a local hotel as a cleaner and receptionist. As we began to talk, I asked him what had motivated him to join.

'A guaranteed job, a good career...' he replied, exuding a sense of grievance. 'And how is it?' I asked.

'I won't say I'm loving it at the moment,' he began. He seemed reluctant to continue, but when I encouraged him to elaborate he admitted, 'It's lots of things, like discrimination – it's all over. The army is all right, but some people in it is making it difficult.... like corporals, the people you work with.'

Clearly something serious had happened fairly recently as he had been moved from one squadron to another on the same base. At this particular camp there was a high proportion of Commonwealth soldiers.

Kwaku had not yet signed off but he was beginning to think about it. He was despondent after failing to improve his personal rating score, despite going to Afghanistan and working hard for promotion, and he was convinced that racism was the reason why he was continually overlooked.

Sometimes even if you come to work, and you are going to work hard, people don't see it. Some people stay in the rest rooms, chill out, have brew, they will get promoted. But you, working so hard, there is no way you're going to get it.

If I work I deserve something... When I came back from Afghan I nearly signed off, but I was waiting to see maybe there'll be changes. At the moment I am not seeing anything.

Kwaku attributed his lack of promotion to racism and a generally negative attitude towards Commonwealth soldiers. 'People don't want us to progress,' he said. 'We all came in the army to work hard and get promotion so that our pay will be increased. But it seems like people are coming straight from training to overtake you. They get promotion and just go, and you still be where you are.'

He was convinced that no one would take him seriously if he complained, and to make matters worse he felt he was being singled out by a corporal.

I was late at work for just three minutes. They put me on three months warning order. I've been on that twice. Sometimes we do silly, silly mistakes, but a three months warning order?

Kwaku had clearly fallen foul of the disciplinary codes and this had been marked on his record. He then described an incident which seemed remarkably petty at first but which escalated into something more serious.

I had this problem with a corporal, he was shouting on me and I didn't like it. He saw me in number two's, without a belt. I was having the belt in my hand to make it a bit tighter. He was like, 'why is your belt not on? ' I said, 'I am making it a bit tighter'. He was like, 'you should have done that in your room, before,' and I was like, 'yeah I know that, but when I was walking I thought it was a bit loose and I was trying to make it tighter.' He was like, 'no we can't take this in the British Army, blah blah blah. You Commonwealth soldiers are taking the piss!'

I was like, 'excuse me?' He was just shouting in front of my face. What happened was, he asked me, 'who is your sergeant major?' I told him the name. He went to him and told him a different story and found a witness about 100 metres from where we had that talk... The witness said he heard everything. I was like, 100 metres away, how could he hear? They wanted me to sign a charge form, but I am not at fault. I wouldn't sign it, so they take me to the OC and he said, 'You again!'

Because people keep reporting... because I was late... they [already] put [me] on a three month warning.

This time the corporal was trying to tell the OC that I was insulting him. The OC told me, 'If you do that again I will send you back to your country.'

I was like, 'The army didn't bring me to this country! I came by myself.'

'You see,' Kwaku explained, 'things like this happen but wherever you take it [to the authorities] you won't win your case. You just have to leave it. There is no point. Sometimes you just have to take it, keep quiet.'

I was curious to know whether he felt that once you are aware of such attitudes you become more sensitive to racism across the organisation.

'Yes,' he replied. 'When I joined first, I didn't know about those things. But as time went on, I know about discrimination. I tell you ma'am, 20 per cent of the British Army are ok with Commonwealth soldiers. Eighty per cent are not.'

'What makes you think that?' I asked. Again he answered with an anecdote drawn from his personal experience, although this time it involved some of his friends too.

Sometimes if you are working with somebody, it's the way a person talks to you. It's like talking to a mad person or someone he don't even care about. For instance, a mate – he was having this bottle of drink in his hands, African drink like Guinness, sweet, but not alcohol. Somebody saw him holding that bottle and was following him. He drove to my house, and the guy was still following him.

It turned out that the man who followed his friend all the way to his house was a Lance Corporal (a junior NCO) who suspected him of driving with alcohol. He had insisted on seeing the bottle and tasting the drink. The next day, the LCpl had approached the friend, who was with Kwaku and a couple of other African soldiers, and told him he was lucky that it wasn't alcohol, or else he would have been charged. When someone asked why he had followed them all the way to their house, the LCpl had apparently answered, 'We need to set our eyes on you black guys.'

Kwaku was clearly disgusted, and I would hear the same story from one of the other witnesses later in the day, without solicitation. He said, resignedly,

> You can't win the case. Better you leave the army. That's why too many Commonwealth soldiers leave the army, because the way we were told about the army is not the way. We get inside... it's the opposite way. Sometimes people, they just think we've got no sense to do anything.

I asked about the citizenship issue, and he had another example of being insulted by a British soldier who had said, 'why are "you people" here? You are just here for the passport.'

He recounted how he had told the man that it was good to have a passport if you were living in someone else's country, but that was not the point.

> We are here to get money. That why we are all here. I can tell you we've got white people in our country working as well and we don't ask them, 'why are you here?'

Kwaku described the rest of the conversation in some detail. He was genuinely hurt by the individual being so ready to label all black people as criminals. He had tried to remonstrate by explaining that Commonwealth soldiers had only joined the army because British people didn't want to.

> 'That's why we are doing it, we are doing you a favour,' that's what I told him. 'We are doing you a favour!'
> He said, 'we don't need any favours, we want you out of this country because you've been doing all the criminal things in this country, you've been doing fraud, you've been killing people in London, it's always black people killing people.'

One reason Kwaku felt so bitterly about this particular exchange was that the man in question was one of the few British colleagues that he used to get on with. He was disappointed at his response and had told him,

> It's not the end of the world, maybe one day you'll be in my country.
> 'I'll never come to a poor country, to a country that's got nothing, that always begs for money,' he said.
> I was like, 'all right, just leave it,' that was it, I couldn't speak any more.
> Since then I talk to him but there's a gap. You can't even trust the people you are working with... 'cos you don't know if that person likes you or hates you. Even if you go to the cookhouse to eat and you see Commonwealth soldiers here and British people here, or if you go on exercise, it's like Commonwealth soldiers here and British here. It's not supposed

to be like that. I asked somebody, why it is always like that? That person [a white British] told me, "you can never mix water with petrol. If you mix it, no matter how much you mix it, it will still separate." '

'Why are we in the army then?' asked Kwaku, exasperated. He had picked up his car keys by then and was getting ready to go on to his next task. 'It's better we all leave. That's why people just leave. Some of my mates just call me in London, [saying] they want to join and I tell them no. Just leave it because I am coming out very soon.'

Flipping the chart

Ampah, who was also Ghanaian, was scathing in his opinion of army equality policy. 'The army could do so much better by investing in diversity, by educating soldiers. It should be part of army structure where you get like ... in MATTS training.'

MATTs, short for Military Annual Training Tests, are forms of continuous assessment covering a range of different subjects, introduced in 2006. Ampah was referring to MATT 6, which tests knowledge of internal policies on bullying and harassment as part of the Law of Armed Training (LOAC) syllabus.[20] It is an annual requirement based around understanding of the Values and Standards.

'Last year,' he went on, 'the instructor was doing it without paying attention. He was just flipping the chart, giving the impression that it was not a necessary thing for soldiers to go through. "Don't do this, don't do that".'

Brian, who was from Jamaica, had served in the Jamaican Defence Force for 10 years before joining the British Army in 2003. He had originally wanted to do air traffic control in the RAF but had not met the residency requirement for that particular job. Now he was in the RLC. He gave an example from his experience:

> I was in Iraq. It's a general conception you are not British, they think of you in a certain way, especially if you are coloured. I was on MATTs training and ... the sergeant was delivering a lesson on hygiene and he had made a statement – he was talking about diarrhoea and he said, 'that's why you mustn't accept food from those niggers.' I didn't even notice.
>
> I was called back and he apologised. I was the only black person there and he thought I was offended. After that I went into the diversity part of the lesson, taken by an officer. She asked this question and [this time] I was really offended.
>
> 'What do you call blacks? she was asking, 'or homosexuals – gays and lesbians?' The guys were saying what they were calling them – rats or whatever.

Then she said, 'what do you call straight white guys?'...they said, 'mates, brothers.' So I said, 'what about straight black guys? Are they classed with homosexuals?'

At this, one of the other people sitting round the table interrupted.

'Are you saying there's something wrong to be homosexual?' Penny, a captain who was working as an exchange officer from New Zealand, was very quick to question the points that the soldiers were making.

'No,' said Brian patiently. 'I am saying blacks were classed with homosexuals and the guys were calling them names. I was trying to make a point about...'

Penny wasn't having it. 'I can see where she was coming from', she interrupted. 'Those are minorities within the army. It was not anything racist, though she made the point poorly.'

This was a mixed group of men and women from Fiji, Hong Kong, Jamaica, Sierra Leone and Ghana who were mostly in the RLC. It had begun as an interview with me asking the questions but quickly evolved into an animated discussion in which most of the participants had an axe to grind. Some had been injured in the course of training or duty and were either waiting to hear about their future in the army or had already decided to leave. Those who had signed off were experiencing a sense of victimisation as a result. The presence of Penny in the room had an interesting effect. She too was a Commonwealth soldier who also admitted to being treated as a foreigner by her peers, but as a commissioned officer she was superior in rank and felt a responsibility to correct, advise and challenge the others round the table. Normally I would talk to groups in the same rank so the question of deference or reticence would not arise.

Ampah was saying that he thought the training was more serious in Pirbright.

> I took it in more. Colleagues around me took it more seriously. Now in the field army, it's not that deep when it comes to diversity. Hopefully more and more Commonwealth guys are coming. How many times have we been having diversity days? I don't think that's good enough.
>
> I [would] like for them to have actual lessons, from senior ranks to junior ranks. Everyone should get it explained, how to deal with issues likes this.

The meeting was taking place just a few weeks after the Prince Harry video leak and I couldn't resist asking whether people talked much about it at the time. They clearly hadn't.

'We tend to hold royals in respect as this is the Queen's army,' Ampah went on. 'It's not really our business. My thought is that we need education and to change behaviour patterns.'

Brian disagreed: 'I don't think that will help one bit. As soon as we finish in this room we tend to go back to same old ways. I said "we" as I am not going to say "whites" or "blacks". We are human beings, no matter how we go back to diversity training. As I said, if you go back to [some of] the rest rooms you see whites and blacks.' He gestured to indicate the degree of segregation.

Brian had been posted to the unit as a lance corporal and he had just described how, when he went on the course, he was told by the staff sergeant:

> Another one! I hope you are not like so and so who was from [somewhere in] Africa.
>
> He started to stereotype me just then. For me within the British Army, as far as I am concerned, we are human beings. We are all God's people, the same blood runs through the veins. I am not going to let somebody step on me.

It's how they think

Time and time again I heard crude generalisations from ordinary soldiers and NCOs as well as officers. Some stayed with me, like the young English woman, for instance, who said with a toss of her head, 'the Jamaicans only join to get passports!' when I told her that I was researching Commonwealth soldiers. The Corporal in the training centre who assured me it was harder for Commonwealth recruits as they tend to be laid back and don't want to exert themselves in training.

'They give up very easily,' he said cheerfully as we sat chatting during a tea break. When I mentioned that the OPT was about to return to Jamaica to select more recruits, he laughed good-naturedly, 'Another laid-back race!' Over in the corner a member of the teaching staff was ironing, dressed in a tunic and a pair of boxer shorts, while a female instructor was studying her computer screen. The Corporal's views on women were no less perceptive: 'Females are better in classroom and on the drill square,' he said in a matter of fact tone. 'They're not so good at shooting and PT.'

A few weeks later I watched a platoon of young women preparing to practise their night firing on the outdoor range. One of the instructors came over to talk to me and I was grateful to have company as the recruits had gone forward to their firing positions, leaving me standing on my own. It was cold and dank, although it was only just gone 3 pm. The young man informed me that when the platoon did their practice later that evening, they would be tested without their knowledge. 'Some of them will pass easily and be told that they don't have to do it again. Some won't,' he said. He volunteered the information that the ones from the Caribbean, particularly St Lucia, St Vincent and Antigua, were liable to fail. I asked him why he thought that was the case. 'They can't retain information,' he explained, 'and they blink a lot, and can't get in the right position. They can't aim straight, and have to be given more time.'

I asked him to describe any other differences he had observed and he was more than willing to oblige. 'I've found that they are often very intelligent in things like Home Economics and can talk in a lot of detail, a lot of detail,' he repeated. 'But when it comes to shooting they are slower to pick things up.'

I was interested in the Corporal's own background and he volunteered the information that he was from Burnley, and that he was 'brought up racial'. When he first joined, his section commander was Jamaican and he had found that very difficult. But, he assured me, he had quickly got used to mixing with different kinds of people and racism was no longer an issue for him.

When I met Carla, the young Jamaican woman in the RLC who was temporarily seconded to the DART team, I asked her whether she had come across instructors with set preconceptions about people's abilities, based on nationality and gender. Was she familiar, for example, with the theory that people from the Caribbean were not able to shoot as well as Brits? I told her a few of the things I had been hearing.

She reacted immediately, as though she had heard it all a million times.

Those are generalisations, of course, but it's about the difference in learning and training. Most kids here in the UK have video games or go to arcades. When we were growing up we didn't have arcades.

It's the same with swimming too. It's not part of our school curriculum. We went to the beach on occasions, but they always call you back and tell you not to let the water go over the knee. We were over-protected. So it's not necessarily true [that we can't learn quickly] but it's how they think.

Yap, yap, yap

Tavi had begun in a more restrained fashion, complaining about the stigma attached to being a Fijian, 'that we drink too much, abuse our women. This has to change,' he announced. 'I am a married man, but I'm going through separation.' His wife was also a soldier in the same squadron, and they had two children.

'I don't drink! And it was always there in Phase 1. We were branded as alcoholic.'

We had been sitting in the community centre for a while, and the group seemed to be enjoying a break from routine and the chance to get things off their chests. They were in the RLC, employed as cooks or suppliers, and most of them had joined in 2002. It was a Wednesday afternoon and we were in the middle of the English countryside. Grilling weary and, frankly, bored soldiers about their experience of being minorities was bound to lead to some negative comments.

Tavi could barely hide his disgust about what had happened to the British Army. 'In the Fijian army you need a high calibre of fitness and mentality,' he said scornfully, 'They break you. Here it's all this, "yap yap yap", it's nothing, a piece of piss.'

He pointed to his head. 'It's all up in here.'

But the prospect of 'human rights culture' spoiling the army, making it 'soft', was a theme I was to hear countless times. Some explained that they had been tipped off about 'broken Britain' from their UK instructors when they started training. Sometimes it was a result of seeing teenage British kids treated differently from how they remembered their own early days in uniform, or a perception of how the training regime had been amended to suit the shortcomings of a new generation.

'If they made the army how it was,' went on Tavi, who had been to Iraq three times and to Afghanistan once, 'the British would all sign off. It's the British government's fault. They make the policies, bringing in human rights and all that. Equal opportunities. It doesn't work.'

Just before this outburst, he had asked me: 'Excuse me – this research, is it for own benefit? It's OK thinking about it, but if the book doesn't change anything there's no point.'

John, from Malawi, was training to be a PT instructor. In 2005 he had originally applied to join the Army Air Corps, but when he turned up for his Phase 1 training they told him that he was not eligible because of his Commonwealth background. The AAC was one area that needed full security clearance, requiring an applicant to be resident in the UK for up to five years before enlistment. The recruiting office in Scotland where he was processed had not known the rules, so the mistake was not his alone. One option was to join the Infantry instead, but he was not interested.

Now he was planning to write his own book. When I answered Tavi's question about my research, John was receptive. 'I am interested in talking...as long as it benefits us. I am trying to write "My life in the army",' he told us. 'I would love to publish in future time. What happened to me, innit.'

It turned out that this was the first time any of them had been interviewed or asked for their opinions. Since I was interested in their experiences as minorities we had quickly got on to the subject of differential treatment.

The issue that exercised John was that levels of fitness really varied with age.

A lot of Commonwealth join when they are older. When they get injured, they are already 30–31. They might get a back injury 'cos their bones are old – over 27 you will get injuries, like back problems. As soon as they know you're injured, that's you. That's the only problem. I work in the gym. I don't complain if people are injured. I will tell him to do it, 'cos it's the army but at that age they should think about it.

There was a consensus that people with injuries were not treated well, that they were encouraged to sign off so they didn't have to be given medical discharge. 'They treat you bad for you to give up,' they said.

After Tavi's outburst at the way Fijians were frequently stigmatised he was prepared to make his own claims about his compatriots.

> We don't complain about anything. As long as we have the four walls and a ceiling and food. If we have a good leader, we respect them and everything will go smooth. Once he doesn't treat us right...we wouldn't care whether he's a leader or not, we wouldn't follow him to battle. I would like to write about that. We look for that! Fijians look at the head.

His forthright opinions on leadership were represented in the cultural guidance notes under the heading, 'what is hidden?'

> Fijians especially respect strong leaders and are often fine judges of leadership qualities. Because of this they respond well to leaders who are seen to have the welfare of their charges at heart and are ready to listen to soldiers' concerns. Weak leadership, especially inconsistency, aloofness or lack of good character, may result in dissension and poor morale.[21]

In an earlier session with a different group we had discussed the cultural guidance notes and I had shown them a copy I happened to have with me. Mawuli was from Ghana, and had joined in 2005. He took a cursory look and said dismissively,

> When you are coming here you are given a paper. But some of these things are more theoretical than practical. At least in the paperwork. On the ground it's not happening. Just like you are learning to drive but when you pass your test you realise that a lot of people do practical advice not theoretical and vice versa. Lot of policies, they cover their back, whatever, but practically it doesn't happen.

He was emphatic that their superiors would get more work out of them if they showed more respect and appreciation for their efforts. He was also philosophical about the prejudice they regularly encountered, claiming that racism or 'imbalance of treatment' is natural. 'For instance,' he said,

> Back home where I come from, we are all Ghanaians but we got tribes. If one tribe is in power, like a president, you find out that all the people from that tribe is getting favoured, put in high positions, what have you. Even though we are from the same country, the same motherland. You still get that sort of favour, that racism.

No matter how you look at it, even the so-called British here. You say, you're Scouse, you from Scottish, you from Ireland, you do that. Me personally, I am not too much bothered, but if you treat me with respect, if you talk to me with respect and say: this is the army so if you are not happy, sign off, I am more than happy to say at the end of the day, I do understand, it's not my motherland. Even if back home they've still got that favouritism and it does happen, it's part of human life.

Moving the goalposts

These extracts from wide-ranging discussions reveal differing reactions to perceptions of racism within the working environment, including the solidarity – and resentment – that comes with shared experience of being made to feel inferior, different or negatively stereotyped. On some occasions, however, when gratuitous racist insults or violent acts are proved to have taken place, the penalties are felt not just by the individuals involved but also by the MoD which is made financially liable. In the previous chapter we noted that a British Muslim soldier had taken his case to an employment tribunal, although the hearing was held in secret.

In January 2010, Kerry Hylton, a Jamaican chef working with the Welsh Guards, acquired a great deal more publicity. He was awarded £22,000 compensation after his complaint about repeated racist bullying went to an employment tribunal. He had left the army two years earlier after claiming that officers locked his family in their married army quarters by super-gluing the door shut, an incident which forced him, his wife and their two young children to move out of their home.[22]

According to legal papers submitted to the tribunal, evidence showed that Hylton was racially abused on a regular basis and was punched by an officer. Among the list of grievances was the fact that the RMP arrested him when he reported the officer's abuse, and that his superiors had nicknamed him 'Paris Hilton' even though he had told them he found it offensive. One racist Lance Corporal, barely above him in rank, caused particular offence. On one occasion he saw him and two other Jamaicans together and asked: 'Is this kitchen becoming a black kitchen?' Pte Hylton said: 'It made me feel really bad being spoken to like that. I had never been spoken to like that before I joined the British Army.'

More damaging for the army's image was the claim that racist insults were made in front of NCOs who did nothing. This indictment of the chain of command system as a mechanism for checking, preventing and reporting abuse forced the institution to address how the culture might be changed throughout the hierarchy. The interventions of the CRE and the MoD in the late 1990s were supposed to herald a new era of reform, yet the reports of beasting, persecution and the condoning of violence had continued. In 2000, after a court case involving a young soldier who had absconded to avoid systematic violent bullying in his regimental unit, journalist Jason Burke attempted to analyse the underlying issues in the brief interlude before the autumn of 2001.[23] After giving details of other cases of desertion and savage initiation rites, and discussing the army's recent efforts to change its reputation – citing Defence Secretary Geoff Hoon's assurance that an 'up-to-date' army promised an 'up-to-date' career – Burke turned his attention away from the armed forces, focusing instead on the impact of social changes on soldiering as an occupation. With the army only just returned from Sierra Leone, he wrote, recruiting officers throughout the country would be able to relax: 'For the days when the prospect of a glorious death on the battlefield thrilled the nation's youth are long since gone.'

Experts, he continued, all agree 'that any army reflects the society that produces it'. Quoting Professor John A. Jackson, a sociologist specialising in military studies at Trinity College, Dublin, he described the way that in the US the experience of war had brought home to the army the impact of social and cultural shifts in the wider society. Just as the American Army had been forced to adapt as a result, the British Army was now going through the same thing.

'The old structures imposing discipline are breaking down,' said Jackson, 'and that poses great difficulties for an organisation that relies on unthinking and unquestioning obedience to orders.'

Those from minority backgrounds who had begun to move up the ladder were no more convinced that racism could be ironed out of the army than anywhere else in UK society. Ken, a corporal who was recruited in St Vincent in 2001, reflected on the reforms he had witnessed over the decade since he had joined.

All this has done is paint this room from red to green and move the goal posts a bit wider, so somebody kick it in the net making it easier for you to score, I close it so it's harder for you to score. That's not even a change in policy.

In his view, there was a limit to how much the army could change because, he pointed out,

It's society that makes the army, the people on the street, the people on the trains, on the bus and in factories: they become the army. So before the army can change, society has to change.

While this study has concentrated on the experiences of Commonwealth soldiers, the observations of UK-born minority colleagues are valuable because they are well-placed to testify to this continuity between inside and outside. Mel was forthright in her opinions about racism in the army. The fact that she was both female and of English–Jamaican parentage gave her a particular vantage point from which to observe her colleagues' ability to deal with what counted as difference. Speaking with an unmistakable Yorkshire accent, she was understandably irritated by questions about which village she was from in Fiji.

> I wouldn't mind if it was people who are kind of … I mean the other day it was a nine-year old girl which was OK, bless her, but the Padre asked me what village I was from and I said, 'Excuse me?' And he said, 'What village are you from?' And I said, 'but Sir, I'm from Barnsley, this little town near Sheffield.'

For Mel, who had been promoted to the rank of corporal, the issue was really one of ignorance. 'Just listen to me talking and you'd know that or at least you could say something about my accent or even just ask me where I'm from. They don't have to ask which village in Fiji I'm from, it just bugs me.'

She was frank about her lack of patience with behaviour she encountered outside and in. On the one hand she had to deal with a range of recalcitrant attitudes to women, especially when she was ordering men around. On the other, she was also annoyed by people making racist comments about African and Jamaican soldiers in front of her, as if she was not black herself.

> And then you get people who refer to people as coloured, and they ask me what I prefer and I say, 'Well, I prefer if you call me mixed,' and, 'If you don't know that I'm mixed and you call me black, I'm not offended.' And then they say, 'Why not coloured?' and I say, 'Because it makes me think you want me to sit at the back of the bus every time you get on. It's a 1950s thing, it doesn't sit well with me to be honest.' 'But it sounds better coloured.' 'No it doesn't! It makes *you* feel better.'

Mel conceded that 'army-wise, I think we have changed a lot', but she was still alarmed by the degree of animosity.

> I still think people have got their collars up and are sticking to their own groups which scares me, it really does scare me. I hate being tarred. I hate having to take a side and I can't stand it when people don't think before they speak. Everybody's obviously entitled to their opinion but being a mixed girl, a black girl, and people see you as white and actually don't realize that you do have some history and do have something about you, it bothers me but they're just ignorant.

In another example, Rabia Siddique, once described as the 'poster girl' of the British Army, filed a race and sex discrimination case against the MoD in 2008 and resigned her commission.[24] Born to an Indian father and Australian mother, she had joined the Army in 2001 as a captain in

Army Legal Services. Although not the first Muslim woman to graduate from Sandhurst,[25] her Arabic language skills meant that she was promoted to Major and drafted in as legal adviser to the 12 Mechanised Brigade in Basra in April 2005.[26] The following September she was involved in an attempt to negotiate the release of two British SAS men from the police station at Al-Jameat after a male colleague radioed a message from an Iraqi judge that they would only speak to 'Major Rabia'. As a hostile crowd surrounded the station, the British soldiers narrowly escaped execution after hours of fruitless negotiations. Afterwards Siddique claimed that she was given a hug by her commanding officer and 'sent to her room for a good night's sleep'. Although she was awarded the Queen's Commendation for Valuable Service, she later discovered that this related to her work before the event and when she made inquiries, she was demoted to a job she had performed three years earlier. Meanwhile the colleague who accompanied her was given the Military Cross for 'courageous leadership and exceptional presence of mind in the face of extreme danger'. Her claim for discrimination on grounds of race and sex was settled just minutes before her case was due to be heard at London Central Employment Tribunal, but her complaint was vindicated in a letter she subsequently received from General Sir Richard Dannatt, who wrote: 'The Army will consider carefully your perception of the way that you were treated in the period that followed the Al Jameat incident with a view to ensuring that appropriate lessons are learned.'[27]

The scandal of Prince Harry's casually racist remark appears to have been blown out of all proportion when placed alongside the cases brought to employment tribunals by Siddique, Hylton and other successful claimants. However, each event revealed a different facet of the institution, proving how vulnerable it was to charges that it had not done enough either to purge military culture of racism and bullying, or to punish the culprits. The level of compensation offered by the employment tribunals as a result of the damages suffered was an indication of how important it was for the army, as an employer, to take racism seriously throughout the hierarchy. This meant a commitment to address racism and other aspects of 'diversity management' at every level of the chain of command, from new recruits to commanding officers. As we continue to explore the process of an army undergoing modernisation, in the next chapter we look at some of the strategies adopted as a result of this external pressure.

7
The Force of the Law

The 12 men are from various parts of the UK and have been in the army for at least 15 years. By the time I arrive they are already seated around three sides of the square table, and since there is no room next to them I have to sit behind them at the back of the room. They are not comfortable with me being there at all and there is not much I can do to change that. Andy, the officer teaching the class, is welcoming and enthusiastic, and as he introduces me he checks that it's ok if they use expletives as things can get quite 'emotional' at times. Someone wants to know if I am recording the session, and I try to reassure them that I am just there to listen.

Andy begins by saying that he is mandated to tell us that equality and diversity (E&D) is all black and white. 'There is no grey,' he insists,

> It's the law. It's about the right for everyone to be treated equally and in an environment free from discrimination, harassment and bullying. It's also LAW.

He shows the first slide in the obligatory Power Point presentation, asking the men to list the values and standards, the 'super six', commenting that it was all common sense. 'How do they fit into E&D?' No one wants to talk.

'Individuals are all links in the chain,' he says. 'If one breaks, it affects everything else.'

Between them the reluctant students list the six values, but they are not keen to explore how they relate to E&D.

'Selfless commitment?' he asks. 'What does that mean?'

'Give yourself to the team,' murmurs a voice.

'Respect? Loyalty? Is there a bad side?' asks Andy. He is not getting much response. He mentions the portrayal of bullying in the army in the BBC drama, Accused, shown the previous night. Although no one in the class admits to having watched the programme, written by Jimmy McGovern, it had received a lot of media attention because General Sir Peter Wall, the

Chief of the General Staff, had written to the BBC director general, Mark Thompson, calling the drama 'inaccurate and misleading', as well as being 'deeply distasteful and offensive' to the families of soldiers in Helmand.[1] Unlike his superiors, Andy does not seem bothered by the negative representation of army life, and tries to discuss the plot as a likely scenario. Again, no one talks.

'Integrity? Discipline?' he continues.

'Firm and fair,' I hear someone say.

> Do we do it equally across the board?
> Courage? Meaning moral courage, intervening in bullying, for example.

As Andy works his way through the slides, his students, experienced soldiers who must have recited the list of army values countless times before, appear to be engaged in passive resistance by refusing to react. Unperturbed, he goes on to list the grounds on which people must be treated fairly: race, religion and belief, gender, age, sexual orientation and disability.

He gets to the subject of banter. 'It's good,' he says, 'but you need to know when to stop. If you get all this right you'll have mutual trust.'

He ploughs on through the question of unfair treatment, searching for examples. 'Direct discrimination?' he asks, before supplying the correct answer himself.

> When someone is singled out.
> Indirect? For example, not taking account of a single parent's needs.
> The definition of harassment is 'when person receiving it feels unwelcome or unreasonable – either one incident or repeated'.
> Bullying?

'Repeated harassment,' says one voice but he is corrected.

> No, it's when you use your superiority to hurt or make someone feel uncomfortable – when you use physical or mental strength.
> Prejudice?
> *Silence.*
> When someone forms an opinion that is irrational.
> Victimisation?

After a few attempts it's clear that they don't get this. The answer is when, if someone has complained or acted as witness, you go out of your way to treat them unfairly.

The second part of the session is more lively as Andy presents a series of possible scenarios as a basis for discussion. Afterwards he told me that this was the first day that he had delivered an interactive version of the syllabus and that it was already proving more useful as a way to convince the students about the difference the law made and how they might be responsible for avoiding costly lawsuits. In the past, students were obliged to sit through the session without making any contribution themselves. I once met a Fijian sergeant who struggled to remember the E&D class he attended at the same centre. 'Oh yes,' he had recalled, 'it was a Power Point thing.'

The first scenario is about a private who objects to sharing a room with someone who is openly gay. They discuss what to do. The consensus seems to be to allocate the gay guy, a demoted lance corporal, to another room, and to listen to the private's feelings, take them into account. That's the wrong answer. If, in their capacity as managers, they do not move him into that particular designated room, they will have broken the law. It's as simple as that. The private's feelings are irrelevant.

Andy tries to tackle their perceptions of gay men. He points out that gay men don't fancy straight men. He knows that a lot of straight men have a problem because they are offended that gay men don't fancy them.

He advises them that another thing to do is give an E&D briefing to all the men. They should have a session at least once a year. If there is a hearing the company will be at fault if they have not done this.

Someone says, 'Then why couldn't you have a female in that room?'

'Because there are anatomical differences, and because the law says you can't discriminate on the ground of sexual orientation.'

Andy raises the issue of transgender, and then says that's for another day. 'If someone comes to you, and they will, the first thing is you listen, you keep your mouth shut. Get to an E&D adviser and give them the heartache. It's a massive thing.'

He runs through some more scenarios which don't really get them going as much. These men are senior instructors in positions of authority and need to know the complaints procedure by heart: sort it out at lowest level; informal chat; formal complaint; redress of grievance (three months); employment tribunal (within six months of offence).

The last scenario is most controversial of all. It presents a single parent who complains of being left out because she is unable to make training as a result of childcare issues. The men express resistance to changing the timetable to suit one person but Andy insists, 'You have to try, it's the law. If you have PT the same time every morning, you are not giving her the opportunity to join in. Raise your concern with the E&D advisor if the battalion won't change.'

There is a real reluctance to moving things round to suit the school day or a parent's hours. 'She should book her own childcare so she can join in,' says one voice. The resentment is palpable. 'We need to go back to the old rules,' says another indignantly. 'If you get pregnant you should get discharged out the army.'

Andy outlines the difference between E&D issue and a management issue. He has a very clear sense of where the line between them falls.

The final summary is surprisingly simple: Treat people fairly; Stop discrimination and bullying; Value diversity in your team.

'Any questions?'

I hear someone muttering on the way out, 'I want to say something but I won't.'

As Andy prepares for the next batch he confesses: 'it's the hardest subject I've ever taught'.

Another group of warrant officers file in and sit down, and he starts again, using exactly the same format. The men are equally quiet.

'The principle is to make sure that every individual contributes to operational effectiveness. Everyone is a link in the chain.'

When he asks for 'the big six' he is met with silence.

Respect? What about if someone is a Muslim, Jew, Sikh? Homosexual, tall, short?

At the end of the day, you respect him for what he brings.

Loyalty? There's good and bad – which is which?

The silence is broken by the hum of the projector, and a military jet roars overhead. Andy goes over the 'Accused' plot again, saying how they made the guy into a 'bitch' (coward).

The corporal harassed the bitch till he shot himself. The section kept loyal to the corporal. That's an example of bad loyalty.

Integrity?

I notice how scuffed the red lino floor is. In the middle of the room there is a model of a landscape which appears to be made out of papier mache. A large piece of netting covered with dark green plastic leaves is hanging from the screen.

He moves through the Power Point again. 'Everyone knows we don't fight for Queen and Country,' he says. 'We fight for our muckers.

As he wraps the session up, he advises, 'If you have a corporal with moral courage, send him to Swindon to train as an E&D advisor assistant.'

Later Andy, whose voice is giving out, tells me that in his experience, 'people are fine with colour and creed'. He has found that there are 'more misunderstandings with sexual orientation. Or if someone is Muslim.'

As far as he could see, 'Soldiers don't give a shit about colour any more. The country is multicultural, so is the army. It's not an issue.' Some switch off, he concedes, and there is not a lot you can do.

The course is one week, and for some their unit is in Afghanistan and they would rather be there.

Before I went on the course, I would have said, 'put the guy in another room' too. They explained to me about the law and that opened my eyes. My skills are developing. The new law has stuff about third hand discrimination but that doesn't affect the army yet.

Not ordinary employment

Andy's enthusiasm for the legal discourse of E&D, highlighted by his sceptical students, illustrated the unstoppable momentum of institutional reform as well as the force of resistance. The session brought home the degree of external pressure emanating from civil society, creating an obligation to change military procedures that had developed in response to their own organisational logic over many years. As sergeants and warrant officers, the senior NCOs undergoing the training were known as 'the beating heart' of the army, charged with responsibility for keeping traditions alive as well as providing the voice of experience and authority. It was therefore particularly important that they were kept appraised of the new legal framework within which they worked, adapting to new ways of doing things regardless of their personal opinions.

In the previous chapter we heard from Ken, a corporal originally recruited in St Vincent in 2001, who was sanguine about the fact that racism in the army was a product of the wider society. 'There are things that happen in the army that happen in the police force, in the passport office, they happen in London Transport', he pointed out. 'They happen in any sort of business, in any major business in the UK.' But the prevalence of racism did not mean that all organisations used the same tools to deal with it, as he went on to explain.

> The difference between them and us, those sort of other institutions and businesses and the army, is that we have policies and the policies are more implemented; there are means and ways of dealing with these things.

His comment did not necessarily imply that he thought the army had cracked the problem. It was more a way of stressing that the organisation practised its own disciplinary codes that, in theory at least, could be made to clamp down on unacceptable behaviour among soldiers. In this chapter we look back over the programme of reform that had resulted from the intervention of the CRE in the 1990s. Had things really changed, and how was this to be measured anyway?

In 1998 the strategies introduced to deal with racist discrimination and bullying fell into four broad categories. The first, as we have seen, directed resources towards increasing the recruitment of minority soldiers as rapidly as possible. The second category of reform aimed to set up improved complaints procedures that would not only investigate alleged instances of racism but also provide victims with counselling and advice through an anonymous hotline service. The Blake Inquiry into the deaths at Deepcut, however, revealed that those who had complained appeared to have had 'little confidence that the system could or would address their grievances'.[2] As a result the Armed Forces Bill 2006 addressed the need for a more stringent process that would allow complaints to be investigated outside the chain of command. In November 2007 the MoD appointed the first Service Complaints Commissioner (SCC) whose job was to monitor the way that the armed forces handled grievances by individuals. Susan Atkins took up the post in January 2008, declaring that she would hold the armed forces and the MoD to their promise that there would be a rigorous, independent and transparent scrutiny of the system. She was determined, she said, to ensure that 'all Service men and women and their families have confidence in the complaints process and are treated properly'.[3]

A third area promised greater 'awareness training' for all soldiers, including recruits and officers across all ranks, while a fourth introduced the collection of statistics and other data needed to monitor the progress of ethnic minorities through the organisation. Before examining in more detail how effective these reforms have been in addressing the problem of institutional racism, it is essential to note, once again, how they have been carried out within a broader context of human resource management (HRM) which has effectively transformed the public, private and voluntary sectors since the 1980s.

The various techniques and technologies devised to implement and validate 'diversity management', as the task had become known, are rooted in a concern to maximise efficiency among the workforce. A raft of ever more stringent equality laws, enacted nationally and in the European Union, has helped to shape this process, and as a result, an industry of E&D advisers and consultancies has mushroomed. Like countless other organisations floundering in the new legalistic environment, the MoD was obliged to turn to such quarters for expertise. As we saw in Chapter 2, Focus Consultancy was employed in 1999 to oversee the British Army's 'multiculturalisation exercise', said to be one of the largest in Europe, acting 'as broker between the British Army and the UK EM communities...to assist the Army with their Ethnic Minority Recruitment Campaign (EMRC)'.[4] While this proved to be a routine transaction it is important to cast a more critical eye over how this story has been told. What might otherwise seem a footnote in the army's development as a multicultural employer is a travesty of what actually happened.

Over 10 years later it was curious to learn from the Focus website that the government's decision to recruit Commonwealth soldiers had been entirely subsumed under the rhetoric of private consultancy expertise. Without mentioning the new government policy of extending eligibility to migrants from 54 countries, Focus claimed to have supported the army 'in understanding the ethnic minority recruitment market, and in its progress from less than 1% ethnic minority recruitment of officers and soldiers to 8% + over a four-year period'. This remark not only gave the impression that the 'expert advice' provided by the consultancy had been able to 'fix' the problem of under-recruiting among UK minorities, but it also made the more pressing issue of politics disappear completely.

Boasting that 'the success of the project has been critically dependent on intensive planning, evaluation and learning about effective interventions in this highly complex area', Focus implied that they were largely responsible. It was to their own credit that the army was the top performer in the public sector 'according to the Race for Opportunity Benchmarking report on race and diversity in corporate Britain (published June 2002)'.[5] Without denying that it has been important to bring military organisations into line with the rest of the public and corporate sector, the suggestion that this process could be reduced to an ever more sophisticated HRM issue is likely further to marginalise the issue of diversity and the armed forces as a matter for public debate. Asking who serves, under what conditions and for what rewards are crucial questions for a post-imperial democracy that cannot agree about its role in the world, and cannot afford to maintain the status to which it aspires. The employment of significant numbers of foreign nationals to provide manpower during a decade of intensive military operations definitely needs to be discussed outside the prosaic terms of the 'ethnic minority recruitment market'.

Continuous attitudes

It is worth emphasising that the E&D policies which protect the rights of minorities were one component of a reform agenda that covered every corner of military life from housing to morale. The extent of violence within the organisation continued to present intractable problems, however, despite the policy of zero tolerance. During the earlier part of the decade in which Commonwealth soldiers were recruited into the army, the MoD struggled to manage a stream of revelations of savage initiation rites, homophobic attacks and endemic bullying, often carried out by junior NCOs but frequently condoned, or overlooked, by more senior ranks. In 2000, for example, the army's Special Investigation Branch (SIB) was running 30 inquiries into such incidents, and, according to a report in the *Observer*, a solicitor specialising in personal injury claims by serving and former personnel confirmed that his firm alone had 60 complaints under way.[6]

Two years later, an internal survey carried out by the MoD indicated that 43 per cent of serving personnel believed that soldiers suffered from bullying, sexual discrimination and harassment.[7] The information emerged in Parliament after Liberal Democrat defence spokesman Paul Keetch tabled a question asking for results of the armed forces' internal 'attitude' surveys. By 2004 the situation appeared to be worse than ever, as the latest survey showed that this figure had almost doubled, reaching 86 per cent.[8] These reports, based on information that had entered the public domain through the auspices of the Defence Analytical Services and Agency (DASA), heightened public concern about the unexplained deaths of four young recruits at Deepcut between 1995 and 2002, and the unsatisfactory inquiries that followed. In 2011 the long-running and still unresolved review into the circumstances surrounding the deaths continued to surface amid allegations that detectives failed to follow crucial leads.[9]

In the meantime, the methods used to monitor soldiers' experience were refined and expanded as a means to harvest feedback from military staff across a wide range of issues. Before 2007, each service conducted its own continuous attitudes surveys on an annual basis, but since this made it difficult to compare results within different areas of policy, a joint project was devised, known as the Armed Forces Continuous Attitudes Survey (AFCAS). This is compiled and analysed by Service Occupational Psychologists as well as statisticians and researchers from DASA. The introduction to the 2008 study stated that the Service Chiefs and the MoD 'place a high value on attitude data' gathered from service personnel, because, 'They are a vital means of understanding how our people feel about key issues.'[10]

One of most important aims of the survey was to probe a variety of issues revealing why individuals might want to leave the services, and what motivated them to stay on. It therefore constituted a prime example of HRM since it was designed to acquire information about employees' feelings and attitudes in order to make the organisation more efficient. At the same time it also indicated that the opinions of the workforce were likely to be taken into account in day-to-day management. In the absence of a trade union, it is possibly one of the few ways that soldiers can make their grievances known to their managers on an anonymous basis.

Correspondents are selected randomly across the three services and divided into two categories: officers and other ranks. The questions cover a wide range of topics ranging from satisfaction with army life, salary and allowances, length of operational tours and the time between them, housing, welfare and other practical matters. They also seek information about levels of commitment to the service and a sense of being valued within it as well as an understanding and appreciation of the service ethos. One set of questions asks: How strongly do you agree with the following statements about your immediate superior?[11] Respondents are given the choice of agreeing, disagreeing or staying neutral to comments such as he/she understands and represents my interests; gives me feedback on my performance; sets a positive example; and recognises my efforts.

The results of these annual surveys are distilled into a report which is freely available to the public. The section on Diversity, Fairness and Equality, Discrimination, Harassment and Bullying, and the Complaints Procedure offers possibly the best way of monitoring changing attitudes and experiences within the army, since figures are available by service as well as rank.

The report analysing the 2008 survey was studiously upbeat, drawing attention to every indication that the new policies and strategies were proving successful.[12] It noted first that officers from all three services held positive views about fairness and equality, pointing out that although the rest of the army – Other Ranks (ORs) – were less positive in comparison, over half held positive views on all aspects of fairness and equality, suggesting that their attitudes towards fairness and equality were more optimistic in 2008 than they had been the previous year.

In 2008, a 'relatively small proportion' of respondents had experienced discrimination, harassment or bullying in the work environment in the last 12 months, and most respondents knew where to get information about the complaints procedure. Although the questions were designed to find out how complaints were dealt with, the analysis admitted that the number of respondents was too small for 'reliable inferences' to be made. However, only 'a relatively small proportion' that had experienced this type of behaviour made a complaint and their main reasons for not doing so were listed as:

- It might adversely affect their career (Officers 51%, ORs 32%)
- It would cause problems in the workplace (Officers 42%, ORs 44%)
- There would be recriminations (Officers 34%, ORs 30%) and
- They did not believe anything would be done (Officers 35%, ORs 33%).[13]

This disjuncture between knowing what the procedure is and being prepared to follow it through provides a snapshot of institutional culture which is unlikely to be different from many other organisations, military or civilian. In addition, the rate of return for completed surveys raises the question of whether the task is taken seriously by those who are randomly asked to participate. In 2007 copies were sent to 1550 officers of whom 61 per cent responded, but out of 4,000 soldiers only 30 per cent bothered to send them back completed. In 2008, fewer than 10,500 responses were received and included in the results, giving an overall response rate of 32 per cent which, according to the report, is comparable to other paper-based surveys of military personnel. It is not far-fetched to say that the findings on the complaints procedures suggest that many of those who rejected the chance to complete the survey might have done so on the basis that it would not change anything as a result.

In addition to the AFCAS, surveys are also used as a tool to monitor trends in the training centres. The Recruit Trainees Survey (RTS) is distributed among Phase 1 recruits and Phase 2 trainees across all training establishments in the three services in order to track their 'perceptions of training, facilities and food, support, fairness of treatment, general perceptions of the course, and hopes for the future'.[14] The feedback allows schools and centres to compare results 'to required standards set by the MoD'.

The report for 2009 provided evidence, for example, that there was widespread knowledge of how to report problems of 'unfair treatment' and where to seek advice. Findings indicated that 'ninety two per cent of recruits (up from 90% in 2008 and 85% in 2007) said that there was a member of staff easily available to talk to outside of training hours'. It also revealed that 'Similarly high proportions said that they had someone they were happy to go to if they had had any personal or emotional problems (89%, down from 90%), if they had problems with administration (92%, up from 91%) or if they had wanted to raise concerns with a person in authority (89%, up from 87%).'[15]

However, while respondents claimed to know about procedures, only half of Phase 1 recruits believed that complaints were dealt with 'in a fair manner at their unit (50%)'. Of those who did not believe that complaints were dealt with fairly, 'over half (56%) said that people were not believed or taken seriously while 46% said that it would have caused problems on the course'. The 2009 report also noted that 'of the 16,166 Phase 1 recruits interviewed, 13% said that they had been badly or unfairly treated, representing a five percentage point increase from last year (8%)'. Just under half of those believed that they were badly or unfairly treated by staff, while the rest said it was fellow trainees.[16]

After listening to one group of Caribbean recruits at ITC describe the behaviour of a notorious bully within their section, their humour tinged with disdain, I asked whether they had ever reported him. None of them had directly experienced any trouble from this individual, perhaps because they were able to look after themselves, but they had observed how he picked on anyone who seemed weak or vulnerable. Their replies indicated that everyone knew about this recruit but the platoon sergeant was also intimidating because of the way he switched between joking and shouting, and they found him hard to read. Had they recorded the bullying on their recruit surveys? They had not used this as a way of making a complaint either. One admitted that he had even written on questionnaire that bullying didn't happen.

'Even though people know about it, it won't really change,' he said, shrugging his shoulders. 'They try to ignore it. They say it's not really bullying. The corporal will give the bully a beasting.'

Studying the result of surveys over a period of time has other limitations in terms of constructing a narrative of progress, as any statistician well knows. The 2010 annual report issued by the Service Complaints Commissioner (SCC) revealed that there had been an increase in complaints across all three services, especially in the army where 302 new complaints had been made in 2010 compared with 123 new complaints at the same level in 2009, an increase of 150 per cent.[17] In her report she pointed out that the significant increase in army figures may have been partly caused by the instigation of more accurate recording practices rather than an increase in the number of complaints. Qualifying or explaining the results of surveys is therefore essential in guiding the reader through the statistics, however graphically they are reconfigured in bar charts or coloured boxes.

In the recommendations contained in the 2010 report, the SCC concluded that the complexity of the system in the interests of fairness was having a detrimental effect and that this was particularly problematic in cases of bullying, harassment and discrimination. In her view, delays regularly lead to 'an increase in case complexity, a hardening of positions within the case and too often a denial of justice'.[18] In many instances, she continued, 'it appears that escalation could have been avoided by handling the case with better care, communication and humanity at the outset'.

Just the way it is

The four soldiers sat in a row facing the audience and prepared to account for their behaviour. Each of them had been involved in a serious situation of bullying and harassment and they now had the opportunity to reflect on the implications in the company of their peers. The mixed group conducting the interrogation was composed mainly of junior ranks, corporals and lance corporals serving in the Royal Artillery who grew increasingly vocal as the culprits struggled to defend themselves. 'Why didn't you make a complaint?' someone asked Jason, a Jamaican soldier who had been bullied by Sergeant Macklin while in Iraq in 2003.

'I didn't want the stigma,' he replied. 'Sergeants stick up for their friends anyway.'

This exchange occurred during a drama workshop organised by the Garnett Foundation as part of the army's Respect for Others programme. The four soldiers were actors who had just been taking part in a dramatisation entitled 'Just the way it is' which was largely scripted from interviews and therefore based on real events. It featured four characters interacting in different locations over a period of almost a decade: Iraq, Afghanistan and a military base in the UK. Seven years after his bullying treatment of Jason, the offending Sgt Macklin had been promoted to warrant officer, and although clearly suffering from Post-Traumatic Stress Disorder (PTSD), he had maintained his job which had brought him into contact with Jason once again. In the meantime, Jason had also been promoted. Now under pressure from the junior NCOs in the audience, the actor playing WO Macklin, still in character, admitted he had never liked him.

'But he was a bloody good soldier,' he said. 'I didn't feel I had any need to develop him [as a soldier].' Then he added, 'he is sullen like a lot of black people'.

This last comment caused a ripple in the audience. The older man was becoming a figure of fun, a stereotype in fact. A woman asked him why he had made a particular comment during the play. She objected to his remark that he would find it difficult serving with British soldiers who wore head-scarves because if he met one in a war situation he wouldn't know who to fight. What difference does it make what headgear she has?

'With all due respect, love', he had begun in response. At this point the workshop leader stepped in to moderate the undue attention the character was receiving. 'He is not a bad guy,' he pleaded. 'He has passion, knowledge, experience, skill. He joined a very different organisation, don't forget.' He had been so convincing in this part that when I talked to the actor during the tea break I found it hard not to feel intimidated myself.

The discussion turned to the politics of gender and the display of sexual harassment we had witnessed. In addition to the conflict between Jason and Macklin, the play dealt with another strand involving the female soldier, a lance corporal who happened to have red hair and a northern accent, and a young male officer, both white and British. It showed how a series of miscommunications allowed the officer to make assumptions about the woman's feelings towards him. It culminated in his attempt to kiss her when she came to his office to lend him a book, an advance which she fiercely rejected. They were both left feeling humiliated and angry.

The female actor had posed the question, in character: did I ask for that to happen? The answer she received depended on the audience. The previous day they had performed to a group of 17- to 18-year-olds in an armoured regiment who had chorused a resoundingly sexist 'yes'. Today the blame was squarely laid at the feet of the young officer who was becoming more arrogant as the exercise went on. But it turned out that he too, like the older working class soldier, had problems that were not easily recognised in the army. He suffered from depression, which earned him the nickname 'Biff', and he was not going to take the criticism without making his own case for deserving greater respect.

The rather incongruous activities taking place within the draughty hangar were partly aimed at revealing what happened when bullying and harassment went unchecked. The role-play was also designed to train junior NCOs on how to recognise, prevent and deal with the potential, but very real, problems that they might come across in their line of duty. The workshop was a one-off session for this particular assembly of would-be managers, but in order to make sense of it the intervention needs to be placed within the much broader context of hiring consultancies outlined earlier in this chapter. The Garnett Foundation, whose website explains how it uses professional actors to 'improve performance' by unlocking talent and releasing staff potential, was built on 16 years of experience, making it one of the longest established NGOs working in the field of diversity management.[19]

In 2009 the Foundation signed a new contract with the MoD after having worked closely with the armed forces, Civil Service and Territorial Army over the previous six years. The 'Respect for Others' programme was one of series of initiatives undertaken jointly with the MoD in order to augment internal training on diversity issues. The brochure handed out before the workshop started clearly illustrated the technical nature of the job, listing the regulations and statutory responsibilities regarding equality and diversity, and providing detailed definitions of bullying and harassment and the complaints procedure.[20] One of the strategies of the workshops was to identify bullying behaviours from the view of the witness in addition to the victim and perpetrator.

A photographic image on the front of the document stressed the conventional view of diversity within the workforce as a composite smiling face made up of differing skin tones and gendered features. The picture inside depicted a white male British soldier, rifle in both hands, surrounded by young Afghan boys as they strolled together down a street. Although the programme was aimed at raising awareness and understanding, and facilitating 'appropriate management of E&D incidents', the second image underlined the fact that 'Respect for Others' was geared towards the counter-insurgency operation as well.

Before it started, the diversity officer introduced the morning's activities, illustrating the fluency with which the language of corporate multiculture, with its emphasis on individual rights, had infiltrated the military vocabulary.

> The army used to think that cohesion depended on everyone looking the same. They had a colour bar till the seventies because they said they were different. They banned gays till 2000 because of 'operational effectiveness'. They said that some people cannot be operationally effective because of cohesion.
>
> Today it is recognised that two things count: your personal commitment to operations and your personal skills and abilities. Race, culture, gender and sexual orientation don't affect those things.
>
> The army has a canteen culture. People feel diversity is imposed on us. Now it's a better army than before but some parts of our culture think in old terms, think E&D have been forced on us. Some see it as a threat or a danger to be resisted.
>
> External organisations have challenged the assertion that the army needs to be that different. The army has claimed the right to be different but how different is it from other organisations? For example, the police and the prison service can't employ anyone in the BNP; Shell have people working on oil rigs for long periods of time. We need to understand why and how the army is different.[21] Otherwise we might get separated from society which employs us, funds us and provides us with new recruits.
>
> The most successful organisations say they have a multicultural workforce. That's where we are going. This is for you, leading a multicultural team.

This endorsement was followed by a short lecture from the workshop leader on why the issue of managing diversity was so important. 'We are an interactive behavioural training company which has worked in every sector – private, voluntary, public, and across the armed forces,' he explained.[22]

> Diversity is not about being pink and fluffy, it is aimed at giving you confidence, awareness, a toolkit. We can't give you answers, or a piece of paper. That doesn't exist.
>
> Managing diversity is going to be on your agenda if you get promoted and will be important in your future employment. Here we have taken some of the worst examples to try to make equality and diversity entertaining.

The session began with a question-and-answer exercise in which members of the audience were invited to reveal their familiarity with the procedures of diversity management. They soon encountered the vexed issue of where 'normal' army behaviour crossed over into definitions of harassment. In this instance, 85 per cent of the 50 or so present declared by means of remote handsets that they understood where the line fell between acceptable and unacceptable behaviour. The graph on the screen revealed that 15 per cent said they neither agreed nor disagreed, and four per cent said they strongly disagreed.

The first time I had seen a version of this training exercise was at Sandhurst (RMAS) where it was presented to an audience of senior officers and colour sergeants. The workshop leader had begun in a similar vein, meeting their sceptical gaze with an energetic insistence that E&D was not dull, but something that they should feel confident about and happy to implement. He spoke about the role of the witness, about how important it was to be able to recognise and challenge problematic situations. The first question he asked the audience was whether they had all the skills to tackle bullying and harassment appropriately. The anonymity of their handsets allowed them to admit that they were far from confident. Just under half thought they did know what to do, but a third were unsure. Participants were reluctant to talk and I wondered to what extent the presence of very senior officers was off-putting. When the definition of harassment flashed up in the screen, however, there was some reaction from the back of the room.

> Offensive, intimidating, malicious and insulting behaviour, an abuse or misuse of power, through means intended to undermine, humiliate, denigrate or injure the recipient. It can take place between individuals of the same or different ranks. Behaviour that is considered bullying by one person may be viewed as, for example, firm management or robust leadership by others.

'It's the nature of our job to intimidate,' growled a voice belonging to someone in my row. Dressed in the signature tartan trousers of a Scottish regiment, his stripes indicated that he was one of the colour sergeants who were responsible for basic officer training at RMAS. Another instructor agreed: 'Intimidate, humiliate, these are part of the job!' There was a brief exchange about the words 'intended to', and the logistics of pushing the least able cadets to go to their limits without using demeaning language, such as 'fat prick'. Then there was another vote, this time for a range of opinions about the causes of bullying and harassment. More than half thought that it was often due to misunderstanding and was actually more likely to be 'robust management' than intentional victimisation. The rest of the responses ranged evenly over explanations such as: that's the way it is, frustration, insecurity, power trip and the fact that some people are weak therefore more likely to be bullied. No one thought that it did not happen at all.

In the discussion at Sandhurst two grounds for consensus emerged. The first was that there were many people in the British Army who were considered to be weak. In that case, asked the workshop leader, 'How do we bring their confidence on? Are we good at looking at those people?'

The second area of agreement was that members of the audience felt that they knew which procedures to follow. At this point the diversity officer who was watching from the back of the room stood up to intervene. 'Theoretically we have a good complaints procedure,' he explained with palpable exasperation in his voice. 'But the junior ranks just don't use it. Surveys and focus groups bear this out.'

Box ticking

The senior officer at RMAS had begun his introduction of the Garnett Foundation with an admission of defeat. 'How do we change attitudes?' he asked the ranks of sceptical faces looking back at him in the lecture theatre. 'It's more than ticking boxes and the MATT 6 programme of training has not been effective.' But the drama workshop that was about to unfold was less concerned with changing attitudes than with establishing procedures. The colonel spoke directly to his audience as he told them: 'There are huge leadership challenges. It's one of those things the army could do better. We haven't cracked it. It's a responsibility for leaders, instructors, trainers, for the chain of command.'

Ollie, a junior officer working as an instructor, explained to me how the chain of command worked from the perspective of a young lieutenant, still in his or her twenties, commanding non-commissioned officers with far more experience and authority. 'You can't go above the next rank,' he said, 'But [if you are a corporal] you can say, "Sir, you need to know that sergeant is a bully". A young officer needs to have the moral courage to say, "This is not acceptable". That's why we teach moral courage.'

We were heading towards the dining room to meet a small number of offi-cer cadets from Commonwealth countries but it was far too noisy to conduct an interview there. In the slightly quieter bar area next door, we were joined by five young men who represented a cross section of the non-UK students at RMAS. Earlier that day the officer who briefed me had spoken enthusias-tically about the overseas cadets flowing through the academy. As we noted in Chapter 1, these students were selected from other national militaries to complete part of their training under the wing of the British Army. In a cohort of 30 UK and Commonwealth candidates, three were likely to have come from the Middle East, particularly the Gulf states, from West Africa and occasionally Francophone Africa too. 'There's a huge diversity,' he had told me, 'ranging from rich Arabs to Africans brought out of their village a week before coming here. They build intense friendships and I hope the [local] cadets will look after them. Some get left in the wake, but it adds value.'

He mentioned that the course had been adapted to suit the changing demographic of UK applicants. Although they too were marked out as the 'playstation generation', the calibre had begun to change of late. They were slightly older and had more experience, particularly of travel. One candidate had already rowed across the Atlantic. 'And there are different challenges now. Officers are meeting NGOs, tribal leaders, the Afghan army, a complex mix of people. He [*sic*] needs to learn how to deal with this complexity.'

Although the presence of the non-UK cadets meant that each cohort (com-prised of 270 recruits) was guaranteed to be mixed culturally and ethnically, the average intake of UK ethnic minorities was comparable to the proportion in the rest of the army. In January 2010 British minorities made up 3.4 per cent, while female cadets were better represented, at 13 per cent.[23] I had come to find out about the Commonwealth cadets, whose nationality made them eligible to join the army on the same basis as the recruits I had met in Catterick and Pirbright. However, Sandhurst entrants required a two-year residency in the UK which meant that it was more difficult for Common-wealth applicants to qualify unless they joined the regular army first and then applied for commission. For this reason, I was told, 'the Common-wealth elements who become officers tend to be South African, Australian, Zimbabwean and occasionally Canadians. They are largely white.'

This was certainly the case among the group I was introduced to in the bar. Three were overseas cadets from Belize and Ghana, but of the Com-monwealth contingent who would be integrated into the British Army, one was from South Africa and the other was Australian. They were all male, and indeed, both Commonwealth cadets were white. Richard, an experi-enced soldier with dual Dutch and South African citizenship, had been in the South African army for four years before joining the British Army in 2003. He applied to Sandhurst in 2007, but because of three consecutive tours it took a couple more years to start the training course and commis-sion as an officer. Initially there were some doubts about whether he could join the British Army as a Dutch citizen. His brother, who also applied in 2003, was turned down on that basis.

Before we assembled I couldn't help noticing that there were numerous decanters full of crimson port lined up along one side of the room. Apparently this was in preparation for a Company social that night, a traditional event in the cadets' calendar when families were invited to visit their offspring during their 48-week course. It was one of several instances of local rituals in which alcohol seemed to feature prominently, and it brought home the fact that RMAS had its own inimitable culture which the overseas cadets might find even more exclusive if not exotic.

The experience and backgrounds of this small group seemed quite disparate and at first it was hard to get a conversation going. I asked whether they had the same training in values and standards, intrigued to know about the ethical aspects of their education. Luis had joined the Belize Defence Force as an officer cadet and said thoughtfully,

> Values are the same everywhere. Some aspects are different though. In Belize, your personal life is up to you, as long as you can do the job. Here it's analysed, scrutinised a bit more. Your relationships, how you dress to go to the supermarket.

Kwasi, seconded from the Ghana Armed Forces, said he thought that the British system was good.

> Some people say that personal life doesn't matter. In Ghana it doesn't matter. In Sandhurst they should go together, as a leader you serve as an example.

I asked Richard what was the main difference, in his experience, between army life in the UK and in South Africa.

> There's a lot of scrutiny of personal life here. To some extent I don't agree because it can be invasive. The South African military is based on the British, so there are lots of similarities. There's a lot more emphasis on welfare in the British Army. Career management is better.

'Is there an emphasis on being British?' I asked.

'No, it's not about being British, it's about doing the right thing.'

'Different countries have their own doctrines,' Kwasi observed. 'Things I learn here don't suit [home] ... '

Luis added: 'I don't know about a British way of life. They just teach ... maybe British society is about being professional.'

We discussed the fact that the overseas cadets had a different academic syllabus, studying British history rather than the intensive academic programme designed for the others. The physical training and the leadership element of the course were the same, however. The conversation was progressing slowly, and there was not much time left. To make matters more difficult, we were all trying to eat our lunch standing at the counter and there was nowhere to put my microphone. Since they would be moving on to positions of authority as junior officers, they would be entering the organisation as managers and therefore would be expected to be acquainted with important aspects of employment law. I asked them to tell me about their education in E&D. Richard spoke first.

> It's not done in depth. It's more about reinforcing and conforming. The UK has been quite a liberal society for a while so it's about guidelines and boundaries. It's mostly taught through power points. Mostly [people] tick the box, not understanding. It's expected that you'll apply the rules.

He had been through deployments as an infantry soldier which meant he was vastly more experienced than most of his fellow UK trainees undergoing the rigorous training. As an English-speaker as well, Richard was confident reflecting as an insider compared to the overseas cadets who clearly felt marginalised. Looking back on his encounters in Iraq and Afghanistan he volunteered the theory that Brits had 'a natural understanding of diversity' in comparison with US soldiers he had met. He described how, in a role-playing exercise about diversity, the Americans had acted out minorities (Afghans) as stereotypes. 'They didn't think they had to think about how other people saw them.'

My question about relationships between the overseas and the local cadets met with a more animated response from the students from Belize and Ghana. Luis spoke up quickly.

> People who've lived British lives, never been out of British towns and villages, stick to themselves. That's not a problem as long as they don't start, don't take it to the next level and insult us.

They seemed to feel strongly about this, as though they had experienced coldness, hostility even, from Brits who didn't want to know them because they were 'foreign'. The conversation was interrupted, typically, just as they began to relax in each other's company although there was no doubt that the differences in age and background coloured their different perspectives. More than nationality, however, it was also a question of experience. While the views of new recruits were able to reveal all-important first impressions, it was more likely to be the considered opinions of older, battle-hardened soldiers that threw light on the progress of reform.

Neutral ignorance

Ken gave a philosophical reply when I asked whether in his view the army had become a more tolerant and enlightened employer during his career.

> If you change the look of the army, it will change the way they do certain things but it won't really *change* the army. We are the army – people are – and if we can't change, then nothing can because we have to make the changes between ourselves. It's like changing from being a non-Christian to a Christian, changing from a Catholic to a Muslim. A Hindu to a Jew. *You* have to change in order for change to be effective.

He was content to accept that the army had 'a strict policy and the guidelines are there', and accepted that fact that a lot of people around him were racist. As long as they didn't bother him he was happy.

'You keep your opinion to yourself and I'll keep mine to myself. It's just their belief.'

He had worked in four different postings and knew that no two places were the same, but he could understand why so many people wanted to leave as a result of racist attitudes from colleagues. He had been spat at by a staff sergeant once and had suffered his fair share of discrimination. He had reported a couple of instances where he felt he had been unfairly treated and the officer dealing with his complaint had asked him whether he wanted to press charges. Ken decided that he would rather the culprits apologised than face punishment.

> I said, 'Just get him to write a letter,' and stuff like that because if I keep going and say, 'Let's punish them for that,' they go away feeling angry and hating black people. As I said to you before, it's about educating, they're not educated and I don't want to go down to the level of punishing people for this, punishing people for that. It's what they're thinking and you can't blame people for thinking what they're thinking.

He had developed a concept of what he called 'neutral ignorance' as a way of explaining routine racism among his UK colleagues. He gave an example of a familiar situation in the canteen where blacks and whites appeared to be sitting separately.

> The instructors come across and shout at the hall, 'What are you doing on that side?' It's not always the case, but it's easier to see the black guys sitting all together because it's a comfort to them, but [the instructors] will never move across and say to another white recruit, 'Why aren't you sitting with those black guys?'

His point was that some people were just not able to analyse this dynamic. For them, two black people sitting together constituted a problem when everyone else in the room was white.

> All this is part of ignorance, not negative ignorance, it's neutral ignorance if you want to call it that. They don't know, or they don't understand and if they don't know and they can't understand, they can't deal with this sort of situation. And there are some people you just can't change. You tell someone something and they know what you're telling them is right and what they're doing is wrong and they still proceed to do it their own way.

Experience could also mean a readiness to accept certain ways of doing things. After 12 years, it was justifiable to claim that the presence of ethnic, religious and linguistic minorities had been instrumental in bringing about internal reform. Just as the analogy of the pipeline served to illustrate the constant flow of human power into the army, it also depicted the process through which individuals passed through the organisation during the course of their careers. During this period, many of those who joined as Commonwealth citizens found themselves on the promotion ladder. They had become part of the changes in organisational culture, trained to guide new recruits and even younger instructors as well. Corporals, for example, played an important role in inducting new members through the culture shock that inevitably awaited them.

Ken was typical of many who saw themselves as role models because when they entered the organisation, there were no black NCOs at all. They used their own example to encourage recruits who were just starting out.

> I always say to them: 'one of these days, it took me ages to get here – standing in front of you, I was in your position eight years ago and there's nothing to say that you, in eight years time, you can't stand here giving a briefing to somebody from exactly where you're from, doing a job like I am.'

For those who had joined soon after 1998 and made the rank of senior NCO, the struggle had been that much harder. Uraia had been a sergeant for 18 months and was aware that the number of Fijian sergeants would increase significantly because of the age structure.

> Most of us joined at 26–27 and have had to work really hard. I was 26. I had to work hard to reach the same rank as a soldier who joined at 18. Now people are realising ... lots are trying to get promoted before their 12 years. It's hard work. You have to put effort in but you get rewarded.

Senior officers often intimated that things might start to change once this inevitable process was underway and the prospect of Fijians infiltrating the Sergeants Mess was something that I had heard mentioned on many occasions. The institution was seen as the backbone of the battalion. Members would have been in the army for about 16 years, one officer told me. 'He remembers history and tradition. His attitudes will change last.'

One reason why sergeants were so influential was that both junior and senior officers relied on their knowledge and experience to run the unit. The Regimental Sergeant Major (RSM) was particularly powerful, and his (or more rarely her) opinion of institutional reform was crucial to how it was received. 'The officers might say that there is no bullying,' I was told, 'but [they] can't implement a no bullying policy without the help of sergeants.' Hence the important role played by WO Macklin in the drama workshop.

The warrant officers attending the E&D group described earlier were evidently a mixed group, and as Andy, their instructor, observed, some of them switched off and were actively hostile. Although on that occasions there were no minority soldiers present, these views were not confined to white heterosexual males. Tony was a sergeant, working as a senior instructor at ITC. In 1998 the Grenadier Guards visited Jamaica, where he was born. He had just finished school when the Guards played a cricket game against his team. From then on he knew what he wanted to do and he subsequently applied through the overseas cell. It was straightforward, he said, and by 2003 he was stationed in Wellington barracks next to the palace. The prospect of belonging to a regiment with such strong sense of pride and identity gave him the ambition to succeed.

Today, he told me, not all Commonwealth applicants were directed into jobs that they applied for. 'We all know Jamaicans have massive attitude problems,' he said, without smiling. 'I'm one too, but there is a problem with guys who have been lied to, told by recruiters what they will face. Then they say, "The Infantry is too hard for me."'

Six in his platoon had transferred after the initial six weeks. Four were from St Vincent and the other two were African. 'The recruiters need to be more honest,' he said, 'but if you're going to be a soldier, then be a soldier.'

I asked him about his views on racism in the army. 'There's zero tolerance,' he replied bluntly. 'I've seen blokes complain, there are people who dwell on it, who pull the race card. I notice that about people. They know if they use it they will have an easy life. But few use it, on the whole.'

The term 'race card' is commonly used in discussions of racism, and the army is no exception. Ollie had mentioned it as well, saying that 'there's always one who puts their hand up and says they don't want to go on a run, and plays the race card'. He too was concerned about the problems of perception, saying it was the biggest barrier. Echoing Tony, he pointed out that Jamaicans were perceived to be more laid back than other nationalities.

'Fijians seem pretty good lads,' he said approvingly, 'they will play rugby, they are boisterous, macho, good fun, drink and are active. Caribbeans do things at slower pace. That's the perception. That they look after themselves. But they might not be doing so well because of the cold, or not robust at running with the pack. They're not as outgoing, won't have natural banter.'

For Ollie, now a captain, the biggest challenge for an officer was how to be inclusive. His regiment recruited heavily from Birmingham and the East Midlands and he spoke tenderly about his young charges, most of whom were recruited from working class backgrounds. He described how one commander in his regiment organised a social with Fijians, St Lucians and South Africans all bringing food. It gave the young men from inner city Birmingham a chance to see something different, he said.

The practice of organising special events to allow soldiers to educate each other by representing their cultures was not uncommon. It was often mentioned as a way to show appreciation of Commonwealth soldiers where there was a significant proportion. It did not always work as an integrating mechanism though. One commander stationed in Germany was perturbed when the British contingent had stayed away from such an event, partly because of lack of interest but also because they were unsure how to represent their own culture. In fact, most of them did not think of themselves as being 'cultural' at all.

Uraia had more sociological theories about ethnic stereotypes. He was very matter-of-fact about the longer-term consequences of having 'foreigners' in the heart of the machine. I had asked him outright, 'Are Fijian soldiers going to change the mess culture?'

'It's no different,' he said authoritatively. 'By then you are all moulded the same.' He was more despondent about his UK peers' grasp of regimental history though, especially those who were still in their late twenties and early thirties. I ask why this might be and he smiled before giving the standard answer: 'Play station generation'.

His ambition was to be a Late Entry officer which meant being commissioned once he reached the end of his 22-year contract.

A Fijian doesn't ask questions. It's the way we are brought up by our mum and dad. So we adapt to the army quite easily. We crack on, we never ask why we are fighting. The Nepalese are the same. But the Caribbeans – and those from African countries – they have a different view of going to war. They ask 'what are we doing here?'

Maybe slavery has something to do with it. Their ancestors were slaves, [so] they look at Europeans differently. In Fiji we were never slaves.

Caribbeans don't like English guys telling them what to do, especially when he tell them to integrate with the others. But it's the British who need to try to integrate.

These fragments indicate widespread views about the differences between ethnic and national groups, particularly where they are accepted as common sense and reified within a military environment. In the context of this chapter about changing attitudes and practices throughout the army, we might still ask, what other measures have been adopted to eradicate the racism that feeds on generalisations and demeaning stereotypes? Ken had described how the army was different from other organisations because 'the policies and the policies are more implemented; there are means and ways of dealing with these things'. But there were other factors affecting both work and social life that made the army a different kind of workplace too.

All about culture

'The job is all day, people live and breathe it,' explained Charles, an officer in charge of diversity policy.

> In other walks of life there is an employer–employee relationship at work. You walk out of the office, and you are yourself again. Because [in the army] people live in the same place, they are flipping from [being a] soldier to [being] themselves. It's a grey area. There is a blurred point between your work attitude and your personal attitude. Being in the army is a vocation; it's a way of life. It is drilled into people, and there is less freedom of expression as an individual.

Mike, his colleague, was wondering if this was the reason why people tended to self-segregate when they had a chance. 'When people are working together and have a break, the black F&Cs go off together and the Fijians are on their own.' He had come to the realisation that there was nothing intrinsically wrong with people wanting to relax with like-minded friends at moments like these, especially if it meant speaking your native tongue. Because of the intensity of the 'way of life' described by Charles, it was understandable that people would gravitate towards those with whom they felt most comfortable.

The notion that racism could be expunged from the army simply because people were used to obeying orders had been pretty much discredited. 'Rather than diktats and policy changes coming down the chain of command,' Charles went on, 'now there's an attempt to encourage soldiers to talk about their experience. There are specific focus groups, with gays and lesbians, women, minorities.'

He pointed to the Armed Forces Muslim Association (AFMA) and the Proud2Serve.net E-Network for lesbian, gay, bisexual and transsexual (LGBT) members of the British Armed Forces as recent examples. There had been other developments too, such as using DVD recordings of soldiers whose faces were blanked out to allow them to speak freely. These materials had evidently been eye-openers for some of the senior staff, bringing home the effects of routine racism and harassment, often unreported. But, as everyone knew, reporting incidents to your chain of command could actually be a disincentive. Those above you in rank were not necessarily the most sympathetic or proactive, as many had discovered to their cost. Accepting this fact meant it was necessary to provide another channel that would allow employees to step outside this framework.

The result was the launch of a new confidential phone service called Speak Out which invited individuals to report unfair treatment of themselves or their colleagues. This was very different from the earlier versions of help-lines promised a decade earlier and never followed up.

'The phone line is a major cultural change,' declared Charles.

The message is going down the chain of command. If you are not happy about bullying, talk to your chain of command. If you are not happy with that, phone this number. They represent the army as an employer and are qualified to know their responsibility. It is not about giving help or advice, but taking action [against] bullying, harassment, discrimination, inappropriate behaviour with the minimum of process.

In the first six months, 50 cases were dealt with, either internally through the chain of command or by direct action. Charles was determined that it would be a permanent fixture, despite the erosion of resources. 'The service expands and contracts,' he said, 'and [at the moment] is all military although there will be some civilian posts.' In 2011, the allocation for E&D work amounted to a mere £3.50 a head, but this figure would only go down as all budgets were under threat. Despite a change in government bringing in its wake the promise to restructure the whole public sector, the obligation to recruit ethnic minorities was still a factor. They confirmed that military chiefs were still called to the Defence Committee in the House of Commons periodically and asked questions about numbers.[24] It was important to remember, though, that racism and culture were just two aspects of a much broader agenda to 'manage' diversity. 'There's a different approach to women, a real pressure on women to be succeeding.' In this concluding section we turn once again to the drama of the employment tribunal where the army's internal battles are sometimes played out on a public stage.

A level playing field

As we have already seen, employment tribunals attract negative publicity for the army but they serve another purpose since they illustrate the fact that military organisations are not exempt from civilian employment law. Extensive media coverage of the more controversial cases, often with salacious details, has the added effect of testing perceptions of what soldiers should look like, how they should behave and what society expects of them. These reactions are not confined to civilians either, as new sources of media such as online blogs, forums and commentaries have greatly facilitated the public airing of once-private observations of serving soldiers, overlapping with more traditional forms of information such as newspapers, radio and TV. It is on these occasions that the reputation of the MoD as an enlightened and progressive employer competes with reactionary views about the principle of equality at work, particularly as it affects gender roles.[25]

The image of the intrepid, flexible woman soldier is a valuable tool for the MoD, both in terms of recruitment and in military operations as well. The military media operation in Afghanistan frequently posted items about female personnel, as in the 'heroine of Helmand', a 20-year-old member of the Royal Military Police who had 'made history' by arresting 17 members of the Taliban in 'a single DAY'.[26] Being a mother of young children need not be an obstacle, and in fact it could indicate her added readiness to serve the nation.[27] However, the reality could often be rather different. In 2010 the EHRC supported a member of the RAF who claimed that she had been removed from her job and had her promotion prospects delayed because she was pregnant.[28] The employment tribunal awarded her £16,000, and recommended several new procedures to ensure that the MoD gave pregnant women better protection from discrimination.

This ruling indicated that falling foul of equality law could be costly for any employer tempted to deny pregnant women their rights. Other landmark cases involving the armed forces have profound effects within the institution by drawing attention to the particular forms of inequality, harassment or intimidation on the basis of gender, ethnicity or sexuality. The case of Kerry Fletcher, an openly lesbian soldier in the British Army, provided a significant example. She joined in 1996, becoming the first woman to ride with the King's Troop, but was forced to leave the army as a result of the corrosive effects of bullying. In 2008 she was awarded £187,000 in compensation after the tribunal accepted her evidence of sexual harassment by a male sergeant. The tribunal commented: 'This is as severe a case of victimisation following an allegation of sexual harassment as one could see in an employment tribunal.'[29] Details revealed once again that the hierarchical chain of command structure served to protect those in authority while intimidating juniors from making complaints, a finding that led to further investigation and monitoring by the EHRC. But although the MoD was obliged to issue an apology to Fletcher, the hostility expressed by some sections of the media reflected a view inside the institution that the concept of individual rights enshrined in European equality legislation was at odds with military culture. This view was to be tested again in another landmark case, one that provided a context for the discussion of single parents that took place in the E&D session in Brecon.

In April 2010 a 28-year-old woman called Tilern Debique achieved notoriety by bringing a complaint against the MoD for discrimination on grounds of sex and race. Having joined through an OPT in St Vincent in 2002, Cpl Debique served in the Royal Signals, rising to the rank of corporal before she signed off on 2007, a year after she had given birth to a daughter. Her grievance was based on her employer's attitude towards her status as single parent; after reporting late for training and then a month later missing a parade, both as a result of childcare issues, she was told she was expected to be available for duty at all times and that the army was 'unsuitable for a single mother who couldn't sort out her childcare arrangements'. At the hearing Debique said that the reaction of her commanding officers left her feeling discriminated against and 'on a path to dismissal'.[30]

The details of the case were hard to discern, such was the torrent of venom that greeted the news of the employment tribunal considering her grievance. Under the front page headline: 'Mother of all defeats!' the *Daily Mail* announced that the army faced a £100,000 payout if it was found that Debique had suffered loss of earnings, injury to feelings and aggravated damages.[31] Hundreds of words were devoted by the *Mail* to ridiculing and undermining her predicament. The leader commented that she had effectively betrayed the many brave female soldiers who, serving in Afghanistan and elsewhere, have 'fought for the right to be treated as equals by the army'.[32] When tribunal ruled in her favour, the paper compared her likely settlement with the compensation received by a paratrooper who was severely disabled as a result of injuries sustained in Afghanistan. During the week of the hearing it continued to run articles about the subversion of British society by 'pseudo-courts' representing human rights culture which had created a 'sanctum for political correctness'.

What made this case a landmark in the history of UK equality law was that it took account of Debique's immigration status as a Commonwealth solider, awarding her damages for racial discrimination. The tribunal ruled she had been discriminated against when immigration laws prevented her sister in St Vincent from travelling to the UK to care for her daughter. Debique, who represented herself, had claimed that she had planned to bring her sister from St Vincent for this purpose but immigration law prevented her from staying for more than six months. This meant that she, Debique, was in a different position from UK personnel who would be able to call on family support with childcare. The tribunal panel chairman suggested that the UKBA should make an exception for serving soldiers and commented: 'We found that such an exception would have put foreign and Commonwealth soldiers, and particularly the complainant, on a level playing field with soldiers with families who have the right of abode in the UK.'[33]

The case was also remarkable for other reasons. As we saw, the reticence shown by some of the warrant officers in the E&D class reflected strong views about women who became pregnant in service, never mind demand-ing schedules to be amended to suit their childcare needs. Some still believed that pregnant women should be discharged, just like in the old days, and they were not alone. A quick glance at Army Rumour Service (ARRSE) aired this perspective in no uncertain terms, with comments on Debique's case such as:

> As evidently she can't do her duty, parades, work etc., she should simply be discharged as a waste of space.
> Just shows how stupid the law is under New Liarbour that a cunt like this can get compensasion [*sic*].[34]

Other comments blamed 'the law' for allowing cases like this to be taken seriously, using the example of Debique's successful hearing to condemn the whole notion of E&D.

> When stuff like this is allowed to happen, we might as well disband the MOD and call it a day. We've had some excellent recruits from Common-wealth countries, but why did we need to go hunting them in the first place? It's a slippery slope to long hair, trade unions and no war after 1700 hours every Friday.[35]

The fact that the tribunal recognised Debique's grievance and that this cost the MoD thousands of pounds in compensation served to underline the E&D instructor's insistence that it was imperative to know the law, regard-less of personal reservations. However, as the media and online forums revealed, there were also resentments expressed outside the confines of the army, although not necessarily about female soldiers' right to be mothers. Debique's ethnicity presented an opportunity to articulate anti-immigration sentiments as a way of undermining the legitimacy of her grievance. For one thing, it enabled her claim for compensation to be denounced as a ploy to 'return home to her poverty-stricken Caribbean village as a rich woman'.[36] The size of the settlement demanded by Debique was regarded as proof of her lack of commitment to her job as a soldier, reflecting that as a migrant, her motives had been pecuniary and self-interested all along. Another report in the *Mail* wrote that: 'The youngest of eight children – six girls and two boys – born to Tilman Jordan and Alina DeBique, Tilern spent her first ten years in a tiny wooden two-room shack, sharing one bedroom. Cooking was outdoors, while a standpipe provided water.'[37]

Debique's Caribbean origins also provided grounds for condemning her child-raising practices as well. The same report told how she had left her baby, apparently conceived under 'mysterious' circumstances, with relatives in St Vincent for the first two years of its life. Instead of interpreting her childcare arrangements as the result of a supportive transnational family struggling to cope in the face of restrictive UK immigration law, this was used as another stick to beat her in public as a fraudulent mother, a charge which only compounded her crimes as a hopelessly unsuitable soldier.

Debique's claim for financial compensation on grounds of loss of earnings, injury to feelings and aggravated damages was portrayed as a form of betrayal since it far exceeded the actual payment awarded to a physically wounded male war-hero. The comparison underlined the level of sacrifice demanded of real soldiers, most of whom are male.[38] However, the case was unique in that it raised the vexed issue of the army's duty to embrace the specific needs and problems of migrant military families as well.[39]

This point directs us to the partners and families of servicemen and women from Commonwealth countries and Nepal. Looking at the army 'way of life' as experienced by partners who are mainly female and predominantly civilian, the next chapter will explore some of the issues entailed in being designated a 'dependant' *as well as* a migrant.

Part IV
Migration

Image 5   Gurkha Variety Store, Tidworth, Hampshire

8
Like Coming to Mars

For a civilian, encountering the different traditions and cultures of army life is strange enough. 'But for someone from a Commonwealth country to come here, it's like taking a human being to the moon or putting a person on Mars.' Salote was well-placed to understand the fate of a service family living far from home. She had left Fiji to join the British Army eight years earlier. Her husband and children followed her once she was settled in her post as a regimental clerk.

Gurinder, who had recently moved from her home in India, would have agreed with Salote's verdict. Her husband Sukhdev confided in me that she had spent the first few months of her new life in tears. She had accused her soldier husband of imprisoning her because she had no friends and no one to talk to when he was at work and she did not speak enough English to travel around on her own. She was also pregnant for the first time. But by the time we met that autumn she was considerably happier. She had learned how to use the local buses, begun the process of obtaining her driving licence and made friends with some of the Gurkha wives stationed nearby in Windsor. On this particular day she and Sukhdev felt like celebrating. They had just heard that his mother had got her visa to join them for six months and had booked her ticket to fly from India the following week. The baby was due within days and Sukhdev was anxious that he only had two weeks leave. 'We don't know what to do, it's our first baby,' he kept saying, mightily relieved that his mother would arrive in time to take control of the situation.

Sukhdev was a Guardsman who had been born in India but was recruited in 2007 while working as a delivery driver in Southall, west London. He had been persuaded to enlist by recruiters who visited the Gurdwara regularly, hoping to sign up young Sikhs. He was 25 at the time and not particularly fit – he even had a minor conviction for drunk driving – but, he said, that did not seem to matter to the recruiters. During his training at ITC he had returned to India to marry Gurinder, but she did not join him until he had been allocated a house in service family accommodation (SFA) the following year. His first attempt at getting a visa for his mother had been unsuccessful, so he had gone to his Company Commander for help. It was a common procedure for soldiers from Commonwealth countries who did not have other family members at hand, and a relatively simple application. This time, with official endorsement from his unit, the request had gone through smoothly.

Bringing relatives into the country to help with childcare was seen as a positive step, the extra support at home regarded as a benefit to the soldier. A paper revising the conditions of service life, issued in 2008, spelled this out: 'the Army believes that stability of family life is of great importance for its personnel and encourages accompanied service wherever practicable'.[1] The same document acknowledged the institution's theoretical commitment to what is known as the Army Family, an overarching community composed of all soldiers, spouses and civil partners to which all newcomers automatically belonged. 'The immediate group you belong to is often called a Regiment, Corps or Unit, and is like a smaller family within the Army family,' explained the paper. 'Most people develop very strong ties of loyalty to this group.' But as single parent Tilern Debique had found, the definition of the word 'practicable' when applied to migrants was severely qualified by immigration law. And for a migrant entering the Army Family on any scale, unused to any kind of life in the UK let alone the particular demands of military culture, the initial degree of isolation and loneliness could be intense.

Abi was a neighbour of Gurinder who lived just a few hundred metres away, but they were not acquainted. She was from Gambia and had recently joined her husband, also a Guardsman, with their five-year-old son. She had no relatives to help with childcare but luckily she was able to enrol her child at the local primary school a short walk away. Her immediate problem was that she had been given the wrong visa which meant that she was not able to start looking for a job. The advice worker in the local HIVE office, part of the Army Welfare Service (AWS), was helping her rectify the situation but Abi was evidently suffering from depression. Although she was encouraged to sign up for classes in the nearby community centre specifically provided for service family members, she told me that apart from going to her son's school, she rarely went out. Her social life consisted of evenings spent with her husband and the colleagues he brought home, fellow West Africans who were either single or unaccompanied. 'They are all black,' she said quietly, 'and they move together.' There was no doubt that in the daytime she was desperately lonely despite having numerous support services within easy reach.

The perspective of partners who are not only ethnic minorities but also foreign nationals can offer a way to test the institution's stated commitment to principles of equality and diversity, as well as to the underlying ideals of an inclusive military family that looks after its own, 'from cradle to grave'. The degree to which migrant households from widely varying backgrounds were integrated into the formal and informal structures of army life depended on many factors, from immigration issues to the quality of community support in any particular place. This chapter begins by exploring the critical role that all civilian partners play in the institution before considering the specific circumstances of those who happened to be migrants as well.

The green machine

The fate of a military spouse, as Salote had observed in her comment about arriving on Mars, meant becoming incorporated into a very different way of life, the dimensions of which were barely visible from outside. It was a role that was invariably portrayed as female, despite increasing numbers of women serving in the army, and one that featured in the news primarily on two occasions: in a collective joyful reunion when the soldier returns from deployment or in a dignified state of grief when the soldier is killed in action. There were exceptions of course, although these tended only to underline the role of women as faithful wives. In 2009 the tabloids promoted a calendar that featured 'army widows' posing naked to raise money for the charity Help for Heroes.[2] In a very different example, the situation of 'military wives' whose husbands were fighting in Afghanistan was thrust into the mainstream media limelight in 2011 as a result of the BBC TV programme 'The Choir'. This three-part series culminated in the women performing at the Royal British Legion's annual Festival of Remembrance at the Royal Albert Hall before going on to launch their single, 'Wherever you are' which became the Christmas best-seller that year.[3]

As this 'reality' documentary revealed, the day-to-day experience of being a wife, girlfriend or partner of a serving soldier takes place in a world within worlds. This was true regardless of whether spouses were active participants in the community or cut off and alienated from the whole institution. For this reason, voluntary organisations like the Army Families Federation (AFF) prefer employees who are at least related to someone in military service.

The AFF was formed in 1995, replacing the Federation of Army Wives' Clubs which had existed since the 1980s. The shift to 'families' rather than 'wives' was not just an effect of feminism or an attempt to recognise the needs of male spouses. It was also a way of including parents and siblings and acknowledging their relationship to the institution as well. Today the AFF claims to function as an independent voice of British Army families worldwide, addressing every aspect of the lifestyle. It was not a requirement that applicants for jobs within the AFF had to be related to a soldier, but it certainly helped. 'Candidates are asked what are the main problems facing army families, and it is likely that you answer better if you have experience,' I was told when I paid a visit to the HQ. The AFF officers whom I met – all women married to soldiers – agreed that the MoD had finally begun to grasp the importance of listening to parents as well as partners rather than seeing them as peripheral to the mental health of the workforce.

Although the organisation was not allowed to intervene in the 'green machine', which was army slang for the chain of command, it played an important part in representing problems and concerns that families brought to their attention. This was done on a systematic basis since all inquiries were logged, collated and published in the quarterly AFF Families' Concerns report, providing statistical evidence of matters affecting 'the global British Army community'. Housing was the biggest issue and the second was family life – deployment, divorce, effects of moving around, and education for kids and spouses. In addition the AFF produce 64,000 copies of the free quarterly *Army Families Journal* which was a rich source of information about the role that military families played both in supporting the institution and in sustaining it under difficult conditions.

Between February and November 2010, the organisation carried out its own survey among the families of soldiers deployed in Afghanistan, the aim of which was to identify issues that arose specifically as a result of separation. The research paid close attention, for example, to respondents' feelings about pre-deployment advice as well as their experience during the period after the soldier returned. Although it is hard to measure the longer-term impact of the report, one example of potential conflict between the AFF and the 'green machine' can be provided by the findings on psychological support. The AFF recommended that army families should have immediate access to counselling before, during and after combat operations. The army's personnel department responded by saying that families were already eligible for counselling at public expense either through the Army Welfare Service or through their GP. The AFF made it clear that this was not sufficient.

The NHS system is not geared up to deal with the unique problems that military families face. If the Army is going to continue to send soldiers on dangerous deployments then it must acknowledge that this can cause mental distress to families, especially if spouse is injured, and give them the mental support they deserve.[4]

One respondent quoted in the report gave a particularly candid account of her experience. 'I guess the only thing that saved me and my children was staying busy. I didn't realise at the time that I was going through a severe depression with the worry of all that was going on.' One of her closest friends lost her husband and she was not able to talk to her own husband about how to deal with this because she did not want him to worry about her.

My family was my rock through everything. It doesn't even have to be blood family. Being close to others in the same unit might be better because they understand what you are going through. Your civilian family will want to help but aren't going through the same thing so they won't really understand.[5]

For Cynthia Enloe, who has analysed the gender politics of military institutions on an international basis, every organisation or employment sector that relies on employees who are married is prone to send out messages about what the ideal spouse should be.[6] She studied the concept of the 'Model Military Wife' over the course of several decades, showing how different national institutions had come to acknowledge the potential benefits that employees' partners bring, not just by supporting their own family member but also by contributing to the well-being of the whole. In an essay entitled 'If a woman is "married to the military" who is the husband?' she wrote, 'What is distinctive about militaries is how clear...that message is. It is spelled out in rituals, in memos, in orders, and in handbooks written by military wives themselves.'[7]

The first requirement was that 'She has come to her own conclusion that the most important thing for her own and her family's well-being is that her husband perform his military job well.'[8] Working through the profile of the ideal army spouse in the contemporary period she included the possibility that 'She accepts that waging war – or keeping the militarized peace – is a high-stress occupation, and so she makes allowances for her husband's moodiness, short temper, and impatience in the weeks and months following his deployment to a conflict zone.'[9]

The value of Enloe's model, which included a much longer list of attributes, was not that it delineated how real women conformed to this mould in practice, or that it precluded the idea that spouses might choose not to become incorporated in such compliant ways. Her point was that many women tried to support their partners in the best way that they could, and that a significant proportion did find it rewarding to work for the benefit of the institution as a whole. By illustrating the parameters of acceptable behaviour associated with being married to a soldier, Enloe emphasised a dimension of military culture that was often neglected in studies of national defence and security issues. Without the unpaid labour and emotional support of thousands of military spouses standing behind their individual soldier, the whole system would grind to a halt.

Conversely, those who refused to play this role might find themselves in danger of harming their partners' careers or of being seen as disloyal or even unpatriotic. Critical commentary from wives, partners, mothers, fathers and sometimes children could also carry devastating weight in the event of a soldier's death. In the US, Cindy Sheehan attracted publicity worldwide when she camped outside Bush's Texas ranch in 2005 after her soldier son Casey was killed in Iraq. In the UK, Military Families against the Iraq War supplied a powerful voice not only in condemning the illegality of the war in which their children were being killed but also in drawing attention to the lack of adequate equipment for troops. When one of the founding members, Reg Keys, whose son Tom was killed along with five others in the Iraqi town of Majar al-Kabir in June 2003, stood against Blair in the 2005 election, he told the prime minister to his face: 'I am here to hold you to account for the human and material costs of this war'.[10]

In many national militaries, spouses, particularly women, are expected to play extraordinary voluntary roles as social event planners, community liaison officers, social workers, pastoral carers and taken-for-granted members of a support network operating in the interests of the soldiers, whether at home or on deployment. The partner needs to function as a single parent while the soldier is away, able to carry out all manner of practical tasks from managing the household economy to dealing with car maintenance, in addition to having their own jobs as well. Military staff are also frequently posted to different locations, both within their own countries and abroad, and families are expected to follow, with all the practical and emotional upheaval that this involves.

Salote's comment about the shock of relocating from the global south to the north was a reaction shared by many of those recruited in Commonwealth countries as we have seen. But her point about intergalactic travel also communicated the alienation that many experienced on entering a military community with its own internal dynamics. It was no wonder that women like Abi and Gurinder were completely disoriented when they arrived, compelled to seek out the company of other minorities whose language and culture they shared in order to orient themselves in this strange new existence. But had the institution adapted sufficiently in order to foster a genuinely inclusive and socially cohesive community, particularly at a local level? After more than a decade of 'multiculturalisation', what was the view of the institution from the standpoint of women who were both soldiers and spouses?

Social networks

My first attempt to attend a coffee morning for 'army wives' was a huge disappointment. Organised by the welfare service in a UK-based RLC regiment that had a significant representation of soldiers from both Gurkha and Commonwealth backgrounds, it was a routine event in the monthly calendar of the base and the main purpose of my visit. When I arrived, however, there was a handful of young English mothers with toddlers but not a Fijian, African, Nepali or Caribbean spouse in sight. 'They don't want to come!' I was told, on this and other similar occasions, as though it was their own fault that they were not participating in this social event.

When I reported this to Salote she agreed with this reaction from the welfare staff, and was surprisingly vehement about the issue. Her experience both as a soldier and an active member of one of the Fijian congregations in the Southampton area had given her a particularly sharp perspective. 'It's true,' she said. 'They just refuse to integrate.'

The network of Fiji expatriates is very strong in the south of England, much of it organised around particular churches. 'The thing is,' she told me when I visited her in her home on her lunch break, 'they have their own little groups also. It's to do with their churches. You'd be surprised that there's about four or five different churches with the Fijians alone. So it depends on their faith, or I don't know, where they're from, so they decide to be part of this group and that's that.'

Salote was critical of the reluctance shown by many of her fellow Fiji citizens to move beyond their comfort zone. 'I mean it's a pity really,' she continued. 'It's not a normal way of life for you not to integrate. You need people and that's one of their biggest downfalls I think.'

She was convinced that some of the younger women were unable to adapt to living in a different country, and that this was contributing to their inevitable isolation and loneliness. Her civilian husband was a chaplain for the UK Fiji community, and she had many relatives both in the army and outside. As we sat and talked, two young men came in and made themselves lunch, both of them cousins who were working on the same base.

> From a wife's point of view, what I find nowadays, the majority of them really, they've just come off school, like they just do their GCSEs or college so they're 18 or 19, they get married and they come straight across here and they try and find their feet. It's communal living back at home, and you've got your aunt just on the other side of the street, you've got your mother living 30 minutes drive away and all that. You've got all this family support [there] and out here they don't.

Salote had observed that many of these young spouses made friends with those who were already established which often meant getting caught up in cliques or tensions within the community. But she had found some of the younger women resistant to going out and was sure that the root of their depression was that they did not know what their husbands were actually doing. 'It's just been throwing them in the deep end really,' she said.

> They come across after getting married and the next few weeks he gets deployed to Afghanistan so they're just sat there, depressed really, and they don't integrate themselves with the community also which just adds to their depression. They don't speak to their neighbours, that just adds to the whole thing.

Salote was the church administrator and therefore at the heart of the social network. She was constantly telling younger women to find out about the courses available at the education centre and urging them to attend the coffee mornings.

Personally I think once you go out for these coffee mornings, you'll be sorted, you'll make friends and you'll find, it's not only you facing the same problems because the others, even though she's from Kenya, you know she's Welsh, Scottish, yes... they'll find at the end of the day we're all human beings, we come through very similar problems anyway.

For partners arriving from Fiji, as from many Commonwealth countries, the question of fluency in English was less of an issue than it was for other migrant spouses. The Commonwealth Guide for Families encouraged English language lessons as a way of getting 'more out of life in the UK' and improving their CVs.[11] But under new guidelines issued by the UK Borders Authority (UKBA) in 2010, the spouse or partner of a member of the armed forces was not required to meet the requirement to show that they could speak and understand English.[12]

Many women, however, had acquired professional qualifications in Fiji which were not transferable, without further studies at least. Understandably this contributed to a sense of disappointment and frustration. 'Some do work, the strong-headed ones,' said Salote, 'but they are also aware of the stigma if it's the wrong kind of job.' Stacking shelves in a supermarket like Asda was considered demeaning for many families, and work in care homes was often seen as preferable.

Childcare was another major problem for those who hoped to work. Salote explained why this was particularly hard for some of the women:

It's just that they've been spoon-fed back at home because you don't pay for child-minding. 'OK, Auntie will come and pick you up' and so and so.

Bringing an aunt or their mother to come and live with them for six months was one way of dealing with this. But Salote was also disturbed by the way that the younger wives were reticent about going to family planning clinics which meant repeated pregnancies. Sex and contraception were taboo topics at home, she told me, and new wives were expected to produce children right away. She could see the pressures from both sides, and had noticed that in recent years a lot more men from Fiji were marrying British women.

The thing is with Fijians you don't only marry the wife, you marry the wife's family so you know you've got 50 less people to worry about, you just worry about your family and that's it.

That's the same now with our Fijian girls in the army, they're marrying English soldiers also and yes, they should really be applauded for that!

Salote was by no means unique in her estimation of the difficulties faced by spouses who had joined their partners from afar. Martha, also originally from Fiji and a clerk in the AGC, was a single parent with three children. The

Army Welfare Service had supported her request for a posting to Germany after her divorce from her soldier husband, but she returned to the UK after a year as she was unable to find suitable childcare. Now a corporal based in Wiltshire, she too was in a position to comment on the experiences of Fijian migrants from the perspective of a soldier and a spouse. Martha had been involved in organising the Commonwealth regimental day in her area, and was sometimes seen as a port of call for local welfare officers. But she had not had a traditional upbringing, she explained, and many of the cultural issues described by Fijians were foreign to her as well.

'Culture is not an excuse,' she said crisply, adding that many of those who came from rural backgrounds were often unprepared for life in the UK.

> They marry someone else in the village and they have no idea about living in a big country and how to integrate. Many have been here for three or four years and are still living like in Fiji, giving the same excuse. They come with no kids, and then their kids live the lifestyle here.

The experience of both women as military administrator, migrant mother, aunt, community organiser and long-term resident of the UK had made them keen ethnographers of the social relations within the institution and I couldn't help wondering whether their employers appreciated them as potential assets. My evidence collected during two years' research suggested that the army welfare services throughout the organisation were unevenly informed and ill-equipped to deal with the particular issues raised by being a cultural minority as well as a migrant.

Third-line citizens

'The sobbing wife plays more than a walk-on part!' remarked one unit welfare officer (UWO) as he explained the importance of role play in their training at Bristol University. He was telling me about the residential courses that the senior NCOs were required to take before being promoted to the rank of colour sergeant and appointed to run the regimental welfare unit, often the last stage of a long career. The first course dealt with policy and regulations while the second addressed interpersonal skills, employing professional actors to breathe life into the many situations the newly trained officer would have to face. The UWO is normally the first port of call for soldiers and family members who want advice, and they are expected to deal with day to day issues from leaking roofs to domestic violence. The inquiries relating to immigration regulations, spousal visas and citizenship applications provided a whole new layer of advice-work, and it was hard to imagine how any amount of role play could equip them to provide the necessary information.

One sympathetic UWO, working in one of the biggest units for employing F&C soldiers, had been in the job for 21 months and found himself dealing with everything 'from visa applications to National Insurance numbers; letters of consent to get family members over; personal problems; cultural difficulties. Especially the wives' side of life.' He was very blunt in his assessment of the situation. As far as he was concerned, the spouses of Commonwealth soldiers were 'third line citizens'.

He echoed the familiar complaint that the army had not anticipated the welfare issues that were entailed in employing non-UK citizens with dependants. For him the biggest thing was adjusting to different cultures, and he had found the cultural guidance document to be helpful. But they had only been produced the previous year and he was of an age to have witnessed the slow pace of institutional change since 1998. 'We had to find out the hard way. It's very much a question of suck it and see.'

The AFF had also been caught unawares. In 2006 a small group of F&C women delegates intervened during the biennial conference, raising the profile of Commonwealth families for the first time. One result was that a new job was created to address their specific concerns. The first to take up this post, a British army spouse married to an officer, quickly discovered that most questions were about immigration, requiring more professional assistance than a sympathetic ear. In 2008, when she started, the dependants of migrant soldiers had been arriving for almost a decade. The wheels had only begun turning within the administrative structure of the army in 2004 when the Adjutant General instructed a task force to investigate the needs of F&C soldiers. By then it had emerged that problems regarding immigration stamps, visas, passports and citizenship were having an impact on their work, let alone their mental health. The inexperience and ignorance on the part of army personnel staff were contributory factors, but many of the issues regarding immigration regulations were beyond their control in any case.

As a result of the investigation into the army's own procedures, however, a new system was put in place which allowed information gathered from families, soldiers and their units to be passed up the chain of command, not just to the MoD but to the Home Office too, in the hope of influencing policy at government level. As the largest employer of Commonwealth citizens among the armed forces, the army was in the best position to identify what it termed 'service need'. The newly reformed Families Welfare team, based in an administrative section known as PS4, became the most significant link in this chain, with a remit to ensure that no serving personnel and their families were disadvantaged by their status as migrants.

Within Army HQ, PS4 operated as the helpdesk for foreign and Commonwealth issues. It was the point of reference for all welfare staff dealing with particularly complicated individual cases, but it also compiled evidence of generic problems which required a more comprehensive solution at a policy level. Most decisions about immigration and settlement rights, for example, were not the army's preserve and had to be referred to the UKBA, through the Land Forces Secretary, as we will see in the next chapter. But over the years PS4 had relied on feedback from internal networks developed among minority soldiers and their dependants wherever there was a critical mass. Where the expertise of F&C personnel had been recognised on a formal basis there was ample evidence that the institution had benefited immeasurably, particularly if and when that person was also an army spouse.

A different career in mind

Catterick is the largest single garrison in the British Army, the home of several infantry regiments employing a significant number of F&C soldiers as well as the Infantry Training Centre (ITC). When Kasa arrived in March 2008 to join her husband who was working as an instructor there, she too had huddled at home, shivering and bored, until she decided to go out and get a job. She discovered firsthand that that the qualifications that many women had earned at home were not recognised. This could be degrading, particularly if they had been to university, as she had. 'I was educated in Australia,' she said, 'although I didn't finish university. I walked up to the job centre and they said "You've got to take GCSEs, or you can't get a job here."'

A few weeks later she saw an advert for the post as F&C adviser within the ITC and applied. This was a position introduced in 2006 to help the Commonwealth recruits streaming through the centre, offering pastoral care as well as practical advice. Having a base within the welfare offices allowed Kasa to learn about the institution from the inside, while at the same time she was becoming acquainted with the Fijian community in the area. When we met, a year after she had first arrived, she had a broad view of the situation for all Fijian wives and families who had moved to the UK to accompany soldiers.

> At home we always can get food. Here the poor wife takes her children to school and sits at home. Most work in care homes, that's all they can do. They are well above that level. In fact, most wives, their educational background is higher than their husbands'. Most of us gave up good jobs back home – in banks, government, airlines, highly qualified jobs. We are doing nothing here.

I asked if many considered joining the army themselves.

'It's not the direction for them,' she replied. 'They had a different career in mind. But we followed our hearts here,' she laughed, patting her chest, 'and we should deal with it. More compromising would make life easier.'

Kasa felt strongly that UWOs needed to do a lot more for Commonwealth women accompanying their husbands. Although her job entailed working with recruits, she was often contacted in emergencies with urgent requests for help. Once, she was called out at three in the morning to a hospital over an hour's drive away where a Gambian woman was in the throes of labour. Her husband was away on exercise, she spoke little English and was terrified at the prospect of being touched by white people. Kasa had to reassure the woman that her life was in expert hands and that she had no choice but to submit. It was hard not to be shocked by the degree of alienation from her surroundings and the terror that it could induce in such potentially dangerous situations. More routine, however, were the late-night calls Kasa received from women whose husbands were abusing them.

The numbers of domestic violence cases among the Fijian community were growing dramatically, she reported, often leading to separation and divorce. She had noticed the particular patterns that she had witnessed among the soldiers returning from combat, especially among those who felt threatened by their partners' growing independence in their absence:

> We have a different method of solving problems. The guys have their own mindset. They are mixing their own culture and what they have picked up here. They have mixed feelings when they come back and wives can become scapegoats.

Levels of domestic violence were known to be significantly higher among soldiers of all backgrounds who had been in combat, a pattern that the AFF had identified in its 2010 survey. This was not just a matter of post-traumatic stress, although that was a significant factor. Sexualised violence operates as a form of control in all societies but relationships between men and women who work inside military organisations are inevitably shaped by the expectations and rewards attached to particular forms of 'militarised masculinity'.[13] In other words, qualities such as toughness, hardness, aggression and prowess in physical pursuits such as rugby, are especially prized in cultures where men are trained to think of themselves as 'warriors'.[14]

Although domestic violence was a criminal offence, for those who already felt insecure or remote, the threat of legal action did not necessarily make it easier to report such behaviour.[15] Technically there was a range of army welfare agencies available for assistance, including some staffed by civilians, but victims were known to feel uncomfortable having to seek help from their husband's employer, especially if it meant going into the barracks to report him. Kasa's concern that welfare personnel were ill-equipped to deal with this type of situation was corroborated by Litia, another Fijian civilian who had worked as an F&C adviser.

> Dependants are the driving force [but] we often put up with violence. There is no special support for wives during deployment and the wives' status is dependent on the husbands. Why should we go to welfare meetings and hear 'we'll look into it'? We are tired of hearing that.

The fact that Fijians had acquired a reputation for higher levels of domestic violence was reproduced in the cultural guidance document:

> Despite the general equality of opportunity for women in Fijian society, it is a traditional expectation for the husband to be the head of the household and for the wife to accept the husband's domestic authority. This can lead to a greater tolerance of controlling behaviour including, sometimes, domestic violence.[16]

However, in addition to flagging up potential problems or culturally unacceptable behaviours, the guide also identified attributes that were thought positive in the context of a military environment. The section on Fijians provided a telling example of the type of characteristics that were highly valued. 'By many accounts,' the notes stated,

> Fijians are an outgoing, physical, community-oriented people. They respond well to team environments... Fijians are welcoming of other ethnic groups and are known for their hospitality and friendliness. Fijians in the British Army fit in easily with people of other cultures... The great majority of Fijians are church-going Christians.

This information helps to explain why Fijians were the largest national group within the Commonwealth contingent. Their inherent suitability, evident from this list of traits, suggested that there was a connection between the ideal qualities of the soldier and the support structure on which he or she relied.

Model communities

We saw in Chapter 5 that the organisation of the Gurkha soldiers represented the historic idea – known as the theory of martial races – that particular ethnic groups produced a blend of ideal qualities required for soldiering, and that these qualities were best protected by nurturing a strong sense of cultural identity. The ideal migrant community is one that performs this role, not just by supporting and servicing the soldier without complaint, but also by reinforcing the uniqueness of their capacity as warriors. The statement that the British Army did not want the Gurkhas to become 'brown Brits' was a reflection of the fact that they were valued precisely for the ethnic traits that distinguished them from their UK counterparts. According to this logic, the existence of a dedicated self-enclosed community was vital in preserving these qualities, preventing them from being corroded or diluted through undue contact with mainstream UK culture.

While the settlement of large numbers of service families from Commonwealth countries had been relatively recent, the 200 years of continuous employment of Gurkha soldiers by the British Army had entailed an extraordinary pattern of transmigration between Nepal and the UK.[17] Throughout the twentieth century at least, the social networks created and sustained by the Gurkha diaspora had been factored into calculations about recruitment, retention, retirement and remuneration, with far-reaching implications for communities in both countries. However, the families of British Gurkha soldiers had remained virtually invisible in the campaigns for equal terms and conditions, including retrospective pension claims and the right to reside in the UK. The spouse of a Gurkha soldier serving in the contemporary British Army was still expected to follow her husband as the invisible counterpart of the 'warrior gentleman', to borrow anthropologist Lionel Caplan's memorable phrase.[18]

Sorrow and happiness

There was a marked contrast between conditions for Commonwealth and Gurkha families in many British Army units and the sense of community for Gurkha families in their regimental centre in Folkestone. 'We are from a Third World country,' Capt P told me on the day I went to visit. 'We always have had disasters and we are used to helping each other through difficult times.' It was hard to miss his implication that the people of Folkestone did not have the same understanding of community because nothing bad ever really happened there. He was escorting me to the coffee morning, the first since the battalion had taken up residency a few weeks earlier.

The Royal Gurkha Rifle regiment (RGR) was based at the historic military camp in Shorncliffe, on the edge of Folkestone, after moving from Church Crookham in Berkshire in 2000. The two battalions, 1 RGR and 2 RGR, alternated every three years between the UK and Brunei. Kent was not as attractive for many of the Nepali families partly for economic reasons, as those in Brunei were eligible for the Local Overseas Allowance (LOA). Apart from financial considerations, Folkestone happens to be situated on the English Channel, just south of Dover and very near the White Cliffs, and there is little protection from the winds blowing off the inhospitable expanse of the North Sea. However, significant numbers of Gurkhas retire in the area around Folkestone which means there is an extensive community with many Nepali-owned convenience stores, a cash-and-carry and at least one travel agent specialising in flights to Nepal. On the way to the base, the radio in the car was playing a Nepali station broadcast from Folkestone. A plumber was being interviewed and the reporter was asking whether he exclusively worked for Nepalis. He said he didn't.

Although I was interested in the lives of Gurkha soldiers on the base, my real motive for visiting Shorncliffe was to hear from their partners about their experience of life in the British Army. Over 90 per cent of soldiers who are married applied to bring their spouses from Nepal and if they were posted anywhere for longer than five months they were expected to move their families to accompany them. The regimental SFA was situated in Dover, Canterbury, Hastings and Ashford as well as Folkestone itself where there was a community centre, welfare office and nursery, catering to around 190 families. When we arrived, the hall was full of women and small children, the noise and general bustle concealing the fact that many other wives were absent, with jobs as teaching assistants, carers, nurses, housekeepers and secretaries as well as service work on the base itself. It was considered desirable for those without kids to augment the men's salaries which were brought into line with the rest of the army in 2007.

The difference between the two coffee mornings could not have been greater. As a guest, I was warmly welcomed by a group that included the Gurkha Major's wife who was the most senior and to whom the others showed deference. Balancing my cup and saucer on my knee as I tried to make notes, it was hard to keep up with the effusive answers to my questions about community life. They emphasised how much they looked after each other, especially when the men were away. 'Our community is very strong. We share sorrow and happiness together. As long as we are in the army we have no serious problems'. Apart from the climate, service life in Kent was little different than it had been in Brunei: disco nights, cooking classes, a mothers-and-toddlers group twice a week and an intricate network to welcome and initiate new arrivals. When I asked if they had exercise classes they admitted to taking part in a fun run in Brunei and to having a yoga class at one point, but otherwise I got the impression they left the fitness to their husbands.

This glimpse of a social structure within the base indicates a tight-knit ethnic group with strong historical and cultural ties. Many were from families with connections to British Gurkhas going back three or four generations, and so were familiar with service life, as they pointed out. The fact that the soldiers were largely recruited from particular areas of Nepal, at least until recently, meant that whole communities were incorporated into a trans-national migrant economy. Meanwhile, within the UK, the image of Gurkhas as a homogenous group rarely revealed evidence of fissures within this 'model community'. The geographical and social distinctions between castes were not just maintained in the UK, but in some cases had become significant in terms of where people lived. According to anthropologist Mitra Pariyar:

> The Rais and Limbus are dominant in Ashford and Oxford, whereas the Gurungs and Magars dominate the Aldershot and Farnborough area. Some small clusters of Bishwakarma families have found their havens – quite aloof from other Nepalese settlements – in smaller towns such as Andover, Bicester and Brize Norton. They openly express that they would be happy if no other castes, particularly the upper castes, came to live close to them. The idea is to escape possible discrimination by fellow Nepalis from other castes.[19]

The degree of social division inside Gurkha communities was rarely discussed in relation to military family life but it is relevant for two reasons here. First, as we saw in Chapter 5, the existence of caste and clan distinctions among particular ethno-cultural groups, like Fijians, was only a problem if it created an alternative chain of command within the army. In many other ways, having strong social structures was another positive asset, making particular groups more likely to submit to the disciplinary regime and patterns of deference required in a military environment.

The second point is that class hierarchies existed to a different degree in all military institutions, not least in the British Army. It hardly needs pointing out that the officers trained at RMAS were drawn from very different social strata than the infantry recruits, many of whom left school at 16. I once asked a mixed group of Commonwealth soldiers how they viewed class differences in British society. One of them had just made a comment about officers going off into their rooms and drinking port, and I wondered what they made of local class warfare which I had assumed was ongoing throughout the organisation. They looked at me with some surprise, not understanding my question. For them, the notion of class they brought from their home countries was a sharper distinction between rich and poor. They did not seem particularly alert to the signs and symbols of class antagonism appearing in everyday exchanges, nor were they acutely sensitive either to the working-class or middle-class identities of their colleagues.

In the context of the 'army family' as a whole, however, and the smaller components of unit life on a base, the combination of social status, ethnic background and military rank meant that spouses were incorporated into the structure of social relations along with their partners. Just as the Gurkha Major's wife was clearly the most important person at the coffee morning I attended, so the wives of the sergeant majors or other senior officers in a regular unit would have been treated with equivalent respect at a gathering of UK spouses. For new partners arriving from other countries, learning to navigate new forms of etiquette in a different culture was not easy. This was just as true for Nepali women as it was for spouses of Commonwealth soldiers. Outside the main bases where Gurkha soldiers were stationed, such as Folkestone, Swindon and Brecon, smaller clusters of Nepali families could experience a much greater degree of isolation in contrast to the inclusiveness on show in Kent. Here again, the perspective of a support worker was able to reveal the differences between belonging to a family within a family, and living on the outside.

From another country

Savita's experience as a Gurkha support worker in Folkestone had made her aware of the isolation that many wives felt, especially when their husbands were away. As a result, she had developed her own theories about being an army spouse. She had had a very different career before she got married over ten years earlier. 'I graduated from Calcutta University,' she told me, 'and now I'm following my husband everywhere.' She laughed as she reeled off all the places where they had been posted: 'from Netheravon to Brunei, from Brunei to Scotland, Scotland back to Brunei, Brunei back to Folkestone, in Kent, then back here (in Berkshire)'. She first worked for an NGO that built libraries in villages, and then for a Fair Trade group in Nepal. She met her husband when she was employed as Chief Clerk in the Gurkha recruiting office in Kathmandu, and when they moved to Folkestone, she worked within the welfare services. Now in a unit with a relatively small number of Gurkha families it was not deemed necessary to have a specialist support worker and she had found herself fulfilling that role on a voluntary basis. Meanwhile she had a part-time job at the nursery on the base and was doing an NVQ in childcare.

When we first met, her two-year-old was being fractious and demanding, making it hard to talk. According to Savita, this was because the child missed her grandmother who had been living with them for the past six months. Savita too was finding it difficult to cope, particularly since her health had been affected by the birth. 'It's really difficult for me to do all the shifting,' she explained, 'and my mum, she's been helping me out with the baby. And now I'm doing my NVQ, my husband's going away [to Iraq], and it's really difficult with her still clinging to me.'

More frustrating than the fact that her mother had to leave the country was the news that although she had a five-year entry permit, she was expected to leave the country every six months and re-enter. 'That's really strange,' Savita said.

> It's a waste of my money, a waste of her time. She's not working; all she's doing is taking care of her. She's an old person, she can't speak English, she can't read or write English, she really feels alienated in the plane, she gets scared.

In her previous job it was not uncommon to be rung in the middle of the night with a plea to accompany someone giving birth in the hospital. But since there were less than 30 Gurkha families in the base where Savita lived now, there was no one to speak up for them. She described the predicament of one woman whom she had brought her to the unit welfare office in desperation to see if they could help her.

> I brought a lady here because she didn't get a school nearer to home and she can't drive and her husband goes away for six months and the council said because the school is not two miles away she won't be able to get a vehicle, a bus, so she said, 'Can the welfare do something for me?' They said, 'No, if the council says no, we can't do anything about it. She's got

another child who comes to our nursery who's quite young as well, three years old, can't talk yet, he's got some troubles, he's very clingy to his father. What to do? Those are the things that should really be looked into shouldn't they? Instead of having all those coffee mornings or cooking classes and stuff.

Her husband's commission in the wider British Army meant that she now lived in officers' quarters where her family was even more isolated. 'Our patch is really a lonely patch,' she said, 'you don't see anybody talking to each other. Only a few "hi's" and "hello's", apart from them, nothing.'

Savita talked about her frustration at the way that minorities were made to feel they were outsiders in Britain.

You know, they all seem so nice [but] you really feel that there's something coming out from them, 'Oh, you're from another country.' We can feel it and I don't like that because you won't get that from my country. You'll always feel welcome. Of course they'll be a bit curious about your colour and your hair colour, eyes colour, but they'll never differentiate you or single you out – never. Things are very different here.

I've got friends from Ghana, Fijian friends. They do feel the same thing, but the thing is they're not as talkative as me. I just – if I feel, I just talk out. I'm strong enough to fight back but there are people who don't fight back.

It was no surprise that the smaller group of Gurkha spouses were suffering from isolation without this extensive social and practical support they might have had in a larger base, especially when their husbands were being deployed. Savita said effusively,

It should be the wives that get the bravery award because the husband just goes to war and all the things they have in mind is how to fight the enemy. Back home the wife worries about the husband getting killed; taking care of the kids, thinking what happens if my husband doesn't come back? All the things they go through!

The ongoing campaigns for pension and residency rights coupled with ever-increasing immigration restrictions meant that Gurkha family members felt even more vulnerable at the prospect of losing their residency status. In December 2008, during the high profile campaign led by Joanna Lumley, the widow of Krishna Dura, an experienced Gurkha soldier killed in Afghanistan, received a communication from the Home Office indicating that she and her children might be required to leave the UK in 2012.[20] Lumley declared that it was 'unthinkable' that they had to worry about whether they would be allowed to stay in Britain: 'This man lost his life fighting in the British Army.' When Cpl Kumar Purja Pun was killed in May

2009, the Home Office was quick to reassure the public that it would not ask the widow of any soldier killed in action to leave.[21] But for dependants whose residential status was linked to the serving soldier, the uncertainty about their future settlement in the UK, including entitlement to public funds, was a heavy burden in addition to the anxiety caused by the nature of their husbands' work.

Round the roundabout

Cpl R had been transferred from the Gurkha Engineers into the RLC and was stationed in Germany where we met over industrialised potato salad and limp lettuce leaves, the only option for vegetarians in the cookhouse. He was telling me how his wife had been affected as a result of the move. Instead of living within easy distance of the Nepali community in south-east England she was now living in a flat with their three-year-old, 45 minutes drive away from the camp. As far as he knew, none of the UK wives had been to visit and she was lonely. Their two older children travelled to school on the bus which meant no contact with the other parents either. When he heard that there would be a meeting for F&C wives the following day he had wanted her to come into the camp but there was no transport available. This meant she would miss an opportunity to socialise with other women and a chance to share her own predicament.

The meeting with 'wives' was scheduled for my last afternoon at the base, and the welfare staff had gone to some lengths to make sure it was well attended. I had never eaten a Mr Kipling cake before, let alone a gaily coloured French Fancy, but there was something iconically British about the array sitting untouched on the plate before us. Six women whose husbands worked either in the RLC or REME had gathered, representing Fiji, South Africa and Gambia, and they were considering my question about the benefits and disadvantages of being posted there rather than in the UK. I was curious to know what it was like not just to be a military spouse but also a foreign national attached to the army in a third country.

'For us wives, when we work, we don't pay tax, that's one of the good things,' said Sula, a young woman from Fiji who had already lived there for five years. The others in the group were equally positive. There was the LOA that their husbands claimed, the cost of food seemed lower, the housing was superior, they preferred the climate even though it could be more extreme, and they found German people friendly and easy to communicate with. Some were learning the language through encounters with people at work and talking to neighbours. And there was more paid employment for spouses in the camp itself. Four of the six had jobs as 'customer services assistants' in the sergeants mess, and a fifth, who had only been living in Germany a few months, was hoping to find a job locally too. The only serious discrepancy seemed to be that spouses who were non-EU nationals were not eligible for the German form of child benefit, or *kindergeld*. Even if their child and the soldier were British or EU citizens, the F&C spouse did not qualify.

This was a very different picture than one might have imagined at first, particularly if one expected a greater degree of isolation among the families of non-UK nationals stationed there. But I had met several Fijian recruits who had opted for regiments based in Germany in order to be closer to friends and relatives, and many people had mentioned the extended Fijian communities spread across the different UK garrisons in Gütersloh, Hohne and Paderborn. In 2011 there were just over 18,000 UK Service Personnel stationed in Germany, over 96 per cent of whom were with the army.[22] During the previous year, however, the Secretary of State for Defence had announced the Strategic Defence and Security Review (SDSR) which mandated the return of half of the UK workforce from Germany by 2015 and the remainder by 2020. This meant that a lot of people were going to be disappointed that their stay in Germany would be permanently curtailed. But apart from the material and social benefits of living there, the everyday difficulties involved in being a non-UK national in a European country were similar to those in the UK itself, only rendered more complicated by extra bureaucracy.

After listening to the group complain that their qualifications earned back home were not recognised, Sona, from Gambia, described other barriers that wives encountered when they arrived.

> It's either one or two things: it's [either] qualifications or you need to get a national insurance number from the UK so sometimes it's hard for us to sort the system and get used to it and sometimes you get to feel that they're giving you the impression that it's either you're being neglected or your voices are not being heard, they don't respect your views or certain things.

Sula had obtained a qualification in IT in Fiji which was worthless in Europe. 'I feel bad,' she replied, 'because we want to continue our knowledge. There's no point in learning something back home and then you come here and you just…' She tailed off as and somebody else finished her sentence 'you just have to start again'.

Although all newcomers were given information packs telling them where to find the services they needed, people still needed advice and practical help too. Jenny who was from South Africa and a no-nonsense kind of person, had developed her own perspective on support for partners within the organisation. 'The military is not very forthcoming for the guys who [want to] drive their wives to interviews…when we do have them.' She added,

> I must say, on my station, if the soldiers have got a problem the welfare staff and senior NCO staff won't let them go.

And being an army wife, I tend to pick up the phone and say my piece. I'm not qualified in it but I do help the wives, help the guys to get their wives to general medical procedures and offer support that they need sometimes. And it's just because I am part of the F&C soldiers, so I see things differently.

I asked if her interventions were appreciated. Both soldiers and their wives thanked her when they knew about what she was doing. 'Otherwise,' she said, 'I just do it because I know how lonely they can feel.' She was famous for her back-garden barbeques and extensive hospitality towards other wives who lived in her quarters.

'Where I stay I've only got two Fijian families, so they meet up at my house,' she laughed. 'We South Africans get along very well with the Fijians.'

The more they shared their experiences of their social lives on the base, the more it appeared that there was an inclusive social network that linked spouses from Commonwealth countries. We have the same way of bringing up, the same culture, they explained. When I asked them to elaborate, Meri, from Fiji, said, 'I think one important thing is we're all brought up to respect each other; it doesn't matter if you are older than this person, you respect them as an individual. Like the respect is reciprocal.'

'There's always respect among Commonwealth soldiers, always,' said Jenny.

'The lifestyle is very different,' continued Meri.

I've got a friend, she was brought up in England, she's also Fijian, but the way she looks at things it's different from – I don't know – probably just different the way we were brought up. Like most of the time all we hear these second words are swearing, that doesn't sound very...like when you talk you don't use the words that often. I think that slowly people are talking like that.

'Yes, especially boys,' interjected Jenny.

Like for us, if I go to the UK, if I see a Fijian person we just say hello to each other and we just talk. Sometimes people say, 'Are you related?' and I say, 'No.' It's just that we feel it's courtesy to say hello and that so, it's different. That's one thing I get questioned about, 'Are you related? Do you know that person?'

It's something to do with our Fijian culture – we always say 'bula' or wave.

Thinking of Corporal R's wife alone in her second-floor flat with a three-year-old, not knowing German and new to the country, I asked whether loneliness was a big thing among the wives here.

'Oh yes,' they said together. 'And not just Commonwealth,' added Jenny.

'It helps if you have good neighbours, you feel at home,' said Sona. 'You can always go in their house or they can take you out, and they make you feel comfortable.'

I asked if they knew any Nepali women in their circles.

'The language barrier's very, very difficult with them,' said Meri, 'because they only speak a little bit of English. It's hard and they're very, very reserved.'

In the discussion that followed there was consensus that not everyone wanted to socialise. 'I think you can get it from all countries,' said Sona.

'Some people are really reserved, they don't want to have anything to do with other families. All they want to do is... stay by themselves.'

But loneliness was a factor in everyone's life once the soldiers were deployed or sent away on exercises.

> You don't expect to get married to someone who's away for six months. Once I followed my husband to work and sat in the car to wait for him. It was the worst thing. It was worse because my husband was only a few metres away.

Jenny's mission was clearly to look after those around her who were more than usually helpless.

> We live next door to a young couple who's pregnant and she's due in four weeks – not that she's going to last four weeks – but we've taken the gate out because her husband's away at the moment so it will be a case of knocking on the wall and going, 'Help! I'm having a baby.' And I'll be like, 'Wake up! Drive!'

The atmosphere of solidarity among the spouses I met was obviously enhanced by the compassion and energy of particular individuals. However, the issue that animated everyone at the meeting, and caused me to weaken my resolve not to touch the Mr Kipling cakes, was the unhappiness caused by their immigration status. Whether this was produced by having to re-apply for visas to travel back to the UK every six months, or the 90-day restriction on bringing relatives to help out with childcare, or the financial pressures caused by having to renew their own visas every few years, this was the largest category of problems facing F&C spouses living on the base. This misery could be exacerbated by a feeling that the welfare services were unwilling to listen or simply unable to help. It was often sheer frustration at the amount of red tape. For many, the issue presented a symbolic burden that made their lives harder than it would have been if they were simply UK citizens.

'Sometimes,' said Moira, one of the older Fijian women, 'you tend to think, is it like that the army is only there for a certain particular group of people from a particular country? But not helping people from the Commonwealth? The emotions build inside you and it's really bad because it's going to make you really hate people.'

At that time, children born to service personnel on a British military base overseas did not automatically acquire British citizenship. This situation was to change shortly after my visit, but in the meantime the logistics of having children with different passports only added to the difficulties. For those spouses joining their partners for the first time from overseas, it was necessary to apply first for a UK visitor's visa and then obtain a German visa from the UK. Occasionally families made the mistake of applying straight to Germany which made it harder to travel to the UK subsequently. Even in this small group there were all kinds of experiences being aired, with Jenny once again adjudicating on the basis of her experience as a South African passport holder.

In one respect there was an additional advantage living in Germany, as far as visas and family life were concerned. Several of the women had brought mothers or other relatives to help with childcare. Although the limit was the same, all they had to do to was to leave the country and then re-enter to begin a new six-month stay. For those stationed in Germany it was far simpler to travel to the UK on a visitor's visa and then come back, or hop over the border to neighbouring Switzerland, than it was to arrange a similar exercise from the UK with only a British visa. In Savita's case her mother was obliged to fly back to India since she did not have a visa for another European country.

Once spouses and families had obtained visas for Germany they were able to travel throughout the Schengen zone without too much difficulty. Although there were rarely any problems in obtaining a visa to visit the UK from Germany, it was necessary to apply every six months which compounded the problems of visiting UK-based families when the husbands were away. Moira's bitterness that they were left to struggle with the regulations when even their husbands could pass to and fro with an exemption stamp was shared by the others.

'Sometimes you feel left out and you can't do anything with no husbands. All we have to do is try and be there for them.'

One put it very graphically as she complained about being given conflicting advice. 'Everyone's travelling in a roundabout, no one's going out!' What was needed was a special person or point of contact who could advise Commonwealth spouses on every aspect of immigration law. 'Then everyone can share their experiences and know where to go or who to see for problems direction-wise.'

This chapter has attempted to describe some of the perennial problems inherent in becoming a dependant of a serving soldier, and to explore some of the forms of solidarity, self-help and community organisation that helped to offset the negative aspects of army life experienced by many family members who were also migrants. Two powerful conclusions emerged from these testimonies from the partners of Commonwealth and Gurkha soldiers. The first was that any improvements in supplying immigration advice and support over the years since 1998 merely underlined the fact that neither the MoD nor the Home Office seemed to have anticipated the extra responsibility entailed in hiring non-UK nationals in the British Army. This was especially negligent since the institution boasted a strong commitment to supporting the families of serving men and women.

The second conclusion was that the British Army owed a great deal to the expertise of migrants themselves, particularly those who felt responsible for the wellbeing of their compatriots. While welfare organisations like the AFF had gradually become more attuned to the specific needs of spouses and children who had migrated from other countries, the level of provision was too uneven and too minimal to contradict the heartfelt belief that 'the army is only there for a certain particular group of people from a particular country'. Against this background, the launch of the Fiji Support Network (FSN) in 2009 represented an unprecedented development in the self-organisation of migrants within the armed forces as a whole.

Forwards and backs

The welfare hall was once again full of Fijian soldiers and their families, although the atmosphere felt very different from the celebrations on Fiji Day, held in the same room six months earlier. This time the soldiers were in uniform, their partners and children in winter coats, and there were no British officers on the raised platform at the front, with or without garlands of flowers. Dressed in a civilian suit in the style of an RAF officer, Marika was introducing the tri-service FSN which he had helped to found in 2009. By February 2011 when this presentation took place, the pressure had been building for two more years, and by then the FSN had developed into a significant organisation in its own right. But this was not how Marika was describing their aims and objectives. The accumulated experience of Fijians serving within the three services had taught them how to advance tactically using the MoD's own institutional language to describe their mission.

'The FSN aims to act as a conduit,' he said, pointing to the statement on the screen behind him. 'To act as a conduit on policy, information delivery and dialogue between the MoD and Fijian citizens serving in the UK Armed Forces. So what do we mean by that?'

He turned back to face the audience before resorting to more familiar terminology. 'In a game of rugby you have forwards and backs. Who is the link man? That's the conduit. He looks at the spaces, where support is needed.'

As he outlined their objectives, beginning with the need to create awareness within the community, I studied the faces of the people in the room. This presentation was one of a series of 'road shows' scheduled to take place in military bases with high numbers of Fijian soldiers who were given permission to attend the meetings in work time. I later learned that the level of attendance would vary from place to place, depending on the extent to which senior officers felt it was important and therefore gave their staff permission to attend. The mood in this particular room was serious; there was no doubt about that. Even the toddlers were quiet as they climbed on and off the empty chairs.

The second objective was to establish a 'point of contact' network with the chain of command. In other words, this was about making the organisation known by identifying the welfare officers who needed particular assistance with Fijian or wider Commonwealth issues. Third, the FSN sought to 'capture and elevate' questions that were relevant to the organisation, particularly those which might lead to changes in policy. Here, matters involving 'cultural nuance' would be channelled through the FSN in order to avoid confusion and maintain 'uniformity of approach'. This was a significant area of their work since it entailed guiding the authorities at difficult times like bereavement or breaches of military law.

'When a Fijian soldier dies on ops,' Marika explained, 'we produce a guide for the Casualty Visiting Officer. We help in courts, for example, when guys go AWOL and we can provide context, background. Their village might be far from internet, for example, and there might be a problem.'

The fourth objective was to promote understanding of what the FSN actually did and to identify those functions that the organisation did not aspire to, such as working outside the military welfare system, dispensing funds, making policy or working for the benefit of particular groups of Fijians. Finally, the FSN was committed to 'delivering' understanding of MoD policies, either by translating them into Fijian or by holding briefings to explain particular aspects of policy.

Although the objectives looked reasonably generic, couched in military acronyms and management-speak, the founding of such an organisation represented an extraordinary achievement on the part of the people who negotiated for its existence. The creation of the FSN was basically an acknowledgement by the MoD that their own welfare and advice systems within the three services could not guarantee that Commonwealth personnel and their families would not be disadvantaged by their non-UK status and backgrounds. As the largest national group, Fijians had borne the brunt of this failure to anticipate and then meet the demands caused by their non-national status. When, during an animated discussion of visa costs, a member of the audience cracked a joke about setting up a Fijian Help for Heroes, the spontaneous laughter that erupted needed no translation. The combined experience of the men and women, soldiers and spouses, in that room confirmed the fact that it was being a migrant – not a minority – that was the most pressing issue.

The regiments that hosted the first waves of Commonwealth soldiers in 1998, many of whom happened to be from Fiji, were utterly ill-equipped to deal with the immigration issues that the employment of these new recruits inevitably entailed. As we shall see below, the impact of the wider institutional failure to introduce specialist training for welfare staff had untold consequences on soldiers' lives. But the government that made the decision to widen recruitment to include non-national citizens, and subsequent administrations that had inherited the problems, were all culpable of a different order of neglect. The eagerness with which New Labour ministers opened the depleted ranks of the armed forces to Commonwealth citizens in 1998 was not matched by a readiness to accept that, without UK citizenship, this new category of military servants would be functioning on unequal terms with their so-called indigenous peers. This discrepancy had little to do with cultural values, racial harassment or the promotion of cultural diversity. As the next chapter will reveal, it was about the underlying contradiction entailed in working for a national military institution without either the protection or the rewards of a British passport.

9
Caught in the Crossfire

The Fiji Support Network road show was drawing to a close but the questions were still coming thick and fast. The soldiers who had slumped in their chairs during the earlier Power Point presentation were now sitting upright and taking part in the discussion. Marika's encouragement that 'no question is a stupid question', had not really been necessary. Earlier he had provided an update on immigration regulations and exemptions, although there was no good news to impart. 'They are bending over backwards but not far enough,' he said, referring to the UKBA.

> Government policy is trying to control immigration. One way is to raise visa fees to discourage people from coming. So we are caught in the cross-fire. We are soldiers, [but] at the moment ministers are not willing to fight this case. If they do it for you, they say, you have to do it for the NHS, or for education. If they give us too much concessions they can be taken to court. An Indian doctor can say, 'I save British lives every day'. It's a powerful argument.

The owner of the first hand to be raised had posed a question about divorce. Fortunately there was a UWO present who was able to give her a detailed answer. He was due to retire in a few days' time after more than two decades of service, and in a relaxed frame of mind. Estrangement and divorce were routine casework for welfare staff and the procedures were well worn. If the couple lived in married quarters, the soldier would be expected to move back to single accommodation to allow the spouse a period of 93 days to find alternative housing. But it was not hard to detect another layer of anxiety in this question since for a Commonwealth citizen, the spouse's residency status was linked to the soldier's work.

The Leave to Remain status (LTR), which was the normal condition of residency for the accompanying spouse, included eligibility for allowances and benefits in the UK. However, in the event of separation, this status expired and the estranged spouse and family were likely to find themselves without permission to stay in the UK, without recourse to public funds or the right to work. As far as the army was concerned, the serving soldier remained responsible for providing financial support for the family, estranged or temporarily separated. For a soldier whose dependants were UK citizens, expenses such as medical treatment, unemployment benefit or child benefit could be taken for granted. For those who were not eligible for public funds, or who did not know where to turn to get accurate advice, the situation could be extremely bleak. The woman who asked the question commented that 'the army could be your best friend or your worst enemy'.

Although this part of the session was mostly conducted in Fijian, the main points were being translated. Questions ranged over vital issues such as compassionate leave; banks and remittances; the length of time that widows were permitted to stay in SFA; and the cost and duration of visas. Fees were skyrocketing, and there was a consensus that the FSN should tell policymakers to subsidise costs, or provide interest-free loans to help serving soldiers. A group of men from a particular battalion asked about the procedure in the case of non-operational death. It turned out that one of their colleagues had recently died and the CO was unwilling to pay for the body to be repatriated to Fiji in case the regiment had to pay for deaths on operation in Afghanistan. There were several questions about dual nationality and it was established that Fijians were now able to retain their citizenship, but they had to pay the government in Fiji the equivalent of £1,000.

This was also a forum for discussing rumours of changes in policy, such as the possibility of obtaining 10-year visas for spouses instead of the standard two or four years. Kasa, who was responsible for dealing with family issues, was adamant that there were a lot of reviews to be done. 'We cannot change policy overnight,' she conceded, 'but we can create awareness in the policy makers.'

The session ended on an optimistic note because, despite the intractable difficulties and the unanswered questions, the launch of the FSN meant that individuals could not only get more accurate information and advice, but they could also operate as a pressure group. 'Today we planted a seed,' said the organisers. 'Our hope is that it would grow into a large tree. The Gurkhas proved it. They worked together and used Joanna Lumley to make the government listen. We need one voice, so let's work together.'

Patriotic principles

The relationship between military service and immigration status can offer a key to understanding any nation's settlement with its past. The surge of public sympathy in response to Lumley's advocacy stirred up a deep sediment of responsibility towards those who had fought in Britain's historic battles. The Campaign for Gurkha Justice (CGJ) simply re-stated the patriotic principle that those who have proved their loyalty to Britain ought to be allowed to retire there, supported by taxpayers' money. In this scenario, the retired Gurkhas' status as would-be immigrants was trumped by their past record as loyal warriors. However, for volunteers from Commonwealth countries currently serving in the armed forces there was no comparable narrative being shaped for public consumption. Their status as foreign citizens overlapped too readily with another sinew of national identity, one that reacted to immigration as a threat. As the FSN officer put it, 'we are caught in the crossfire', lauded as heroes but penalised as immigrants.

Asking who is eligible or qualified to serve in the armed forces can reveal the terms and limits of national citizenship. In that sense, a multicultural army represents more than an attempt to obey the law by mirroring the society from which it recruits. It can also provide military institutions with legitimacy in the eyes of numerous parties, from politicians to members of minority groups themselves. However, as this book has tried to show, nothing was quite as simple as the theory might imply. Commonwealth soldiers were recruited primarily as a means to increase the recruitment pool, with the happy coincidence that this would import minorities into the armed forces. Although anti-immigration sentiment is rife in many countries, the comparisons between different national arrangements are useful in revealing the extent to which military service underpins national identity and the right to belong.

Within Europe, where many countries have scrapped conscription relatively recently,[1] it was possible to see divergent approaches towards recruiting ethnic and cultural minorities, whether citizens or not. Closer inspection, however, revealed that the justification for each national policy was derived from a similar compound of colonial history *and* domestic politics.[2] We have already noted that the example of the French Foreign Legion, discussed in Chapter 3, pointed back to the methods of military organisation under French imperial rule. In contrast to the model of multiculturalism associated with the US and UK, with their emphasis on ethnic monitoring and equal opportunities, the contemporary ideal of the universal citizen-soldier in the Armèe de Terre continued to assert that the ethnic, religious or cultural identity of recruits was irrelevant as long as they were French nationals. Meanwhile ethnographic research among soldiers has been able to offer a more realistic picture of the way that racism infused postcolonial military culture in France, as it did elsewhere.[3]

In Spain, where there was a legacy of fascist dictatorship and civil war within living memory, a more pragmatic approach had been adopted, not unlike the UK strategy. The Socialist Workers Party (PSOE) which came to power in 2004 inherited a military institution faced with huge recruitment problems as it struggled to re-establish itself as a professional and democratically accountable all-volunteer force.[4] PSOE gradually lifted restrictions on recruiting male and female foreigners, setting a new upper limit of 9 per cent. Under the previous government, non-nationals recruited from Spanish-speaking countries could sign a single contract for three years.[5] In 2005 this was changed to six years with the possibility of three more if they applied for citizenship. But in terms of the relationship between military service and migrant status, it was the US Armed Forces that provided the most striking comparison with all these examples, and, as the UK's closest ally, the contrast was one that did not escape the attention of soldiers on the ground.

One of the founding stories of the US was that it was a nation rooted in the identities, aspirations and labour of many different peoples. The particular brand of 'militarized republicanism' that characterises US society helps to explain why, in spite of acrid debates about immigration, when the president declares that the nation is at war there is a rush of patriot fervour that sanctions expedited citizenship rights for all those who serve.[6] This is not just about a residual commitment to the figure of the citizen-soldier found in many republics, but a measure regularly updated in the law of the land. The legislation enacted after 11 September 2001 illustrated the state's calculations about the amount and type of military 'manpower' required for an extended period of war. The strategy of rewarding military service with citizenship ensured a ready supply of young and physically fit recruits. It also channelled the tide of patriotism induced by the attacks on the twin towers into support for military ventures that might have encountered more opposition if it was found necessary to re-introduce conscription.

Until 2001, those with green cards, or Lawful Permanent Residency (LPR), were eligible for recruitment (as well as being potentially subject to the draft) and permitted to apply for citizenship after three years in military service as opposed to the statutory five for civilians. In July 2002 President Bush proclaimed that all green card holders (known as resident aliens) who had served with honour on active duty after 11 September 2001 would be eligible to apply immediately for US citizenship, *regardless* of the length of their service. In January 2006, Congress passed a new statute that overrode all previous bills, sweeping away the old distinction between times of war and times of peace. In addition to clarifying expedited citizenship rights to immigrants in the forces, it also authorised the recruitment of hundreds of legal non-citizens with appropriate skills, as we noted in Chapter 4.[7] From August 2009, immigrant recruits were permitted to apply for citizenship and start the application process during their basic combat training. By 2010 about 1,000 soldiers had been naturalised at this stage, and the following year it was announced that officials from the United States Citizenship and Immigration Services (USCIS) would be permanently stationed at training centres in order to facilitate the naturalisation process, not just for soldiers but their spouses as well.[8] President Obama repeatedly drew attention to the contributions of naturalised service members by pointing out 'their dedication' to the nation.

'Nothing can be more inspiring,' he said on a trip to a military base in Texas in 2011. 'Even though they were not yet citizens when they joined our military, these men and women signed up to serve ... It doesn't matter where you come from, it doesn't matter what you look like, it doesn't matter what faith you worship, what matters is that you believe in the ideals on which we were founded.'[9]

The rhetorical power of the US model, which swept not-yet citizens into the arms of the nation even before they had begun their training, emerged out of a long history of enlisting minorities into the armed forces, but the carrot of full citizenship offered to immigrants who were willing to work in the military sector was only one striking point of contrast with the British Army. Since both countries employed volunteer forces whose members exchanged views on terms and conditions when they met on operations, the discrepancies were not only significant at a theoretical level. Discussed against a backdrop of armed combat where US immigration officials regularly visited troops in order to process applications, periodically holding citizenship ceremonies in Kandahar, for example, the practical and symbolic differences between the two national militaries were self-evident.[10]

While all these various arrangements reveal the divergent histories of nation-making when displayed on a broad canvas, the finer details of policy change in each country often reflect more subtle shifts in the relationship between civil and military spheres on a local scale. In the UK, apart from having immediate impact on the lives of soldiers and their families, the exemptions, dispensations and rulings agreed by the Home Office also revealed the elasticity of the idea that military work was an exceptional form of public service that required commensurate rewards.

In July 2008 the New Labour government published a Service Personnel Command paper providing details of a cross-departmental initiative that examined ways to improve conditions for all armed forces personnel, families and veterans, regardless of nationality. Entitled 'The Nation's Commitment: Cross-Government Support to our Armed Forces, their Families and Veterans' the report had been commissioned partly in response to the Military Covenant campaign which had been launched the previous year by the *Independent on Sunday* with the support of high-ranking military chiefs. The resulting recommendations were derived from two important principles stated at the outset by ministers Des Browne and Bob Ainsworth. The first was the need 'to counter the difficulties that follow from being required to move around the country or the world' and to identify those areas 'where special treatment is needed to achieve this'. The second was a recognition that public anger about the human costs of the wars in Iraq and Afghanistan could no longer be ignored. One plank of the reforms addressed the question: 'how we can better support and recognise those who have been wounded in the service of their country'.[11]

The situation of F&C personnel was addressed in the body of this report, marking an important step towards acknowledging the way that they were particularly disadvantaged as a result of their status as migrants. The relevant section was prefaced in the Command Paper by another statement of principle that managed to say everything and nothing at the same time. It was also nearly 10 years late.

> Foreign and Commonwealth (F&C) citizens have a long and distinguished history of Service. Nearly 12,000 of today's Service personnel, including Gurkhas, are from F&C countries. We recognise their unique circumstances. UK Borders Agency (UKBA), an agency of the Home Office, will continue to work closely with MOD to resolve immigration and nationality issues affecting F&C Service personnel.[12]

This recognition had been a long time coming. When recruitment had begun in 1998, for instance, those planning to apply for naturalisation quickly discovered that the time spent on deployment or in overseas bases disqualified them from claiming continuous residency in the UK, thereby making it impossible to begin the process of applying for citizenship until after they had left the army. In another example, a child born during an overseas posting to serving personnel who were foreign nationals was not automatically eligible for UK citizenship. Inevitably this meant that children in some families might have different nationalities, depending on where they were born, or, as it often happened, that expectant parents were forced to calculate how to spend their leave in the UK in the hope that their baby would arrive on British soil.

The 2008 report identified five areas for reform 'as soon as practicable' among which was the resolution of the qualifying period required for naturalisation, a measure which had already been put in place in 2006,[13] and the decision to allow children born on overseas postings to be eligible immediately for UK citizenship, a change that came into effect in 2010. While these examples represented less of a reward for those migrants serving in the British armed forces, and more of an ironing out of potential disadvantages, every concession – or exemption – had to be fought for clause by clause. But this was a hidden process, one that has received much less publicity than other interventions aimed at raising the overall profile of the armed forces. Before examining the impact of the disadvantages that men and women from Commonwealth countries have faced and continued to endure, we must now consider why it is that passports, permits, residency rights and visas play such a huge role in determining how soldiers do their job.

Foreign travel

> *I keep my Pakistan passport at the moment. If the Pakistan government calls me up I have to go. I cannot be bonded to two governments at the same time. That is what the issue is with most of the guys around here. We keep our passports – I am not saying that we should give them up – but there should be something on those passports that should properly bind us to this country because that stamp what we have in our passport – it*

means nothing. If something happens to me, the British government is going to ask what am I? Am I Pakistani or British? If I am Pakistani – you see the conditions going on everywhere in Pakistan – so what are they going to call me, as a traitor? I am working for the British government and the British government is not accepting me because my passport is still Pakistani and there is a stamp which shows, what? Nothing! If I lost my ID I can't go anywhere.

(Ahmed, Pakistan, 2006)

The invitation to travel to 'exotic distant lands' and meet 'exciting unusual people' was not just a slogan hi-jacked by US anti-war activists in the 1970s to counter the lure of the army's recruitment ads. Foreign travel is a basic premise of military work. In official terms, 'the British Army is actively engaged in operational duties across the globe...and is currently deployed in over 80 countries across the world'. In addition to combat duties, soldiers are required to travel abroad on exercises from the Arctic to the equatorial rainforests, and to offer their services as trainers in countries with which the UK has a strategic alliance, such as Kenya and Sierra Leone. The MoD also maintains substantial bases in Germany, Cyprus, the South Atlantic, Brunei and Gibraltar. The recruitment videos depicting soldiers operating in extreme climates and harsh terrains are not merely advertising fodder to entice Britain's more adventurous youth, they are a reminder that mobility is a condition of military service. For that reason, soldiers are required to keep their travel documents up to date, although most of the practical arrangements for work-related trips are made on their behalf. If their passports are red, they can circumnavigate the globe with relative ease, in or out of uniform. If not, it is a nightmare. Non UK-passport holders, even with an official army ID card, can expect to be scrutinised, hauled aside, humiliated and delayed by zealous border officials, including those who greet them when they re-enter the UK. In some countries they can be refused entry altogether, even if they are simply passing through in transit as part of a UK military contingent.

Marcus, who was black and from Zimbabwe, was travelling with a team to Egypt when he was stopped at Cairo airport. Foreign visitors normally purchase their visas on arrival, and his fellow soldiers, all UK passports holders in civilian dress, duly queued up and passed through without a hitch. It was only when their commanding officer realised that Marcus was no longer in the party that he returned to find that he had been refused a visa because of his nationality. 'Because it was a Muslim country,' Marcus explained, 'I was scared to show my Army ID.'

He told this anecdote at a briefing for F&C soldiers that took place in his RLC unit in Gütersloh, Germany, in 2009. The Power Point presentation had ended, but a group of Fijians, Ghanaians, Zimbabweans, St Vincentians and others had stayed behind to compare their own experiences and discuss common problems. It was hard to keep up with all the different stories that came out at once. Kojo, from Ghana, was travelling from Germany to Switzerland to compete in an athletic competition. When their minibus reached the border, the Swiss authorities allowed all the other members of the team to enter the country, but he and the other competitor, also a non UK passport holder, were refused. The officers in charge tried to explain that the two were athletes and that everyone else was providing support, but to no avail. The team returned without taking part in the games.

When a soldier who was a non-UK passport holder signed the British Army contract, he or she became exempt from UK immigration control under Section 8 (4) (a) of the Immigration Act 1971. At that point the UK Border Agency provides an 'Exempt UK Immigration Control' endorsement in the individual's passport which suspends any existing UK visa restrictions. Until 2010, this status was registered in the form of a stamp which was notorious for arousing the suspicions of border guards. It was a particular nuisance for those who were stationed in Germany and needing to make frequent trips back to the UK. Kojo was coming through Stansted airport when he ran into trouble at the immigration desk. He waited while the young woman perused his passport, slowly reading through every page.

> I asked to see her manager. An older woman came out and I was standing with hands on hips looking at her. 'Why the attitude?' she asked me. 'I want you to see the kind of people who work here.' I told her.

The manager looked at the stamp in the passport and asked the young woman: 'did you see this?' According to Kojo she had not bothered to read the page, despite the fact that he pointed it out when he handed her the passport. The manager apologised on that occasion but it was an example of routine conflict. Another time, the immigration officer asked Kojo: 'where did you get this?'

He replied sarcastically 'I made the stamp at home in Ghana.'

'Why are you getting angry?' asked the guard as Kojo was starting to fume. 'The officer backed off,' he said.

His annoyance was understandable, not just because he had perfectly legal travel documents but also because of the irony at being treated as a suspected interloper. Travelling to Germany was no problem despite the notoriously strict Schengen border controls because officials recognised the NATO Status of Forces Agreement document (SOFA) which all service personnel carried with them. Obtaining Schengen visas in order to travel within Europe was relatively simple too. Rather than apply through UK-based channels, it was common for those based in Germany to buy their own visas from the local town hall at an affordable price and avoid the hassle.

But there was a consensus that the UK exemption stamp was, in all honesty, not very convincing. 'It could easily be forgeable,' said someone at the briefing and the group laughed in agreement.

'It could be done in Nigeria!' said a voice. 'Nigeria?' someone retorted. 'It could be done in downtown London.'

While many of these stories were fuelled by memories of personal inconvenience or humiliation, an important principle emerged from similar discussions whenever there was an opportunity to air this particular category of grievance. The fact that foreign nationals were physically separated from UK citizens at border crossings indicated that they were not equal employees of the British Army. This point was driven home during my first encounter with soldiers in an infantry unit. Sitting round the table with men and women with many years of service between them, it was hard to miss the sense of injury caused by the segregation that they routinely experienced as a result of their nationality.

Tivo, from Fiji, was talking about a recent trip to Canada on exercise with his platoon, particularly annoyed by what happened when they passed through the Canadian immigration controls on leaving the country. 'One minute you are talking to your mates, the next you are standing there looking at them on the other side. You have the same cap badge, the same uniform, but...'

His attempt to describe how it made him feel was summed up by his next remark. 'I am a British soldier holding a Fijian passport,' he said. 'It doesn't mean I am British.' Like many others, he was angry that asylum seekers appeared to have priority when it came to immigration rights. 'It hurts when people who are illegal get benefits from the taxes I pay,' he continued, venting an opinion I was to hear frequently.

> British friends urge us to get UK citizenship so we can go through immigration with them. They don't understand why it is not given. When you are mates, after everything we go through...It makes you wonder some times – are you a British soldier or Fijian soldier?
> People at home look at me – 'are you in the British Army?'
> 'No, I am just Fijian.'

Steven, a young man from South Africa who worked in the AGC, added his weight to Tivo's complaint.

> When you come back from these things, you are going through immigration and being separated like cattle. We have learned to live with it. I consider myself an F&C soldier serving in the British Army. At the end of the day are you really exempt from immigration?

Steven's discomfort was compounded by the effects of the Mercenary Act in his home country which threatened to criminalise all South African citizens working in other national armies. 'They consider us to be mercenaries,' he mused. 'Sometimes I wonder if we do qualify as mercenaries, as hired hands.'

The indignation that the British Army was powerless to prevent this differential treatment by border officials was not confined to Commonwealth soldiers either. Gurkhas too experience similar levels of scrutiny at all borders and object to the routine segregation that takes place on return to the UK.

'I was twice delayed coming in,' said one member of a group I met during a training session at the regiment's base in Shorncliffe. 'I had lots of interviews and they had to contact my unit to confirm. They don't trust us. We feel like we are in the British Army, but…'

The delay had meant that he missed his train and was unable to make his appointment. 'I wasted the ticket and it cost me. Honestly I felt like an asylum seeker, like a refugee. Coming from Afghanistan!'

The men had been told to take a break from shooting practice in order to come and talk to me and we were all rather taken by surprise. Standing around in the biting wind was not the most natural starting point for a conversation and I had tried to break the ice by asking if they had their families with them. Their answers had quickly brought us to the subject of travel, proving once again that their frustration was close to the surface.

> When you come with British soldiers they go through the UK passport line and we have to queue.
> It automatically separates us.

Don't your officers help by confirming who you are?

> They say: 'it's the job of the border officials. They have to do their job.'

It was not just when they entered the UK that Gurkhas encountered difficulties.

> In European countries, we ask for visa and we don't get visa. They don't recognise the NATO travel card or army ID. It's a problem!

Memories of differential treatment could still rankle years after the event. 'In 2001,' said one, 'I flew with the RAF and we had a break in South Africa. The Brits went through. Four hours later I got a three-days' visa. What kind of life is that?'

Nowhere to go

There were other issues that affected the quality of life for soldiers who were not UK citizens, some of which were logistical as well as a result of their immigration status. For those who were single, spending periods of leave on the base, like one I visited in Warminster, a small military town on the edge of Salisbury Plain, could be achingly dull because they were not able to go home to their families, like their British colleagues. Earlier the welfare officer had alluded to this discrepancy as well, adding that it often caused problems when single men were left in the camp over the long weekend. He would arrange outings to the safari park or to rugby matches to compensate, but this could not compete with the freedom enjoyed by their friends. There were only so many times you could enjoy visiting the lions at Longleat.

'Every weekend the British go away to see their families,' said Tivo and the others agreed.

> We can't afford to go to Fiji. They talk about going [on holiday] to Turkey. We from Fiji keep our heads down. We have nowhere to go, we can't go anywhere without visas.
> During the break there will be loads of Fijians here. English lads spend all their money in the first week and go home every weekend.
> We've got money, even though we send money to our families, but we've got nowhere to go.

It was particularly galling when the platoon was in Canada as they were not able to transit through the US, or cross the border to take a vacation, unlike their mates. 'We had to stay in Canada and drink up,' said Tivo bitterly.

> When the lads came back they were on about it. They went to Vegas, New York – it is terrible when you are standing there. You feel you want to slap them. And tell them 'shut up'!

Armed forces employees are entitled to travel subsidies within the UK, including annual rail vouchers and allowances based on the expectation that soldiers would be stationed at a distance from families. Many F&C soldiers did not make full use of these vouchers and argued instead that the money could be transferred to a savings account to allow them to buy air tickets home. The cost of return flights for a family travelling to Fiji or Nepal could be prohibitively expensive. One Gurkha corporal, recently transferred to Germany, told me that his family aimed to go back every two or three years, but for three kids and his wife it cost over £3,000 for the flights. Although he found this difficult, he was at pains to point out that he was still committed to the career he had chosen.

'We fight for the UK, and feel proud,' he assured me. 'We made our choice. Even though we were not born in this country, we made a choice for Britain. [I have] no regret for fight for other country.'

He did voice one other complaint that I was to hear on several occasions. 'When you do a six-month tour the British Army are allowed two weeks leave. Gurkhas are [also] allowed two weeks to come to the UK, but they are not allowed to go to Nepal.' This was particularly galling since the geographical distance between Kabul and Kathmandu was comparatively short. But rules were rules, and as employees of the British Army they were forced to accept that they were bound by the same logic that their base was in the UK.

The red passport

Jamaica 2003; Ghana 2007; Nigeria 2003; Ghana 2003; Nepal 1995; Nepal 1994; Ghana 2008; Gambia 2005; Uganda 2005; Nepal 1993. It was my first group interview in Germany and I had asked to see a maximum of five people at a time. The fact that there was twice that number, in a period where many were away in Afghanistan, was another sign that people were eager to talk to anyone investigating their experiences as minorities and migrants. As usual with a larger group, it took a little time to get going but on this occasion, after finding out when they had all joined, we began with the usual grumbles about careers and promotion. Most of the men and women round the table worked as suppliers which often meant sitting at a computer terminal, as I discovered when I asked if I could observe them at work the following day. The only exciting thing that happened was when the English Corporal strolled into the room with a guitar and regaled them with a song. For all the world like a scene from a military version of 'The Office', the main reaction the David Brent character received from the workers, all from F&C backgrounds, was a few muttered comments like 'the army's got talent' and a fair amount of eye-rolling. As if anticipating this frivolity, the discussion around the table the previous day reflected on the age difference among them and their UK peers.

'Joining at 25 plus after living in another culture makes it harder to adjust to military culture,' said one. 'It can be hard to adjust quickly anyway.'

'Those who are educated have visions of becoming officers, getting qualifications in medical or dental trades, and it can be a big problem when it doesn't happen,' said a former Gurkha, now transferred into the British Army.

A Ugandan woman was annoyed at not getting promoted after five years or so. 'You think, why bother?' she said.

'Recruiters drive you into certain careers,' complained someone. 'What you get is totally different as well.'

There was general agreement that some people definitely had a longer-term career plan and saw the army as a stepping stone. For that reason, issues of promotion, training and job satisfaction were likely to have a profound effect on their futures. Then a voice mentioned passports, and from then on it was even harder to tell who said what. The consensus seemed to be that although it was wrong to join the army simply in order to obtain UK citizenship, being in possession of 'the red passport' certainly made it easier to do the job.

There was the usual chorus of complaints about the disadvantages of crossing borders with non-UK passports. Some had been subjected to travelling in cargo planes to destinations that did not accept non-UK troops at all, even in transit. This situation had produced instances of segregation that were particularly demeaning, as I would discover on other occasions.

During a session with RLC soldiers on a different base, a young Ghanaian man described how he was a member of a group travelling to Kuwait.

All the British guys flew on a civilian flight to Qatar but the Common-wealth had to go on a cargo plane from Brize Norton to Iraq and then to Kuwait.

We were told it would be sorted out on the way home, but on the day we got dressed up ready to go with the Brits [they told us we couldn't]...so we had to come on a cargo plane to Basra. Then the flight was cancelled and we had to sleep in Iraq, then we had to go to Turkey and then England. It was a nightmare.

There were four of us in the cargo plane. Luckily there was a British guy who was too late for the civvy plane but he nearly shed tears. He was complaining about what we had to go through!

He chuckled, remembering the man's distress and the way that the plane had rattled all the way back to Brize Norton.

'Did you complain?' I asked.

'No, we took it on the chin.'

The reason for this differential treatment was that Qatar border officials were barring all foreign nationals with a few exceptions from entering the country. I first heard this account in 2009, just days after it had just happened – although it was clearly a common experience. Another version entailed the 'non-British contingent', a designation that was clearly disliked, being ejected from a group being flown out to a special operation in Kuwait.

A private expense

The issues that infuriated the group sitting round the table in Germany ranged wider than this occasional discrimination. There was an underlying consensus that the question of citizenship was intrinsically related to their occupation. Although they shared the view that joining for the sole pur-pose of getting a British passport was wrong, they argued that the nature of their work ought to earn them a less expensive route to naturalisation, if not a faster one. At that time the process cost roughly £600, constitut-ing a large proportion of their salary. Over the next few years it would rise steadily in line with increases in dependants' visa costs as well. Apply-ing for naturalisation was regarded as a personal option by their employers and therefore treated as a private expense. The only thing the army paid for was the passport itself, at the final step. 'It's wrong that we have to pay for cost of UK citizenship ourselves,' the group agreed. But it was not just a matter of expense. There were important principles at stake as these extracts from other group discussions show. One infantry soldier from Fiji complained,

> The army is quite helpful when it comes to applying, with signatures, but in terms of information, we have to go ourselves to the internet, and we have to find finances... and once you get the passport, it makes things very easy for the army.
>
> When you go on tours, they don't have to get you visas, so they benefit from the [money] you have to pay but no one lifts a finger, no one advises you how to go about it. No one actually comes up and tells you.

Colin, who was recruited in Jamaica, said he thought it was 'disgraceful' that they had to pay for everything. 'I've gone to Iraq, Afghanistan and Northern Ireland,' he said scornfully. 'That's Britishness enough for me.'

Echoing the opinions of many others he listed the financial implications of applying, as well as the humiliating process of preparing for the 'Life in the UK' test: 'We need fuel money, a day's leave, the cost of the test and training material.'[14] As usual, the person with a particular grievance was able to articulate issues that others might feel but not be able to express. His gripe about naturalisation costs revealed that he was dealing with complicated immigration procedures in order to bring his family to the UK.

'The major thing is with immigration,' he began. 'You come as a mature person, so you have family, but there is so much red tape. You are left to sort it out yourself.' I asked him to explain.

> My wife and kids are back in Jamaica [but] I am trying to get them up. She was my girlfriend at the time. I had to send them back down to Jamaica, 'cos I couldn't get married in the UK. I had to go back and marry her there, and then come back. She didn't have much time on her visa but [in order to reapply as a serving spouse], she was sent back again and I had to bring her back again – this was three years ago.

As we discussed the implications of dealing with immigration headaches with little support from his employers, he went on,

> Another thing: what are we? I class myself as a British soldier. I am doing nothing different. Why can't you define my role? It is like being auxiliaries. I am doing my full whack and I've got more on my plate.
>
> No, I am not a UK citizen, [but] I view myself as a professional. I joined the British army, I am proud to be a British soldier. But we are boxed in,

classed as non-British, foreign and Commonwealth. And as much as we are classed as one, we are all from different countries.

Gesturing to a Fijian colleague, he added,

My concern might not be the same as his. I have different concerns. I've had problems with the Home Office. What time have I got to ring the Home Office? It's like you are asking for favouritism.

Family reunion

Any discussion of problems caused as a result of citizenship and immigration status invariably led in two directions. The first was connected to the practical issues involved in travelling without the red passport and the principle of paying the full fee for naturalisation, as these testimonies illustrate. The second related to personal life, and the host of potential difficulties, costs and heartaches involved in setting up and maintaining family settlement in the UK. It is important to reiterate that by no means all Commonwealth soldiers enlisted with the aim of acquiring UK citizenship. For a significant number, their nationality was intrinsic to their identity; many were not committed to staying in the UK for the rest of their lives. Those from countries that did not allow dual citizenship were reluctant to have to apply for visas to return home. They also feared losing property rights or a connection with their cultural heritage. Attitudes often depended on length of service and the contingencies of family life.

On one occasion I met a small group of Fijian women whose husbands served together in an infantry regiment. Over the past decade they had accompanied them in a variety of postings, including Northern Ireland, and their palpable sense of solidarity and friendship reflected their shared experience of service life. They did not have UK citizenship because they were not sure they wanted to lose the 'blue passport', but now they were considering it because they were so alarmed by the rising cost of visas. I asked whether their husbands would agree. They glanced at each other and one said with a smile, 'In Fiji men do what women tell them.'

Being posted in Germany presented its own disadvantages for spouses, despite the compensations of enjoying a slightly higher standard of living. As we saw in the previous chapter, living inside the Schengen area necessitated obtaining short-term visas for travel back to the UK. It also made it more complicated for the soldier to bring a spouse from a Commonwealth country since they were obliged to travel to the UK first and then apply for a visa to Germany, all of which took time and cost money.

One of the corporals taking part in the group discussion in Germany, a Ghanaian woman called Anne, felt particular compassion for the spouses she was meeting in the course of her work as a clerk. 'Wives are the backbone of soldiers,' she pointed out. 'If the army is not doing much for them, they will want to leave. Visas are expensive. The army helps the soldier but tells him or her they must sort out their family themselves.'

A Jamaican woman agreed: 'You as an individual need to sort yourself out. I am all right, taking one day as it comes. It's what you make of it. Change will not happen in a day.'

'You go to the welfare office,' continued Anne, 'and they tell you to sort out your own family. Soldiers' wives are struggling. They are treated like crap.'

The problems of being a non-UK national who was not a Commonwealth citizen were even worse, according to one participant. 'Some wives can't go to UK [at all],' he said. He knew an Irish guy whose wife was a Thai national who was refused a visa to visit the UK. In desperation the soldier had tried to drive home but they were stopped at French border and turned back.

More than anything else, the sheer cost of visas and the necessity of renewing them at regular intervals was causing immense resentment. It was another aspect of their life as migrants which meant that they were not being treated on an equal basis with the UK peers. Salote, the Fijian corporal who was training to become an F&C adviser in the welfare services, explained the situation when I visited her in Southampton. She told me that people whom she met frequently said, 'Oh, you're in the British Army, how nice!'

'They [think we're] treated equally!' she said, exasperated.

Like with me, my pay is no different than with the other corporal there but there are issues like when my dependants' visas get expired, it's my responsibility to get them renewed or they get sent back to Fiji.

And I'm serving in the army; I'm paying the same amount of taxes you know? I go and do deployment like them. Like I said, these things cannot be solved overnight but I think it's gone on for long [enough] really. Paying £495 every so often, that's plenty money and it increases by the year.

For Salote it was important to bring these matters to the attention of the chain of command. 'Some of them,' she went on, 'I think they are aware of it but it takes people to be constantly pushing. Like visa cases, and also with children being born in Germany.'

We met before the UKBA changed the law relating to children born to service personnel on overseas postings. She explained that this was an example of an anomaly that was indefensible.

A Fijian lady gives birth in Germany and the child gets a Fijian passport. A Fijian lady bears a child here in the UK, the child gets a UK passport, things like that. Realistically, well from my own point of view, if the father of a child is a British Army soldier, if he's paying taxes to the British government irrespective of where he is based, it's I think it's the law itself, you know. Equality.

There was one aspect of their entitlements and allowances that benefited Commonwealth personnel that was not enjoyed by their British peers. This was a dispensation known as 'domcol', an abbreviation for Domestic Collective Overseas Leave, which was granted to eligible service personnel who either enlisted in a Commonwealth country or travelled to the UK with the sole purpose of joining the armed forces. Domcol was basically a continuation of a practice from an earlier era when government employees in or from the colonies were faced with travelling long distances by boat, thereby requiring significant periods away from their work. It entitled soldiers to 45 days leave and a flight home at public expense every 5 years of service for as long as he or she remained unmarried, and/or their next of kin lived in their home country.[15]

In order to be eligible for domcol, they had to meet certain other stipulations which often caused confusion unless there was reliable support and accurate advice from the unit welfare office. Understandably it was a topic that was frequently raised in conversation about the perks and problems of being a Commonwealth soldier. The prospect of a free flight and an extended period of home leave motivated many of those who were not married or who had decided not to bring family with them. For a couple struggling to stay connected while they lived on the opposite sides of the globe, however, it was small consolation.

Freddie was from Fiji, a quiet man who was recruited in 2007. It was only when I was able to speak to him alone that he began to talk about his situation. Before that he had sat quietly at the table while his colleagues, all gunners in the RA, had their say.

'I haven't seen my wife and kids for two years,' he told me. His youngest child was just one year and five months, and he had never even met him. This was May and he was due to go to Afghanistan in September. That would mean it would be at least another nine months before he could visit Fiji or bring his family to the UK. His predicament was made more difficult because he came from a poor background, he said. His parents had separated when he was young and he was supporting his mother now as well as his immediate family, sending most of his wages home. Unlike many others, he did not own a computer and therefore could not contact them on Skype. Instead he had to use the telephone which he said cost him £200 every month. Meanwhile he was saving to go back on leave, a trip which would cost £1,200.

As he was telling me this, Sophie, also a gunner, put her head round the door. I had wanted to speak to her as we had met once before at Pirbright during her basic training but now a quick exchange revealed that she did not have much to report. She was happier in the regimental unit because she had more time for herself. 'My room is more private,' she said, 'and I can spend hours on the phone.'

This was important because her children, who were five and two, were living in St Vincent in their father's care. She was not planning to bring her family to the UK until she knew where she would be living, but she had managed to visit a few weeks earlier and was planning another trip in August.

Her situation was in stark contrast to Freddie who seemed to be really struggling, emotionally as well as financially. 'I am not good at expressing myself,' he admitted. 'Sometimes I have the thought of what's going on, I can't express it.'

He had spoken to the sergeant major about his situation and learned about the possibility of domcol, but the thought of waiting for five years to qualify did not fill him with much hope. I asked him how he got on with his colleagues.

'Sometimes it is hard in the work environment,' he said in a subdued voice.

I am the only Fijian in the battery and they treat me as 'our Fijian'. Sometimes I get the feeling of segregation. They put you down.

Sometimes I can't take it, I walk away. When you come back you really need somebody to talk to. I need family especially in this environment. Most of us hardly speak out, maybe because of our background. I was brought up not to say a lot of things. I accept what is given to me. I just cope with it.

He was resigned to his situation but there were times when he was overwhelmed by homesickness.

I am a big boy, I play rugby, [but] I cry to myself in my room. I am a Christian; it gives me backbone to overcome things. Maybe it's all about sacrifice. Forward ever, backward never! That's my motto.

The plight of soldiers who, like Freddie, decided for one reason or another to defer bringing their families to the UK, added another dimension to the issue of migrant status and military service. Like countless other global migrants, Freddie was indeed making a form of sacrifice by working far from home in order to support his family. But the British Army was not an ordinary employer, even according to their own recruitment materials. As we saw in the previous chapter, the Guide for Commonwealth Citizens and their Families, published in 2008 by PS4, the central welfare team responsible for negotiating and delivering the organisation's policy for service families, stated that a soldier's spouse or partner was automatically considered part of the 'Army Family' on the basis that 'that the stability of family life is of great importance for its personnel'.[16] But when a couple was separated by many miles and the spouse was only able to accompany the soldier at their own expense, this commitment looked increasingly strained.

Reactive maintenance

In the same way that the MoD had not anticipated the welfare issues entailed in supporting spouses and other dependants from ethnic minorities, it had certainly not foreseen the extra burden that Commonwealth soldiers found themselves shouldering as a result of their status as migrants. The 'suck it and see' response must be considered a positive one against a background of apathy, ignorance and even resentment. Some of the unit welfare officers I spoke to were candid about their lack of knowledge.

'There's a lot unknown by us,' said Jim, a Warrant Officer who worked in a UWO with a high percentage of non-UK citizens. 'In the welfare teams, we come into this job with life skills behind us. Even our welfare officers' course doesn't really teach you a lot and this Foreign and Commonwealth piece is ever revolving through reactive maintenance.'

His frankness about the difficulties of the job helped to explain why so many individuals I had met were frustrated by the lack of expertise in their unit welfare offices. 'It's getting bigger and bigger every week here,' he continued, 'every time we get recruits in. I can't say all of them are from the Foreign and Commonwealth but there are a massive amount.'

The main problems were caused by their complete inexperience in dealing with immigration law. Just as the act of joining the armed forces did not entail an expedited right to UK citizenship, so the decision to leave after four years did not provide any guarantees that an application to remain in the UK would be successful. Individuals who had signed off were permitted to start the process of gaining settlement 10 weeks before they were discharged. Although not all would want to stay in the UK, for those who did, and especially those with families, this was a complicated and expensive process. In order to qualify for settlement they not only had to meet the UKBA criteria, whether in terms of residency and having no criminal convictions, but they also faced paying hundreds of pounds in fees. In theory, unit welfare services were briefed to pre-empt and to advise on this aspect of preparing for discharge, as on any other, but if they were inexperienced, like Jim, this only added to the difficulties.

He was ready to admit that, when soldiers signed off and started to investigate using the credits earned during military service that enabled them to take higher education courses, he was not in a position to advise.

I don't know whether they're still entitled to stay or leave, if you know what I mean. The majority of the people that leave are around the five-year point so they can already have their naturalisation under way to become British citizens.

Some of the husbands have been naturalised but the wives haven't. And it's like if they're not naturalised, are they still entitled to stay because they're spouses of a naturalised person?

It's questions like this... I've actually emailed the immigration control for answers and they've gone, 'Yeah, look at this on the website,' and the document doesn't actually match what you're trying to get the answers for.

Jim had asked one of the soldiers who had gone through naturalisation to write out a description of all the different stages so that he could use it for others. He had confided in him that because he was a British citizen he had no idea of the process.

It's a little bit strange for us trying to understand all of the stuff that goes on for the Commonwealth, because they pay for their own visa applications and all that sort of stuff.

I mean you get the odd one or two that come in and know exactly what they're talking about because they've read new policy, bits and pieces on-line, and there are some Commonwealth soldiers – sparkling bright – that have checked all of this, double-checked and triple-checked.

Applications for settlement, family visas or citizenship were not all about filling in forms correctly. Sometimes there were problems caused by missing documents, such as marriage certificates, that could not be solved by research alone. Timothy was a retired chaplain who worked as a voluntary welfare officer in a unit in Salisbury Plain. He virtually ambushed me on one of my visits to a Phase 2 training centre once he heard I was interviewing Commonwealth soldiers. Our conversation brought home some of the effects of the organisation's failure to predict the hardship caused either by the lack of specialist knowledge or the complexity inherent in the process.

Timothy presented himself as a relic from an earlier era, who was making himself very useful in the current one. He joined the army in 1961 and served both as a regimental officer and as an army chaplain. After semi-retiring in 2001, he then took up a post as chaplain on a voluntary basis where he had discovered that his expertise in spiritual matters was appreciated less than his readiness to roll up his sleeves and get acquainted with immigration procedures. Too elderly to bother about finding the right terminology but willing to reflect critically on his long service with the British Army, the Padre spoke from the heart as he explained what he had learned from his latest role in the organisation.

He believed that the army had made great advances, compared with 'the old days' at least. 'The first black man joined our regiment in 1969,' he confessed. 'It was known as the White Lancers and we called him the Black Lancer.' Although he had worked in welfare for several years he felt that the problems had escalated in 2007. The number of F&C soldiers at the base had reached 33 per cent at one point, although by the time we met it had fallen to below 20 per cent. 'There has been a huge increase in the last 18 months to two years. There are a lot of problems the army is not alert to.' High on the list was the question of bringing spouses and children to the UK as dependants. In this particular establishment, most of the soldiers had not been home for over six months. All recruits were permitted to apply for family quarters at this stage so that their accommodation would be sorted out by the time they were sent to their unit.

> There is one Gambian whose wife has been here for 15 years and has a child of five or six. They are sending him to Germany but there's a problem with his wife because she can't apply for a stamp to the HO – they have no record of her – she is a 'late stayer'. It's causing a lot of problems.

Waving a blue plastic ring-binder, thick with pages and pages of forms, he explained that in the last six months he had written 50 letters supporting the sponsorship of wives and husbands.

> They see me as a grey haired civvy, someone confidential. I collect notes every day that say, 'Can I see you?' It has doubled my non-chaplaincy workload and I spend less time on spiritual welfare.
>
> I've taken this on as no one else has. If they are training in Ukraine for the UK army, how to get their wife and kids to join them? I have to look on the internet. The army doesn't take this on [but] they talk the talk!

One of the reasons his services were in such demand was that he had obtained a licence to conduct weddings. 'I regularised 11 marriages this year,' he said brightly, explaining that individuals needed to produce a marriage certificate to qualify for SFA.

> If they can't, it's difficult for them. Muslim marriages don't produce a certificate, for example. Or some spouses came as students and stayed. One Zimbabwean met his wife in Southend-on-Sea. He went back for a traditional wedding and now wants married quarters.

In his experience, most applications and appeals went through, but it varied from one country to another. He showed me another file, pointing to a page showing names, addresses and phone numbers of High Commissions in 20 different capitals. 'It is very time consuming. We really could do with an immigration-Home Office cell,' he said.

There were plans to apply for a full-time officer to take on the job that clearly needed filling, but it was clear by 2009 that funds would be more limited than ever. The Padre was doubtful that his role as chaplain would be continued after he left, but clearly felt vindicated that as a marginal figure he had been able to offer practical help in changing individuals' lives. 'I feel pride at getting visas for them – it's like converting people!' he said, eyes twinkling. But he was no pushover. 'They are good at telling porkies, like Anglo-Saxons. If they can work the system they will.'

Unintended consequences

In 2009 an African soldier was discovered to have joined the army under a false identity. At the time he was serving in the Irish Guards and had recently taken part in a 'Trooping the Colour' parade in the course of his duties, but his duplicity was revealed after he was involved in a car accident. Police found that he had a number of aliases, one of which he had used successfully to hoodwink recruiters. The tabloids predictably went to town. 'Illegal squaddie guards Queen', barked the *Sun*'s headlines; 'Revealed: One of the Queen's guards is an illegal immigrant', triumphed the *Daily Mail*, proving that the heroism normally attributed to those who served Her Majesty was no match for the hatred roused by the foreigner who was in the country on false pretences.[17]

The fact that the individual was a guardsman provided an excuse to fantasise about his proximity to the Queen as though his training as a soldier was merely a mask concealing nefarious and treasonable intent. It was the opposite of the situation described to me by a senior officer meditating on the recruitment of soldiers who travelled to the UK as migrants.

'You see an immigrant in uniform, and you think, ah, he's a soldier, he's ok. You see him out of uniform and you don't know what you've got!'

As his words hung in the air he added hastily, 'Well, I suppose it's the same with anyone really.'

The assumption that anyone who volunteered to be a soldier was bound to be honourable and disciplined might have worked for military staff, but for the UKBA, neither an army uniform nor even a valid ID document necessarily ruled out the possibility of fraud. For those who worked in PS4, negotiating the interface between immigration control and military employment policy, there was room neither for honour nor for sentiment. They were well aware from focus groups that many felt humiliated, let alone inconvenienced, by their experiences at UK border controls and frustrated that they did not have more identifiable travel documents. But the officer in charge was quick to underline the policy line that the UKBA 'have a job to do' which is 'to identify that the individuals coming in are who they say they are'.

As head of PS4 he was responsible for briefing welfare officers on how to advise Commonwealth citizens and their families, stressing that they were told to travel with appropriate travel documentation, including the telephone number of an army duty officer that they could give to the border control officer in order to verify their identity. But as far as he was concerned, decisions about immigration control were the prerogative of the UKBA. 'As long as you remain someone who is not a European Union citizen, there will be border controls and additional scrutiny,' he admitted, before adding, 'And in the past, sadly, there has been fraud.' Any changes happened at glacial speed. From February 2010 exemption stamps issued by the UKBA contained a photographic vignette which added a welcome degree of authenticity to a migrant's passport.

PS4 had been centrally involved in negotiating the specific points contained in the 'Nation's Commitment', and the role of the unit was to continue to identify any 'unintended consequence' of army service by providing evidence of disadvantage to the Home Office. One of the contested areas identified by the Task Force in 2004 was the fact that soldiers' partners who were also Commonwealth citizens were disadvantaged in comparison with their civilian counterparts who could seek settlement in their own right after five years' residency in the UK. The situation for a military spouse or partner was different because the government was, in effect, funding their exemption from immigration control as long as the soldier remained in the army. According to a PS4 officer, one example of the discrepancy might be:

> Say you've got a Pakistani doctor in the National Health Service and, in those days, if his contract ran past the five-year point, then potentially he and his family could seek settlement in the United Kingdom and that would give them recourse to public funds.
>
> On the other hand, if a family member came into the United Kingdom [to join] a serving soldier, subject to immigration control, they would remain on the same Exempt Armed Forces Dependants' visa without the opportunity to seek settlement until the soldier left.

Although it took several years to take effect, this welcome decision was intended to offer partners greater autonomy as well as security. It meant that if the couple could meet all the other Home Office criteria, the partner could then seek settlement in their own right after two years. This was an important concession since, apart from anything else, it would permit them to make a life for themselves in the UK and plan for their children's future separately from their soldier partner, from whom they might be estranged or divorced. Another benefit was that any dependant children who were about to go to university would be entitled to pay home fees rather than overseas fees, providing they had obtained settlement as well. Needless to say, the prospect of paying university fees on a soldier's salary was out of the question if the children did not qualify for a home-student loan.

Brown envelopes

Colin's analysis cut straight to the heart of the problem, as he saw it.

> The bottom line is that I don't think the army is equipped. They have manning problems, and seek out people from different backgrounds, but they have not investigated deeply enough. It's unforgivable when they do active recruitment in countries.

Like many of his fellow Jamaicans, he had undergone his pre-selection tests in his home country during a visit by the OPT, and his sense of outrage was fuelled by the belief that the British Army had gone out of its way to recruit Commonwealth citizens as a way of employing ethnic minorities as well as filling the ranks. His resentment was aimed at his employers who, he felt, had not bothered to research the implications of recruiting people from outside the UK to perform a job that was in the national interest. He continued angrily,

> I can see no reason why, [if] I am willing to give my life, this entitles me to come and be given whatever rights. The fact that I am willing to put my life on the line entitles me to have rights of other citizens.

Colin did not say whether he had compared his situation with that of US soldiers whom he had met in Iraq or Afghanistan, but his sense of entitlement was not simply plucked out of the air as a bad-tempered gesture. As a Jamaican national, citizen of a former colony, he would have been well aware of his country's contribution to Britain's twentieth-century wars. The link between the struggle for national independence and military service had been particularly strong in Jamaica as we observed in Chapter 1. He would undoubtedly have learned in school that Caribbean peoples who volunteered to fight on behalf of the 'Motherland' expected positive benefits in return, despite being excluded from the British Army itself.[18]

While the paths to national independence varied among what are now Commonwealth countries, British Army recruitment in the twenty-first century inevitably summoned up memories of those imperial connections. Contrary to the young South African's fears expressed above, F&C soldiers were not classified as mercenaries because they swore allegiance to the Queen when they joined up, thereby reasserting and recognising historic colonial ties between their own nation and the UK. The importance of that legacy was briefly expressed in terms of British citizenship too when, in 1948, the Conservative government created a new category available to all those in the United Kingdom and the colonies. The 1948 British Nationality Act 'was seen by many as a mark of gratitude for the support – including significant military service – of Commonwealth and imperial citizens during the Second World War'.[19]

The 2008 command paper noted this 'long and distinguished history of Service' in the briefest of terms as it prepared to qualify its proposals to address the 'unique' situation of F&C citizens in the armed forces today. However, in the 50 years between the 1948 Nationality Act and the decision to recruit Commonwealth citizens in 1998, their rights to enter the UK in order to live and work as civilians had been inexorably curtailed through successive immigration and nationality legislation. The inclusion of some basic principles in the Service Command paper was significant but it did not affect the intransigent problems at unit level. The fundamental issue of who was responsible for providing information and guidance was at least clarified when, in 2011, the relevant section of the British Army website was redesigned for that purpose. Where the US immigration services collaborated with the US army to provide 'customer service channels exclusively to assist members of the military and their families', the best that the UK armed forces could offer was to point migrants directly to the relevant UKBA documents so they could do their own research.[20]

On the page outlining personnel support for F&C citizens a number of contact points were now listed, with links to briefings produced by army welfare organisations, the UKBA and countries such as Fiji (which by then had been suspended from the Commonwealth) and Nepal. However, the clarification was not just a belated attempt to provide information for prospective employees. As time went on it was clear that the MoD had chosen another option: to emphasise the extra hurdles entailed in applying as a citizen of a Commonwealth country and to signal that the onus for sorting out immigration issues had officially passed over to the soldiers themselves. Nowhere was this redefined relationship more clearly specified than in the section on 'Paying for UK visas and British citizenship applications'.

'This is normally a personal responsibility,' the advice began, directing readers to the UKBA website. 'The UK Armed Forces only pays for UK visas or passports required for official travel. This does not include any visas required by you or your family first moving to and remaining in the UK, settlement or UK citizenship applications.'

The point is not that the situation was effectively different, since it was always the case that Commonwealth citizens paid for their families' visas as well as for the cost of naturalisation. This information was simply a warning: unless you are single, think twice about the economic disadvantages. The advice continued,

> The average cost of UK visas for a family of four to move from country of origin to the UK, apply for settlement and subsequently UK citizenship is currently about £7,000. You are strongly advised to budget and put money aside to save for the costs of UK visas.

For a private beginning a military career on an annual salary of £17,265, this amount would be prohibitive, even though it did not have to be paid all at once.[21] It represented a level of expense that would be entirely absent from a British soldier's calculations, unless she or he was planning to marry or cohabit with a citizen from another non-EU country. 'Our terms and conditions might be the same as our British counterparts,' as one Fijian put it bluntly, 'but we still have to pay to have our families living in the UK.'

The provision of signposts for individuals trying to sort out their immigration issues was obviously a welcome development when compared to the services of a welfare officer who simply could not imagine what it was like *not* to be a British citizen. Nevertheless, as Colin and others pointed out, contacting the UKBA was a time-consuming business which had its own frustrations and hiring an immigration lawyer was another significant expense. The information was constantly changing and visas costs rising too as successive governments sought to show how closely they were attending to the task of capping immigration. But by 2011 there were other problems on the horizon, ones that were increasingly flagged up by the FSN as they trawled the bases and garrisons offering advice to Fijians and others from Commonwealth countries. Following the publication of the government's plans to cut thousands of jobs from the army, soldiers and their partners wanted to know one thing: what would redundancy mean for those who were neither settled nor citizens?

It was common knowledge that the ominous brown envelopes would be delivered to the first round of employees in the late summer of 2011. There was talk of generous redundancy packages and a promise that no one actually serving in Afghanistan would return to unemployment, but no mention of what the cuts might mean for those with migrant status. As the new focal point for raising the concerns of Fijian soldiers, the FSN was well aware that there were numerous young men who had lost everything in Fiji, either as a result of the political instability or because of the length of time being away. They had no other homes to return to if their contracts were terminated prematurely. The threat of unemployment was especially alarming for families who had been putting down roots in the UK, hoping to remain in the country until the soldiers had worked through their long contract. Those who had not yet earned or secured the right to remain felt vulnerable even though they had been assured that their situation would be still considered as 'unique'.

This sense of insecurity was not helped by rumours circulating about particular cases where either settlement or full access to public funds, including housing, was denied. One example was the case of two Fijian soldiers who had received redundancy notices and who had their applications to settle turned down on the basis that they had been stationed in Germany for their entire service. While this was not considered a problem for the men's status, their wives had apparently not qualified for residency in the UK. Their children, on the other hand, were born in Germany and either had been granted or were eligible for 'red passports'. If the families were to return to Fiji they would have to pay for visas for the children who would be classified as visitors from the UK. The families were said to be seeking help from veterans' agencies which had taken up their case.[22]

The creation of the FSN meant that at least the F&Cs had a voice within the welfare infrastructure of the armed forces. But what of other nationalities who were not represented in such direct manner? In 2007 the BBC reported the formation of the British Commonwealth Soldiers' Union (BCSU), quoting its founder, Belize-born Marlon Clancy, saying that 'Commonwealth soldiers are third-class soldiers'.[23] The BCSU subsequently disappeared from view[24] but clearly the problems that inspired its creation continued to affect the experience of F&C soldiers and their families. As the evidence in this chapter suggests, the capacity of the British Army to deal with the issues and problems entailed in employing soldiers with migrant status had been extremely limited. However, the administrative problems of employing migrants were eclipsed by the wider politics of UK immigration control which were producing ever-tightening regulations as well as rising visa and naturalisation costs.

Seen in this light, the phenomenon of Commonwealth soldiers in the British Army identifies pressing questions that reached into the heart of contemporary debates about national identity, citizenship and multiculturalism at home, as well as the future of the UK's role as a global military power. In the concluding chapter we move away from a discussion of institutional practices and policies to consider some of these wider consequences of maintaining Britain's multi-national and culturally diverse army.

10
Conclusion: Militarised Multiculture

Image 6   Members of the Household Cavalry Mounted Regiment
MoD.

One of the more unexpected features of the Royal Wedding in April 2011 was a news item that appeared in the *Mail* under the following headline: 'By Royal Appointment: The skateboarding, punk-loving boy from Harlem who made America proud'.[1] The story provided a perfect example of the role that a visibly diverse army was able to play in projecting a particular image of Britishness. In this instance, the message was directed not so much at British citizens inside the UK as to US readers online who might be lured by a local connection to the event. The boy in question was Denton John, described as a 'son of immigrants from Grenada' who grew up in Harlem, New York. He had returned to Grenada after finishing high school and decided to join the British Army from there. It is likely, given the timing, that he was in the country when the OPT visited in 2008 and that he went through the same pre-selection process as some of the young men and women I had met in Catterick and Pirbright. In any event, at the age of 23 John found himself a member of the Household Cavalry Mounted Regiment, the unit charged with responsibility to protect the Queen.

The *Mail* account was culled from a short item on the CNN website that had set the agenda a few days earlier with an understandably partisan spin: 'Royal wedding's lone American will guard Queen on horseback'.[2] The more craven local version was updated as the day proceeded. As the procession left the Abbey, the *Mail* reported that the young man was taking 'centre stage', with his breastplate resplendent in the glorious sun. Photographs of the event were interspersed with captions such as 'Pride of America: The Queen's carriage makes its way to Buckingham Palace with Harlem boy Denton John believed to be riding next to the monarch'. His US connections were repeated over and over again. ' ... riding on horseback with his gleaming boots, red plume, sword and immaculately-pressed uniform on Friday, the New Yorker made the country proud as the only American in the wedding procession'. His commanding officer was quoted as saying, 'He is the only American in the Household Cavalry, and as far as we know, the only American in the Royal Wedding, It's our version of the "American Dream".'

It was a marvel that the young man did not collapse under the weight of symbolic value he was carrying on his head. Whether he knew it or not, he was fulfilling many dreams and expectations as well as proving that racism was no longer an obstacle to social mobility, either in Britain or in the US. The fact that he was black was just as significant as his Grenadan passport or his American high school certificate and, presumably, his accent. But what US audiences would not have known was that the Household Cavalry had its own reasons for enjoying this young man as a trophy.

As we saw in Chapter 2, the regiment was the subject of the CRE's inquiry in the mid-1990s following repeated instances of racist bullying and discrimination. Prince Charles had famously complained about the lack of black soldiers in the unit to which he belonged, demanding that they actively target ethnic minorities for recruitment. The red-coated guardsmen are one of London's classic tourist attractions and therefore the degree of diversity in their elite ranks is not only more visible but also more significant than it might be in other infantry regiments. The attention drawn to 'the only American in the Royal Wedding' was evidence that the deployment of one black soldier was enough to convey the virtue of multiculture in a military setting.

Clasped hands

Minority soldiers were all too aware of the photogenic aspect of diversity, often based on their own encounters with journalists and politicians.

Understandably many were reluctant to be used for PR purposes. I asked Ken whether he had ever been pulled into a photo shoot in order to represent the fact that there were black people in the army. He knew exactly what I meant.

> I hate it myself. You know if you're in a certain situation, if you have a group of people here, and there are white people and black people. They seem to think sometimes that even to have one or two black people [makes] it look good.

On one occasion it had happened to him on tour. A press photographer had called him over to join a group 'to balance it out' and he had refused. 'I'm a very open-minded person,' he told me, 'I'm an approachable person. I just think if you're good enough for something you should be chosen [for that reason], not because of your face.' Ken had similar views about women being displayed in media representations of the troops and other manifestations of what he called positive discrimination. He felt that these were political issues that had little to do with the actual capabilities of the people involved. 'I'm not being funny or disrespectful to women,' he insisted, but he clearly thought that it was harder for female soldiers to work on an equal footing with men and therefore wrong to pretend otherwise.

The experience of being told to stand near a senior officer during a press conference or take part in a group chat with a minister was a hazard of being a minority soldier. Some officers mentioned that they tried to put a stop to this, particularly when there was only one black soldier present and they could see how demeaning it could be for the individual. But a quick search through Google images of politicians visiting troops on operations illustrates the importance of the subliminal shot proving that a multicultural army represented the country's best interests. One such staged picture shows Blair on a surprise visit to troops in Iraq in 2004. While the British public at home were raging about the legality of that wretched war, their prime minister was photographed in jovial conversation with a group of soldiers, his arm stretched across the frame to clasp the hand of the one who was black.[3]

Although this pattern could be supported by anecdotes from individuals, including testimonies from memoirs written by soldiers themselves, the question of strategic representation did not mean that minorities necessarily felt valued as a result. As the number of TV documentaries showing life on operations increased, some were aggrieved that black soldiers were virtually invisible.

'When you watch these programmes, you don't see us,' said Colin, who was Jamaican. 'Ross Kemp and all that. I find it well weird. I don't want to be paranoid, [but] you look at it, you don't see us. It's not my reality.'

He recalled an early tour in Iraq when journalists from the BBC came and interviewed everyone. 'No one thought, what is the Commonwealth point of view? What is he going through? No one ever came to me.'

It wasn't just the lack of interest. He was annoyed that the journalists were arranging for people to make phone calls to the UK. 'What about my family in Jamaica?' he asked, remembering that 'the Brits in the army would be more outspoken – they could afford to be'.

His complaint highlighted what it felt like to be a minority, either selected for inclusion simply because of what he or she looked like rather than on the basis of achievement or ability. Or, possibly even worse, rejected as an example of an ordinary British squaddie and therefore not deemed to be of interest to the armchair war-spectator at home. But leaving aside the wounded pride of those who had either been co-opted or ignored, the significance of diversity in its military context required a more elaborate analysis. Apart from proving that the British Army was as multicultural as the rest of the UK, what else was at stake?

Down the line

Ken had been recruited in the first OPT to visit St Vincent, back in 2001, and had seen first hand the effects of institutional reform over the intervening decade. Having been promoted to the rank of corporal he was now a junior manager on the promotion ladder, but he had also had plenty of time to experience life outside the organisation too. His impression of what life might be like 'down the line', as he put it, was partly based on the way people reacted to him out of uniform. 'Normally, if people see me in the pub, they don't know who I am, what I do, but they just judge me and see me as another outsider.' In civilian clothes he had experienced racist insults in the street as well as discrimination in bars and pubs. It often happened when he was with army friends who were white who would spring to his defence, even getting into fights on his behalf. But in uniform it was a different matter.

> It's a different attitude when you wear uniform to when you wear civilian clothes. The uniform is like a cover; it's like a shield. If I go places in my uniform, people will greet you because they can identify the uniform. But if I take my uniform off and go in the same places, they look at you differently, talk to you differently and speak to you in different ways.

This conversation with Ken stayed with me because it echoed the thoughts of the senior commander who had remarked about the difference between seeing a migrant in and out of uniform. Only this time, Ken was telling me how it actually felt to experience that dichotomy in person. There was no denying it was disconcerting for young men and women to be recruited to fight for a country they had never been to, only to find when they arrived that they were not welcome – not unless they were wearing battle dress. Several months later I caught up with the young men, also from the

Caribbean, whose attestation ceremony I had witnessed at Pirbright. They had been regaling me with stories of their life as trainees at ITC, with widely varying accounts of trying to integrate with their peers. I had asked whether they had ventured outside the base on their occasional weekend breaks.

Dennis had been invited to Manchester by one of his English section mates and welcomed into his family. Ben preferred either to visit his mother in London or to stay in Catterick and keep out of harm's way. Carlos and Albert, both from Belize City, had sampled the clubs in York and Newcastle and one evening found themselves in Stockton where they decided to stay overnight. As they entered the bar of their hotel, a group of men, young and middle aged, turned on them and told them to get out.

Carlos pulled out his army ID card and held it up. 'Does this make any difference?' he demanded. The men backed off immediately, mumbling their apologies. 'Wow mate, you're a hero,' they heard someone say, according to Carlos who had a great ear for a story.

As the two recruits ordered their drinks at the bar, a woman whom they described as 'a little old lady' told them, 'don't listen', a gesture that they found touching. 'She took our part,' they said, nonplussed at the way that the men had reacted violently on seeing the colour of their skin.

Being stigmatised as immigrants or outsiders gave some of them insights into the way their UK colleagues treated them. At the same time, a regular diet of racist propaganda from the tabloids inevitably shaped all their views, regardless of where they were born or the colour of their passports. Asylum seekers provided an easy target of resentment and hatred for soldiers, especially when they were caricatured walking into the country and eating up benefits handed to them on a plate. As a result of a particularly virulent outburst in the *Sun*, one man from Fiji confided that he had recently come to doubt whether he wanted his family to settle in the UK. 'Do I want my kids to grow up here?' he found himself asking. He was worried about the possibility that they would never be allowed to fit in.

Gurkha communities were not exempt from anti-immigrant vitriol either, despite the groundswell of public support they had received in 2009. The recruits experienced hostility in Darlington when they attempted to converse with other young people, but in the garrison town of Aldershot, Nepalis were growing more fearful after an increase in racist attacks.[4] This was attributed to the rise in unemployment, and the tension exacerbated by a statement made by the local MP Gerald Howarth in 2011. Calling for a policy of dispersal, he warned that his constituency was in danger of being overwhelmed by elderly Nepalis arriving as a result of the change in government ruling.[5]

It was Jan, a young white recruit from South Africa, who was able to articulate the defensive, defiant viewpoint of migrant soldiers who found themselves labelled as outsiders. He too was at pains to point out a distinction between those who deserved respect and those who were regarded as scroungers.

That's the way I see it ma'am, there's a lot of immigrants in this country but there's a lot of them are hanging round doing nothing but then you get us that work here, we provide a service for the country. I always tell the people who tell me I'm a foreign bastard or joke with me like that, I tell them at least I'm here doing your countrymen's job – because how many millions of people in Britain and look how the army's advertising because they need soldiers? We come over here to do the job, so we expect to be treated with respect!

He shook his head and added scornfully, 'We are fighting for *their* country!'
Simon, a fellow guardsman who was from New Zealand and also white, had agreed with him.

Even when I was living in London, the amount of people who said, 'Jeez, I could never join the army!' And this is British-born people, and they could never ever do it, and they get such a surprise that people like us come from so far away with a single goal to fight for a country that's not theirs.

Multicultural drift

The irritation that young men like Jan and Simon expressed may have masked a sense of entitlement on the grounds that they were not only 'providing a service' but they were also white as opposed to those 'immigrants' and asylum seekers who were visibly not. They were both fully aware of the irony that they were made to feel like foreigners and given ethnic minority status on a par with black recruits, many of whom had grown up in the UK. Jan's fate was to be an important statistic in whichever army he joined, British or South African. For the South African National Defence Force (SANDF), the question of diversity was just one factor. Rebuilding the institution in accordance with the principle of equality in the Bill of Rights also entailed integrating no less than seven military forces with their different histories, traditions and mutual enmities.

In her assessment of the first decade of reform Lindy Heinecken suggested that 'the lack of a mutually acceptable military culture' had failed to bridge the divide between black and white as well as between those of different military backgrounds. One particular issue, she wrote, was that 'In the SANDF it appears that loyalty and "struggle credentials" have become more important than individual competency, skills and experience.'[6]

The example of South Africa indicated that the terminology of 'diversity management' was woefully inappropriate in capturing all the different elements of national reconstruction. Once again, however, a comparative approach is invaluable in demonstrating a range of reasons why recruitment, representation and the institutional response to racism are so important in articulating the relationship between civil and military in different national contexts. Writing about the treatment of Muslims in the Indian Army, for example, Omar Khalidi concluded that the Indian political leadership's successful subordination of the military to civilian control was one of the exceptional achievements of the country, 'in shining contrast to neighbouring Pakistan, Bangladesh, Myanmar and the like'. His research indicated that 'As long as politicians share the vision of India as a multi-religious and secular state, the minorities have nothing to fear from a military composed of any one or more ethnic or caste groups.'[7] However, he warned, 'if groups representing extreme views of homogeneity come to power – even through democratic means – they can pose a clear and manifest danger to the physical security of the minorities'.

These two examples show that the composition of national armed forces in democratic countries involves more than a symbolic relationship with civil society. The issue of diversity acknowledges patterns of group identity, citizenship and belonging that have been forged in the course of civil wars as well as social movements of the twentieth century. As a result of those struggles, women and minorities had succeeded in widening access to almost all areas of employment, including education, business and politics. Why should the armed forces be any different?[8]

In Chapter 2 we noted that the 'multiculturalisation' of the British Army was propelled by a combination of governmental and non-governmental forces. The process conformed to an agenda set by a corporate version of multiculturalism, defined as an attempt 'to "manage" minority cultural differences in the interests of the centre'.[9] During the intervening decade the army was obliged to adopt a series of standard institutional reforms from ethnic monitoring to the more sophisticated strategies of HRM that were being introduced across the private and public sectors during this period.

While it is possible to look back and assemble all these measures in a chronological pattern, we should also note that it has been a more chaotic, uneven and contested development, characterised in the famous Parekh Report on the future of multi-ethnic Britain as 'multicultural drift'.[10] Although in hindsight this process has often been represented as a coherent programme driven by ideology, the reality was far more complex, requiring a precise analysis if we are to grasp not just what actually happened, but also what the implications have been for civil society.[11] In this chapter we will consider other factors that have influenced the standing of the armed forces as a national institution, interrogating the role of values as a device to re-centre the figure of the heroic soldier in British public life. As we draw together the various strands of this book, we can begin to see how the concept *militarised multiculture* is able to connect the project of 'diversifying the uniform' with this extraordinary shift in attitudes to military work.

Recognising *militarised multiculture* as a distinct entity is an acknowledgement that this haphazard programme of national institutional reform had taken place during a period of apparently endless wars in a world shaped by the rapid globalisation of security. Like the official term 'diversity manage-ment', *militarised multiculture* is applicable in different national contexts, and certainly valid in all NATO countries, regardless of how many troops were deployed in Afghanistan. But unlike the polite labelling of diversity as some-thing to be managed and contained, the concept is able to sharpen the rela-tionship between civil and military, revealing connections between domestic racism, cultural plurality, migration, social cohesion, national identity and foreign policy. But more than this, *militarised multiculture* also has a bearing on the changing practices of war, not least the behaviour of soldiers within the conflict zones and the treatment of civilians as well as detainees. This last point directs us once again to the subject of state-sanctioned killing, fighting, dying and death.

The cardboard box

It's an image of everyday life that's hard to get out of your mind. Wayne, a young man from St Vincent, is packing up his possessions in a giant card-board box, ready for his posting to Afghanistan. He had joined the army only eight months earlier and it's hard to imagine he would have enough possessions to fill it, but he tells me that these are the things that will be returned to his family if he does not come back alive. He has been instructed to talk to me and to let me follow him round but it was impossible to get a sense of a daily work routine because there wasn't one. I had been warned by a senior officer that infantry soldiers were renowned for living like lions, either working physically hard or sleeping for hours on end.

Wayne was doing neither, and nor was Josaia, from Fiji, who was in the same boat, but they had offered to show me the block where they lived. The adjutant had stressed on the phone that life had been very hectic and many of the soldiers were away on training exercises. These two had volunteered for deployment on the basis that their regiment had been asked to supply men to replace casualties in Afghanistan. They were among a group of 35 who were on five days notice, and they had just been filling out all the forms necessary for the life insurance policy they were obliged to take out. Earlier I had tried to find out what motivated them to put their names forward since they had so little experience.

The financial incentive was the most compelling since salaries were increased during deployment by a daily bonus and a lump sum. Wayne had been working in a car welding shop and was looking for something more out of life when the OPT visited Kingstown in 2008. His formal education had been minimal and he was ordered to attend the numeracy course for under-qualified recruits in Darlington. I noticed that his handwriting was weak and that he had lip read the consent form I gave him. 'Most people in the Caribbean join out of poverty,' he told me, but 'the reality sinks in once you get in and see the danger side'. His main concern was the improvised explosive devices (IEDs) but his mind was already made up to go. He was not the first in his family either to travel to the UK or to join the armed forces. His great uncle had been in the RLC and his sister joined the navy six years before. His brother worked night shifts in London as a delivery driver.

As he showed me his cubicle, Wayne pointed to the pictures of naked women plastered on the wall around his bed. Without a trace of embarrassment he explained that the sergeant major had encouraged them do this in order to 'make themselves at home'. Josaia was less comfortable and indicated that he had not taken the advice. There was a glossy union jack stuck on the locker too, and I asked them both about what it meant to fight a war on behalf of another country. There was no other way to put it: were they ready to kill and to risk their lives for Britain?

'This is what we are trained for,' said Wayne, stoically. 'It's not about killing for someone else's country it's about saving your own life.'

The pair had been on special pre-deployment exercises in Thetford where bona fide Afghans gave them a lesson on culture and language, they told me. The course was very tough, especially when they had to go through swamps with 70 kilos on their backs. And that was not even in hostile territory. More seasoned soldiers were inclined to be scornful at questions about their work, letting me know there was no way a civvy could understand how physically demanding their training could be until they had tried it themselves. For these two novices, the reality of what they had let themselves in for had already begun to sink in. I asked both men whether they were homesick, and they glanced at each other briefly. When times were hard 'you think about going back to your own country', they admitted. They missed the food and the weather, and worried constantly about their families. Both sent money home and Josaia was in regular contact by phone and email. Wayne rang twice a month as his mother did not have access to a computer. And both knew that their families were anxious.

Josaia was following in the footsteps of his great uncle who had served in the same regiment from 1960 to the 1980s, and who was the first Fijian RSM in the British Army. He was the youngest of a big family with several cousins currently serving in the armed forces. Barely a month after he had gone through the pass-off ceremony at Catterick, one of these relatives, Petero 'Pat' Suesue, was killed by an IED in Afghanistan. Josaia had lined the route of the repatriation parade in Wootton Bassett and attended his memorial service which drew Fijians from all over the country. He knew exactly what risks he was taking by volunteering to go to Helmand Province.

The home front

Josaia's cousin, Fusilier Petero 'Pat' Suesue, of 2nd Battalion The Royal Regiment of Fusiliers, was shot while on foot patrol in Sangin on 22 May 2009. He was the 160th member of the UK armed forces to die in Afghanistan. He had joined in 2002, and served in Northern Ireland and Iraq before being deployed there, and he was also a prized rugby player, like so many of his compatriots in the forces. In 2006 Suesue had returned to Fiji to marry, and two years later the couple moved into a house in Hounslow. The tributes from families, friends and colleagues posted on the MoD news site were typically moving and heartfelt.[12] On the day after he was killed, another young man, Sapper Jordan Rossi of 38 Engineer Regiment, died in an explosion. The *Mail* reported their deaths in one article, describing Suesue as 'a Fijian soldier', explaining that he was 'one of a growing number of Fijians serving with British forces'.[13] It was over a decade since the army had begun to recruit heavily in Fiji and the paper had had plenty of time to acknowledge that Fijians served 'in' and not 'with' British forces.

Media coverage of British military fatalities since 2003 deserves a separate study in order to grasp the seismic shifts in public attitudes to military work. In general, the management of news about soldier fatalities is intrinsic to the way that audiences at home become habituated to the principle that death in combat is 'the ultimate sacrifice'. But when a population is deeply divided about the morality of a particular war, or unconvinced that a military occupation is worth the price in life and resources, the deaths of servicemen and women can be made to mean very different things. During the first Gulf War, President George Bush Sr banned media coverage of the return of combat casualties, claiming that he wanted to spare their families the extra distress. The ban was lifted in 2009 after President Obama asked for a review. Critics had long campaigned against the prohibition arguing that it was an attempt to conceal the true effects of war from American citizens. The spectacle of flag-draped coffins being unloaded from a military plane made war 'real', raising concerns about whether the cause was worth the sacrifice of 'our' sons and daughters.

Despite the absence of a similar ban in the UK, the increasing rate of British military fatalities was, for a few years at least, an important focus for opposition to the war in Iraq. In 2005 anti-war campaigners tried to draw attention to the silence surrounding the deaths of soldiers, suggesting that they too were victims of an illegal war along with countless Iraqi civilian casualties.[14] In 2007 artist Steve McQueen, commissioned to document the Iraq war, created an exhibition entitled 'Queen and Country' based on the idea that stamps bearing portraits of the deceased should be issued to commemorate their sacrifice. He worked with more than a hundred of the bereaved families who supplied him with the photos he used to make the stamps. Both the Ministry of Defence and Royal Mail rejected the proposal, giving a variety of reasons why this would not be possible, including their concern for the victims' relatives. Their refusal to co-operate gave a strong signal that the government was wary of being led into this unpredictable terrain.

When Gordon Brown assumed control as prime minister his government was struggling to gain the moral high ground and needed to convince the population that it had the armed forces' best interest at heart. The *Sun*, which had supported the invasion of Iraq, moved into position as the chief backer of the campaign, Help for Heroes, and set up a dedicated Forces website to monitor the travails of troops at home as well as abroad. The phenomenon of civilian repatriation ceremonies at Wootton Bassett, beginning in late 2007, offered a focus for a more ambivalent reflection on soldiers' deaths which by then had become utterly routine events in the life of the nation. In June 2008 the *Telegraph* reported that more than 5,000 paid their respects when the body of Corporal Sarah Bryant was among those repatriated, calling it 'a very British way of mourning'.[15] Meanwhile, by December 2007 a homecoming parade by returning soldiers was greeted for the first time in years by streets lined with people, a transformation clearly brought about by political intervention for which the *Sun* claimed all the credit.[16]

Given the centrality of the media in orchestrating public reaction to the rising number of military casualties, it was not surprising that it was a newspaper that led the campaign to reinstate the Military Covenant as a focal point for intervention. The *Independent on Sunday* launched the initiative in the offices of the Adjutant General, bringing together a host of organisations and powerful individuals including senior military figures and politicians from all parties. Although it sounded like a formal constitutional document, the Covenant could be traced to an army doctrine publication, codified in 2000, where it laid out the relationship between the state and the soldiers who were contracted to fight on its behalf.[17]

> Soldiers will be called upon to make personal sacrifices – including the ultimate sacrifice – in the service of the Nation. In putting the needs of the Nation and the Army before their own, they forego some of the rights enjoyed by those outside the Armed Forces.
>
> In return, British soldiers must always be able to expect fair treatment, to be valued and respected as individuals, and that they (and their families) will be sustained and rewarded by commensurate terms and conditions of service.

In its opening statement, the campaign used the terms of the Covenant to define what this 'fair treatment' might mean:

> ... in return for putting their lives on the line, British troops, airmen and sailors should be given adequate equipment to do their jobs, the best treatment possible if wounded and the assurance that their families will be looked after if they die in their country's service.[18]

This was a concerted attempt to bring to public attention the conditions under which military employees were expected to work. For one thing it helped to reconnect the conditions of armed service to the founding principles of the welfare state as it was developed in the post-1945 period. But the campaign also rode the crest of a wave of sympathy for soldiers who were being cast almost as casualties of war themselves. By reminding the nation of the debt of honour it owed to the soldiers who fought on its behalf, 'the concept paradoxically broke the link in the public mind between the army and the unpopular intervention in Iraq: it separated the men from the mission, thereby letting loose large-scale but hitherto fairly latent support for "our boys" '.[19]

There was no doubt that the government was forced to address the terms and conditions of military service as a result of the Military Covenant campaign.[20] One of Brown's first steps in 2007 was to commission the inquiry that produced 'The Nation's Commitment: Cross-Government Support to our Armed Forces, their Families and Veterans'. As we saw in the previous chapter, this set of recommendations formally recognised the potential disadvantages faced by F&C personnel and their families and made specific promises to address them. But there was another inquiry, launched around the same time that was to have significant impact on the profile of the armed forces in the country as a whole.

Entitled 'National Recognition of our Armed Forces', the resulting report proposed a new programme of outreach based on the fundamental principle that the military uniform was to be treated with respect. Detailed suggestions were made on how to improve communications with media, schools, politicians and business leaders; on the importance of providing more systematic support for homecoming parades and public award ceremonies; and of facilitating greater levels of military support for civil operations, such as search and rescue missions. In a further effort to win public approval for these attempts to 'mend' the civil–military relationship, the report's authors suggested that the government should incorporate the little-known Veterans Day, which had been introduced in 2006, into an annual public holiday henceforth to be known as Armed Forces Day.[21]

In justifying these measures to an electorate that was judged to have grown weary of continuous war, the government re-activated the language of patriotic sacrifice and heroism: '... it is vital for our serving men and women, especially those engaged in difficult and dangerous overseas campaigns, to know that the whole of Britain understands and appreciates the work that they do in their name', declared Brown as he endorsed the recommendations.[22] Commenting on plans for the first Armed Forces Day to be held on 28 June 2009, Veterans Minister Kevan Jones repeated the same theme: 'The armed forces are a force for good in terms of protecting us and this day is an opportunity for the public to say thank you to those men and women and their families for the sacrifices they have made.'[23]

These measures, described in minimal detail here, indicate some of the political consequences of taking the country to war and keeping it there. As a result, civil society in the UK has undergone a radical process of militarisation that has been insufficiently tracked and analysed, the effects of which will be felt for many years to come. But as the equilibrium between public sympathy, apathy, hostility and support for the troops moved this way and that, the aspirations and experiences of ordinary Commonwealth soldiers provoked little interest. The fact that migrant workers had been ready to put their lives on the line in the service of the nation received scant comment or investigation outside the framework of the British Empire that was used to explain their presence.[24]

Mercenaries and media wars

An infantryman moonlighting as a taxi driver in Bulford, Wiltshire, feigned surprise when I answered his question about what I was doing on a military base. When, in return, I asked if he knew that 13 Fijians had been killed during the Iraq war, he simply said, 'It makes you think, doesn't it?'

There was something about his demeanour that indicated this was not a reflexive man. He had already told me how he signed up after wandering into a recruiting centre one day on a whim. 'Makes you think what?' I asked.

'That perhaps they are not very good at their job?' he ventured.

He had clearly never given the matter a moment's thought, but his attitude reminded me of some of the young English and Welsh men's reactions when I asked if they might consider joining an army in another country. 'No,' they said with some distaste. The thought had not occurred to them and they evidently found something unnatural about the prospect. But this response was not unusual outside the army too. Pat Suesue, Josaia's cousin, was certainly not the first Fijian to die in Britain's twenty-first century wars, but the lack of curiosity about what made non-citizens sign up, demonstrated by the *Mail*'s ambiguous remark about Fijians serving with British forces, had been a striking feature of their employment. In the absence of informed discussion about the contribution of non-citizens, the language of patriotism could easily exclude those not thought to belong. In addition, harking back to Britain's colonial connections only added to the mystification of its military recruitment process, throwing a damp towel over any spark of curiosity about what has really been going on.

The failure to perceive the recruitment of Commonwealth citizens as an index of something more pragmatic had resulted in a ghostly, almost embarrassed silence. That void was easily filled with the sound of British imperialist nostalgia, larded with militarist pride and gratitude: they are still here because we were there, and without them we would be nothing. They fought for us then and they fight for us now, for as long as we need them.

When the death of Fijian Pte Tukatukawaqa was announced in 2004, a notice in the *Guardian* merely stated that 'As a result of colonial links, Fijian soldiers...have a traditional role in the British army, similar to that served by the more famous Nepalese Gurkhas.'[25] A BBC News report declared that

Fijian soldiers have a reputation of physical strength and spirit and have been quietly serving in the British Army for several generations. Long colonial links have seen the South Pacific islanders serve alongside British troops for more than a century. Some observers say their physical robustness and boundless bravery echoes the famous Gurkhas.[26]

This style of reporting did nothing to challenge the belief that the UK was still a global power, one that could draw on a loyal workforce from its former colonies to fight its modern-day battles. As we have seen throughout this book, the repetition of words like tradition and loyalty, combined with the elevation of the Gurkhas under Lumley's banner, also reiterated the notion that certain types of warriors, defined by ethnicity, temperament and physique, were queuing up to make themselves available.

There were occasional glimpses of a more complex explanation. In 2006 BBC News reported the deaths of Gunner Samuela Vanua in Iraq and Ranger Anare Draiva in Afghanistan in a short feature about why Fijians were drawn to the UK armed forces.[27] The gist of the piece was that the deaths of individuals in combat were not enough to deter Fijians from applying in droves. They were motivated by 'wages and pride', justified by the standard line that 'long colonial links have seen their ancestors serve alongside British troops for more than a century'. Only a brief quote from an editor at the *Fiji Times* provided a material reason for the migration pattern. Almost half of Fijians were reported to live below the poverty line, earning an average of about £2,500 a year.

> Despite the number of deaths in the conflicts, there are hundreds more Fijians who are prepared to go to the region, either as part of the British Army or to get jobs in security. They are young men and hope to acquire money for their families and come back in one piece.[28]

The fact that there were many young Fijians prepared to work abroad suggested that the old mantra of colonial links was insufficient as an explanation for Britain's migrant soldiers. In fact the rapid growth of the global security industry was a defining feature of contemporary warfare. In his study of the topic, *Corporate Warriors*, Peter Singer attributed this to the break up of the state monopoly of the military profession which began to manifest itself in the 1990s.[29] Privatised military firms (PMFs) were essentially 'private business entities that delivered to consumers a wide spectrum of military and security services, once generally assumed to be exclusively inside the public context'.[30] What was more shocking, he suggested, was that PMFs were now active in every continent except Antarctica, 'including in relative backwaters and key strategic zones where the superpowers once vied for influence'.[31] In a study of the notorious private security firm,

Blackwater, Jeremy Scahill drew attention to the lack of accountability inherent in their operations. 'Even though tens of thousands of mercenaries have deployed in Iraq,' he wrote, 'private security forces faced no legal consequences for their deadly actions in the first five years of the Iraq occupation.'[32]

The term 'mercenary' is widely used to describe the terms of employment in PMFs which recruit from a global pool of recruits. Those with previous military training and experience are often drawn to this more lucrative job market, and inevitably there is an informal hierarchy of migrant workers from particular places, providing an endless supply of labour as well as contributing to national economies that rely on remittances. Fiji happens to be one of the main sources of this global martial force, along with Nepal and South Africa. In an extraordinary report on the marketing of young militarised Fijians, a journalist from Bloomberg news agency witnessed what he called a 'mercenary harvest' in 2007.[33] The article explained how 'Since the 1970s, this impoverished and remote remnant of the British Empire has positioned itself as a discount-soldier surplus store.' Following independence, Fiji's rulers had 'pedigreed and unleashed their dogs of war' as a strategy to reduce chronically high unemployment. The national military was increased from 200 to more than 2,000 'to protect a tourist destination the size of New Jersey with a population of 918,000 and no enemy other than sunburn'.

One result, according to calculations by Lt Col Mosese Tikoitoga, a senior officer and 'private-army sales liaison' for the ruling party, was that Fiji had outsourced more than 25,000 troops to the UN, the British Army and independent mercenary contractors since 1978. The issue of remittances in the form of wages from returning soldiers, as well as money from the UN for leasing peacekeepers, was calculated into the national budget, a factor recognised by the UN Working Group on the use of mercenaries. A report in 2007 acknowledged 'the important contributions of remittances from Fijian migrant workers in the field of security to the economy of the country'. Remittances were estimated to have reached $300 million over almost 30 years.[34]

This information helps to paint a very different picture of the contingencies of martial labour and the restructuring of the global security industry that has taken place over the last two decades. For young migrants from countries like Fiji, jobs in the UK armed services were viewed as highly desirable. The salary may fall well below its equivalent in the privatised military sector, but the fact that the British Army insisted on a highly trained and disciplined force convinced many that there would be greater protection of life and limb. There was also the prospect of the full army pension that attracted those ready to sign up for 22 years. However, individuals of all nationalities, including former Gurkha soldiers, often went on to work as 'security providers' with qualifications that were embellished not just by their military training but also by their particular regimental background. One example might be Everest Security which advertised itself as 'one of the UK's fastest growing providers of integrated security and cleaning solutions', claiming to be 'forged from the Gurkhas ethos for energy, loyalty, hard work, dedication and customer satisfaction'.[35]

The figure of the 'corporate warrior', just a fraction of the workforce involved in the privatisation of war economies, explains why the employment of Commonwealth soldiers in the British armed forces deserves to be assessed in an updated global context. In earlier chapters we explored some of the personal motivations of migrants who joined after 1998. Regardless of their individual circumstances, they could be also viewed as actors within contemporary circuits of militarised work that operated not only within, but also far beyond the boundaries that defined national interests. But by recognising the convergence of the privatised security sector with the forces of poverty, unemployment and ambition that propel migration I am not suggesting that the residues of colonial history or the military connections forged in the twentieth century were less important. On the contrary, we have already seen how military institutions presented one area of British national life where the memory of empire not only survived as a living connection to the past but was also cherished through institutional rituals, symbols and artefacts.

The modern history of the British Army can only be understood against the backdrop of Britain's transition from a once imperial power to its current status within NATO because it is here, at the intersection of defence, security and foreign policy, that the country's adjustment to the loss of empire is registered on multiple levels. Governmental decisions affecting Britain's future role as a military power have clear implications for debates about national identity, as analysts like Hutton had pointed out before Lehman Brothers crashed in 2008. It is a mistake to dismiss political and intellectual scrutiny of the armed forces as a task for specialists. Without a more engaged debate about the resources entailed in maintaining a large standing army there will be fewer opportunities to understand the pivotal role of militarism in shaping British national identity.

Approaching military service through the framework of the state-funded public sector offers insights into concepts of citizenship and national belonging because it raises in acute form the question of what the country owes those who volunteer to join the armed forces, particularly at a time of war. This mutual obligation, laid out by the Military Covenant, draws us back, once again, to the figure of the fallen soldier. The fullest expression of this pact takes place 'when the Nation keeps covenant with those who have given their lives in its service'. A year after I had watched the Remembrance ceremony on an army base in the company of the four young Caribbean recruits, I made my way to the heart of London to witness the spectacle of Armistice Day in a more public setting.

National values

The scene in Trafalgar Square that I described in the preface drew on the timeless notions of military sacrifice that keep the idea of nation alive, rooting it in the collective past and breathing new life into the relationship between armed forces and civilian society in an uncertain present. In the eerie quiet that descended as the traffic came to a halt, this ritual form of respect for fallen soldiers was expected to embrace as well as to mute the deep reservations felt towards all wars, and especially the conflicts that had taken place since 2001. In this ambivalent space, the battle cry of a demonised enemy could be heard over the rooftops, proving that British democracy was alive and kicking.

Setting fire to a giant poppy during the two minutes silence on Armistice Day was just about the most spectacular act of profanation conceivable, placing it at the other end of the spectrum from the more conventional activities underway in the Square at exactly the same time. Yet both these events could be made to illustrate the extent to which the concept of *militarised multiculture* had become inseparable from the imperatives of democracy and national security.

This was not the first time that an Islamist group had tested the limits of political dissent. An earlier manifestation had appeared in Luton where a similar assembly, calling themselves 'Islam4UK', had staged a protest during a homecoming parade, denouncing British soldiers as butchers and killers of Muslims. The combination of provocative chants and shrouded women amplified a wholesale rejection of British values in favour of an alternative polity that was committed to waging war on western civilisation. The English Defence League (EDL), which also began life in Luton, gave voice to another kind of violence, an offensive nativism masquerading as a patriotic stance against the threat of Islamic tyranny. Their counter-demonstrations reflected a symbiosis between the two clusters, one section of British society refusing to belong and the other objecting to their right to belong.

On that day in November 2010, the same armed forces that were the target of the militant Islamists' wrath were being hailed for defending the very democratic values that allowed dissidents a legitimate right to protest against the war. There were implications for security too. The protestors' abuse, combined with their demand for an Islamic caliphate, could be interpreted as proof that this particular minority was 'the enemy within' in yet another guise.[36] When, the following year, they threatened to hold a similar demonstration under the banner, 'Hell for Heroes', the coalition government banned them under the Terrorism Act 2000 on the grounds that they were glorifying terrorism and that Muslims Against Crusades (MAC) was another name for a proscribed terrorist organisation.

Arguably then, the provocations of the group's leader, Anjem Choudary, and his colleagues intervened to produce a symbolic alignment between the military and the ultra-nationalists. The EDL was seen to be defending the integrity of the armed forces, and together they were standing steadfastly against the threat of terrorism represented by the Islamists. In this context, minority soldiers became a strategic asset. Their visibility was able to signify that the army reflected the diversity of British society and could therefore claim to be positioned as neutral in the face of animosity between these two extremes.[37] Sir General David Richards, Chief of the Defence Staff, made this very point when asked in an interview whether he thought that the decision to ban MAC was a problem for people who were fighting so that other people could have their freedoms. His frank answer revealed the importance of employing not merely a diverse military workforce that symbolised a national commitment to multiculturalism, but also one that included and embraced Muslims:

> I agree and I think funnily enough we do take that point very seriously, it is important to us we fight for people's freedoms. From my perspective I think the right decision was taken and I have amongst other things, I'm President of the Armed Forces Muslim Association. Indeed, on Friday, I went to their Eid celebrations, I have done for a number of years. So I know that the vast, vast majority of Muslims are very patriotic, enjoy living here, indeed many of them are in the armed forces. We all have fringe, problem children and I think they were in that category.[38]

The question of racism – and specifically hatred of Islam – was at the centre of this highly politicised territory of democratic protest and proscribed organisations. Throughout 2010 and 2011, for example, the EDL too faced the prospect of government intervention since the organisation thrived on deliberately provocative marches through areas with high Muslim populations. In most instances, the Home Secretary Theresa May placed a blanket ban on all marches for a limited period, ostensibly in the interests of ensuring 'local communities and property are protected'.[39] However, the role of the national armed forces, which represent British sovereign power in the context of international relations, must not be confused with that of the police who are responsible for law and order in civil society. Thinking about the two institutions side by side helps to illuminate their different but related functions. For those who are familiar with the history of racism in the British police force over the past decade, the comparison will have a certain resonance.

One of the main recommendations of the Macpherson report in 1999 was a rapid increase in the number of ethnic minority police officers.[40] In fact numerous inquiries and investigations over the past three decades had suggested that employing significant numbers of ethnic minorities had played a part in winning the trust of communities that had felt systematically marginalised and harassed by their local police. Reforming the institution

by making it more diverse was also considered vital if racism was to be erad-
icated from the ranks, a goal that has had predictably uneven results.[41] But
while the police mandate covers crime and justice in the UK, the armed
forces are employed to represent the country's defence and security interests
abroad.

In 1998, when the first cohorts of Commonwealth citizens were recruited
into the British Army, the Strategic Defence Review issued by the New Labour
government redefined Britain's role as a military power. In the memorable
words of George Robertson, then Secretary of State for Defence, who wrote
the introduction to the document:

> The British are, by instinct, an internationalist people. We believe that
> as well as defending our rights, we should discharge our responsibilities
> in the world. We do not want to stand idly by and watch humanitarian
> disasters or the aggression of dictators go unchecked. We want to give a
> lead; we want to be a force for good.

The Military Covenant campaign was one result of Blair's wars that followed
on from this declaration. Along with Wootton Bassett, Help for Heroes, the
Military Wives Choir and all the other unexpected domestic, political out-
comes of continuous foreign intervention, the demand that soldiers deserve
fair treatment proved that the armed forces were a societal institution as well
as a national one. This returns us to a theme that runs through this account:
the importance of values as a mediating device.

Human rights

The question of values was discussed in Chapter 4 in connection with the
shift towards value-based learning in training institutions. I pointed out that
one of the ways in which the armed forces had been influenced by changes
in civilian society was that they had adopted elements of Human Resources
Management (HRM) that had become commonplace in corporate and public
bodies. The reassertion of values was a mechanism that helped to orient the
armed forces in two directions at once: both inwardly towards the domestic
population and outwardly into the sphere of international politics. There
was a moment when it also chimed with Gordon Brown's attempt to define
British values as a way of restoring civic patriotism.

In 2011, former CGS General Dannatt illustrated how far the concept of
values had been absorbed as a defining characteristic of military culture, dif-
ferentiating it from civilian society which was perceived as individualistic
and even amoral. Speaking to a theological think-tank he argued that society
was no longer providing new recruits with 'an understanding of the core values and standards of behaviour required by the military'.[42] The mental and
moral preparation of our soldiers was as important as their physical training,

he declared. 'They must be able to kill and show compassion at the same time; they must be loyal to their country, their regiment and their friends without compromising their own integrity.' One implication of his speech was that the army could not be blamed if individual soldiers failed to live up to these values. Much more controversial was his claim that civil society could benefit from adopting the values espoused by the military.

His intervention took place scarcely two months after the Gage inquiry into the unlawful killing of Iraqi citizen Baha Mousa had concluded that his death had involved 'an appalling episode of serious gratuitous violence'.[43] The inquiry, ordered in 2009, revealed that the chain of command, right up to the MoD, was heavily implicated in blocking subsequent attempts to investigate what had happened. Dannatt's successor, CGS General Sir Peter Wall, admitted that Mousa's death in 2004 cast a 'dark shadow' over the Army's reputation. In an interview with *Guardian* journalists, Lieutenant Colonel Nicholas Mercer, the army's former chief legal adviser in Iraq, accused the MoD of 'moral ambivalence' and a 'cultural resistance to human rights' that allowed British troops to abuse detainees.[44] While Dannatt had fully condemned what had happened in Iraq, he would also have known that further revelations would continue to emerge as other families who suffered abuse at the hands of British soldiers sought compensation.

Lawyers were already pursuing two further inquiries with wide-ranging remits to investigate allegations that UK forces abused and unlawfully killed Iraqi civilians while they controlled parts of southern Iraq.[45] The Al-Sweady Inquiry, for example, was examining claims that UK soldiers murdered 20 or more Iraqis and tortured others after the 'Battle of Danny Boy' in Maysan Province, southern Iraq, in May 2004. The MoD was vigorously denying the allegations on the grounds that those who died were killed on the battlefield.[46] However, after more than a decade of military operations in Afghanistan it was likely that the UK armed forces would continue to face legal challenges of abuse and unlawful killing for many years to come.[47]

In 2009 the Aitken Report, the result of the army's internal inquiry into the unlawful killing of Mousa, had advocated the strengthening of military core values and standards as well as emphasising the importance of cultural awareness. This recommendation illustrated the convergence of equality and diversity reform with the legal pressure, in the shape of human rights legis-lation, to prevent the violent abuse and torture of prisoners in the war zone. The disciplining of racist behaviour was central to both these objectives. But where did anti-racism figure in this restatement of military values, aside from the requirement to 'treat people as you'd want to be treated'?[48]

In trying to answer this question it is worth revisiting the sequence of events in 2009, described in Chapter 1, in which a group of retired generals and former army chiefs made a public statement dissociating the armed forces from the far right. In their open letter objecting to the BNP's dis-missal of Johnson Beharry as a token black hero, singled out by a 'pc-mad government', they stated: 'The values of these extremists – many of whom are essentially racist – are fundamentally at odds with the values of the modern British military, such as tolerance and fairness.'[49] But they went further than a ritual condemnation in the name of liberal values. They cited the presence of a significant proportion of Commonwealth soldiers as an illustration of those values in practice:

> The reputation of our Armed Forces was won over centuries of service in some of the most difficult areas of the world. Political extremists should claim no right to share in this proud heritage.

That same week, the *Guardian's* political commentator Michael White speculated that the BNP might find eager recruits among ex-servicemen who were 'angry about the loss of life in ill-conceived and underfunded campaigns overseas, embittered by the treatment on return to civvy life'.[50] For this reason, he suggested, it really did matter that the generals took a stand on racism and equality in the armed forces, even if it meant risking accusations of meddling in politics.

> If the armed forces, police and prison service are more integrated to reflect society at large than they used to be – it's a work in progress – then the risk of soldiers, serving and retired, being drawn into the doomed politics of racial purity diminish.

A year later, the three soldiers in the square, two Fijian and one Nepalese, would personify this dual role, representing the vestigial traces of Britain's history as a global military power but also holding up a sign that the army was not as 'hideously white' as it once was, to borrow Greg Dyke's phrase about the BBC. But as the BNP was quick to point out at the time, the generals were guilty of hypocrisy. Some of those same names, notably that of General Sir Richard Dannatt, were involved in lobbying the government to limit the number of non-UK soldiers. The negotiations, which lasted for several years, stressed the importance of 'ensuring that the norms and values of society are reflected in its armed forces'. In 2007 they borrowed the notion of Britishness, promoted by Brown's government during that period, to legitimise the idea that *numbers* were critical in achieving the right mix of home-grown 'norms and values'. The whole episode deserves closer scrutiny for what it reveals about the endorsement of *militarised multiculture* by a wider array of participants drawn into the political fray.

Nothing British

The publication of the generals' letter in 2009 coincided with the launch of a new campaign against the BNP, coordinated not by the conventional anti-racist organisations preparing for the coming elections, but a different grouping particularly enraged by the BNP's attempts to co-opt military history into their fascist fantasies. One such initiative, called 'Operation Stolen Valour', consisted of video statements by public figures associated with the military, including best-selling author and film-maker Andy McNab who discovered that his name had been used by BNP fans of his work. The group's mission statement said that 'The BNP are cynically exploiting the reputation of Britain's military to promote their nasty brand of racism, segregation and intolerance.'[51] This was linked to another, related website, 'There is Nothing British about the BNP', which provided more of a monitoring and analytical role, promoting British values such as 'democracy, tolerance, fair-play and respect for one another' instead of the politics of hate.[52] Writing in the *Spectator*, columnist Charles Moore explained why he had agreed to support the campaign, arguing that it was only because it gave him a chance to defend the armed forces that he was prepared to endorse it. 'We do not know how lucky we are to have non-political armed forces,' he said, 'and that political detachment needs constant policing.'[53]

Moore, whose views on the politics of race and immigration were well known to readers of the *Telegraph* and the *Spectator* over several decades, elaborated on his belief that the armed forces should distance themselves from the BNP. 'The current chaos in defence policy makes the ranks vulnerable to the politics of resentment,' he went on. Citing the precedent of ex-servicemen voting for a Labour government after 1945, he expressed a concern that the BNP would harness the frustrations of soldiers leaving the forces today, vulnerable to their appeal to a racist agenda. ' ... They are socialists – national socialists – peddling illusions about equality – for white people – and a siege economy. It is conservatives, not the left, who are best placed to oppose them.'[54]

One of the more significant aspects of the mobilisation from the right was the fact that the tabloid media positioned itself alongside to sing from the same hymn-sheet. In October 2009 it was announced that a statue of Sergeant Talaiasi Labalaba, the legendary Fijian SAS soldier gunned down in Oman in 1972, would be unveiled at the headquarters of the SAS in Hereford in time for the remembrance ceremony that same year. One of the 200 Fijians recruited in 1961, Labalaba was given a posthumous Mention in Despatches but never awarded a medal. In an article entitled 'Forces fight BNP hate merchants', the *Sun* began a report of the coming event with the announcement that 'A BLACK hero of the SAS is to be honoured with a statue – in a stinging rebuke to the racists of the British National Party'.[55]

The article explained that the belated acknowledgement was intended as a 'kick in the face' for the 'twisted hate merchants who have hijacked images of Britain's proud military tradition, including Sir Winston Churchill and spitfires, to win voters'. It revealed that General The Lord Guthrie, former head of the Armed Forces and Colonel Commandant of the SAS, had 'praised Labalaba's selfless example as he attacked the BNP'. Each sentence reiterated the fact that the decision to honour the Fijian hero was intended as a blow to the forces of the far right.

Guthrie articulated the same message in a column written 'exclusively' for the same issue of the *Sun*, explaining why he was supporting the Nothing British campaign.

> Thinking of Labalaba and the other courageous overseas combatants in the British Army, it makes me so angry to see the British National Party and their surrogates seek to use the good name of our Armed Forces to promote the pernicious politics of racism.

He castigated the BNP, not just for their 'rubbish' claims that they were alone in fighting a 'battle for Britain', but also for wanting an all-white British Army. Recalling the contribution of overseas soldiers in the Second World War, the General went on:

> This would deprive our military effectiveness of an important source of personnel and expertise ... particularly Jewish soldiers – both British-born and those from overseas – who fought with outstanding bravery on the frontline despite fearful risks if captured.
>
> More than that, I know from my experience in the military in a number of overseas postings that serving alongside people from different cultures and nationalities gives you a strong sense of admiration for other peoples' ways of doing things.

The *Daily Mail* addressed similar themes of racism and diversity in its account but instead of denouncing the BNP, the writer put a slightly different spin on the decision to honour the Fijian soldier.

> It is also some small recompense to thousands of ethnic minority servicemen, many from Commonwealth countries, who feel their courage and devotion has not been recognised in the same way as their white counterparts.[56]

The article cited the example of Walter Tull, a British-born black soldier of Barbadian descent who was killed during the First World War, and whose military career was 'blighted by prejudice'. Having worked his way through the ranks as a soldier, he became the first black man to be commissioned at a time when army regulations banned non-whites from serving as officers.[57] For the *Mail*, awarding the VC to LCpl Johnson Beharry was proof of the fundamental changes that had taken place in the mentality of the armed forces – and in society as well. But it was the death of Jabron Hashmi in 2006 that 'brought the role of ethnic minority personnel in the military into sharp relief' because Hashmi, just 24 at the time, 'was the first British Muslim to be killed during the so-called War On Terror'. The article ended with a comment from the young man's brother Zeeshan, who, as we saw in Chapter 5, was also a former soldier. He was quoted as saying: '[Jabron] felt he was fulfilling two roles and duties; as a Muslim and as a British citizen.... He felt very privileged to be linked with two different cultures.'

National interest?

We can draw several conclusions from the manner in which this sequence of events was reported. First, the distinction between being a Muslim and a British citizen was precisely the kind of mentality that normally infuriated papers like the *Mail*, but here it was doing a very different kind of job. Anyone who volunteered for military service was qualified to sit at the high table of patriotism, as long as they were supervised by their hosts who were renowned for condemning anything that smacked of multiculturalism or political correctness. However, it bears repeating that the participation of British citizens who were also Muslim was particularly important in demonstrating that the armed forces represented the nation as a whole. In this theatre of war, their presence indicated a triumph for the forces of 'democracy, tolerance, fair-play and respect for one another' that were ranged against the 'politics of hate' articulated not just by the BNP but by those other extremists, the EDL and MAC. The project to include the British Muslim soldier within this version of *militarised multiculture* was a tactical victory in the ongoing battle of Britishness.

Second, as we saw in the discussion of military culture in Chapter 4, naming a set of values as a governmental tool to delineate British national identity converged in useful ways with the promotion of values and standards in army education. It provided one means by which the military was repositioned in the centre of national life, the commitment to anti-racism and cultural diversity serving to underline its efforts to adopt a modern, progressive outlook. This process arguably played a role in galvanising support for unpopular foreign policies, or at least allaying public unease at the horrific costs entailed in endless deployments. But the past was important too as we saw earlier in this chapter.

The appreciation of Commonwealth troops as a positive asset was a third reason why the generals' intervention in 2009 can be made to reveal the strategic role of *militarised multiculture*. Guthrie made noises about 'an important source of personnel and expertise' but the fact was that the UK government would not have been able to conduct military operations from 1999 onwards without recruiting soldiers from Commonwealth countries. It would certainly not have been able to sustain continuous deployments in Iraq and Afghanistan without this source of global migrant labour, often garnered directly through overseas recruiting operations. But nowhere is this link between migration and military service made explicit.

In defence terms, the reliance on a military workforce drawn from Britain's former empire has been presented as a feature of the UK's aspiration to remain a global power. In 2000 the MoD released an exhibition entitled, 'We Were There' which was created as part of the joint 'Action Plan' with the CRE, outlined in Chapter 2. In 2010 the website hosting the exhibition was updated, placing the whole project within a revised historical perspective. The first incarnation was intended as 'a significant statement about the contribution of Britain's ethnic minority communities to UK defence over the last 250 years', explained the new introduction. The initiative was seen at the time as an educational resource describing the benefits of cultural diversity as well as helping to promote 'better understanding between communities by showing how men and women from Africa, Asia, the West Indies and other Commonwealth countries fought and served alongside British forces during many major conflicts'.[58]

In 2010 a new dimension was added, providing evidence that the role of military history in asserting the rights of minorities had become more important in the meantime, particularly in the context of debates about Britishness and national identity. 'For students of history and citizenship,' the new website suggested,

the exhibition offers a wider and more inclusive perspective of our military past. It demonstrates how people from different religions, races and cultures came together at times of great social, political, military and geographical change to help create and then defend the British Empire and democratic freedom. What has surprised many people is that most of those who served from the colonies were volunteers, including the whole of the Indian Army.

The contrast between the two versions deserves a longer discussion, but the final panel of the current exhibition is the most relevant here because it illustrated another convergence: this time, of *militarised multiculture* with national security and foreign policy.

The MOD and the Armed Forces now operate on a global scale in a wide variety of roles such as war fighting, counter-terrorism, defence diplomacy, peace-keeping and the delivery of humanitarian aid. Altogether about 290,000 civilian and military personnel are employed.

Men and women from ethnic minorities make up 5.6% of the Armed Forces and 2.9% of the MOD and Civil Service. They all contribute to the common aim of defending their country through strengthening international peace and stability and being a force for good in the world.[59]

The expanded list of military roles from war-fighting to peace-keeping and the ambition to be 'a force for good' in the world reflected the transformations in global warcraft that had taken place in the intervening years. The constellation of geopolitical, technological, economic and moral factors that were used to sanction the deployment of NATO forces was neatly compressed under the heading of international peace and stability, thus concealing the true costs of the global counter-insurgency, aggressive nuclear proliferation and the inexorable privatisation of military work. The same combination of bravado and virtue was illustrated that same year in PM David Cameron's speech announcing the terms of the 2010 Strategic Defence and Security Review:

> Our national interest requires our full and active engagement in world affairs.... And it requires too that we stand up for the values we believe in. Britain has punched above its weight in the world. And we should have no less ambition for our country in the decades to come.[60]

Just weeks after this speech, Cameron was to make another statement about defence, this time using it as an opportunity to signal his government's agenda on national security at home. 'We will still have the fourth largest military defence budget in the world,' he stated at the European Security conference, held in Munich.[61]

> .... But the biggest threat that we face comes from terrorist attacks, some of which are, sadly, carried out by our own citizens. It is important to stress that terrorism is not linked exclusively to any one religion or ethnic group.... Nevertheless we should acknowledge that this threat comes in Europe overwhelmingly from young men who follow a completely perverse, warped interpretation of Islam, and who are prepared to blow themselves up and kill their fellow citizens.

Against this background, the exhibition, 'We Were There', evoked a version of multiculturalism that was inseparable from security. The panel continued:

> The MOD is keen to reflect the multicultural nature of society today and to draw on the widest possible pool of diverse talents available. It is committed to recruit greater numbers of men and women from ethnic minority backgrounds into military and civilian professions.

The accompanying image showed the back view of a uniformed man giving the thumbs up to a Chinook helicopter delivering aid, explained by a caption that read: 'Flight Lieutenant Sohail Khan in Pakistan where he helped with the earthquake relief effort'. Never mind that Flt Lt Khan was an airman in the RAF which had a very different history of employing minorities.

The illustration implied that military service was not about *fighting* Muslim antagonists, it was about *helping* them, bringing aid to the vulnerable in the interests of British security. It was an example of *militarised multiculture* being employed as a weapon with two prongs: one to enhance and update Britain's status as a global power and the other to manage the risk of 'home-grown terrorism'.[62]

The crimson thread

The topic of black British and Asian attitudes towards military service is raised by another detail of the same panel discussed above, one that deserves equal scrutiny. The enthusiasm and commitment professed by the MoD towards 'drawing on' the 'widest possible pool of diverse talents' confirmed that, despite the cuts imposed by the Tory government, the recruitment pipeline was constantly hungry for prospective candidates.

Young ethnic minorities born in the UK provide a hugely significant source for socio-demographic reasons alone, but, as we have seen, the levels of recruitment into the army continued to remain low throughout this period, constituting less than half of the overall minority personnel. There is some irony in the fact that the origin of *militarised multiculture* as a concept could be traced to the struggles of civilian migrant-settlers for inclusion in all aspects of British life. Just as the first cohorts of Commonwealth soldiers were signing up in 1998, the country was marking the 50th anniversary of the Empire Windrush which famously docked in Southampton in June 1948. But as Dandeker and Mason suggested in 2007, the concept of 'representativeness' used in calibrating the requisite proportion of minorities did not match the socio-demographic profile of minorities actually born in the UK. To explore the implications of this and to do justice to the politics of British minorities and military service – in the past, present and future – would require another volume, much less a chapter of its own.

Returning to the Commonwealth and Gurkha soldiers who are the subject of this study, there is no doubt that the history of their incorporation into the UK armed forces underpinned the entire edifice of British nationalism in its current form. The diverse spectrum of Commonwealth soldiers may not accurately represent, in ethno-cultural terms, the particular array of minorities growing up in the country, but their inclusion ensured that the sinuous thread of military history that connected Britain's imperial past to its present remained unbroken.

European nation states and empires were built and maintained through military conquest over a period of several centuries. The question of who served in those colonial armies remains of extreme importance in the contemporary negotiation of citizenship, immigration and national identities. In Britain's case, this vital thread connects the enlistment of African 'slaves in red coats', purchased by army recruiters to fill the ranks of the West India

Regiments at the end of the eighteenth century, to the last OPTs dispatched to the eastern Caribbean in 2008. It includes that anomalous source of modern British soldiers, the Brigade of Gurkhas, whose successful campaign for parity in 2009 guaranteed their inevitable reduction, if not the end of their employment contract altogether.[63] Throughout the history of slavery and imperialism to the present day, Britain's military recruiters have been guided by all manner of contingencies in their unceasing quest to fill their global armies. The persistence of martial racism, the belief that racial type, military prowess, faith and culture were all connected, has stained this thread a deeper hue of crimson, surfacing again and again as a motif within this dreadful fabric.

There are some who would argue that turning to Commonwealth countries to supply Britain with soldiers as a solution to its recruiting crisis was no different to hiring migrants to work in any other sector. This book poses the question whether military labour is intrinsically different from any other sector, and therefore whether migrant soldiers are due special rewards or exemptions. One index might be the views and reactions of those who took the Oath of Allegiance, like those described in the first chapter. As the rate of overseas recruitment fluctuated with the pressures of supply and demand, many found themselves asking in whose interests they signed up.

Perhaps the last word belonged to Ken, reflecting on the news that the last OPT destined for Jamaica in late 2008 had been suspended indefinitely in response to higher numbers of UK recruits.[64] 'That makes you feel used – if I could use such a strong word, very much used,' he said. 'Because I feel like, in the first place, if you had enough people to come in from the United Kingdom, there would have been no need to recruit in the Caribbean. I don't like to say it's like modern-day slave labour because you get paid for it. But if there was a credit crunch at the time when I joined up, I probably would not have been looked at.'

'Now,' he reflected, 'There are people I know who are still in the Caribbean who have done their paperwork, done their medical, all that sort of stuff and they tell them, "Oh no, we have enough people now, you can't come." '

Appendix

Trained UK Regular Forces[1] by service and nationality[2] on 1 April 2011

	All services	Naval service	Army	RAF
Total	**172,580**	**35,250**	**97,270**	**40,070**
UK Nationals	**163,940**	**34,400**	**89,650**	**39,880**
Bermudan	–	–	–	–
British	163,630	34,390	89,360	39,880
British Hong Kong	90	–	90	–
British Overseas Territory Citizen	200	10	190	10
Gibraltarian	–	–	–	–
St Helenian	10	–	10	–
Irish[3] and Commonwealth[4]	**8,050**	**790**	**7,150**	**120**
Antiguan	–	–	–	–
Australian	80	20	60	–
Bahamian	–	–	–	–
Bangladeshi	–	–	–	–
Barbadian	10	–	10	–
Belizean	50	–	50	–
Botswanian	30	–	30	–
British Singapore	–	–	–	–
Cameroonian	60	–	60	–
Canadian	60	20	40	–
Citizen of Fiji	2,240	130	2,100	10
Citizen of Seychelles	20	–	20	–
Citizen of Sri Lanka	10	–	10	–
Citizen of St Christopher (St Kitts) and Nevis	–	–	–	–
Dominican	30	10	20	–
Gambian	260	20	240	–
Ghanaian	820	10	800	–
Grenadian	140	10	130	–
Guyanese	30	–	20	–
Indian	100	10	90	–
Irish	370	60	280	30
Jamaican	480	30	440	10
Kenyan	210	20	190	–
Lesotho	–	–	–	–
Malawian	230	10	220	–
Malaysian	10	–	–	–
Maltese	10	–	–	–
Mauritian	60	–	60	–

Namibian	–	–	–	–
New Zealander	80	10	60	10
Nigerian	180	10	170	–
Pakistani	10	–	10	–
Papua New Guinean	–	–	–	–
Sierra Leonean	40	–	40	–
Singaporean	–	–	–	–
South African	890	90	790	10
St Lucian	280	10	270	–
Swazi	20	–	20	–
Tanzanian	10	–	10	–
Tongan	10	–	10	–
Trinidad and Tobago citizen	100	30	60	10
Ugandan	80	–	80	–
Vincentian	570	240	330	–
Zambian	40	10	40	–
Zimbabwean	400	20	360	10
Foreign	**10**	**10**	–	–
Nepalese	**460**	–	**460**	–
Unknown[5]	**130**	**50**	**20**	**70**

1. UK Regular Forces comprises trained personnel. It does not include Gurkhas, Full Time Reserve Service (FTRS) personnel and mobilised reservists.
2. Nationality data for all three Services is only available from 1 April 2007 due to the introduction of the Joint Personnel Administration System.
3. Citizens of the Republic of Ireland.
4. Includes Zimbabwean and Fijian citizens, who continue to retain Commonwealth status under the British Nationality Act 1981.
5. Includes those with an unrecorded nationality.

Due to ongoing validation of data from the Joint Personnel Administration System, all statistics are provisional and subject to review.
All numbers are rounded to nearest ten, except numbers ending in '5' which are rounded to the nearest 20 in order to avoid systematic bias. Due to the rounding methods used totals may not equal the sum of the parts.
"–" denotes zero or rounded to zero.
Source: DASA, Ministry of Defence dasa.mod.uk.

Notes

Preface

1. Alex Kleiderman, 'Armistice silence comes to Trafalgar Square', BBC News, 11 November 2006. http://goo.gl/la540 (accessed 25 August 2011).
2. Harry Wallop, 'Two minutes' silence released as a charity single', *Telegraph*, 7 November 2010. http://goo.gl/s3GBx (accessed 7 September 2011).
3. Ram Patten, a former Royal Marines Commando who suffered severe PTSD as a result of his experiences, launched the fundraising campaign March for Honour in 2010. Details, including photos of Patten meeting PM David Cameron, can be found on his website: http://www.marchforhonour.com/ (accessed 22 September 2011). Patten is a citizen of the UK.
4. Hansard, Parliamentary Business, Publications and Records, Commons Debates. 'Armed Forces: Foreign Workers', 4 October 2010: Column 1310W. http://goo.gl/s6y0S (accessed 30 September 2011).

1 Introduction: For Queen and Commonwealth

1. John Harris, 'Your country needs you...' *Guardian*, 2 February 2006. http://goo.gl/O0w2G (accessed 10 December 2011).
2. 'Recruitment drive fails to halt exodus as the army suffers shortfall of 1,500', Scotsman.com, Saturday 19 August 2006. http://goo.gl/bNI3x (accessed 14 March 2012).
3. Christopher Dandeker and David Mason, 'Echoes of Empire: Addressing gaps in recruitment and retention in the British Army by diversifying recruitment pools', in Tibor Szvircsev Tresch and Christian Leuprecht, Eds, *Europe Without Soldiers? Recruitment and Retention across the Armed Forces of Europe*, Montreal and Kingston: McGill-Queen's University Press, 2011, pp. 209–231.
4. 'Forces Housing must be improved', BBC News, UK, Thursday, 4 January 2007. http://goo.gl/Y7ihN (accessed 27 September 2011).
5. The percentage of the UK Regular Forces from an ethnic minority background increased every year from 4.9 per cent in 2004 to 6.5 per cent in 2009. Edition – 2009. Released on – 30 September 2009, Key points. http://goo.gl/5JqsB (accessed 22 October 2011) In the army, the figure was 9.4 per cent – Officers 3 per cent and Other Ranks 10.4 per cent.Service and Civilian Personnel, Females and Ethnic Minorities. UK Defence Statistics. Pocket Cards, 9b. http://goo.gl/e054M (accessed 22 October 2011).
6. Hutton, Will, 'Britain's no longer a world power, so let's be a better, fairer nation', *The Observer*, 26 April 2009. http://goo.gl/fZHj5 (accessed 27 September 2011).
7. Stuart Hall, 'The Neoliberal Revolution', *Soundings*, Issue 48, Summer 2011. http://goo.gl/HQ4FB (accessed 27 September 2011).
8. Thomas Hardin, 'Britain no longer has the cash to defend itself from every threat, says Liam Fox', *Telegraph*, 22 July 2010. http://goo.gl/6ELqz (accessed 18 September 2011).
9. 'A "great hero" who saved comrades – full citation', BBC News, 18 March 2005. http://goo.gl/lZZJP (accessed 5 November 2010).

10. George L. Mosse, *Fallen Soldiers: Reshaping the Memory of the World Wars*, Oxford: OUP, 1990, pp. 94–96.
11. Benedict Anderson, *Imagined Communities: Reflections on the Origins and Spread of Nationalism*, London: Verso, 1983, p. 17.
12. John H. Morrow Jr, *The Great War: An Imperial History*, London: Routledge, 2004, p. xii.
13. Ibid., p. 322.
14. 'With the Indian Troops at the Front'. 1916. Imperial War Museum, ID: IWM 202-1. http://goo.gl/pcg6y (accessed 31 October 2011).
15. Brian Dyde, *The Empty Sleeve: The Story of the West India Regiments of the British Army*, St John's: Hansib Caribbean, 1997.
16. Richard Gott, *Britain's Empire: Resistance, Repression and Revolt*, London: Verso, 2012, p. 102.
17. Morrow, *The Great War*, p. 312.
18. Ibid.
19. Richard Smith, *Jamaican Volunteers in the First World War: Race, Masculinity and the Development of National Consciousness*, Manchester: Manchester University Press, 2004.
20. Dandeker and Mason, 'Echoes of Empire'.
21. Kathleen Paul, 'From Subjects to Immigrants', in Weight, R. and Beach, A., Eds, *The Right to Belong: Citizenship and National Identity, 1930–1969*, London: I. B. Tauris, 1998, pp. 223–248.
22. Dandeker and Mason, 'Echoes of Empire', p. 227.
23. Field Marshal Erwin Rommel was a German commander who was admired by many in the Allied forces because of his military tactics, particularly in North Africa where they gave him the nickname 'Desert Fox'. After his death Churchill pronounced him a foe worthy of respect, 'because, although a loyal German soldier, he came to hate Hitler and all his works, and took part in the conspiracy to rescue Germany by displacing the maniac and tyrant.'
24. See Memorial Gates Trust, http://www.mgtrust.org/ (accessed 27 September 2011).
25. The BNP website contains many items that indicate their support for soldiers, particularly throughout 2009–2011. See, for example, 'Cumbria British National Party sends parcels to support our troops', BNP News, 24 July 2011. (accessed 4 March 2012).
26. Kim Sengupta, 'Griffin branded "despicable" for attacks on Army top brass', Independent, 21 October 2009. http://goo.gl/QH1xQ (accessed 26 October 2011).
27. Matthew Taylor, Jenny Percival and Vikram Dodd, 'Muslim group pledges more protests against UK soldiers', *Guardian*, 11 March 2009. http://goo.gl/xwtH6 (accessed 31 October 2011).
28. Vanessa Allen, 'Treachery! The government unveils new residency test for Gurkhas…that almost NONE of them can pass', Mail Online, 24 April 2009. http://goo.gl/tuaJo (accessed 31 October 2011).
29. 'BNP leader Nick Griffin: lots of Hindus, Sikhs and ethnic minority Britons support my anti-immigrant views', Mail Online, 20 October 2009. http://goo.gl/ 82iWn (accessed 31 October 2011).
30. A Freedom of Information request revealed that UK military institutions had trained officers in countries committing human rights abuses during the uprisings of 2011. 'The Syrian officers trained by the MoD were among hundreds from Middle Eastern countries whose governments pay for them to attend Britain's world-renowned officer-training colleges each year. It trained 104 Bahraini officers over

the same period, seven from Libya, three from Tunisia and 56 from Yemen, according to MoD figures.' Robert Booth and Ben Quinn, 'Syrian officers received training in Britain', *Guardian*, Wednesday 27 April. http://goo.gl/ykVpV (accessed 29 April 2011).

In April 2011, an inquiry about the UK's defence training engagement with Gulf states, made under the Freedom of Information Act, revealed that 61 cadets from Bahrain had been trained since 1995, and that five were currently enrolled at Sandhurst. Chris Millward, Land Forces Secretariat, 21 April 2011. FOI Ref: 21-02-2011-095411-005. http://goo.gl/wQpqy (accessed 20 June 2011).

31. MoD, 'Afghan Army chief returns to Sandhurst', *MoD Defence News*, 19 April 2011. http://goo.gl/fFxAg (accessed 19 April 2011).

32. Apart from a Roman Catholic chapel, there are no other religious buildings, like mosques or temples, to be found inside the extensive grounds; Muslims and those of other faiths are obliged to find places of worship outside RMAS.

33. Stephen Deakin, 'Britain's Defence and Cosmopolitan Ideals', Sandhurst Occasional Paper, no. 3. Royal Military Academy Sandhurst, 2010, p. 6.

34. Ibid.

35. See 'Ayo Gorkhali' for further information about the history and legacy of the relationship between Britain and its Gurkha soldiers. This website began as a Welsh-Nepali community engagement project, commissioned by the Brecknock Museum and Art Gallery in Brecon and is endorsed by the Winchester Gurkha Museum.'. http://www.ayo-gorkhali.org/ (accessed 24 April 2012).

36. According to the website 'Ayo Gorkhali', a number of Gorkhali warriors also fought with the British against the Nepalese army. Gorkhali mercenaries had also been recruited by the Sikh leader, Ranjit Singh, in Lahore, and served under him until 1823 when their entire unit was wiped out by Afghan artillery in the Sikh–Afghan War. In other words, the simple history of British imperialists co-opting a group of soldiers for their own ends can be made to reveal a much more complex account of regional affiliations and military work as a form of livelihood rather than loyalty. http://goo.gl/EyRRE (accessed 31 October 2011).

37. David Omissi, *The Sepoy and the Raj: The Indian Army 1860–1940*, London: Macmillan Press, 1994, pp. 23–24.

38. Tarak Barkawi, *Globalisation and War*, London: Rowman and Littlefield, 2006, p. 74. See also Jahan Mahmood, 'Remembrance Sunday – From Allies to Terrorists', 10 November 2010. http://goo.gl/70eoa (accessed 10 November 2010).

39. John Parker, *The Gurkhas*, London: Headline Book Publishing, 2005, pp. 79–80.

40. Barkawi, *Globalisation and War*, p. 72.

41. Wolseley, 'The Negro as a soldier', *The Fortnightly Review*, No. CCLXIV. New series – 1 December 1888. Visit http://goo.gl/1GYKw (accessed 8 February 2011) for more information about the journal.

42. Wolseley, 'The Negro as a soldier', p. 699.

43. In a 1943 edition of *The African Standard*, the publication of the West African Youth League (Sierre Leone section), the London correspondent noted that the Basutos of South Africa, 'who are a fighting race, love drill and spend much of their leisure time in practicing it. This makes it hard to find suitable punishment for them when it is necessary, since the customary award of extra guards and drill is regarded as a privilege'. Our London correspondent, 'Britain's Coloured Army in the Middle East: African native auxiliaries helping to defend Egypt against Rommel's Africa Korps', *The African Standard*, the publication of the West African Youth League (Sierre Leone section), Vol. V. No. 5. Friday, 29 January 1943, p. 5.

44. Hew Strachan, 'Reassessing Recruiting Strategies for the Armed Services', in A. Alexandrou, R. Bartle and R. Holmes, Eds, *New People Strategies for the British Armed Forces*, London: Frank Cass, 2001, p. 110.
45. Ibid. p. 110.
46. Wolseley, 'The Negro as a soldier', p. 700.
47. David Killingray, 'Race and rank in the British Army', *Ethnic and Racial Studies* 10, 3 (1987), pp. 278–90. See also Killingray, *Fighting for Britain: African soldiers in the Second World War* Woodbridge, James Currey, 2012.

2 The Race to Recruit

1. From the archive, 'Kilts sway grass skirt soldiers away from Fiji home', *Herald*, Scotland, 19 September 1998. http://goo.gl/V7ywa (accessed 28 September 2011).
2. Terri Judd, 'A fruitful recruiting land for the army', *The Independent*. Friday, 8 September 2006. http://goo.gl/Nh8ZE (accessed 5 October 2010).
3. Tanya Thompson, 'Tattoo bandsmen decide to stay', *The Scotsman*, Saturday, 12 December 1998.
4. Stuart Hall defined corporate (public or private) multiculturalism as seeking 'to "manage" minority cultural differences in the interests of the centre'. Barnor Hesse, ed., *Un/settled Multiculturalisms: Diasporas, Entanglements, Transruptions*, London: Zed Books, 2000, p. 210.
5. House of Commons HC Deb 28 October 1997, vol. 299, cc728–730. http://goo.gl/jJGFk (accessed 15 February 2012).
6. Ibid.
7. House of Commons HC Deb 28 October 1997, vol. 299, cc728–729. http://goo.gl/PntWc (accessed 15 February 2012).
8. House of Commons HC deb22 January 1998, cc621–622w. http://goo.gl/SAzn9 (accessed 29 October 2010).
9. House of Commons, Publications and Records, 18 February 1998, column 663. http://goo.gl/iL2ba (accessed 29 October 2011).
10. The Princess of Wales Royal Regiment (PWRR) recruits many of its officers and soldiers from Kent, Sussex, Surrey, London, Middlesex and Hampshire as well as the Isle of Wight and the Channel Islands. As armoured infantry, the majority of the soldiers are mounted in Warrior Infantry Fighting Vehicles.
11. Publications and records, *Hansard*, Army: recruitment. 13 May 2009: Column 765W – continued. http://goo.gl/3jjcJ (accessed 28 September 2011).
12. Paul Cornish and Andrew Dorman, 'Blair's Wars and Brown's Budgets: from Strategic Defence Review to strategic decay in less than a decade', *International Affairs* 85: 2 (2009) 247–261, p. 248.
13. Modern Forces for the Modern World, Strategic Defence Review, July 1998. Supporting Essay Nine, 'A Policy for People'. Section 41, p. 214.
14. Ibid., Introduction, p. 205.
15. http://goo.gl/YA9XS (accessed 20 October 2011).
16. Select Committee on Defence. Minutes of evidence. Memorandum for the Commission for Racial Equality, 2 October 2000. http://goo.gl/V5yw (accessed 29 October 2011).
17. Christopher Bellamy, 'Army pledges to stamp out racism in ranks', *Independent*, 28 March 1996. http://goo.gl/DAVtt (accessed 11 December 2011).
18. 'Oldest regiment serves dual role', BBC News, 25 January 2006. http://goo.gl/1Ui1n (accessed 6 October 2010).

19. In 1988 Richard Stokes was appointed first black guardsman in the Grenadier Guards. He left in 1990 complaining of endless racist abuse. http://goo.gl/kq5AR (accessed 7 October 2010).

20. The Armed Forces Bill. Bill 4 of 2000–2001. Research Paper 01/03. 8 January 2001. House of Commons Library. P. 29.

21. The exhibition was launched by The Minister of State for the Armed Forces, Mr John Spellar and the Chair of the Commission for Racial Equality, Mr Gurbux Singh. The 'We Were There' exhibition. Ministry of Defence, launched 28 November 2000. http://goo.gl/le88K (accessed 30 October 2011).

22. http://goo.gl/mtxTj (accessed 15 March 2011).

23. 'My memory is of a huge placard somewhere in the city in which I worked. It was very glowing. "Do you want to help the War cause?" it read, "England Needs You", with a finger pointing at you, so when you stood and looked at this thing, it became personalised. England, that great country, needs me. Of course, it had a terrific psychological effect.' Extract from Robert N. Murray, *The Experiences of World War II Westindian Ex-Service Personnel*, Nottingham Westindian Combined Ex-Services Association, Hansib Publishing (Caribbean), 1996, p. 27.

24. Focus Consultancy. Some of our clients: The British Army. http://goo.gl/hgfhP (accessed 20 October 2010).

25. About Defence: equal opportunities in the armed forces. http://goo.gl/5df7j (accessed 20 October 2010).

26. The Macpherson report defined 'institutional racism' as 'The collective failure of an organisation to provide an appropriate and professional service to people because of their colour, culture, or ethnic origin. It can be seen or detected in processes, attitudes and behaviour which amount to discrimination through unwitting prejudice, ignorance, thoughtlessness and racist stereotyping which disadvantage minority ethnic people.' 'What is institutional racism?' *Guardian*, Wednesday, 24 February 1999. http://goo.gl/0nJbW (accessed 20 October 2010).

27. Race Relations (Amendment) Act 2000. http://goo.gl/d2Nqz (accessed 20 October 2010).

28. Ibid.

29. Christopher Dandeker and David Mason, 'Ethnic diversity in the British armed forces', in *Cultural Diversity in the Armed Forces: An International Comparison*, Joseph Soeters and Jan van der Meulen, eds London: Routledge, 2007, pp. 142–3.

30. Comparison of eligibility criteria for entry into the Armed Forces. Parliamentary Business, Publications and Records. 14 March 2005. http://goo.gl/uJS5g (accessed 28 October 2011).

31. Rachel Woodward and Patricia Winter, 'Discourses of gender in the contemporary British Army', *Armed Forces and Society*, vol. 30, No. 2, 2004, p. 284.

32. MoD, 'Women in the Armed Forces: A Report by the Employment of Women in the Armed Forces Steering Group', (London, MoD, 2002), p. 6.

33. Ibid, p. 3. The MoD was allowed to derogate from the principle of equal treatment in the interests of combat effectiveness but such derogation must be 'necessary and appropriate'.

34. The Armed Forces Bill. Bill 4 of 2000–2001. Research Paper 01/03. 8 January 2001. House of Commons Library. p. 23.

35. Michael Smith, 'Guthrie launches final assault on "PC" forces', *Daily Telegraph*, 16 February 2001.

36. Gerald Frost, 'How to destroy an army: the cultural subversion of Britain's armed forces', in Alexandrou, Bartle and Holmes, *New People Strategies for the British Armed Forces*, London: Frank Cass, 2002. p. 37.

37. People in Defence, 'Forces LGBT networking site wins European Diversity Award', Defence News, MoD, 28 September 2011. http://goo.gl/3NcuK (accessed 28 September 2011).

38. HC Deb 09 March 1960, vol. 619, cc426–592. http://goo.gl/AJWCH (2 November 2010).

39. See, for example, the historical account of racism in the British Army in the 'We Were There' exhibition. http://goo.gl/86GDT (28 October 2011).

40. Richard Weight. *Patriots: National Identity in Britain 1940–2000.* London: Macmillan, 2002, pp. 307–312.

41. The quote continues: 'An Army Council report concluded that the loyalty of black and Asian soldiers could not be relied upon in wartime: to sum up, the enlistment of coloured men into the Army, and *a fortiori*, the grant of commission in the British Army to them, constitutes, in the view of the Army Council, a threat to the discipline and well-being of the Army which might be a very serious matter in time of war' (Ibid., p. 308).

42. Mark Smalley, 'Colour barred? Unknown warriors', BBC Radio 4, 11 September 2006. http://goo.gl/8ihHx (accessed 28 October 2011).

43. From our military correspondent 'Fijian recruits for army', *The Times*, 7 November 1961; Issue 55232; col. G.

44. Ibid.

45. Black Asian British Army, *Relate: The Story* 'Equality: racism' National Army Museum. http://goo.gl/fTwUW (accessed 16 December 2010).

46. Owen Bowcott, 'MoD kept race details on troops', *Guardian*, Tuesday 4 January 2005. http://goo.gl/eseYh (accessed 15 February 2011).

47. WRAC Association. http://www.wracassociation.co.uk/history (accessed 16 December 2010).

48. From our military correspondent 'Fijian recruits for army,' *The Times*, 7 November 1961; Issue 55232; col. G.

49. Teresia K. Teaiwa, ' "Fijian Women Soldiers: Challenging or confirming concepts of culture and citizenship?" Discussion paper contributing to the project: "What are we fighting for? Fijian women soldiers at home and abroad" '. Victoria University of Wellington, January 2009.

50. Fiji in World War 1: the soldiers from Fiji in the Great War. http://www.freewebs.com/fiji/fijianlabourcorps.htm (accessed 28 October 2011).

51. Christopher Bayly and Tim Harper, *Forgotten Wars: The End of Britain's Asian Empire*, London: Allen Lane, 2007, p. 522.

52. HC Deb 09 December 1963, vol. 686, cc34–117. http://goo.gl/G11TR (accessed 20 October 2010).

53. Ibid. See c59.

54. From our military correspondent 'Fijian recruits for army', *The Times*, 7 November 1961; Issue 55232; col. G.

55. HC Deb 09 December 1963, vol. 686, See cc70–72. http://goo.gl/G11TR (accessed 20 October 2010). During this debate MPs discussed at length why recruitment was posing such difficulties. Emrys Hughes, Labour MP for South Ayrshire, suggested that it was because the army was competing unfavourably with other sectors of employment. 'I do not know that a rational case for appealing to recruits to join the Army in 1963 can be made out...I understand that the

modern Army must be a part of a great organisation, equipped with modern transport, and that, because it must be mechanised, it must contain skilled mechanics, electricians, fitters and so on. Those who advance this argument must realise that these are exactly the people we urgently need in industry.' See cc70–72.

56. Ibid. cc97–100. http://goo.gl/G11TR (accessed 20 October 2010).
57. Hew Strachan, *The Politics of the British Army*, Oxford: Clarendon Press, 1997, p. 232.
58. 'Fiji's unsung heroes of UK army', BBC News, 9 November 2004. http://goo.gl/gctR9 (accessed 28 October 2011).
59. One article often cited was by the defence correspondent of the *Daily Telegraph*, Michael Smith. 'Foreign legion boosts Army' 24 July 2001. http://goo.gl/Aw15s (accessed 20 October 2011).
60. The Times 100. Summary of case study 2008–2009. Tesco: recruitment and selection. http://goo.gl/Ods8k (accessed 25 November 2010).
61. Statistics for nationality as opposed to ethnic minority status are harder to access. See for example, discussion in the House of Commons, 9 March 2007: Column 2296Wv: Iraq: Peace Keeping Operations. Nick Harvey: To ask the Secretary of State for Defence if he will estimate the number of soldiers serving with UK forces from each country of the Commonwealth in (a) Iraq and (b) Afghanistan. [125566].

   Derek Twigg: Data on the nationality of armed forces personnel deployed on operation are not held centrally in databases of individual records and it is therefore not possible to give figures by Nationality. http://goo.gl/fuoBb (accessed 12 February 2011).
62. The MoD report on Equality and Diversity issued at the end of 2009 stated that the intake from ethnic minorities into the UK Regular Armed Forces was provisionally for the 12 months ending 30 September 2009 4.8 per cent for the Royal Navy, 11 per cent for the Army and 2.6 per cent for the RAF. The aim was to reach 8 per cent ethnic minority representation by 2013 (in order to reflect ethnic minority representation in UK society). As 1 October 2009 this figure was 6.6 per cent. http://goo.gl/YXOQ2 (accessed 7 October 2010).
63. DASA. UK Armed Forces Quarterly Manning Statistics. 1 April 2010. Graph 4.3 (Table 2.1). Ethnic minorities as a percentage of intake to UK Regular Forces by Service. http://goo.gl/asauZ (accessed 7 October 2010).
64. DASA. UK Armed Forces Quarterly Manning Statistics. 1 April 2010. Graph 3.2 (Table 2.2). Ethnic minorities as a percentage of strength by Service. http://goo.gl/GtVP2 (accessed 7 October 2010).
65. HC. Select Committee on Defence Fourteenth Report. 3: Recruitment. 30 July 2008. http://www.publications.parliament.uk/pa/cm200708/cmselect/cmdfence/424/42406.htm#note84 (accessed 20 October 2010).
66. David Gee, *Informed Choice? Armed Forces Recruitment Practice in the United Kingdom*. Research and publication funded by the Joseph Rowntree Charitable Trust. November, 2007. www.informedchoice.org.uk (accessed 27 October 2010).
67. Michael Evans, 'They don't mention the warfare – Army adverts come under attack', *The Times*, 7 January 2008.

3   The Promised Land

1. The army training centre at Pirbright (ATC) is the main establishment for delivering the core training available to the majority of recruits who were not destined

for the infantry. The infantry regiments make up only 24 per cent of the field army as a whole, supplemented by nearly 20 other 'trades'.

See also, Richard Norton-Taylor, 'Women still banned from combat roles after Ministry of Defence review', *Guardian*, Monday, 29 October 2010. http://goo.gl/hqQMY (accessed 26 February 2012).

2. Britain is the only European country to recruit into the regular army at 16. In 2007 it was discovered that fifteen 17-year-old British soldiers had been sent to Iraq between 2003 and 2005 despite a UN convention (Optional Protocol to the Convention on the Rights of the Child on the involvement of children in armed conflict) to keep children away from armed conflict. BBC News, 'Under-18s were deployed to Iraq', Sunday, 4 February 2007. http://goo.gl/yd0xB (accessed 2 October 2011).

There were four members of the armed forces who were under the age of 18 years and deployed to operational theatres between April 2008 and March 2010. Hansard Written Answers, Armed Forces: Young People, 18 October 2011: Column 868W. http://www.publications.parliament.uk/pa/cm201011/cmhansrd/cm111018/text/111018w0003.htm#column_866W (accessed 23 October 2011).

3. For certain jobs there is a residency requirement so that backgrounds can be checked.

4. Government Gazette, 16 November 2007. No. 30477. Act no. 27, 2006. http://goo.gl/eVa6w (accessed 27 February 2011).

5. Liz Ward and Alana Diamond 'Tackling Knives Action Programme (TKAP) Phase 1: Overview of key trends from a monitoring programme' Research Report 18. 2009. http://goo.gl/9p6cO (accessed 4 November 2010) See also Christine Jeavans, 'Mapping UK's teen murder toll' BBC News, Monday, 15 December 2008. http://goo.gl/jgOgl (accessed 15 December 2010).

6. During a lecture on value-based learning at the Infantry Battle School, Brecon, the instructor suggested that 50 per cent of Infantry recruits were from 'council estates', and 70 per cent from 'broken homes'.

7. Select Committee on Defence. Third Report. Recruitment.14 March 2005. http://goo.gl/XGY69 (accessed 4 February 2011).

8. Johnson Beharry and Nick Cook, *Barefoot Soldier*, London: Little, Brown Book Group, 2006, p. 198.

9. DASA 1 April 2009 (Infantry presentation, May 2009).

10. Army.mod.uk. The Mercian Regiment. http://goo.gl/h707c (accessed 26 January 2011).

11. Army.mod.uk. Welsh Guards. Recruiting. http://goo.gl/Q6AQT (accessed 26 January 2011).

12. Army.mod.uk. The Royal Regiment of Scotland. http://goo.gl/xMt9P (accessed 26 January 2011).

13. Army.mod.uk. Irish Guards. Contact us. http://goo.gl/H3dGc (accessed 26 January 2011).

14. 'Irish recruits flock to join British Army', *Belfast Telegraph*, 4 September 2008. http://goo.gl/byUbf (accessed 13 September 2011).

15. '15% rise in recruits from Wales to Armed Forces' BBC News Channel, Wales. Thursday, 28 January 2010. http://goo.gl/pNr8V (accessed 30 November 2010).

16. Elite UK Forces. Parachute Company. http://goo.gl/q94wB (accessed 4 January 2011).

17. One index of the contribution of Fijian rugby players was displayed in the October 2010 edition of *Soldier* magazine. That year, the army won all four

inter-service titles, and out of six players mentioned by name for their star contribution, five were Fijian. Richard Long, 'History Makers', *Soldier*, October 2010, p. 96.

18. Daniel Foggo and Roger Waite, 'Commonwealth cousins prop up the British Army', *The Sunday Times*, 26 April 2009.
19. Richard Norton-Taylor, 'Army puts cap on number of foreign recruits', *The Guardian*, Tuesday, 3 February 2009. http://goo.gl/LozNQ (accessed 7 January 2011).
20. Michael Evans, 'How British Army is fast becoming foreign legion', *The Times*, 14 November 2005.
21. See for example, Michael Smith, 'Foreign legion boosts army', *Daily Telegraph*, 24 July 2001. http://goo.gl/JIPTD (accessed 8 February 2011) and Ian Bruce, 'UK overseas armed forces match French Foreign Legion', *The Herald*, Wednesday 11 February 2008. http://goo.gl/0Vmcn (accessed 11 May 2011).
22. Richard Norton-Taylor, 'MoD may halt surge in Commonwealth recruits to army', *Guardian*, Saturday, 5 April 2008. http://goo.gl/a4dJy (accessed 5 February 2011).
23. Foggo and Waite, 'Commonwealth cousins prop up the British Army'.
24. Ibid.
25. Christopher Leake, 'Race uproar over Army troop quota', *Mail Online*, 1 April 2007. http://goo.gl/k9C59 (accessed 7 January 2011).

4 Culture Shock

1. Sean Rayment, defence correspondent, 'Ex-prisoners "make better Army recruits than today's teenagers"', *Telegraph*, 23 April 2006. http://goo.gl/uib5o (accessed 9 February 2011).
2. Richard Norton-Taylor, 'Two thirds of teenagers too fat to be soldiers', *Guardian*, Friday 3 November 2006. http://goo.gl/U0Tm7 (accessed 18 February 2011).
3. See, for example, Keith Ajegbo, Dina Kiwan & Seema Sharma, *Diversity and Citizenship. A Curriculum Review*, DfES Publication, Nottingham, 2007.
4. In 2009 the MoD acknowledged liability for permitting physical injuries to individuals on account of inadequate equipment in cold temperatures. An article in the *Telegraph* revealed that 'Lawyers acting for the soldiers, many from warmer Commonwealth countries who are far more susceptible, said failures of equipment and training were to blame for cases of Non Freezing Cold Injury (NFCI)'. It also quotes a Nigerian ex-soldier who was discharged after suffering NFCI, who contracted it on winter exercises in Wales. When he complained that his feet were swollen and stuck in his boots, and that his fingers were too stiff to move he was told, 'Soldier on, and stop being a wimp'. He also reported that the Home Office had refused him a visa to return to the UK for the final medical he required in order to get receive £150,000 compensation. 'MoD facing £5m claim from troops for cold injuries', *Telegraph*, 16 June 2009. http://goo.gl/iBzJx (accessed 4 October 2011).
5. P. A. J. Waddington, 'Police (Canteen) Sub-culture: an appreciation', *British Journal of Criminology*, 39 (2), 1999, pp. 287–309.
6. Anthony King, 'The Word of Command: Communication and Cohesion in the Military', *Armed Forces & Society*, 32 (4), 2006, 493–512, p. 493. See also Robert J. MacCoun, Elizabeth Kier, Aaron Belkin, 'Does Social Cohesion Determine Motivation in Combat? An Old Question with an Old Answer', *Armed Forces & Society*, 32 (4), 2006, pp. 646–654.

7. King, p. 503.
8. Guy L. Siebold, 'The Essence of Military Group Cohesion', *Armed Forces & Society*, 33 (2), 2007, pp. 286–295.
9. Ibid., pp. 4–5.
10. Charles Kirke, 'Group Cohesion, Culture, and Practice', *Armed Forces & Society* 35, 2009, p. 745.
11. Ibid., p. 747.
12. Ibid.
13. General Sir Richard Dannatt KCB CBE MC. The Chief of The General Staff's Equality and Diversity Directive for the Army. Army Code 64340. 1 April 2008, p. 2.
14. David Mason and Christopher Dandeker, 'Evolving UK Policy on Diversity in the Armed Services: Multiculturalism and its Discontents', *Commonwealth & Comparative Politics*, 47 (4), November 2009, 393–410, p. 403.
15. Timothy Edmunds and Anthony Forster, *Out of Step: The Case for Change in the British Armed Forces*, London: Demos, 2007.
16. Gordon Brown, 'Who do we want to be? The future of Britishness', speech delivered at the Fabian New Year Conference, Imperial College, London, Saturday 14 January 2006. http://goo.gl/7xMV5 (accessed 16 November 2011).
17. See, for example, the Tesco website: http://goo.gl/xY8g3 (accessed 14 February 2011).
18. See http://goo.gl/YXnOf (accessed 12 March 2011) Sodexo (UK and Ireland) provide the catering, retail, mess management and cleaning services for the MoD in many locations.
19. Alex Alexandrou and Roger Darby, 'Human Resource Management', in Laura R. Cleary and Teri McConville, eds. *Managing Defence in a Democracy*, London: Routledge, 2006, p. 157.
20. Ibid., p. 168.
21. The standards of behaviour are listed as lawful, appropriate and totally professional.
22. Values and Standards Action Plan (VSAP). DEP2008-0476. February 2008.
23. Values and Standards of the British Army, 2008. AC 64813.
24. As one of three chaplains responsible for providing spiritual welfare and Sunday worship the Padre had a privileged view of the recruits' religious needs across a range of ethno-cultural backgrounds. The choir in the training centre was almost exclusively made up of Fijians, with members singing in Fijian. 'I try not to call it the Fijian choir', he said, 'But the soldiers love it.'
25. See Rachel Woodward's essay arguing this same point: R. Woodward, 'Not for Queen and Country or any of that shit...': reflections on citizenship and military participation in contemporary British soldier narratives', in Gilbert, E. and Cowan, D. (Eds) *War, Citizenship, Territory*. Routledge, London, 2008, pp. 363–384.
26. 'Taliban losing local support in Helmand', A military operations news article, Ministry of Defence, 17 March 2011. http://goo.gl/8nYHO (accessed 17 March 2011).
27. The Aitken Report, An Investigation into Cases of Deliberate Abuse and Unlawful Killing in Iraq in 2003 and 2004, MoD, 25 January 2008. http://goo.gl/T1poe (accessed 1 April 2011).
28. Ibid., pp. 4–5.
29. Ibid., p. 32.

30. Hugh Gusterson, 'The Cultural Turn in the War on Terror', in John D. Kelly, Beatrice Jauregui, Sean T. Mitchell, and Jeremy Walton, Eds, *Anthropology and Global Counterinsurgency*, Chicago: University of Chicago Press, 2010, 280.
31. David Kilcullen, 'Twenty-Eight Articles: Fundamentals of Company-level Counterinsurgency', Edition 1, March 2006. http://goo.gl/VsIoY (accessed 6 November 2011).
32. Ibid., p. 1.
33. Julia Preston, 'The US military will offer path to citizenship', *New York Times*, February 4, 2009. http://goo.gl/3vTK3 (8 August 2011).
34. David H. Price, *Weaponizing Anthropology: Social Science in the Service of the Militarized State*, Oakland: AK Press, 2011.
35. 'MoD opens Afghan village in Norfolk', *Telegraph*, 1 May 2009. http://goo.gl/1kPxl (accessed 8 April 2011).
36. MoD News, First infantry troops train in replica Afghan village 12 June 2009. http://goo.gl/bXpWo (accessed 4 May 2011).
37. Christopher Leake, 'Afghan refugees on £200 a day – to pose as Taliban', *Daily Mail*, 14 July 2007. http://goo.gl/YxtN1 (accessed 6 May 2011).
38. Interview with members of 3 Yorks Regiment, sometimes referred to as the 'Yorkshire Taliban', June 2009.

5 Keeping the Faith

1. Sarah Percy, *Mercenaries: the history of a norm in international relations*, Oxford: Oxford University Press, 2007, p. 104.
2. Ibid.
3. Army.mod.uk. 1st Infantry Training Battalion. http://goo.gl/rsH4V (accessed 5 October 2011).
4. In 2008, 17,349 applied and 230 were selected to begin training in January 2009. The Singapore police take 30–40 of these for the Gurkha Contingent. (presentation from Brigade of Gurkhas, August 2009).
5. 'The recruitment process of the Brigade of Gurkhas ... has been highly caste-sensitive. Owing to their reified views of different castes, the British recruited mostly from selected castes – the Gurungs, Magars, Rais and Limbus (and Chhetris, most of whom went to the Indian army in 1947) – and then placed them in caste-specific regiments. Of course, a few other castes were also involved, especially when the number of recruits was massively increased for the First and Second World Wars. The Tamangs, Sherpas, Newars, Thakali were the other castes used during these wars. At most other times, however, only those considered "martial races" have been employed in Gurkha regiments.' Mitra Pariyar, 'Cast(e) in Bone: The Perpetuation of Social Hierarchy among Nepalis in Britain', COMPAS, Centre on Migration, Policy and Society, University of Oxford, Working Paper No. 85, University of Oxford, 2011, p. 13.
6. The Royal Gurkha Rifles: A young officer's guide, p. 15 (no date).
7. According to a Gurkha officer: 'We used to do that in every battalion, wherever we were, including in the UK but Health and Safety and, quite rightly, Rights of Animals, said you're not doing that. So in Pokhara a bull is dispatched on behalf of the Brigade and it's done with one clean cut through the neck, so it dies instantly. If it's two cuts it's going to be a bad year for the Brigade, so there's a lot of pressure on the young lad that's supposed to be doing this. That result

is then signalled throughout the Brigade. The chop's been done on their behalf, been blessed and then the Brigade can relax and enjoy the following year.'

8. Army Basic Skills Provision: Whole Organisation Approach, Lessons Learnt. The Basic Skills Agency, London, 2007, p. 6. http://goo.gl/JWsYo (accessed 17 December 2010).

9. Army.mod.uk. Skills for life (Basic skills). http://goo.gl/EzRBD (accessed 30 December 2010).

10. Diane Taylor, 'Assault Course: When Andy McNab went into the Army, his reading age was less than 11. Now he is helping new recruits', *Guardian*, 5 December, 2006. http://goo.gl/DMRm9 (accessed 11 May 2011).

11. General Sir Richard Dannatt KCB CBE MC. The Chief of The General Staff's Equality and Diversity Directive for the Army. Army Code 64340. 1 April 2008, p. 2.

12. Briefing by ARTD personnel, July 2008.

13. BRITISH ARMY CULTURAL GUIDANCE. Reference: A. DPS (A)/28/9 dated 21 January 2008. B. DPS (A)/28/9 dated 31 March 2008 (Edition 5) p. 2.

14. Ibid., p. 5. http://goo.gl/w1Gu8 (accessed 11 December 2011).

15. Ibid.

16. 'Religious leaders meet and forge relationships in Helmand', People in defence news article, Ministry of Defence, 30 June 2011. http://goo.gl/eSzGA (accessed 30 June 2011).

17. The promotion of the traditional Hindu order, together with its caste structure, has been emphasised by the British who have been 'complicit with the high-caste interpretation of Hinduism as the national religion of Nepal, with its links to sustaining and promoting caste hierarchy.' Pariyar, 'Cast(e) in Bone: The Perpetuation of Social Hierarchy among Nepalis in Britain', p. 14.

18. In August the Battalion Pundit (Hindu Chaplain) visited the Gurkhas in Nahr-e Saraj, holding temple services and blessing each soldier with a tikka (red dot on the forehead). <http://goo.gl/7lwpk> (accessed 24 February 2011).

19. 'Dalai Lama sends message of support for Armed Forces Day', Department of Defence UK. 18.06.2010. http://goo.gl/oqapM (accessed 6 October 2011).

20. Defence Academy. The Armed Forces Chaplaincy Centre. http://www.da.mod.uk/colleges/afcc.

21. The MoD revised their policies on religion following the 2010 Equality Act. The new guide stated that, 'Our policy is that religion is a private life matter lived out by individuals and communities within the public arena. In order to recognise and harness individual difference and to remove any barriers which might prevent people from joining the Armed Forces or MOD Civil Service, we endeavour to give those who wish to do so the opportunity to practise their religious observances wherever possible subject to vital considerations of operational effectiveness, health and safety and business needs. It is important that in applying this policy the needs of individuals are balanced with those of their colleagues and the organisation as a whole.' Ministry of Defence, 'Guide on Religion and Belief in the Armed Forces'. June 2011. http://goo.gl/U95US (accessed 10 February 2012).

22. Ministry of Defence, 'Guide on Religion and Belief in the MoD and Armed Forces'. Designed and produced by TES-TI Media. Bath, 2004–2005. http://goo.gl/FZ6Is (accessed 11 February 2012).

23. Ibid. para 6, p. 5.

24. The Buddhist spiritual adviser employed to work at the Gurkha training centre in Catterick had been a monk since the age of eight. He patiently explained to me that for Buddhists, it was important to act with compassion. Using violent means to counteract enemies, or defeat those who are doing harm to innocent people, was permitted as long as it was performed with compassion for those who are suffering as well as those who do wrong. The message from the Dalai Lama supporting the UK's Armed Forces Day, delivered at the AFBS conference, confirmed this stance towards violence and retribution, a position he reiterated on the assassination of Osama bin Laden in May 2011.

25. United Kingdom Defence Statistics, Ministry of Defence, Published: 29 September 2010. Table 2.13 Strength of UK Regular Forces by Service and religion, at 1 April each year. Note: The percentage of Christians serving in the Armed Forces has reduced from 89.7 per cent in 2007 to 85.8 per cent in 2010. The number of UK Regular Forces citing 'No Religion' has increased from 9.5 per cent in 2007 to 12.6 per cent in 2010. At 1 April 2010, the Army has the highest proportion of Hindus (0.6%) and Muslims (0.5%). These have increased gradually over the past 4 years from 0.2 per cent and 0.3 per cent respectively.

26. Riazat Butt, 'Church of England attendance falls for fifth year in row', *Guardian*, Friday 22 January 2010. http://goo.gl/pDPwO (accessed 11 May 2011).
    'The average weekly attendance in 2008 fell to 1.145 million from 1.16 million in 2007, while the average Sunday attendance fell from 978,000 in 2007 to 960,000 in 2008.'

27. A note on the BA website reads, 'Armed with a bible and a cross, life for a padre on Operations can be tough. They go out on patrols and live in Forward Operating Bases, on hand for when they might be needed.' http://www.army.mod.uk/home. aspx (accessed 5 October 2011).

28. Ibid. See also the story by Michael Evans, 'How the devil do you get a Satanist in the Navy?' *The Times*, October 25, 2004.

29. Chris Holden, 'Last Post', *New Humanist*, November–December 2011, vol. 126, No. 6, pp. 23–25.

30. 'Continued exclusion of the non-religious on Remembrance Day', British Humanist Association, 11 November 2011. http://www.armedforceshumanists.org.uk/node/39 (accessed 21 November 2011).

31. Emma Bondor, 'Jews in HM Forces: Multicultural and Multinational', *Renaissance*, January 2011, p. 7.

32. Daily Mail reporter, 'Britain's finest moment: the pomp and pageantry of the Royal Wedding in all its glory', *Mail*, 29 April 2011. http://goo.gl/lqBKU (accessed 12 May 2011).

33. Daily Mail reporter, 'Touching tribute from a Royal bride: Kate's bouquet returns to Westminster Abbey to lie on the grave of the unknown soldier', *Mail*, 1 May 2011. http://goo.gl/Y38DJ (accessed 1 May 2011).

34. Stephen Deakin, 'British Military Ethos and Christianity', *British Army Review*, no. 138. Winter 2005, pp. 97–105.

35. Paul Robinson, Nigel De Lee, Don Carrick, Eds, *Ethics Education in the Military*, Aldershot: Ashgate, 2008, p. 20.

36. Quoted in Deakin, 'British Military Ethos and Christianity'.

37. Sarah Sands, 'Sir Richard Dannatt: A very honest General', *Mail*, 13 October 2006. http://goo.gl/DDzCc (accessed 21 November 2011).

38. Tony Thompson, 'Armed forces try an ethnic tactic', *Guardian*, Sunday 13 March 2005. http://goo.gl/5Izxn (accessed 6 March 2012).

39. UK Defence Statistics 2011. Chapter 2.13: Strength of UK Regular Forces by Service and religion, at 1 April each year. http://goo.gl/VgA86 (accessed 10 February 2012). See also Esther Addley, 'Allah, queen and the country', *Guardian*, Saturday, 21 April 2007. http://goo.gl/T2xyL (accessed 6 March 2012).
40. 'Armed Forces Muslim Association launched', *Hillingdon and Uxbridge Times*, Saturday, 10 October 2010.
41. Ahmed J. Versi, 'Army chief admits failure to convince Muslims over Afghan policy', *The Muslim News*, Issue 247, Friday, 27 November 2009 – 10 Dhu al-Hijjah 1430. http://goo.gl/OZ1Vs (accessed 23 February 2011). In the same interview Richards also said, 'It is very important for the Muslim community to be exposed to an alternative view as it is for the rest of the nation. The Taliban kill many more Muslims than we do.'
42. Army Rumour Service. http://www.arrse.co.uk/intelligence-cell/154437-armed-forces-muslim-association.html (accessed 24 February 2011).
43. 'British Imam leads Eid celebrations in Kandahar'. Ministry of Defence, Defence News. 19.November 2010. A Military Operations news article. http://goo.gl/Eg4l1 (accessed 10 March 2011).
44. Ibid.
45. Andy Bloxham, 'Muslims clash with police after burning poppy in anti-Armistice Day protest', *Telegraph*, 11 November 2010. http://goo.gl/4KKqU (accessed 10 March 2011).
46. 'Fresh race row for MoD as British Muslim soldier claims he was branded a "Paki" and was throttled by sergeant', *Daily Mail*, 16 February 2009. http://goo.gl/ekLCP (7 March 2011).
47. Lucy Cockroft, 'Muslim SAS soldier sues MoD for racial discrimination', *Telegraph*, 6 September 2009. http://goo.gl/kOQ5B (accessed 10 March 2011).
48. Poonam Taneja, 'UK's Muslim soldiers "fighting extremists not Muslims"', BBC News, 21 February 2011. http://goo.gl/hvZC1 (accessed 30 March 2011); 'Muslims on the Frontline', Asian Network Reports Special, BBC Asian Network, 21 February 2011, 18.00.
49. '"Our little Paki friend": MOD to investigate Harry after racial slurs on Asian colleague', *Daily Mail*, 11 January 2009. http://goo.gl/ZLvgk (accessed 6 October 2011).
50. Ibid.
51. 'Howard calls for Harry Nazi costume apology', *Daily Mail*, 13 January 2005. http://goo.gl/uoD9U (accessed 7 March 2011).
52. Paul Lewis, 'Harry escapes bashing for "Paki" remark', The *Guardian*, Monday, 12 January 2009. http://goo.gl/F6oqP (accessed 7 March 2011).
53. Sam Greenhill, 'Prince Harry's "little Paki friend" Ahmed has captain's role in the war on terror', *Daily Mail*, Monday 12 January 2009. http://goo.gl/x7Fv0 (accessed 10 March 2011).

6 Crossing the Line

1. 'British Army takes the lead with new application for Apple iPad', British Army website, 26 May 2010. http://goo.gl/S9cKr (accessed 14 March 2011).
2. By 2009, simulators and replica operations rooms had been installed at the giant Sennelager Training Centre in Germany ready for pre-deployment exercises that would involve driving virtual vehicles and commanding computer-generated ground patrols. Commenting on the state of the art facility which utilised X-box

technology, the officer in charge, Major Edward Whishaw of the Corps of Royal Engineers, said, "It's a modern gaming environment that, hopefully, a young 18- or 19-year-old soldier will appreciate; replicating theatre with a carbon copy of reality"'. Defence News, 'Gaming technology helping UK forces prepare for Afghanistan', Ministry of Defence, 4 July 2011. See also Chris Cole, Mary Dobbing and Amy Hailwood, *Convenient Killing: Armed Drones and the 'Playstation' Mentality*, Oxford: The Fellowship of Reconciliation, September 2010. http://goo.gl/A09Pr (accessed 24 October 2011).

3. In 2002 it was reported that more veterans of the Falklands War had killed themselves in the years since the 1982 conflict ended than died during hostilities, according to the South Atlantic Medal Association, a veterans support group. The group said they were 'almost certain' that the suicide toll was greater than 255 – the number of men killed in the war. BBC News, 'Falklands Veterans claim suicide toll', 13 January 2002. http://goo.gl/QqdnX (accessed 13 September 2011).

4. Stephen Bates and Richard Norton-Taylor, 'Video nasty: Prince Harry faces racism inquiry over footage of "Paki" remark', The *Guardian*, Monday 12 January, 2009. http://goo.gl/Wppfw (accessed 27 February 2011).

5. Matthew Taylor and Audrey Gillan, 'Racist slur or army Banter? What the soldiers say', *Guardian*, 13 January 2009. http://goo.gl/aF1gP (accessed 12 March 2011).

6. The ethos of the British Army states that 'Soldiers have the responsibility and legal right to use lethal force, and may be required to lay down their own lives and risk those of their comrades.' Therefore it is in the interests of 'operational effectiveness' that the Army must maintain values and standards that are different from society. Values and Standards of the British Army, 2008. AC 64813.

7. Donna Winslow, 'Military organization and culture', in Giuseppe Caforio, ed. *Social Sciences and the Military: An interdisciplinary overview*, London: Routledge, 2007, p. 84.

8. John Hockey, *Squaddies: Portrait of a subculture*, Exeter: University of Exeter press, 1986.

9. It is interesting to compare banter in the army with corresponding behaviour in football where racism between players on the pitch came to light in 2011. The Secret Footballer, 'Brawls and insults – we are all at it', *Guardian*, 11 November 2011. http://goo.gl/0SU3g (accessed 21 November 2011).

10. BRITISH ARMY CULTURAL GUIDANCE. Reference: A. DPS (A)/28/9 dated 21 January 2008. B. DPS (A)/28/9 dated 31 March 2008 (Edition 5), p. 16. http://goo.gl/7EGEy (accessed 21 February 2011).

11. Ibid, p. 7.

12. The Stephen Lawrence Inquiry: Report of an Inquiry By Sir William Macpherson of Cluny, February 1999. 46.25: 6.34, 321.

13. Bearing in mind that online forums for military personnel are often open to non-military participants, the definition in ARRSEpedia has a useful definition of beasting: A punishment ritual, usually involving physical violence to some degree but can be verbal, carried out by one or more persons and used to intimidate or reinforce hierarchical status within a group. Can be anything from a Regimental Bath to a good shoeing. <http://www.arrse.co.uk/wiki/Beasting> (accessed 4 January 2011).

14. 'Soldiers went AWOL from barracks after "unbearable bullying"', *Telegraph*, 14 March 2009. http://goo.gl/qBBWb (accessed 27 April 2011).

15. 'Runaway soldiers', BBC Panorama, 27 March 2007. <http://goo.gl/fzKFp> (accessed 9 March 2011).
16. Michael Savage, 'More than 17,000 episodes of troops going AWOL since 2003', *Independent*, Sunday, 20 February 2010. http://goo.gl/g0H8g (accessed 27 April 2011).
17. Michael Bartlet, 'Britain's child soldiers', *Guardian*, 11 March 2011. http://goo.gl/hsL3g (accessed 10 October 2011).
18. Staff writers, 'Quakers and Unitarians call for a change to the Armed Forces Bill', *Ekklesia*, 16 April 2011. http://www.ekklesia.co.uk/node/14581 (accessed 21 April 2011).
19. 'Campaigners welcome new right to leave the armed forces for under-18s', Forceswatch, 19 May 2011. http://goo.gl/CrpF4 (accessed 7 July 2011).
20. JSP383. The Joint Service Manual of the Law of Armed Conflict. Joint Service Publication 383, 2004 Edition.
21. British Army Cultural Guidance, Ibid. p.7.
22. Nick Britten, 'Racially abused soldier awarded £22,000 compensation by MoD', *Telegraph*, 9 January 2010. http://goo.gl/CYRE6 (accessed 20 June 2011). See also 'Racially abused Army chef awarded £22,000 by tribunal', *Personnel Today*, 11 January 2010. http://goo.gl/GnVPb (accessed 10 October 2011).
23. Jason Burke, 'Bullied Army recruits are being forced to desert', *Observer*, Sunday 4 June 2000. http://goo.gl/vUmX7 (accessed 10 February 2011).
24. Sean Rayment, 'Hero lawyer sues Army over sex discrimination', *Telegraph*, 31 May 2008. http://goo.gl/Plqy9 (accessed 21 November 2011).
25. Saleyha Ahsan, commissioned in 1996, was the first British Muslim woman to graduate from RMAS, joining the Royal Army Medical Corps and deployed to Bosnia in 1997. Supplement to the London Gazette, January 1997, p. 473. After leaving the army in 2000 she qualified as a doctor. The Wellcome Collection. http://goo.gl/mzS9s (accessed 21 November 2011).
26. Barbara Davis, 'My war against Army sexists was WORSE than being held hostage and nearly executed in Iraq', *Mail*, date not given, http://goo.gl/OErS3 (accessed 21 November 2011).
27. Ibid.

7 The Force of the Law

1. 'BBC defends army bullying drama "Accused"', *New Statesman*, 23 November 2010. http://goo.gl/F2F5o (accessed 1 April 2011).
2. BBC News, 'Commissioner plan after Deepcut', Tuesday, 13 June 2006. http://goo.gl/3Xgle (accessed 15 May 2011).
3. Defence Policy and Business News, 'First ever Service Personnel Complaints Commissioner appointed', MoD, 7 November 2007. http://goo.gl/uh4HS (accessed 15 May 2011).
4. Focus Consultancy, 'Some of our Clients: The British Army'. http://goo.gl/tc9o4 (accessed 28 April 2011).
5. Ibid.
6. Jason Burke, 'Bullied army recruits being forced to desert'. *Observer*, Sunday, 4 June 2000. http://goo.gl/oY8g2 (accessed 15 March 2011).
7. Richard Norton-Taylor, 'Army acts as 43% of troops condemn bullying', *Guardian*, 12 November 2002. http://goo.gl/0rp2W (accessed 15 March 2011).

8. Richard Norton-Taylor, 'Most soldiers say the army still has bullies', *Guardian*, Monday 6 December 2004. http://goo.gl/lUYQd (accessed 15 March 2011).
9. Deepcut deaths investigation 'failed to follow leads', BBC News UK, 11 March 2011. http://goo.gl/jJZHs (accessed 15 March 2011).
10. Armed Forces Continuous Attitude Surveys, 2008 Main Results. Published 1 June 2009, p. 13.
11. Ibid., 4.2, p. 31.
12. Ibid., Executive Summary, p. 6.
13. Ibid., 10.16, p. 68.
14. Recruit Trainee Survey. Annual report: January 2009 to December 2009. Ministry of Defence. July 2010, p. 4. http://goo.gl/MZ3sj (accessed 29 April 2011).
15. Ibid., pp. 6–7.
16. Ibid.
17. Service Complaints Commissioner for the Armed Forces, Annual Report, 2010. 1. Facts and Figures, p. 20. http://goo.gl/bsMeM (accessed 15 May 2011).
18. Ibid., 4. Improvements for the Future, p. 53.
19. The Garnett Foundation. Online. http://goo.gl/23DMs (accessed 31 March 2011).
20. *Respect for Others – Your Guide to Fair Play in the Army*, Booklet – Army Code 64325, Edition 5, July 2009.
21. Members of the armed forces are permitted to belong to political organisations as long as this does not interfere with or enter into their professional activities.
22. The group has worked with Johnsons Cleaners, Ford, King's College Hospital, Essex County Council, Hyde Housing, HM Prison Service, Kent Fire & Rescue Service, Arriva, MoD, NHS, Remploy, Metropolitan Police, Cabinet Office, Pitney Bowes, Irwin Mitchell Lawyers, Sanctuary Housing, Guide Dogs for the Blind and many others.
23. Figures for the year 2010 are available in United Kingdom Defence Statistics, 2010, Chapter Two: Personnel, 29 September 2010. Ministry of Defence. http://goo.gl/8UCQd (accessed 20 April 2011).
24. See the remark made by CGS General Peter Wall in January 2012 where he admitted: 'We do not have a brilliant track record in the army of recruiting from certain ethnic communities across the UK...If we want to sustain a fully manned regular and reserve manpower complement, then we are going to have to be better at doing that.' Nick Hopkins, 'Army to cut 20,000 jobs two years earlier than expected', *Guardian*, 31 January 2012. http://goo.gl/D7yIt (accessed 21 February 2012).
25. Patricia Winter and Rachel Woodward, *Sexing the Soldier: The Politics of Gender and the Contemporary British Army*, London: Routledge, 2007.
26. Ian Drury, 'The heroine of Helmand: Young military police officer makes a record 17 Taliban arrests in single DAY', *Mail*, 3 April 2011. Online. Available HTTP http://goo.gl/g4cMg (accessed 6 April 2011).
27. Jenny Stocks, 'Men wear their war wounds with pride, it's different for us women', *Daily Mail*, 6 January, 2011. http://goo.gl/adByS (accessed 28 March 2011).
28. Equality and Human Right Commission, Victory for pregnant women in the armed forces, 3 June 2010. http://goo.gl/e6pWS (accessed 7 June 2011).
29. 'Lesbian soldier Kerry Fletcher wins £187,000 harassment payout', *The Times*, 27 November 2008.
30. Adam Gabbatt, 'MoD faces payout after female soldier wins discrimination case', *Guardian*, 14 April 2010. http://goo.gl/iDTF9 (accessed 14 March 2011).

31. Vanessa Allen, 'Mother of all defeats!', *Daily Mail*, 13 April 2010. http://goo.gl/KW14W (accessed 14 March 2011).

32. Comment, 'Act of Betrayal', *Daily Mail*, 14 April 2010, http://goo.gl/7nqNP (accessed 14 March 2011).

33. Press Association, 'Female soldier awarded £17,000 by employment tribunal', *Guardian*, 16 April 2010. http://goo.gl/SfwXu (accessed 14 March 2011).

34. Army Rumour Service (ARRSE) Thread: 'Now she wants Â£500,000.........Sexy T', 14 April 2010. http://goo.gl/Qe2o1 (accessed 28 March 2011).

35. Ibid.

36. Dan Newling and Katherine Knight, 'Single mother soldier who claimed £1.1million over childcare left her baby after two years', *Mail*, 16 April 2010. http://goo.gl/f8T2F (accessed 30 March 2011).

37. Ibid.

38. Allen, 'Mother of all defeats'.

39. 'The Army has a vested interest in helping soldiers balance the needs of their employment with their family life. However as soldiers, serving parents must be available for deployment at anytime and so have personal responsibility for ensuring that they have robust arrangements in place to care for their children, should they need to be away from home.' A Regular Army Interim Guide for Commonwealth Citizens and their Families, Section 5, p. 7. Ministry of Defence, Edition No 1 dated 8 February 2008. http://goo.gl/wOcbL (accessed 17 June 2011).

8   Like Coming to Mars

1. 'A Regular Army Interim Guide for Commonwealth Citizens and their Families', SO2b PS4(A) DPS(A), Edition No 1, dated 8 February 2008, p. 7.

2. Daily Mail reporter, 'Army widow joins Calendar Girls-style effort to raise cash for Help For Heroes charity', *Daily Mail*, 15 December 2009. http://goo.gl/m2LaE (accessed 8 June 2011).

3. Entitled 'Wherever you are', the song was composed by Royal Wedding composer Paul Mealor, and included lyrics compiled from letters to and from the women and their soldier partners. Paul Kendall, 'Military Wives choir: "We've found our voices"', *Telegraph*, 11 December 2011. http://goo.gl/VgfDp (accessed 12 December 2011).

4. Op Herrick 12, Survey of Families, Army Families Federation. 2011, p. 7. <http://goo.gl/ZHxdE> (accessed 16 June 2011).

5. Ibid., p. 33.

6. Cynthia Enloe, *Maneuvers: the international politics of militarizing women's lives*, Berkeley: University of California Press, 2000, pp. 162–166.

7. Ibid., p. 162.

8. Ibid.

9. Ibid., p. 163.

10. 'Reg's Words', Vote for Reg Keys, 2005. http://goo.gl/VHvaf (accessed 24 November 2011).

11. Commonwealth Families Guide, op cit, p. 21.

12. Home Office UK Border Agency, Information for applicants on the new English language requirement for partners. <http://goo.gl/cGtyh> (accessed 22 June 2011).

13. Paul Higate, 'Peacekeepers, Masculinities and Sexual Exploitation', *Men and Masculinities*, 10 (1), pp. 99–119, 2007.

14. Cynthia Cockburn, who had studied peace movements in a variety of regional settings, expressed the continuum between domestic abuse and war succinctly: 'Put briefly, violence in our everyday cultures, deeply gendered, predisposes societies to accept war as normal. And the violence of militarisation and war, profoundly gendered, spills back into everyday life and increases the quotient of violence in it'. Cynthia Cockburn, 'Don't talk to me about war. My life's a battlefield', open Democracy, 25 November 2011. http://goo.gl/8g5Ni (accessed 25 November 2011).

15. The Commonwealth Families Guide issued by the MoD stipulated that UK laws to prevent domestic abuse 'were designed to ensure equal treatment of all irrespective of gender, race, religion, belief or sexual orientation and tolerance towards minority cultures and the protection of children', drawing attention to the fact that anyone found committing physical violence towards partners, married or unmarried, and towards children was liable for prosecution. Commonwealth Families Guide, op cit, p. 10.

16. British Army Cultural Guidance. Reference: A. DPS (A)/28/9 dated 21 January 2008. B. DPS (A)/28/9 dated 31 March 2008 (Edition 5) p. 7.

17. The phenomenon of Gurkha military migration and settlement is, of course, much more dispersed than this. In addition to the Indian Brigade of Gurkhas, British Gurkha soldiers are stationed in Brunei and Singapore. Veterans and private security operators can be found worldwide, with significant impact on the Nepalese economy.

18. Lionel Caplan, *Warrior Gentlemen: "Gurkhas" in the Western Imagination*, Providence & Oxford: Berghahn Books, 1995.

19. Mitra Pariyar, 'Cast(e) in Bone: The Perpetuation of Social Hierarchy among Nepalis in Britain', COMPAS Centre on Migration, Policy and Society, University of Oxford, Working Paper No. 85, p. 7.

20. Graham Brough, 'My husband died for this country ... now they want to deport me', *Mirror*, 16 December 2008. http://goo.gl/K7pa1 (accessed 12 December 2011).

21. Michael Smith and Kevin Dowling, 'Gurkha's widow told she can stay', *The Sunday Times*, 10 May 2009.

22. British Forces Germany (BFG) is the composite name given to the British Army, Royal Air Force and supporting civil elements stationed in Germany. The British Army, Formations. Armedforces.co.uk http://goo.gl/AofRu (accessed 4 July 2011).

9 Caught in the Crossfire

1. Kate Connolly, 'Germany to abolish compulsory military service', *Guardian*, 22 November 2010. http://goo.gl/xBDL9 (accessed 19 October 2011).

2. See, for example, Joseph Soeters and Jan van der Meulen (eds), *Cultural Diversity in the Armed Forces: An International Comparison*, London: Routledge, 2007.

3. Christophe Bertossi, 'French "Muslim" soldiers? Social change and pragmatism in a military institution', in Bowen, J., Bertossi, C., Duyvendak, J. W. and Krook, M. (eds), *European States and their Muslim Citizens: The Impact of Institutions on Perceptions and Boundaries*, Cambridge: University of Cambridge Press, 2013.

4. Beatriz Frieyro de Lara, 'The professionalization process of the Spanish Armed Forces', in Tibor Szvircsev Tresch and Christian Leuprecht (eds), *Europe Without Soldiers? Recruitment and Retention across the Armed Forces of Europe*, Montreal and Kingston: McGill-Queen's University Press, 2011, pp. 181–193.

5. In 2002 foreign nationals were allowed to make up two per cent of the army. Initially this was limited to non-nationals living in Spain. When the cap was increased candidates from Equatorial Guinea and Latin America were given preferential treatment, despite being inconsistent with EU employment policy. Ibid., p. 183.

6. Ronald R. Krebs, 'The Citizen-Soldier tradition in the United States: Has its demise been greatly exaggerated?' *Armed Forces & Society*, Volume 36 Number 1, October 2009, pp. 153–174.

7. Julia Preston, 'The US military will offer path to citizenship.' *New York Times*, 4 February 2009. http://goo.gl/yfQga (accessed 8 August 2011).

   In September 2003, there were approximately 30,000 foreign born, non-US citizens in the US armed forces, including Mexicans and other Hispanics. The US Army's cyber-recruiting operation holds daily online chat sessions in English and Spanish. Between October 2002 and December 2007, some 31,200 members of the US Armed Forces were sworn in as citizens, while in February 2008, 7,200 recently discharged service members had citizenship applications pending. Tarak Barkawi, 'State and Armed Force in International Context', in Alejandro Colás and Bryan Mabee (eds), *Mercenaries, Pirates, Bandits and Empires*, London: C. Hurst & Co., 2011, pp. 49–50.

8. Erin O. Stattel, 'Basic combat training now includes naturalization', ARNEWS, 27 April 2011. http://goo.gl/naqsy (accessed 7 August 2011).

9. Lt Col Deanna Bague, Fort Bliss Public Affairs, 'Obama speaks on contributions of naturalized Soldiers', US Army homepage. 11 May 2011. http://goo.gl/wvUd4 (accessed 6 August 2011).

10. Air Force Chief Master Sgt Julie Brummund, Task Force White Eagle, 'Face of Defense: Deployed Soldier becomes US citizen', US Army homepage. 19 May 2011. http://goo.gl/DYhdw (accessed 7 August 2011).

11. 'The Nation's Commitment: Cross-Government Support to our Armed Forces, their Families and Veterans', Ministry of Defence, July 2008. http://goo.gl/EfApL (accessed 5 August 2011).

12. Ibid., Chapter 2: What we will do, Section 2.42, Foreign and Commonwealth Personnel, p. 18.

13. 'New rules for troops' citizenship', *BBC News* (2006). http://goo.gl/UK5Mg (accessed 27 October 2011).

14. A letter to the AFF encapsulated this viewpoint: 'Why do Foreign & Commonwealth soldiers have to do a Life in the UK test? They have already been indoctrinated into the life and culture during basic training and serving with their unit? Furthermore, why do they need to pay a fee to become a British citizen, while they are sacrificing their lives on operational tours – isn't that a good enough test? I hold the Queen's Commission, yet to become a British National, I have to complete the same test asylum seekers have to complete. I feel rather insulted.' The response from Land Forces Secretariat was that applying for citizenship was regarded as a personal decision and therefore individuals were obliged to fund themselves. The test was a legal requirement and there were no exceptions for UK armed forces. *AFF Journal*, 85, Winter 2011, p. 66.

15. DOMCOL Substitute allows those personnel who are not eligible for DOMCOL to accumulate up to 25 per cent of annual leave to enable them to visit their home country at their own expense. Service personnel in their first three years of service serving in the UK can make use of the Get You Home (Early Years) (Overseas Assistance) scheme which provides a contribution towards one return

journey a year for the first three years of service to a qualifying address abroad. 'Armed Forces: Leave', Written answers, Lords, Hansard, 5 October 2009. http://goo.gl/c5qBb (accessed 4 August 2011).

16. 'A Regular Army Interim Guide for Commonwealth Citizens and their Families', SO2b PS4(A) DPS(A), Edition No. 1 dated 8 February 2008, p. 7.

17. Alex West and Tom Newton-Dunn, 'Illegal squaddie guards Queen', *Sun*, 24 July 2009. http://goo.gl/uxiKc (accessed 29 July 2011).
    Neil Sears, 'Revealed: one of the Queen's guards is an illegal immigrant', *Daily Mail*, 24 July 2009. http://goo.gl/NeSkk (accessed 29 July 2011).

18. 'There was certainly a sense of these values in black Jamaicans who came forward as volunteers to defend the British Empire. But, as a sense of Jamaican national identity began to emerge, it was the ex-servicemen's exclusion from both the material and symbolic rewards of military manhood that became a key issue in nationalist agitation: the non-recognition of male sacrifice that became a significant component of the nationalist narrative.' Richard Smith, *Jamaican Volunteers in the First World War: Race, Masculinity and the Development of National Consciousness*, Manchester: Manchester University Press, 2004, p. 6.

19. Christopher Dandeker and David Mason, 'Echoes of Empire: addressing gaps in recruitment and retention in the British Army by diversifying recruitment pools', in Tibor Szvircsev Tresch and Christian Leuprecht (eds), *Europe Without Soldiers? Recruitment and Retention across the Armed Forces of Europe*, Kingston, Canada: McGill-Queen's University Press, 2011, p. 211.

20. The USCIS web page can be found at: http://www.uscis.gov/military (accessed 19 August 2011). The UKBA does not have a dedicated section for members of the British Armed Forces, but the British Army website provides information under the heading Welfare and Support, Personnel support, Foreign and Commonwealth citizens: http://www.army.mod.uk/welfare-support/23209.aspx (accessed 19 August 2011).
    Information for members of the armed forces can also be found on the UKBA website under 'Immigration Directorate Instructions, chapter 15 – Armed Forces'. http://goo.gl/2dBVf (accessed 23 August 2011).

21. Army Pay Scales (1 April 2011–31 March 2012), The Defence Supplies Directory. http://goo.gl/9bojz (accessed 1 August 2011).

22. Of the 900 or so Servicemen and women selected in Tranche 1 of the Armed Forces Redundancy Programme, at least 16 per cent were Foreign or Commonwealth citizens. *AFF Journal*, 85, Winter 2011, p. 16.

23. BBC News (2007) 'Commonwealth soldiers form union', 7 March. http://goo.gl/KCKP3 (accessed 7 January 2008).

24. See, for example, a post on ARRSE.com (28 May 2009): 'Anyone know how to get in touch with them, or if they even exist anymore?' There were four replies but none of them were able to provide an answer. http://goo.gl/io1dp (accessed 27 October 2011).

10 Conclusion: Militarised Multiculture

1. John Stevens and David Gardner, 'By Royal Appointment: The skateboarding, punk-loving boy from Harlem who made America proud', *Mail*, 30 April 2011. http://goo.gl/v2EVA (accessed 28 October 2011).

2. Richard Allen Greene, 'Royal wedding's lone American will guard Queen on horseback', CNN, 26 April 2011. http://goo.gl/ucEAC (accessed 28 October 2011).

3. James Chapman, 'Balls indicates U-turn on Iraq War inquiry after revelation that Blair "demanded privacy"', *Mail*, 22 June 2009. http://goo.gl/EyhxS (accessed 7 September 2011).
4. In May 2011, a group of 20 youths surrounded a Nepali youth and beat him unconscious. Nabin Pokharel, 'Emigrants' woes: Nepalis in UK rue "racist" attacks', Ekantipur.com, 1 July 2011. http://goo.gl/ERzUE> (accessed 25 October 2011).
5. Martin Evans, 'Disperse Gurkhas like asylum seekers, urges minister', *Telegraph*, 20 September 2011. http://goo.gl/PbfcT (accessed 25 October 2011).
6. Lindy Heinecken, 'Diversity in the South African armed forces', in Joseph Soeters and Jan van der Meulen, *Cultural Diversity in the Armed Forces: An International Comparison*, Abingdon: Routledge Military Studies, 2007, p. 91.
7. Omar Khalidi, *Khaki and Ethnic Violence in India*, New Delhi: Three Essays Collective, 2003. p. 40.
8. Soeters and van der Meulen, p. 5.
9. Barnor Hesse, ed., *Un/settled Multiculturalisms: Diasporas, Entanglements, Transruptions*, London: Zed Books, 2000, p. 210.
10. 'Multicultural drift' was a term first used by Stuart Hall (see Hesse, Ibid) It appeared in the *The Future of Multi-Ethnic Britain: The Parekh Report*, London: Profile Books, 2000, p. 14.
11. 'Multiculturalism, as almost everybody recognizes, is a slippery and fluid term, and it has accrued a vast range of associations and accents through decades of political, contextual and linguistic translations. It may retain a fairly useful if limited descriptive sense in post-colonial, migration societies, but it also skitters off to index normative debates, real and imagined policies, mainstream political rhetorics, consumerist desires, and resistant political appropriations'.

    Alana Lentin and Gavin Titley, *The Crises of Multiculturalism: Racism in a Neo-liberal Age*, London: Zed Books, 2011, p. 2.
12. MoD Defence News, 'Fusilier Petero "Pat" Suesue killed in Afghanistan', 24 May 2009. http://goo.gl/orria (accessed 7 September 2011).
13. Matthew Hickley, 'Mother pays tribute to "fun-loving" son killed in Afghanistan as second soldier killed on patrol is named' *Mail*, 25 May 2009. http://goo.gl/d1cWd (accessed 7 September 2011).
14. In 2005 Maya Evans became the first person to be convicted under Section 132 of the Serious Organised Crime and Police Act, the controversial new law that banned unauthorised protests from taking place within half a mile of Westminster. Standing near the Cenotaph in Whitehall she read out the names of the 97 British soldiers who had died in Iraq.
15. Cassandra Jardine and Richard Savill, 'Wootton Bassett: A very British way of mourning', *Telegraph*, 7 July 2009. http://goo.gl/rPkmH (accessed 7 September 2011).
16. 'Heroes' warmer welcome home', *The Sun*, 14 December 2007. http://goo.gl/TYoz5 (accessed 7 September 2011).
17. Army Doctrine Publication, Volume 5: Soldiering – The Military Covenant. http://goo.gl/2RQiZ (accessed 12 September 2011).
18. Andrew Johnson, 'IoS campaign: honour our troops', *Independent*, Sunday, 7 September 2007. http://goo.gl/i2dBm (accessed 8 September 2011).
19. Sarah Ingham and Christopher Dandeker, 'The covenant we must protect from the lawyers', Parliamentary Brief Online, 24 June 2010. http://goo.gl/P9RHq (accessed 8 September 2011).

20. George Jones, 'We need to spend more on armed forces, admits Blair', *Telegraph*, 13 January 2007. http://goo.gl/QHjFy (accessed 28 November 2011).

21. Quentin Davies MP, Bill Clark OBE Ministry of Defence, Air Commodore Martin Sharp OBE MA RAF, 'Report of Inquiry into National Recognition of Our Armed Forces'. May 2008. http://goo.gl/D0kjk (accessed 28 October 2011).

22. Ibid.

23. Daily Mail reporter, 'Armed forces and veterans to be honoured in new national day', *Mail*, 22 January 2009. http://goo.gl/Fqtxp (accessed 28 October 2011).

24. Another example of the lack of curiosity was exemplified in a *Guardian* review of the reality series 'Fighting on the Frontline'. Sam Wollaston wrote: 'Then, as a reminder that what they're talking about isn't just lad-chat but a reality, Del gets hit by a bullet... Del's not Scottish, he's from Saint Lucia. What the hell is he even doing there? But then you could say that about all of them.' In 'TV review: fighting on the frontline; Boardwalk Empire; Downton Abbey', *Guardian*, 9 October 2011. http://goo.gl/liMQM (accessed 13 December 2011).

25. 'Black Watch names fourth Iraq casualty', *Guardian*, Tuesday 9 November 2004.

26. 'Fiji's unsung heroes of UK army', BBC News, 9 November 2004. http://goo.gl/iylWf (accessed 28 October 2011).

27. BBC News, 'Wages and pride draw Fijians to UK army', 6 September, 2006. http://goo.gl/N2uWl (accessed 7 September 2011).

28. Ibid.

29. P. W. Singer, *Corporate Warriors: The Rise of the Privatized Military Industry*, Ithaca and London: Cornell University Press, 2008.

30. Ibid., p. 8.

31. Ibid., p. 9.

32. Jeremy Scahill, *Blackwater: The Rise of the World's Most Powerful Mercenary Army*, London: Serpents' Tail, 2008, p. 9.

33. Craig Copetas, 'Dogs of war unleashed by Fiji at right price for UN, Blackwater', Bloomberg, 29 October 2007. http://goo.gl/9CWwm (accessed 6 September 2011).

34. For a more substantial account of the recruitment of Fijians in the privatised security sector see Nic MacClellan, 'From Fiji to Fallujah: The war in Iraq and the privatisation of Pacific security', *Pacific Journalism Review*, 12(2), 2006. For a wider global analysis see Paul Higate, 'Martial races and enforcement masculinities of the global south: weaponising Fijian, Chilean, and Salvadoran Postcoloniality in the Mercenary Sector', *Globalizations*, 2012, 9(1), 35–52.

35. Everest Security Manned Guarding (Gurkha Services). http://www.everestsecurity. co.uk/ (accessed 25 October 2011).

36. Individual members of MAC had also belonged to Islam4UK which was banned earlier that year under the Terrorism Act 2000 after it threatened to hold a protest at a repatriation ceremony in Wootton Bassett. 'Islam4UK cancels plans for Wootton Bassett march', *Guardian*, 10 January 2010. http://goo.gl/YAON6 (accessed 31 October 2011).

37. Soeters and van der Meulen, Cultural Diversity in the Armed Forces, pp. 5–10.

38. Sky News Press Office, 'General Sir David Richards interview with Dermot Murnaghan', 13 November 2011. http://goo.gl/r7TKM (accessed 13 December 2011).

39. Peter Walker, 'English Defence League march through Tower Hamlets banned by Theresa May', *Guardian*, 26 August 2011. http://goo.gl/MiZxw (accessed 13 December 2011).

40. Vikram Dodd and Sally James Gregory, 'Decline in ethnic recruits for police', *Guardian*, Saturday 24 February 2001. http://goo.gl/26lza (accessed 25 October 2011).

41. Two examples of the BBC News, 'Police stop and search powers "target minorities"'. BBC News, Monday 15 March 2010. http://goo.gl/5hPWa (accessed 4 March 2012). Vikram Dodd, 'Police played "spot the black officer in the dark", tribunal hears', *Guardian*, 2 March 2009. http://goo.gl/R88DE (accessed 28 November 2011). Telegraph View, 'Racism and the Met', *Telegraph*, 9 April 2012. http://goo.glG3zRy (accessed 18 May 2012).

42. 'Given that much of our society is pretty unstructured these days, and given that the military has the unique opportunity to educate its own into the importance of a proper moral understanding, then perhaps the military community may have a wider contribution that it can make to the nation.' Dannatt: Military must teach morals', *Defence Management*, 8 November 2011. http://goo.gl/nRAX4 (accessed 28 November 2011).

43. Nicholas Cecil and Paul Cheston, 'Day of shame for British army as 14 soldiers suspended over horrific killing', London *Evening Standard*, 8 September 2011. http://goo.gl/AOnUr (accessed 8 September 2011).

44. Richard Norton-Taylor, 'MoD's resistance to human rights in Iraq blamed for death of Baha Mousa', *Guardian*, 24 November 2011. http://goo.gl/shcPq (accessed 28 November 2011).

45. Sam Marsden, 'New Iraq War inquiry set to open', *Independent*, Monday, 2 January 2012. http://goo.gl/vb5BY (accessed 3 January 2012).

46. Ibid.

47. Ian Cobain, 'RAF helicopter death revelation leads to secret Iraq detention camp', *Guardian*, Tuesday, 7 February 2012. http://goo.gl/xFuYk (accessed 7 February 2012).

48. British Army website. Army Life. Values to live by. http://www.army.mod.uk/join/20217.aspx (accessed 24 February 2012).

49. James Kirkup, 'BNP: British generals should be hanged for war crimes', *Telegraph*, 20 October 2009. http://goo.gl/wK7eo (accessed 26 October 2011).

50. Michael White, 'BNP and the armed forces: a colour-blind military is the best defence', *Guardian*, politics blog, Tuesday, 20 October 2009. http://goo.gl/a9CfH (accessed 27 February 2012).

51. There is Nothing British about the BNP: Stolen Valour. See archival website at http://goo.gl/rmmmW (accessed 26 October 2011).

52. http://www.nothing british.com/ (accessed 26 October 2011).

53. Charles Moore, 'The Spectator's notes', *The Spectator*, 24 October 2009. http://goo.gl/0rrVP (accessed 26 October).

54. Ibid.

55. David Willetts, 'Forces fight BNP hate merchants', *Sun*, 21 October 2009. http://goo.gl/Ijhck (accessed 26 October 2011).

56. Daily Mail reporter, 'Black SAS war hero who held off 250 rebels single-handed to be immortalised in statue', *Mail*, 10 November 2009. http://goo.gl/owHnG (accessed 26 October 2011).

57. See Walter Tull Sports and Arts Society for further details. http://goo.gl/rWdzZ (accessed 26 October 2011).

58. Introduction, 'We Were There'. MoD, http://goo.gl/6iLtl (accessed 30 October 2011).

59. 'We Were There' home page. http://goo.gl/OJoN0 (accessed 31 October 2011).

60. 10. The official site of the Prime Minister, 'Statement on Strategic Defence and Security Review', Tuesday 19 October 2010. http://goo.gl/NplVY (accessed 31 October 2011).

61. 10. The official site of the Prime Minister, 'PM's speech at Munich Security Conference', Saturday 5 February 2011. http://goo.gl/EO8oc (accessed 31 October 2011).

62. The exhibition was subsequently updated to provide short biographical accounts of individuals, including Sohail Khan. However, underneath his personal entry, the same image of Khan working in Pakistan was featured, with the caption: a Chinook Helicopter. http://goo.gl/ll2LU (accessed 28 February 2012).

63. 'Gurkha cuts disproportionate, says ex-Army chief', BBC News, 1 September 2011. http://goo.gl/Bbf29 (accessed 31 October 2011).

64. In 2012 the advice to F&C nationals given on the British Army website stated that Commonwealth citizens were still able to apply online from overseas but were required to travel to the UK at their own risk if they were considered eligible to start the recruitment process. Meanwhile it had become clear that F&C numbers were likely to fall as a result of cuts to battalions with a high proportion. See, for example, Thomas Harding and James Kirkup, 'Battalions with foreign bias face axe in Army cuts', Telegraph, 29 June 2012. http://goo.gl/gtBgm (accessed 29 June 2012).

Select Bibliography

Alexandrou, A., Bartle, R. & Holmes, R. (2001) *New People Strategies for the British Armed Forces* (London: Frank Cass).

Anderson, B. (1983) *Imagined Communities: Reflections on the Origins and Spread of Nationalism* (London: Verso).

Barkawi, T. (2006) *Globalisation and War* (London: Rowman & Littlefield).

Barnett, A. (2012) *Iron Britannia: Time to Take the Great Out of Britain* (London: Faber & Faber).

Bayly, C. & Harper, T. (2007) *Forgotten Wars: The End of Britain's Asian Empire* (London: Allen Lane).

Beharry, J. & Cook, N. (2006) *Barefoot Soldier* (London: Little, Brown Book Group).

Caforio, G. (ed.) (2007) *Social Sciences and the Military: An Interdisciplinary Overview* (London: Routledge).

Caplan, L. (1995) *Warrior Gentlemen: 'Gurkhas' in the Western Imagination* (Providence: Berghahn Books).

Cleary, L. R. & McConville, T. (eds.) (2006) *Managing Defence in a Democracy* (London: Routledge).

Colás, A. & Mabee, B. (eds.) (2011) *Mercenaries, Pirates, Bandits and Empires* (London: Hurst).

Cole, C., Dobbing, M. & Hailwood, A. (2010) *Convenient Killing: Armed Drones and the 'Playstation' Mentality* (Oxford: The Fellowship of Reconciliation).

Cowen, D. (2008) *Military Workfare: The Soldier and Social Citizenship in Canada* (Toronto: University of Buffalo Press).

Dyde, B. (1997) *The Empty Sleeve: The Story of the West India Regiments of the British Army* (St John's: Hansib Caribbean).

Edmunds, T. & Forster, A. (2007) *Out of Step: The Case for Change in the British Armed Forces* (London: Demos).

Enloe, C. H. (1980) *Ethnic Soldiers: State Security in a Divided Society* (New York: Pelican).

Enloe, C. H. (2000) *Maneuvers: The International Politics of Militarizing Women's Lives* (Berkeley: University of California Press).

Gilbert, E. & Cowan, D. (eds.) (2008) *War, Citizenship, Territory* (Routledge: London).

Gilroy, P. (1987) *There Ain't No Black in the Union Jack: The Cultural Politics of Race and Nation* (London: Hutchinson).

Gilroy, P. (2004) *After Empire: Melancholia or Convivial Culture?* (London: Routledge).

Gott, R. (2012) *Britain's Empire: Resistance, Repression and Revolt* (London: Verso).

Hesse, B. (ed.) (2000) *Un/settled Multiculturalisms: Diasporas, Entanglements, Transruptions* (London: Zed).

Hockey, H. (1986) *Squaddies: Portrait of a Subculture* (Exeter: University of Exeter Press).

Howe, G. (2002) *Race, War & Nationalism: A Social History of West Indians in the First World War* (Oxford: James Currey).

Khalidi, O. (2003) *Khaki and Ethnic Violence in India* (New Delhi: Three Essays Collective).

Kelly, J. D., Jauregui, B., Mitchell, S. T. & Walton, J. (eds.) (2010) *Anthropology and Global Counterinsurgency* (Chicago: University of Chicago Press).

Killingray, D. (2010) *Fighting for Britain: African Soldiers in the Second World War* (Woodbridge: James Currey).

Lentin, A. & Titley, G. (2011) *The Crises of Multiculturalism: Racism in a Neo-Liberal Age* (London: Zed).

Morrow Jr, J. H. (2004) *The Great War: An Imperial History* (London: Routledge).

Mosse, G. L. (1990) *Fallen Soldiers: Reshaping the Memory of the World Wars* (Oxford: Oxford University Press).

Murray, R. N. (1996) *Lest We Forget: The Experiences of World War II Westindian Ex-Service Personnel* (Nottingham Westindian Combined Ex-Services Association, Hansib Publishing (Caribbean)).

Myerly, S. H. (1996) *British Military Spectacle: From the Napoleonic Wars through the Crimea* (London: Harvard University Press).

Omissi, D. (1994) *The Sepoy and the Raj: The Indian Army 1860–1940* (London: Macmillan Press).

Parker, J. (2005) *The Gurkhas* (London: Headline Book Publishing).

Percy, S. (2007) *Mercenaries: The History of a Norm in International Relations* (Oxford: Oxford University Press).

Price, D. H. (2011) *Weaponizing Anthropology: Social Science in the Service of the Militarized State* (Oakland: AK Press).

Robinson, P., Lee, N. D. & Carrick, D. (eds.) (2008) *Ethics Education in the Military* (Aldershot: Ashgate).

Scahill, J. (2008) *Blackwater: The Rise of the World's Most Powerful Mercenary Army* (London: Serpents' Tail).

Shaw, M. (2005) *The New Western Way of War* (Cambridge: Polity).

Singer, P. W. (2008) *Corporate Warriors: The Rise of the Privatized Military Industry* (Ithaca: Cornell University Press).

Smith, R. (2004) *Jamaican Volunteers in the First World War: Race, Masculinity and the Development of National Consciousness* (Manchester: Manchester University Press).

Soeters, J. & Meulen, J. van der (eds.) (2007) *Cultural Diversity in the Armed Forces: An International Comparison* (London: Routledge).

Strachan, H. (1997) *The Politics of the British Army* (Oxford: Clarendon Press).

Tresch, T. S. & Leuprecht, C. (eds.) (2011) *Europe without Soldiers? Recruitment and Retention across the Armed Forces of Europe* (Montreal and Kingston: McGill-Queen's University Press).

Weight, R. (2002) *Patriots: National Identity in Britain 1940–2000* (London: Macmillan).

Weight, R. & Beach, A. (eds.) (2008) *The Right to Belong: Citizenship and National Identity, 1930–1969* (London: IB Taurus).

Winter, P. & Woodward, R. (2007) *Sexing the Soldier: The Politics of Gender and the Contemporary British Army* (London: Routledge).

Index